A LETTER FROM OGGI

A LETTER FROM OGGI

The Letters of Olga Franklin

Edited by Richard Jaffa

Book Guild Publishing
Sussex, England

First published in Great Britain in 2015 by
The Book Guild Ltd
The Werks
45 Church Road
Hove, BN3 2BE

Typesetting in Garamond by
Keyboard Services, Luton, Bedfordshire

Printed and bound in Great Britain by
CPI Group (UK) Ltd, Croydon, CR0 4YY

A catalogue record for this book is available from
The British Library.

ISBN 978 1 910298 93 0

In memory of Olga's big sister, Beryl Jaffa (née Davis),
the recipient of these letters.

Contents

Acknowledgements

I would like to thank everyone who has assisted me in this wonderful task. I am especially grateful to my cousin Derek Davis who was always close to Olga and whose family knowledge and erudition has helped with many obscure references and the historical background. Finally I wouldn't achieve anything without the support and love of my dear wife, Jane. It was a great joy to me that from the moment they met, Jane and Olga became great friends and, when in the last few months of Olga's life she needed help and advice, it was to Jane that she turned. My children, Simon and Sarah, had the chance to know Olga in their teens and I still treasure in my bookcase the Bat Mitzvah project that Sarah did as a 12-year-old, where she chose her Aunt Olga as her subject for 'A Jewish Woman of Courage and Lifetime Achievement'. Sarah sat by Olga's bedside in the hospice as she narrated her story. These letters confirm the excitement that story generated.

Introduction

'There's a letter from Oggi!'

The arrival of the post including a letter from my Aunt Olga was always an event in our household when I was growing up. Whether the letter contained the latest scandal in Fleet Street or the eccentricities of the Royal Family or simply the strange behaviour of some of our relatives, it was rapidly assimilated. The envelopes lying on the doormat, whether handwritten or typed, were instantly recognisable. All of life was here. To our quiet, suburban, Birmingham existence Olga's life seemed utterly romantic. She mixed with kings and film stars, travelled the world and knew all those secrets that didn't even get into the newspapers.

Coming back to her letters some years after her death, I was struck by how they retained that same vitality that had entertained my family all those years ago. When writing in a national newspaper she was surrounded by teams of libel lawyers who sometimes cramped her style, but in her missives to my mother she could write the otherwise unprintable. Her letters recreate for us many of the famous and notorious from the thirties through to the seventies and we see figures from those decades, warts and all.

I can see her shambling along Park Lane with Groucho Marx, sympathising with his complaints, flirting with Nikita Khrushchev in a railway carriage in the USA, and hiding in the Duke of Windsor's couchette en route to London – even the most forward of modern reporters would blanch at some of the tactics required by our popular papers in the 1950s and 1960s.

Olga combined the audacity required for a good reporter with limitless curiosity and often a surprising degree of innocence for someone in the national media. As her letters show, she was fascinated by people and what made them tick. Her letters were not just a diary; they are living history. We can read Olga describing Warsaw in the last days before the Nazi invasion; the Blitz in London is all too vivid; she paints life in immediate post-Stalin Russia; she conjures up the misery of 1950s Rumania. Even before she entered Fleet Street her letters show the build up to the Second World War through the parliamentary debates she attended. She connects to so many of the tumultuous events of the twentieth century. We see her on the balcony of Hitler's Chancellery, suffering the worst of the Cold War, introducing Prince Philip of Greece to the British public and performing endless stunts to increase newspaper circulation.

Olga was born Olga Rose Davis in Pershore Road, Edgbaston, Birmingham in 1912, second of four sisters and two brothers. Her grandfather, Lewis Davis, had come to Birmingham as an impoverished immigrant in the 1870s and her grandmother, Betsy, took in washing and mending for the rich Jews who had settled earlier in England. Olga's father, Izzy, was one of nine children and born in 1877 literally as the cattle boat from Eastern Europe landed in Grimsby. Some of Izzy's siblings prospered and became wealthy but he had an up and mostly down business career. Olga, who was the brainy one of the family, got a place at King Edward's School, the most prestigious girls' school in Birmingham, but had to leave after one of Izzy's financial disasters. Languages were her thing and on leaving school she attended a language course at Birmingham University. By the time these letters start in 1932 Olga's mother, Becky, had already died and Izzy would follow her in 1937. At age eighteen Olga got her first job working for Sir Herbert Austin at Longbridge doing French and German shorthand. From Austin Motors she moved to BSA Tools, Small Heath, then to two other industrial businesses before she spent three years at Joseph Lucas Ltd in Great King Street.

In 1934 she married Norbert Franklin but her marriage was tragically short. Within two years he was diagnosed with lung cancer and died in 1937. In her first book, *Born Twice*, she describes the breakdown that followed his death and her attempted suicide.

Recovering from that, she went to work as a German interpreter for Birmetals Ltd in Quinton, Birmingham, who had begun manufacturing aluminium for the Spitfire. In 1938 she decided to try her luck in London and found a job with a refugee German firm representing British armament manufacturers and selling heavy guns and tank materials to the Polish government. She describes in her letters how they got paid by the Poles but they never delivered their arms – the Germans invaded too quickly. She was one of the last people out of Warsaw and escaped Poland on 1st September 1939, three days before the invasion.

Her ambition had always been to become a journalist, but it took the war to create the opportunity and finally in 1940 she landed a position with Reuters. From there she went to the *Oxford Mail*, then to the *Newcastle Evening Chronicle* and finally to Fleet Street when she joined the *Daily Sketch* in 1945. Her last major job was with the *Daily Mail* in 1956, where she remained until 1970.

She was the first Russian-speaking reporter in the British press, and in the 1940s and 1950s she travelled frequently to Russia accompanying Billy Wright and Wolves to Moscow, and later reporting on the Russian leaders, as for example when she shadowed Khrushchev across the USA. The newspapers also used her as a stunt girl and royal reporter at different periods of her career. She was the first British journalist to meet the future Duke of Edinburgh; she door-stepped the Duke of Windsor and picked up Groucho Marx in Park Lane; her letters detail all the historic events she covered and the seemingly endless list of famous people that she met or interviewed. After she left the *Daily Mail*, she worked freelance in newspapers, TV and radio for the rest of her life. Apart from her books, she wrote for the *Daily Telegraph*, the *Guardian*, the *Daily Mirror*, *The Spectator*, *Punch* and many other periodicals. She was a regular on *Woman's Hour*, *World at One* and the BBC World Service, in addition to panel shows and games, such as *Call My Bluff* and *The Tennis Elbow Foot Game*, frequently using her knowledge of Russian affairs. She wrote plays and talks for radio and published a highly successful series of self-help books.

In her pre-war letters, she describes the atmosphere in London as one of hope for peace and shows how that optimism dissolved after Munich. She made regular visits to the House of Commons to listen to the great debates. On a lighter note she produced a wonderful record of life among a small group of single women, mostly her cousins, in London, seeking husbands. Her own private life was quite racy for the 1930s and 1940s.

She doesn't avoid the errors and mishaps she suffered as a reporter and we read how a mistake about Mussolini's son nearly got her fired from her first press job at Reuters; similarly, how a story about Harold Pinter's first wife landed her in hot water.

Olga, although born and educated in Birmingham, was often mistaken for a Russian. Her colleague Bernard Levin even called her 'Grand Duchess'. She cultivated this impression by her appearance. Her long hair, inevitably unravelling despite innumerable pins, was usually contained by the kind of scarf more commonly seen on a Moscow factory worker. She had no interest in clothes. Only the fact that she had a sister, Beryl, who worked in the rag trade, ensured that periodically her wardrobe was supplemented. As a student, I once arranged to meet Olga at the Savoy Hotel, but seeing her enter the lobby, I hid behind a pillar until I had overcome the shock of her appearance.

Fortunately for us, her many hundreds of letters were preserved by my mother and later Olga herself always kept carbon copies, so these volumes represent a small part of her output over nearly forty years. This volume mostly contains many of the letters she wrote to my mother. She also corresponded periodically with some of the people about whom she wrote. She enjoyed exchanges with Dame Rebecca West, Alan Searle, Auberon Waugh and even Sir Isaiah Berlin. The cartoonists Illingworth and Emwood caught her likeness brilliantly.

Her letters not only cover national and international events and personalities but are also a highly personal record. After her early widowhood she embarked on a series of relationships, which she continued, despite the disapproval of her sisters, until finally she met Alfred W, and although he remained a married man, that relationship was sustained until his death thirty years later.

She was a remarkable linguist. In her lifetime, at various stages of her career, she managed probably a dozen languages. She could visit a country and have a working knowledge of their language within a few days. Her zest for life was enormous. I speak for all her nephews and nieces when I say that she was an integral part of our childhood, adolescence and adult years and that we all hold memories of her that range from the funny to the downright embarrassing.

I think I can best sum up her attitude to life by quoting from the last broadcast she did for the BBC, which she actually recorded for *Woman's Hour* from the bed of the hospice in Birmingham a week or two before she died. Asked by the interviewer how she felt about her imminent mortality (she was dying from a brain tumour and had refused any surgery), she replied that she had thoroughly enjoyed her life and had no regrets. She viewed life as rather like a party which had come to an end; when a party came to an end someone had to do the washing-up and it was now her turn to do it.

In editing Olga's letters I have tried to preserve their immediacy. Most of these letters were written late at night or in strange hotel rooms. They are colloquial, informal and a little salacious. Often they were hurriedly written on the same paper used in the newsroom for journalists' copy and they were left unfinished, sometimes without an opening greeting or a sign-off. Olga was writing to her eldest sister, with whom she enjoyed a close and very honest relationship. She addressed her sisters by several names; Beryl was B, Bella, Berylline, etc. and Cora was often Coralie or Cork. I have added capitals where occasionally it offers more consistency and I hope the footnotes are not intrusive or disruptive.

During her early years in London Olga was generally short of cash and there are many references to money. With so much inflation since the 1930s/40s we can lose track of values. One pound in 1936 would now be worth £62. So when Olga reached a salary of £4 per week in the early 1940s it would be worth £150 a week now – just subsistence living. I have put decimal conversions in where money amounts appear but you can multiply them by forty to get near a modern equivalent. Where she uses German, Yiddish or other languages, I have added a translation where appropriate. Many of the people she met were famous in their day but are now less well known. Olga was very frank and unashamed about her private life and would have retained the references if she were still alive. I have not censored anything.

In 1983, Olga started editing her letters and in her draft introduction wrote that she had not done it sooner because many of the characters were still alive. She was particularly keen to show the new generation of young women how, before the war and immediately after it, marriage was the only real choice available to women. That search for a man to marry is a strong theme through all her early letters from 1938 until 1950.

Having embarked on the task of editing her letters, she then left it to write a book about her experiences in Russia and interpreting the Russian mind. Sadly her final illness overtook her before that was completed but fortunately we are all more than adequately compensated by these wonderful letters

I must admit I adored my aunt and she was a great influence on me. After university I became a journalist and worked on two provincial papers before joining the *Daily Mail*. It was a proud day for me when both Olga and I had a byline on the same features page. But I found that I didn't really like life on a national newspaper and although I learnt much from it, I decided that I wanted a different type of career and found the law much more to my liking. But I wouldn't have missed it!

Richard Jaffa, Birmingham 2014.

Olga's family as they appear in her letters

Father: Izzy Davis

Mother: Rebecca (née Bernstein), who died before the correspondence started

Sisters and brothers: **Beryl** (married to Frank Jaffa)
                                 Cora (married to Ivan Lieberman, killed in North Africa in WWII, and later to Max Teofil and Leslie Jacobs)
                                 Betty (married to Louis Mintz)
                                 Felix and George (twins)

Nephews and nieces: Beryl's children: Richard and Lucille (Lucy) Jaffa (later Cohen)
                                 Cora's children: Vivienne (Viv) Lieberman (later Szekeres), Annette Teofil (Zera) and Rachel Teofil (now Symons)
                                 Betty's children: Henry, Bernard and Simon Mintz

Her Davis aunts: Phoebe Cave, Sally Gorch, Polly Rainbow

Her cousins: Rita, Rosalie, Harold (Cave)

1

Lost in London (Part I)

1932

In 1932, Olga, twenty years old, is working for Sir Herbert Austin at Longbridge and is about to meet her husband-to-be, Norbert Franklin. Norbert was originally from Poland but most of his family had settled in France. In the meantime, Olga is living in Edgbaston with Cora and her six-year-old sister, Betty. Her oldest sister, Beryl, had married Frank Jaffa in 1930. Her father, Izzy, had been a naughty boy as may be obvious from the first letter. Grandpa Izzy Davis had given his wife and children a difficult time. Olga's two cousins, Rosalie and Rita Cave, who we will meet throughout her correspondence, appear in the first letter. They fancied themselves as a bit posh and Birmingham far too parochial for them. They had gone off to London husband-hunting. It would be a protracted hunt! But Rosalie later married Paul Gottl (Gough), the Queen's patisserie chef, and Rita married the Austrian composer Hans May. But that was a lot later.

February 1932
46, Vernon Road
Edgbaston, Birmingham

Dear Beryl,

Our cousins Ros and Rit came to tea with Aunt Phoebe. It wasn't a good day for it. We'd scarcely got rid of that awful girl smirking on the front doorstep with a baby in her arms and her 'don't you think he's just like your Dad?'

Remember her? The girl with the vague look who was our cook-housekeeper before the last one? We just said Father wasn't at home and pretended not to understand. Then an hour later, the cousins come,

1

dressed to the nines on a day's outing in somebody's big car from their new home in St John's Wood, London.

Aunt rested her stomach on her knees and accepted our offering, such as it was, of anchovy-egg sandwiches, macaroons and tea, and asked after YOU, saying what a blessing it was that at least one of us Davis girls was now safely married and if only Ros and Rit could find good steady husbands, she could retire happily to Juan les Pins and never return to the dull Midlands. The cousins sort of snorted. 'Thank you, you needn't worry on my account,' said Ros and Rit just giggled and said, 'I wouldn't even LOOK at any Birmingham beau, Mamushka, so you can give up THAT idea.'

Rit has evidently picked up a bit of Russian from Aunt Phoebe's aristocratic friends in Juan les Pins and Ros has an important job as a German translator-typist. They wore smart hats; you know the mode now with huge bow over one eye which meant I had to walk right round the other side of the table to hand Rit her tea as she couldn't see me coming otherwise.

We talked about Cousin Jane who is also off to live in London. It's a proper exodus. Ros was sympathetic that we had to stay on in dull Brummagem; 'It's not really the beating heart of the Empire, is it?' Annoyed, I pointed out of the window at the lake and wood opposite. 'We've got the reservoir,' I said, feeling a bit on the defensive. 'Oh that,' said Ros. 'Can you skate on it in winter?' Rit asked. Honest, B, it wasn't worth wasting our best home-made macaroons on them.

Still, Ros admired our Betty which pleased me. 'She's not very big for six,' said Rit, but I could see they were both jealous of her long curls because they kept pulling them every time she went by with the sandwiches.

They left early to return to London which was a relief and you can thank me for not giving them your address. Aunt Phoebe thanked Cora for making a nice tea and told Betty to kiss her goodbye. Then she said she hoped Cora and I would soon find good husbands to take care of us and we must come to see her in Grove End Gardens, St John's Wood one day where she would introduce us to people and so on. Their car arrived, a big Austin sixteen horsepower and off they went. Our brothers were watching from their room upstairs and crept down to finish off the tea remains before we could even get back into the house.

Your affec. sister, Olga

46 Vernon Road, Edgbaston
April 1932

Dear B,

Thank you for a nice evening. Norbert Franklin* is very keen on both
you and Frank. 'Such a nice couple,' he said, 'it's very conducive.'

What do you think he means? Father says it means he's fallen and
will ask me to marry him and gave me such a lecture about it. Said I
must keep my big mouth tight shut most of the time; men don't like
girls who talk or girls who ask questions or girls who say clever things
or who think they're clever. Father went on and on. And, especially <u>not</u>
to tell my beau anything about Father and his business. Or rather his
lack of business. Because it might frighten N off and spoil everything.
I said stop it, Dad; you make it sound like a plot to catch the poor man.
Father said, a bit gloomy I thought, 'You just have to catch him at the
right moment. That's what every woman does. No man would ever marry
otherwise, except some clever woman knows the right moment... when
he's not on his guard; then it's done and by the time he realises it's too
late and he's caught.'

Is that true? Is that how you caught Frank? I don't believe it somehow.
Anyway I told Dad that you and I were going to spend the Bank Holiday
weekend at Llandudno and N was hoping to join us there, and I hope
he didn't mind.

'Mind?!' said Father, 'it's just ideal. You can walk him up the Great
Orme and then the Little Orme and he'll pop the question when he's
weak from walking. I know it. Mind? I'll even give you five bob towards
your train fare third-class.'

We're taking Betty with us of course; we'll teach her to swim.
Yours affec. O.

---

*Olga and Norbert were married in 1934. It was a very brief idyll. Within a year
or so of the marriage he was diagnosed with lung cancer. There are no letters at this
period as she was living only a few hundred yards from Beryl.

1935

13th September 1935
323, Lordswood Road
Harborne, Birmingham

Dear B,

Sorry to have kept you waiting for a reply. My various careers, viz.,
domestic, commercial and affectionate, occupy a good deal of my time,
leaving little leisure for sisterly interchange of thoughts.

We went to see La Bergner* in Escape-me-Never, Marvellous. If you
are very good, I will tell you how to make Consomme Saint-Gervais; it's
a soup. The gardener found a wasp nest and was wounded[...]

Elizabeth Bergner starred in the film directed by her husband Paul C. Zinner.

16th September 1935
Fort Anne Hotel, Douglas, I.O.M.

Dear B,

Nobby's chief treat was to see the soldiers marching up and down the
promenade on parade and hear the bands playing and watch the salute
and the changing of the guard. The sight of uniforms, the band and a
Major spitting 'Left, Left, Left' and my Nobby goes wild with excitement.
I suppose this comes from years living in Germany. The sound of the
bagpipes of the Scottish Grenadiers in their blue and green, (also
represented) sends him into raptures. We took a snap of the Governor
of the Isle of Man who looks like the Aga Khan and attended one of
the Parades[...]

1936

Christmas Eve
Palm Court Hotel, Torquay

Dear B,

The medicine had gone to the wrong hotel; the Pine Court and the Post Office were so busy with the Christmas rush that they simply would not speak to anyone. N was suffering horribly. I was desperate. I got the telephone book and found the TB hospital and asked them to recommend me a good Doctor in Torquay who specialised in lung illnesses.

I spent about two hours alone with Dr. Robinson. He said he thought it was definitely cancer. That growth on the lung was unknown before the war but cases were increasing rapidly in his opinion due to the increase in motoring – petrol fumes, the smell of tar and the fume-laden atmosphere.

That's the position up to date except for one or two other things he told me by way of encouragement and by God I needed some encouragement after that. Said he's lived since 1919 with only one lung, due to after-war Spanish 'flu and was so fit; thought he'd certainly be called up in the next war.

Are you getting very fed up with this letter? The weather is still much like summer; the Christmas hotel programme is hectic, dances and talking pictures, games, competitions, fancy-dress balls, concerts and mystery drives. Owing to Nob's not being well, they have allowed us to retain the best room in the place.

More next time and all my love. O.

1937

Norbert Franklin died of lung cancer after two years of marriage in May 1937 at the age of thirty-five. Olga, then aged twenty-four, attempted suicide on the same day, 'which had consequences' (her own words). She described those events in her first book, Born Twice, *published by Peter Garnett in 1951. After her suicide attempt, Olga was unconscious for five days. Norbert had been a patient of Dr. Ilya Margolin. When Beryl called and told him she could not wake Olga, Dr. Margolin rushed to her and his prompt action undoubtedly saved her life. In those days, attitudes to suicide and the law relating to it were very different. She spent several weeks in a*

Birmingham mental institution. Beryl fought to get her released. She had done quite serious damage to her lungs and Margolin recommended she go to Switzerland to recuperate.

Askona, Switzerland

Dear B,

You need not have worried about my travelling alone. I have to get used to being on my own from now on. Right from Victoria on I was with Cecil and we've been together ever since.

She is pretty, nice, related to the Writer E. Arnot Robertson whom you've read. We cycled to Milan yesterday. The heat was terrific. It's a fine city, reminiscent of Paris, except for the soldiers and officers everywhere, very dashing in grey uniforms with black silk shirts and ties, grey hats with gold braid, white teeth blazing in their dark faces. Soldiers everywhere, to the right, left and on top of you, in the sun outside the cafes, quatsching* [sic] with the girls in shady arcades; they strut, they parade, smirk at you over their shoulders. Fraulein Paulentz, typical flaxen-haired Aryan German girl, received a lot of attention, I went about with her and my London girl-friend Cecil Asbridge.

In this hotel she is called Signorina Asbridge. The girls in Milan go in for novel brassieres and swing their hips. We were taken first to see the Cemetery which is considered to be one of the Wonders of the world. It is divided up into three parts, Protestant, Catholic and Jewish. It is a triumph of architecture and bad taste. On top of enormous family vaults lie, in various attitudes of torment, the bronze figures of those who lie below. Each monstrosity is more incredible than the last. In the end Cecil got quite upset with it all and we had to leave. After that we saw the Cathedral and inspected every relic, particularly the dead but still intact body of Saint Ambrose lying in state under glass and adorned with gems and jewels so costly that the net value would probably settle all Mussolini's financial problems for the next 20 years. We saw the people kneeling before the picture of Mary and the Child, in front of the great shimmer of lighted candles and praying desperately. When their prayers are granted, they come again and drop a few lira in the money-box because they feel that a miracle has been performed.

We visited the shops which were much more chic than anything in Paris or London, but they were not cheap. Cecil wanted some nice black

6

and white gloves but THEY wanted 74 lira about 12/-!

We swam often in Lake Lugano. Sometimes the water is warm and sometimes icily cold because it is fed from the mountain snows.

Cecil and I cycled into Italy on Monday; we arrived at Pontetresa and after showing our passports, declaring our money and depositing our bikes, we crossed the frontier. The soldiers are cheeky and try to caress you as you pass. The Swiss half of Pontetresa is gay with flowers and cafes with their little check tablecloths but on the Italian side, it is very poor, shabby and depressed-looking. They had no tea to offer; when asked for cafe cream they looked shocked as though we asked for gold.

Coffee was provided but of exceedingly poor quality, with coffee grains dirtying the rim, sour and yellowish milk and no cakes to be had. We got tired very quickly of Italy and went back almost directly across the frontier. The soldiers did not seem surprised to see us return so promptly.

I am going to Zurich in the morning and hope to be able to stay until Sunday afternoon if my money holds out. I had to go to the British Consul for more. He was very charming; he is a Tessina named Senor Anastasi and he has an English wife. He said last year there were 3,000 English people in Lugano, but this year there are none because of the 'politische Sachen', (politics) he says.

Cecil and I had our hair washed today and a manicure. Our hair was filthy with lake-water. It was a bit tough describing in German what we wanted doing to our hair. But how efficient they are; you can't get your hair washed so cleanly or set so well or so quickly and efficiently in London, wherever you might go … and all for Swiss Frs. 4.50 for hair and 2.50 for manicure. Billig ja?

Cecil and I have been pestered by all sorts of men; some we have been out with to dance, but they are all so fearfully passionate that we just have to run for it. Cecil says she is longing to get back to our nice cold Englishmen; she is sick of being pulled about.

Cecil thinks it funny that I should be a widow at only 24 but she doesn't ask questions. She has a doctor boyfriend in London and she is far more experienced than I ever imagined a girlfriend of mine could be, so I am learning a lot from her. I mean I learn not to be surprised at anything though I think you might be shocked. Such little 'provincials' we are, you and I Bella, in spite of being Old Married Women.

No word from you. Why so stuck-up? Everyone dresses like mad in Lugano. Trousers are not worn it appears, but I wear yours; they make almost too much impression.

Switzerland is a wonderful country; it serves to prove to the world that a non-mixable variety of nations can live together happily. They speak four languages and God knows how many dialects. But they are passionately patriotic towards their beloved Switzerland. They speak French, German, Italian Tessina Romanisch, and they hate the Germans and the Italians. At the English they merely laugh, and rightly so. I'll try and write you again from Zurich.

Love, O.

On her return from Switzerland to Birmingham, Olga found an advertisement for a German interpreter at the Birmingham factory.
*Quatsching – Yiddish slang for gossiping.

September 1937
c/o Birmetals Ltd, Woodgate, Quinton
Birmingham 32

Dear Bella Bella,

Still no word from you young couple at the seaside, what are you doing? (Archly speaking) We are orlrite [sic] thank you.

Annie was anxious in case I should not have enough to eat last night. (Because of your instructions to fatten me). So she only gave me two cutlets, one whole cauliflower, a bath-size dish of spaghetti, two tomatoes, one grapefruit and three baked potatoes, followed by damson tart and have a cup of tea....

I don't like it one bit with you away. There is nobody to fuss over me and I like to be fussed over.

Betty has two big blisters on her ankle but she insists on going skating tonight just the same; she is obstinate like a block of our own best Aluminium Hardener manufactured by this firm; so can I help it if she busts her blisters?

Alec says his friend the moneylender has fallen for me in a big way. Aren't I the Little Heartbreaker? Do you think the funny little creature would lend me any money? Probably not.

Quite a lot of people are not going to the Panto because of 'flu breaking out, but I hope you will come just the same because I have spent 3/6d on you though you are not worth it because you go away and neglect me and doan [sic] care if I starve...

Please, the house is quite CLEAN and we haven't used the geyser. We don't wash. We can wash next week. There is no news and Rita Rainbow gave Betty sausages. Do you think I talk too much about Food? I hope you are having good food.

At Birmetals today, the new hat didn't go down too well.

The girls in our office all said; 'What has she got on?' and the Export Manager Mr. Simcox said, 'Oh, Irish' ... and Mr. Ripley said, 'My God, a Spanish Bullfighter.'

Your loving sister, ORF.

1938

After recovering from her suicide attempt, Olga describes in her autobiography how she became restless and decided she had to get away from Birmingham.

30th March 1938
c/o Birmetals Ltd, Woodgate, Quinton
Birmingham 32

Dear B,

Leaving Birmetals was so complicated. Lordy!

They collected £3.10s and gave me a present. I was embarrassed. I bought a fireside chair and a linen basket. Don't ask me why a fireside chair and a linen basket becos I don't know. They have such loving hearts these Black Country girls; knowing a bit of the story they made such a fuss of me always; their special pet; a bit like you do. Mr. Boyles offered me another job at Birmid Industries at Smethwick and I said I'd see. Mr. Smith said he wouldn't be surprised to see me come back to Birmetals but my boss Handforth never spoke a word to me for about 4 days and never even said goodbye; after a lot of damp, clinging handshakes and exhausting farewells I left. I keep thinking about that long report Handforth dictated about the metallurgical foundries and factories in Germany... all with electrical equipment and England has hardly any at all.

Dr. Margolin was so upset when I told him my boss in the laboratory was a leading member of the Nazi Party. Actually Herr Dipl.Ing. Weisse came to work one day in his brown Stormtrooper uniform complete with dog-whip! One of the Directors tactfully suggested he change into ordinary business suit before the Board meeting.

Mind you, the Monteure (the German engineers) did liven up the place

9

a bit. When Hitler suddenly ordered the whole lot to return at the weekend, it got very boring and quiet. For one thing, no one seemed to know how to get the Rolling Mill and Extrusion Press going again[...]

2nd August 1938
6 Grove End Gardens
NW8

Dear B,

I stayed at the Royal Hotel, Woburn Place from Sunday until Tuesday ... of all the horrible places I'd like to smack Frank's bottom for suggesting it .... it cost 5/9d bed and breakfast.

I stared across the street until Moons' petrol-filling station got on my nerves and I came over here and Cousins Rosalie and Rita Cave invited me to sleep in their Ma's bed until Friday; then they are going away for the weekend, so I'll have to find a room somewhere else.

I suppose I ought to be depressed. London is hot and lonely and I haven't got a job yet, not to speak of but I am not depressed though it is going to be a grisly job to carve my little chunk of flesh out of the backside of this God-forsaken City. I got sacked from one job I got on the second day. He was a German and nearly went mad when he arrived to find me opening his morning mail and putting it ready for him. He said it was secret and I had no right. Rather nasty really.

I seem to have wasted a lot of money and I would like some of your nice stew but they don't make stew here. I stayed a few nights at the Hen & Chickens and the Cobden, Ugh[...]

10th August 1938
Cobden Hotel, Holborn

I rang up the Daily Express of course ..... I hadn't spoken to a soul from Sunday morning till Tuesday. Fancy: If I forgot how to talk. But Henry Rose* is still in the U.S.A. and won't be back till next week. I went to see Neville Laski** K.C., in the Temple but he simply started right in to make love to me and I saw it was no use even trying to get him to talk sense .... the poor mutt simply wanted to be kissed.... Imagine! I was very nasty with him ... you know me, 1937/38 edition[...]

*Henry Rose was a well-known Manchester sports journalist and family friend who died in the Munich plane crash in 1958 with members of the Manchester United FC.
** Neville Laski was a leading barrister and another Manchester connection.*

In 1938, Cora married Ivan Lieberman. Olga was by now settled (after a fashion) in London.

August 1938
17 St Ann's Terrace
St John's Wood, NW8

Dear Bee,

Well you do see life in London. I can't see myself ever coming back to Brum. I really enjoy London and I'm never bored; there's always something to do, see or go to or from or be at and so.

This week I've had quite fun. Tuesday I got the sack, Wednesday I got a genuine proposal of marriage and Thursday I got another job.

I was as pleased as punch for getting the sack; at least it wasn't quite the sack because I gave simultaneous notice and just walked out. Lovely! I got it for being cheeky.

I didn't really want to go back to work; think I'm a born loafer ... I like it too much loafing around and sunbathing in the parks; it's been hellish hot again and the sun simply scorching. But much against my will I landed a job this morning an' I s'pose I'll have to work for a bit now. But this time it's not a dark and dirty frowsty little office with a nasty fat man in Moorgate in the East, but luxury offices in Australia House, just between Aldwych and the Strand, right West Central about a minute or so from Haymarket and Piccadilly Circus. They're all German Jews this time but it's the metal trade which I know something about or oughtn't I. I had a long test but tankyou [sic] made no mistakes. The same money as before. Business is considered to be so bad this year (by all the employment bureaux who have dropped their terms) that £4 a week is considered to be the tip-top wage now and it's a helluva struggle to get that.

One job was funny; was advertised at £4 and for private-secretary, 'smart, attractive personality' etc., and gosh you oughta seen the girls run after it. Some hundred odd girls stormed the offices of the Fenchurch Street bureau and the poor creature-in-charge, a Mr. Alabaster was very

11

limp and alabaster by the time those naughty girls, all the six hundred but not all 'smart, attractive, personable' had finished with him. Not to mention the odd thousand telephone calls he received and the odd million written applications all for the same job and coming from all over England, from Birmingham, Manchester, Wales, Brighton, Jersey and all round London.

Most of these girls .... no nearly all of them he told me, are IN work but they go mad at the idea of getting £4 per week and at the same time dazzling somebody with their smart attractive personalities.

But, at the Laurie Employment bureau it was funnier still; they also advertised a secretarial job at £4 odd and got the usual stampede first thing in the morning, but when I arrived later about 10 am, I found one solitary girl sitting all forlorn in the waiting-office. It appears someone came in and informed the waiting queue that the terms were 10% on the first year's salary that is about £11 TO BE PAID IN FULL and AT ONCE. She said, you oughta seen the dust those girls raised trying to get outa the place quick enough.

I picked up a Canadian fellow in St James's Park whilst I was typing there some weeks ago. Then I met him again in the same place (p'raps he was still looking for me) and he begged me so hard and passionately to have dinner with him, that I did. It was Wednesday when I had no job, no money to spare and had eaten no lunch (I enjoy life but I doan eat when I got no job, on principle) so he bought me a seventeen course meal in the Regent Palace, bought me flowers, took me out to coffee and the pictures.

In the Regent Palace we got talking to an American woman and he asked her to join us for coffee so we went to a Honeydew bar and drinking more coffee we got talking to a German refugee, so we all joined up.

My, we were a funny mixed sort of party but it was fun; you meet such interesting people all the time, you've no idea. The Canadian was for five years assistant to STEPHEN LEACOCK, who as well as a Writer is a famous Economics expert. This chappie has also been an Aviator and is now a Mathematics tutor privately. He's been all over the world.

He insists on wanting to marry me. Of course he's quite mad and I told him so. This evening he rang up again and asked me to have dinner and I had to tell him pretty sharply that I wouldn't and then I hung up. So I dined with Aunt Sally in Baker Street. Sally gets more spiritualist every day; she went tonight to a 'physical' meeting; that means the Medium makes the spirits materialise into ghost form, and this costs 5 bob if you please.

Cousin Rita Cave told Aunt Sally she quite enjoyed the wedding and Cora and everyone looked very nice. She was disappointed Dr. Margolin* wasn't there and she wanted to know who the best man was, because she liked him rather.

By the way, I've got a date with the best man in Brum on Saturday night and I'm taking the opportunity of coming to Brum tomorrow (Friday) that's if you don't mind ... (since I'm free to travel) ... but if you don't want me you can just turf me out on my ear.

Here's a laugh for you; I got dates with both my dentist and chiropodist but I'm leaving my doctor (Margolin) out this time. With a connection like that, you can get plenty of health treatment free of charge, don't you think: Look what you get all for nothing; I'll be able to run the hundred yards in record time, breathe through my nose and break nuts with my teeth. Oh Boy!

Whilst I was typing all this rubbish, a knock came at my door.

Who's that quoth I, knocking, knocking at my chamber door? It was a handsome, (but oh how handsome!) blonde blue-eyed man from the floor above, who was also typing (and doing German translations too!) and wanted to borrow some carbon and typing paper.

Thank God my nose was powdered and I was not completely naked. He was joined later at my door by an equally blonde blue-eyed girl (I don't know what relation if any) and they both came in and sat on my bed (next to the huge picture of the Assyrian horsemen which is a popular feature of this bed-and-breakfast boarding-house) ... and we talked and talked. The man is not German but an English Engineer named Mr. Schneider which is a bit difficult to believe. The girl was a German Jew and an exile, not pretty but nice. They've only just gone and he says I must come upstairs and have coffee some time. Gee but they're such nice people. How do you exist in Birmingham where all the people are so dull, so deadly dull. It's so exciting here; something happens every day and you meet someone new every single day and they're all interesting. Yesterday morning on the bus I bumped into the son of an old pal of Frank's and he is also going to ring me up.

Well I hope you won't mind if I turn up tomorrow, I mean today. I haven't had much grub this week but that's a detail. Have you heard from Cora? I heard from Miss Adams at Birmetals in Quinton that Mr. Boyles has got the sack. She says that Birmetals is now run completely by the Nazis, and in fact by Dipl.Ing Herr Weisse himself, complete with his brown shirt, leather boots and dog-whip. She says the workmen in the Rolling-mill had a meeting and threatened to call a strike unless he took those clothes off. In fact he puts his civvy suit on to walk through the factory and metallurgical laboratory and foundry and wears his 'best' brown Stormtrooper outfit for Board meetings....

I'll be seeing you, if you let me. Oggi

* Olga and Dr. Margolin remained in touch and were probably lovers briefly.

12th August 1938
17 St Ann's Terrace
St John's Wood, NW8

Dear B,

I was invited to Cousin Rosalie's and Rita's for supper Wednesday night and turned up an hour late when it was all over. My own fault, I get lost and I'm vague, haphazard I know. Anyway I got it in the neck like you wouldn't believe. Say .... you know you when you're annoyed or if you don't, ask Frank,

Say! you haven't even got the first idea about it, you don't even know how to try and get mad ... well finally Rosalie reduced me to tears ... partly because I was so tired I could have howled anyway and partly because even the brittle shell I've built around me gets a bit shattered if it's hammered at long and hard enough. However, I survived. Cousin Harold arrived later and we all went to the Zoo in Regent's Park and watched the sea-lions bathing. Friday there was a sort of farewell party for the Max Kawa's of Berlin* who are going to America.

I have a temporary job working for some Germans which is quite hard work.

Aunt Sally is taking me to see a family called Genyon who take care of most of the German refugees in London. And next Sunday I am supposed to be going to a ramble with the Left Book Club** to whom Louis Genyon, the brother belongs. I think they're red-hot Communists all so I suppose you'll say 'I thought so'.

I didn't write this week on account of working hard and being talked at by Rita and Rosalie and getting lost and all. But I did write to Aunt Becky*** and asked if she would like me to come and visit her in Pilsen; perhaps she could get me an au pair job in Czechoslovakia; aren't I the restless bugger? I landed in a hell of a mess on Monday. I was in London with just 5/6d in the world, enough for fares for a couple of days but not enough for food. Then, Monday night my landlady put a note outside my door she wants two weeks rent in advance.

I wrote to the Bank ... it's a long story but I couldn't get any money until Wednesday morning by which time I was a bit peckish. I tried everything I could think of but no use and believe me that was the nastiest spot I was in so far. (If you turn over the page, you'll find I'm still talking).

What wouldn't I give for a basin of your stew. I do loathe cafe food and so would you if you had it as I do for every blasted meal.

But I like London; it is stimulating; continually meeting new people. It is extraordinary how many people there are here who are very eccentric. I guess it's the strain, the awful strain of life that gets people down and they just have to grab at some sort of outlet or religion or belief to keep going, like Sally with her Spiritualism.

By the way I think you might like me .... I look suddenly right up to the minute – since Saturday. I actually had my hair thinned out ... take a drink now, steady ... and the girl took so much off that the bit that's left I can wind round on to the top of my head in the real 1938 model style and I think you'll like it. Wish I had a few clothes to go with it. Rita and Rosalie pretend to swoon away every time they see me ... and what's worse, to drag out smelly falling-to-pieces garments dating from about 1925 and thrust them into my arms despite my protests which they ignore. I now have a drawer full of horrible outfits from which all vestige of colour or shape has long since faded .... really pitiful rags. And for these I have to utter a constant stream of feeble thankyous until my voice (never strong in spite of Sally having put it on the Absent-healing list and prayers being offered up for its sweet sake by qualified psychic mediums at Meetings) ceases to register and sinks to a tired whisper ... dating back to August 1937....

All the German Jews for whom I work, including the office girl and cashier to the Managing Director are frightfully religious and in winter they leave at 3-30 on Fridays. The girls are so nice; one gave me a box of candy for my birthday; but these ruddy Deutschers are so tough; they work you to death.

P.S. How much do I owe Frank now? Let me know when you'll be in London and you can 'come and get it'.

Max Kawa was a leading Berlin dress designer and one of the many German Jews fleeing from Hitler
**The Left Book Club was founded in 1936 by Victor Gollanz (later to be one of*

*Olga's publishers) and included a whole range of socialists, communists and members
of the Labour party as a concerted voice against fascism.*
****Olga's Aunt Becky had married Ernest Adler and settled in Palestine in the
1930s. Her descendants still live in and around the kibbutz Mishmar Ha-emek in
Israel, as do other members of the family.*

5th September 1938
c/o Metal Supplies Ltd
Australia House, Strand, London WC2

Dear Beryl,

Thank you for the hairpins. I forgot. I look very tidy this week because
of them. Yes, it is my Saturday off this week-end, would you like me
to come over? Would you please say. Please will you thank Betty for her
lovely letter.

(Dear Betty, it was beautifully written and spelt and worded. I presume
Beryl helped you with the wording. Never mind your dictation was very
good; you will make a good secretary yet. I would like to know what
you want to have for your birthday next month. P'raps you should ask
Beryl because maybe it will have to be something sensible.)

It seems Michael has not yet got tired of me, at least not yet. He is
going to take me to see Lucie Mannheim in Ibsen's 'Nora' (The Doll's
House) if he can get seats for Thursday.

On Sunday, however, he is going to hear Duff Cooper* speak at the
Club and there will be a dinner costing 8/6d for members only, so I
couldn't go in any case. They would let me join, I understand, at half-
price as a country member (30/-d) but I think it is still too much money
to pay for it.

Forgive me if this letter has a tired sound; late nights. I keep showing
Betty's letter to everybody because I am proud of it. I hope people are
not bored with it. The last paragraph where the cry bursts forth from
Betty's soul that 'our lives are dull' reminded me of the youngest of
Chekhov's 'Three Sisters'; remember the ones who were always wanting
to go to Moscow so that they could lead the kind of lives they wanted
to lead. Betty may wear Deanna Durbin frocks and speak with a
Brummagem accent but her soul is pure USSR I am sure of it. But I
ask the question, why is she not comforting your old age that you should
lust after companionship from the sick roysterings of my eternally

16

adolescent spirit?? Perhaps Betty will become a writer; her crisp, tart description of our other sister Cora being dragged from the mud by a horse caused me to raise up my voice in a great and hearty chuckle.

It has gone suddenly very cold again tonight and I am sitting close before my odorific gasfire. I have beautiful tall curls and I am wearing my cyclamen gown. If only I had on the dressing-table a bottle of lavender water together with a bottle of Brandy, a plate of cake and another of pickles on the bed; if my curtains were full of holes and I had a motley audience of dingy lovers then I should feel rather like Lady Caroline Lamb in her declining years. Oh it is a delicious book. I am so sad that I am nearly at the end of it. I think I will now turn back to the beginning again.

Enough of my foolish fancies. I am, you note, still being Carolinish. Now as to the 'fame and fortune' dear Betty speaks of. Does she refer by any chance to Metal Supplies? There, certainly I have much fame, on account of my errors and omissions. Of fortune I have none. Our shipping-clerk, Mr. Albert Johnson born and bred of good solid Birmingham (I think Tyseley) stock is leaving this week to take a better job. This has caused a 'wave of wanting to leave-ness' ... to pass over the entire office staff like a swarm of locusts descending on the crops, and has likewise left us denuded, deflowered and dejected by our fruitless longings.

This morning it suddenly occurred to me that I would do the cousinly and dutiful and proper thing and ring up the Caves after my neglect of some three to four weeks. My reception, however, was unfortunate. First, a cold voice, Rita Cave's, enquired to what might be attributed the honour of my call. She then went on to remark that I was a fine bloody ticket-seller or something to that effect. I am a sad disappointment to my cousins.

I was in fact commissioned to sell tickets (21/-) each, for the Maccabi ball and I not only failed to dispose of any one of them but left them by error in a bus, whereupon they were returned to Rita with a sharp reproof for carelessness. I was informed by her at some length of my unfortunate disabilities and disqualifications; the whole poverty of my character, disposition and activities were enlarged upon and with a few extra sharp reproofs thrown in for good measure, the discourse was brought abruptly to an end and I was summarily handed, telephonically speaking, over to Rosalie and the atmosphere was found to be more equable. Rosalie is still out of work and is attending shorthand classes two evenings a week: Ros is what you might call a worker. She, however, also reproved me at some length for my failings as a ticket-seller and since it did not occur to anybody, I did not suggest pointing out that I had in the first place been reluctant to take on the job. I feel one ticket-seller in the Family is quite sufficient.

Love Og

***Duff Cooper was a government minister who resigned in protest at Neville Chamberlain's policy of appeasing Hitler. He later returned to government when Churchill became Prime Minister.*

19th September 1938
c/o Metal Supplies Ltd
Australia House, Strand, London WC2

Dear Beryl,

How did you and Betty get on with the Kennedy relations* in Manchester? I dined with my doctor boyfriend last Thursday. He is very, very plain, with teeth and glasses and when he talks, he sprays you unless you duck.

He was so lovesick that I finally decided to tell him my story in order to choke him off properly. (By the way, it was Rene and Lee who introduced him to me; he has a thriving medical practice in North London).

I told him my story, truthfully but with a wealth of lurid detail, not leaving anything out hardly … and just to clinch it I told him I was not only Not a Good Girl but a very very Bad Girl indeed. I torked [sic] all evening, I had the grandest time! But the total net result was an awful blow in the eye, for at the end of the evening, quivering with misguided passion, he informs me that 'My Past' does not make any difference and now he wants me more than ever. He is even ready to MARRY! Think of that. I felt that as a raconteur I had failed miserably. If that is the best result I can achieve with a real horror story (and after all my little stay in the 'Snake Pit' WAS, as you yourself witnessed) …then I lay down my pen and ink before I've started. Tenses are a bit mixed there, but you know what I mean.

He has 'phoned twice since and he is ringing today to make a date for his half day tomorrow. But I warned our Miss Campbell to say, as Herr Dr. Mayer says 'I am in dictate' and anyway if I have to speak I shall tell him I am going to evening-class for Journalism.....

Which is true! I started the L.C.C. Journalism class last night at Prince

Henry's Rooms in Fleet Street. The first class was a bit of a disappointment. The Lecturer was painfully slow and dull. And he stood for everything that I most disliked. Imagine.! He is a passionate Godfrey Winn** fan! He was lecturing about how one should never, if possible, introduce abnormal forms of speech in dialogue in a short story and he was of the opinion that one should avoid introducing any stuttering or stammering of a character as this might give offence to a stuttering reader ......
Then one old girl spoke up. She thought there ought to be no hard and fast restrictions like that because if one was writing about LIFE, one ought to stick to reality, however unpleasant.

So up speaks little Ogg (always the stark realist) and says 'I should like to support that point because I think there is quite enough evasiveness in our Daily Press without pandering to it in Literature.' Our Lecturer didn't like that, or me and tells a story of Mr. G. Winn's special kindness to a particular stutterer. Whereupon I suggested that must have given Mr. Winn a good opportunity to be even more sympathetic than usual.....
The class rocked with laughter and I got the heady impression they were all with me. I was cheeky enough to add that Mr. Winn was terribly sincere but sincerity could be misguided. 'Herr Hitler,' I said, 'seems awfully sincere, but look what a nuisance he is with his sincerity.' I felt I had the Class with me and couldn't stop. I just plunged on. 'A true journalist,' I said, 'should not be so passionately sincere because he must keep his balance and be able to see clearly all points of view quite apart from his own.' The Class shouted as one man 'Hear Hear' and I think I got a bit carried away but felt I'd won the first round.

When I got home that night, ...you'll never believe this ... there was a huge parcel waiting for me at Mrs. Mann's flat, with a Birmingham postmark and obviously came from Barrows' famous store in Corporation Street, so I thought naughty Beryl, she's at it again, I bet this time she's sent me a pot of Jugged Hare for my dinner. So I opens the parcel and it is two large, handsome rich plum cakes. And the sender, my dear old doc, Dr. Margolin!

I felt weak with shock ... to think at last ....he must have forgiven me all my wickedness. I had to go to bed from it ... that is after Mrs. Mann and Son (Cyril) and me had hacked deep into one of the cakes.

I won't tell you all my other adventures because some of them are naughty and wouldn't pass the Censor. I saw that film 'March of Time' but it's not just been censored but hacked to pieces.

A terribly attractive but awfully Bad man I went out with on Sunday says that (he is a German) I speak the very finest English he has ever heard. He asks, do all Birmingham people speak like it? Like, he says, in Hanover where you can hear the finest German spoken. Oh but he was a bad man!

I've not seen my Cave Cousins again and now it's so long since I phoned them I'm scared to … lots more to write but Metal Supplies will be after me if I don't stop …. Love to Betty and Frank,

Love, Snogs.

* *Olga's aunt Rachel (Ray) Kennedy (née Bernstein) was a teacher who taught the writer Louis Golding in Manchester and is almost certainly the model for the heroine in his bestseller* Magnolia Street. *She horrified the Manchester Jewish Community by marrying a non-Jewish pilot during World War I. He became a great friend of the Jewish community and his photograph hangs in the Jewish Museum in Manchester.*
** *Godfrey Winn (1906–1971) was a well-known journalist, actor and novelist also born in Birmingham and like Olga, went to King Edward's School.*

20th September 1938
c/o Metal Supplies Ltd
Australia House, Strand, London WC2

Dear Beryl,

Thanks for yours. That is what I wanted, just a bit of gossip about food and whatnot. It was a very interesting letter. I am glad Frank is coming to London. I shall consider it a privilege to have him pay for my luncheon?? Just a bit of my artless, ingenuous pumping, you know. Oh! what a tease the girl is. Tell Cora and Ivan to move into one of the beds and store the other one….

I like my job, and the work is quite interesting. It is nice working in such pleasant surroundings. The other girls are not too friendly, one is German, two are Swiss and there are a couple more. The four Germans here, two Directors and two Managers reFUSE to speak any English and they bark at one another all day long in German. I shall never get used to their temperamental manners.

When they are all collected in the one office I get quite frightened; I guess they can hear the hullabaloo and shouting way down the Strand. Loud Germanic voices raised in altercation, thunderous cries, someone is striding up and down the office, Mr. Suss' (Jew Suss*) voice is now raised in a wail of agony; I begin to sweat; this is the end, I think, someone is getting the sack and is in travail; perhaps they are going to close down or have lost all their money or are going to be sent back to Germany. The explosive sounds come nearer; they are coming in to this office; trembling I look up and concentrating manage to translate the tragic cries. But it is all right, they are discussing whether the copper market will stay firm for another 24 hours.

Have had a quite quiet week and done a bit of reading for a change. Have got 'William & Dorothy'** which is nice. Last night I sat up late reading Dorothy Wordsworth's hopeless passion for the naughty Coleridge and wept shamelessly in full view of the five haughty Assyrian horsemen riding over my bed. I could not come back to my room to read as it is both dark and cold but for the price of a Russian tea (5d) I sat all evening and read in the Strand Palace Lounge. Nice of you to invite me for the weekend. In view of the weather I would much prefer to come to Brum but I am fearful of taking advantage of your generosity. The thought of the roast duck torments me with desire but it's a quid to Brum and anyway I guess you've seen enough of me for a while. I think I am moving my digs next week, to a room in Henry St, just off Circus Road, St John's Wood, N.W.8. Will write.

Love Ogg.

*A novel by Lion Feuchtwanger, made into a film by Birmingham-born Michael Balcon in 1934.
**Possibly a volume of Ernest de Selincourt's Letters of William and Dorothy Wordsworth.

22nd September 1938
5, Park Mansions, Henry St
St John's Wood, London NW8

Dear B,

As I type I can see myself in the long mirror opposite and like Narcissus, I am in love with myself in my long cyclamen dressing-gown which you made me.

London is tonight again disfigured with posters declaring 'Hitler Speaks'. It sounds very novel but I am so blasé these days that I didn't even buy a newspaper. Meanwhile Rita Cave is still driving ambulances and Rosalie wants to be a spy, and the new Spring hats which she's put on show for customers, should be a great help in livening things up a bit.* My plan is to occupy a steel shelter lavatory at the bottom of your neighbour Alec Livingstone's garden and we shall place a notice to warn enemy bombers that we are a Protected Industry.

When a document was returned to me today for re-typing, I moaned loudly that Herr Berlinger was a bleeding liar for saying he said something he didn't say. But when he came in to collect, I merely agreed tamely with his protestation that it was a 'misunderstanding'. When he'd gone, the girls fell on me and called me a gutless Chamberlain and there was an awful fight. I have a bruise.

We talked Sex in the office today. This was because Fraulein Pinkus is away in Switzerland and she is really the only one who gives the office any tone. We ate penny Party Buns and had a nice time. 1d Party Buns are lovely and you can get them from Joe Lyons. Herr Dr. Mayer eats 3 every day between his lunch at 1.30 and his tea at 4pm when he eats his sandwiches.

I think our little sister Betty is very nice. When she is not cross.

Give everyone my love.

* *Cousin Rosalie had a hat shop called Chapeaux Therese which was in George Street.*

September 1938
c/o Metal Supplies Ltd
Australia House, Strand, London WC2

Dear Bella,

Cora and Betty called at the office today and caused a sensation. I was quite anxious beforehand in case it might have been one of Betty's plain days or in case Cora was wearing still her old green coat. My fears were not realised and both children did me such credit and Betty bringing me such 'nachas' [pride] that I nearly burst with pride.

The 'Girls' all think she is JUST like me, ... the image they say, in face, character, everything. Of course, they were impressed by her angelic little whispers. They oughta hear her refusing to wear what she's told sometimes.

Especially admired was her immaculate grey costume and her curls. Fraulein Behrend wants to adopt her. 'Such a Lovely Girl' was their awed murmur all afternoon. Our Corrie was considered very sweet and charming and not a bit plump, though not so attractive as You of course. Herr Dr. Mayer said he did not know I had 'a such small sister'. I think he thinks she is really my child and part of my obscure and murky past.

Please tell Cora that Dr. Mayer's friend Herr Fritz Hirsch from our Associated Company, National Scrap Metals across the way in Lancaster Place knows the Schotts*; he knew the firm from Danzig or something and knew that Walter was living with a nice family in Birmingham. Dr. M wants to place a little refugee girl of 13 but I had to tell him I didn't know anyone.

Betty looked a bit pale but I expect it was because Cora took her in the Ladies' and powdered her nose. I'm afraid Betty made such an impression that the Girls can't talk about much else today.

Soon the good Herr Doktor will be in here screaming for his letters, his tea and more Party Buns.

I should like to come to Brum (uninvited) this weekend but to spend a whole pound does seem sacrilege. I'll have to make up my mind on Friday, won't I?

* *Walter Schott, a German refugee, who settled in Birmingham, later courted Betty (unsuccessfully).*

September 1938
5, Park Mansions, Henry St
St John's Wood, London NW8

Dearest Beryl,

I am as you see now moved into my new little hole. I am quite comfortable.

My landlady has a middle-aged bachelor son named Cyril. When I am in the bathroom she bangs on the door hard and calls out:

'Come out of there; it's time for Cyril to shave.'

London has now heaved a deep-chested sigh of relief. The Thames is swollen high tonight with pride. In Lyons Corner House, people keep bursting out between courses into 'He's a jolly good fellow' and every half-hour whilst the poached egg congeals upon its toast, we rise to God save the King. I'll say no more but let the future say it for me. I take off my straw hat which rather needs pressing, especially the one velvet rose in front, to Mr. Chamberlain. I like his guts even if he is three score years and ten... it is that quality of undefeatableness in a man that one admires....

But everyone must ache a little to think of the hundreds of thousands of nice, so reliable Czech folk turned out of their homes and winter drawing nearer and the nights get colder rapidly. Deprived of their coalmines, their steel works, glass factories, bitumen mines, fortifications, railways, oil supplies, iron foundries and the shadow of their friendly mountains.

In spite of relief, in spite of admiration for a man who is acclaimed by the whole world to have brought off a coup which is not a coup ... my stubborn streak persists; my opinions are unchanged. I sicken still at the pictures of the full-jowled Benito as the beneficent, beatific benefactor of blissful peace .. Time marches on.

One thing also I know. You are and have been good – to me. One excellent thing, my dear, but misguided Father did, he begot you, his eldest daughter.

I was kissed tonight by a strange but handsome young man inside a taxi ... but in spite of temptation and some persuasion, arrived home at Park Mansions intact. Sometimes I think you have brought me up to be too straitlaced. Still I must not bring disgrace upon our house. Sufficient that I hang about disreputable Communist outdoor meetings, rub shoulders with roughnecks, thieves, socialists, anti-gods, liberals and petty pilferers.

Love Og

September 1938
5, Park Mansions, Henry St
St John's Wood, London NW8

Dear B,

Today (Sat) I came out here to Thames side. I took the tube to Richmond and then the bus through Hampton Court across the park where the thick-bellied trees stand at ease like soldiers in regimental rows stretching as far as the eye can see ... whilst the gentle deer, some of them no bigger than dogs, trip delicately in an' out.

The river, where the Mole crosses the Thames at Hampton Court, bears on its left bank a fine Lilliputian village with tiny little wooden houses, supported on trellis-work interlaced with flowers. Following the track along tiny footpaths you can look down or across to these little huts, with tiny little chimneys stuck askew, probably for fun, upon the roofs. These houses and caravans and house-boats have the most extraordinary names, Mumsie Annexe, Hoocha Koocha, Y-worry, Lazy

Land, I wish I could remember some more …. and everywhere hosts of flowers rioting; it makes me think of Rackety-Packety House from our favourite book when we were children. The river is very beautiful but sullied for me by the voices booming along as far as you travel on either bank … to the effect that This is the National Programme and that German troops have today penetrated into Sudetenland and so on, until at last the slice of yellow moon looks down upon still water.

You see I am learning, or rather studying to learn the difficult art – of being alone. But I guess I haven't been at it really long enough yet. It must take years to acquire anything like a standard of proficiency. I thought I was good at it and generally I am very, very, but sometimes a combination of dreary hotel, moonlight on the river and oh that bloody wireless invites a melancholy (it's playing 'Carolina Moon Keep Shining') which makes you think with appetite of drinking deep of the shining river lying at your door. Oddsboddikins, but the radio has much to answer for and if the harpsichords are always playing in heaven I shall refuse to go, in the event of my being invited.

This room is full of monster artificial flowers; I think they are intended to be poppies; there are also many artificial sweet-peas nestling together with paper chrysanthemums. The wireless has just commenced to play 'shananikidah' …… in retrospect my Jewish fiddler or whatever he was, of the night before in the taxi, appears even more attractive than he actually was and I am actually wishing I had not dismissed him so summarily. To such a pass is a still-young girl brought who, without benefit of compass, leads a life with as little direction as have the golden autumn leaves floating outside on old Father Thames.

My present loneliness is due in the first place to my unbelievable conceit; I do not find any companion good enough for me. I am critical of all. I stick my roman-jewish nose in the air, and like the lonely Dictator amongst his desolate Berchtesgarden mountains who also allows no one in his bed, it seems … I want to be alawn [sic] and hobnob with the artificial flowers. The wireless now informs me that She's-got-eyes-of-blue. I-never-cared-for-eyes-of-blue but- that's-his-weakness now. Would you believe it?

It will be absolutely in order for you to ignore entirely the whole of the foregoing. Having belched it up I really feel quite good. The Wireless now reminds me that this is a 'room-with-a-view' and this at least is strictly accurate and cannot be denied. And now, whilst we enjoy Lily-of-Laguna, I wish to remind you that all the foregoing complaints or sad welter of dismalness d'ye ken John Peel is strictly meant to be in the form of satire, Daisy Daisy, and bears no relation whatsoever to my customary state of mind, which is placid, Oh Danny-Boy!

And on Wednesday next, when your stomach rolling over and over from the Fast,* thunderously rebels ... pray for your sinful sister that she may again see the Light....How is my pretty little sister Betty? and what is the news?

Best love, O.

* *Yom Kippur.*

29th September 1938
c/o Metal Supplies Ltd
Australia House, Strand, London WC2

Dear B,

As you will note probably from the papers, London is not what it used to be. What with street-fighting and bombs exploding in the Underground ... and now the Police are to carry guns!

I tell you ... just an ordinary little crook like me won't stand a chance these days, the Police are so active! I guess that's the trouble ... our 'think-you're-wonderful' London Police Force resent it so much that they have to do a little real work for the first time since the War that they go in for a great deal more rough-house than is strictly necessary.

I have some new friends, very eccentric like all the others. One is called Michael; took me to see 'The Good Earth' revived at the Classic last Thursday. I loved all of it and was quite astonished when a loud female voice behind me intoned at full pitch, 'I think it is TOO Depressing.' (This was in the middle of the famine bit). 'Shall we go dear?' she said. And they went. Extraordinary taste some people have.

Another friend is Rene Zeitlin, very sophisticated, has six clever brothers; she appears not to want to be too officially engaged to Lee the lawyer in case she changes her mind. The idea of marriage really rather bores her, particularly marriage to Lee: He is very tall and plain, very kind. Still, the years are flying and marriage is indicated, so what? Then there is Bernard; she is not pretty but awfully intelligent; not everybody's Meat but Lee and Bernard swear they love her to distraction. It seems that the money her brothers are prepared to provide has no influence upon their ardour one way or another. Bernard told me, in strictest confidence, (in the heat of his disappointment, of course) that he wondered what Lee would think if he knew that he (Bernard) and she had been lovers a year ago for a short time, when their blood had been overheated by a stay in Westgate-on-Sea.

EVERYBODY insists on telling me things in STRICTEST confidence. I do wish they wouldn't.. Most of the Londoners I met up till now would probably come under the heading of what you in your own inimitable fashion would describe as 'Yamps'. They yamp on and on. I wonder if I had joined the International Brigade .... would I have met a few people who were not Yamps.

If you are still reading the 'Express', I suppose you don't know much of what is going on in Spain. Some people here say all this street-rioting in London now is because we now have so many foreigners in London. That's silly: No refugee here dares so much as whisper that he does not care very much for Herr Hitler. Just try mentioning one word of politics to a foreigner (of any nationality) in London and they shut up like proverbial oysters. No, I think that public opinion has been outraged by the massacres in Spain. The News Chronicle printed the most pitiful picture the other day of several tiny Spanish children limping along the road from Barcelona, each child having lost a limb, and the expression on those children's faces is haunting everyone who has seen that picture, myself included.

Sunday: Going into the country this afternoon. Rene wants to pick Pussy-willow: She gets these 'turns' occasionally when she fancies she is a wood-fairy[...]

2nd October 1938

Dearest B,

Isn't it bloody cold? Sorry I did not write before to thank you for the delicious stews, which were more than appreciated.

I said: 'my sister sends me stew' and people said; 'what's that?' I think they think it's something to wear.

It tastes like heaven[...]

October 1938
5, Park Mansions, Henry St
St John's Wood, London NW8

Dear Beryl,

I am reluctant to make apologies for I fear there is nothing can excuse my gross neglect. Believe only that every time I sit down to write to you I am prevented and that this is really the first opportunity to communicate

First, let me acknowledge with sincerest thanks receipt of the chicken (surely the major portion of your week-end supplies) and the delightful soup, the fruit, the stew, all of which I enjoyed and appreciated. Please do not think that because I have not written for so long that I am not thinking of you and little Bettina and Frank all the time, but when I do find time to sit down and write I am often too tired to use the typewriter and too tired to think.

Have been out and about a great deal and last week two late nights, one 3am and one nearly 4. Don't remind me how foolish it is to indulge in such freakish hours. I know it, I feel it and my mirror reflecting very pale face with sunken eyes peering under Chinese slits confirms my foolishness. Still it all comes under the heading of nice, clean fun and helps to relieve the monotony of a workaday world. Exhaustion is the price one has to pay for too much popularity and you know only too well how your shmoozy little sister always pulls her weight at a party.

Did you see the beautiful picture of Rita Cave in the News Chronicle last week, together with STRONG article calling for Justice to Rita Cave, because she has been left out of the Alpine Hut* programme because she cannot yodel.

I intend to organise a lie-down strike in Langham Place until she is reinstated. Rosalie has been the last couple of weeks in Paris but returns today. Her young boyfriend Mark, left thus at large, phoned me three times to go out with him. But I was adamant. Think of the risk......

When today I wrote a letter to a firm in Rotterdam, Germany, the Herr Doktor pointed out quite kindly that he thought I was perhaps some six months in advance of my time and that I should endeavour in future to keep this sort of crystal-gazing prophecy out of mere commerce as it was apt to cause delays in the post. He then dismissed me with his customary 'Go with God' whereupon I'm afraid I retorted that God seemed to be rather particular about the sort of company He keeps.

Franco is tonight a bare 17 miles from Barcelona and one shudders to think of the fate awaiting those brave Republicans if Franco and the Junker planes succeed in taking the city. In the newsreel this week, there is a brief but tragic picture of the hungry people in Spain clamouring for food.

There has been no little outcry in London for 'Arms for Spain' and the mob has howled for Chamberlain's blood. I hope to get into the Queen's Hall** on Wednesday if possible to hear J.B. Priestley, Vernon Bartlett, Stafford Cripps and many others on the subject. But what is the use now, it is all over but the shouting.

I have seen the Citadel (most disappointing) Dr. Clitterhouse (quite good) and Angels with Dirty Faces. I went with new friend Michael who knows how to do things properly and have enjoyed with him many good dinners at Czardas in Dean Street.

Michael and I are having a very satisfactory Platonic friendship. I like him very much and he thinks I am entirely Marvellous .... however I am not at all likely ever to 'fall' for him except as a friend, and so far I find this a very satisfactory arrangement.

Rene introduced us. She has seven brothers and £4,000 and is much sought after. Rene is about 27 and no longer innocent, knows just what she wants and though determined to have either one or the other, is very bored and dissatisfied with both her suitors but the seven brothers have impressed upon her it is now time to marry and Snow White has made up her mind to comply for, apparently, this is all London has to offer for the paltry sum of £4,000, though her eyes are black like those of Bess the Landlord's daughter. Meanwhile female competitors look on incredulous and amazed.

For their own bitter experience has taught them that to have secured merely the passing notice of ONE man is amazing and unbelievable, but to have TWO men, supplicants, is something for which To Thank Heaven....

Herr Berlinger and Herr Dr. Mayer were highly entertained at the booklets issued to all German refugees by the Jewish Aid Committee instructing them on how they should Behave in England. I wish the Aid Committee had had the foresight to include a special paragraph instructing Herr Berlinger NOT to strut about the polished corridors of Australia House clutching a thick Salami, garlic-flavoured sandwich to his mouth.

Some amusing mistakes they make in English. The German word for homemade cake is 'haus-gebacken' (home-baked) and when a selection of cakes and pastries was offered to a German refugee at a tea-party, he refused the selection proffered to him and said solemnly, 'No thank you, but I should like to have the housemaid.'

I read that clever, funny book 'With malice towards some' .... being an American woman's opinion of England. It was deliciously amusing but rather silly, especially the latter half and no doubt deserved the flagellation it received in some sections of the Press, notably from Rebecca West*** and others. But the book I am now reading is intensely interesting; 'I married a German' by Madeline Kent. Please try to read both these.

I am not too grand in health, but I survive. When Michael is not taking me out for a drive or to the theatre or pictures or to dinner, then the refugee girls at the office insist on my coming home to their flat in the evening and that means another late night talking and whatnot.

So das Leben geht. Life in the Big City. It is all very entertaining and amusing and fills the time splendidly so that the days flow away like water down a hole and mostly I am not sorry to see them go. I am by now so accustomed to playing the part of the Brave Little Woman that I know the whole works by heart. At the office they shudder to think of the graveyard which was Metal Supplies Ltd., before I came, ... for I turn on a flow of high spirited girlishness with the same facility that I rid myself of my endless cups of tea which I imbibe. The refugee girls are much more hard-driven for they smoke packet after packet of Kensitas. There is no doubt that if I should lose my job, any self-respecting circus would be glad to take me on.

I am looking forward to seeing you again as soon as possible. I really find I quite miss you and F & B.

I really must insist on your buying 'Time and Tide' or 'The New Statesman' on Fridays so that when War breaks out, at least you will know on which side you are fighting.

Much love Olga

*Alpine Hut was a BBC radio series.
**The Queen's Hall in Langham Place was destroyed by bombs in 1941.
***Rebecca West was a successful novelist and the mistress of H.G. Wells. She and Olga corresponded in the 1960s.

October 1938
5, Park Mansions, Henry St
St John's Wood, London NW8

Dear Beryl,

How are you all? I am still waiting for Betty's newsy letter. I hope Frank
is feeling better. How is my sister Cora, several times removed.

There is not much news. I am going round to the Caves tonight.
Expect to get-it-in-the-neck properly. But perhaps they will be lenient
because I am going to sit with Auntie Phoebe until they come home.
Rita says in the evening, there will be a few odd men coming round. I
expect 'odd' will be the word.

What did you think of the Bridgewater election? Hurrah Hurrah.

Good old Vernon Bartlett!* Some Deutschers are taking me to the
House of Commons tomorrow (Monday) evening to hear the debate on
the Jews. Chamberlain is going to raise the question in the House. I will
write and tell you all about it. So think of your little Oggi tomorrow
night, her little rubber neck stretching from side to side and her stomach
rumbling like cannons with excitement.

Please will you FORGIVE me if I don't send the pound I owe until
next Friday? I could do it at a pinch but I should be horribly Embarrassed.
I promise next week without fail. Do you agree? Or do you insist upon
your just due? Write and let me know.

With humble and a contrite heart,

With love, Og

Bartlett had just won a seat as an anti-appeasement candidate.

October 1938,
5, Park Mansions, Henry St
St John's Wood, London NW8

Dear B,

One of my colleagues at the office, a Swiss girl, not Jewish, got the sack
yesterday. I think they really got me to replace her. And only waited until
I was into the work. She used to roll in at quarter to ten of a morning,
take nearly two hours for lunch and leave on the dot; no one ever thought

that it had been noticed at all, but these German Yids have eyes in the back of their heads. Thank God, my German is pretty hotsy totsy now. Australia House is all smothered in dark green curtains for Air Raid Precautions (ARP) and the lavatory windows smeared with black grease to keep out the light. It smells like hell.

It is to be hoped the grease won't have all melted off by the time the Big Four* decide to have another go at splitting the world wide open. Time Marches On.

Best love, Olga

*Olga's own footnote: Hitler, Chamberlain, Deladier, Mussolini.

October 1938
5, Park Mansions, Henry St
St John's Wood, London NW8

Dear Beryl,

Many thanks for your most attractive letter and thanks again for the oxtail which is now in my belly.

I think you ought to make a jumper for yourself first. Are you not simply in Rags? But, of course, if you insist. Could I have Bridal White or if impracticable, nigger brown?

Snow has not yet again visited the Metropolis but you can taste it on every wind that whistles round the block. I think it will be with us for the weekend but I hope not.

Renee and Bernard and Lee and I did not stay very long in the Yiddish theatre in the East End after all.... for during the Second Act when the heroine who was very stout, began to 'sing' ..... 'Wer darf a Mama' (Who needs a Mother?) it got to be very sad and Bernard got the stomach-ache and we had to leave. It seemed very heartless but there isn't anything you can do about stomach-ache except go out. Perhaps it was a bit too sad anyway, for it was all about a Mama who kissed the alter Tata (father) goodbye and takes her kid and schlepps the ganzen Weg mach Amerika to find the kid's Tata and when they find him he is a gangster and he shoots people and then they catch him and take him off to prison whilst the Mama holds on to the little boy and screams Ach weh'se mir (woe is me) and the little boy cries such a lot that a kind lady comes in and takes him away to a school so that the Mama won't see him anymore and that's where she breaks down and sings the title of the play and that was where we had to leave because Bernard got so upset. Afterwards when we'd got over it a bit we had a very nice supper.

I don't know about my cough. Sometimes it is and sometimes it isn't. Now that Herr Dr. Mayer has got one he is having the week in bed and I am remembering how he told me I was not to go to bed with mine because I had to work. That is ganz typikal. Yesterday t'was funny. I got sort of mixed up with Herr Berlinger (who is also my boss) going to lunch and he insisted on my going with him to the Strand Palace Hotel along the road and he told me all about The Beautiful Girl who followed him all the way from Paris to Amsterdam, and the Beautiful Girl who chased him from Switzerland to London and the one in Le Touquet beautiful as a Dream who was offered to him along with £7,000, but when he had worked it out with the French Franc at the present Rate of exchange, it only worked out at £5,000 and he had to turn it down. He says all the women are out to catch him, he knows it, but he is Too Smart for Them. I thought it was a bit odd and I wondered if perhaps he might not have been mistaken about their intentions for he stands billowing in fat to the height of about five feet one and the large head which houses the Great Brain is protected by thick bristle which has to be scratched from time to time. His eyes are blue and have the expression of a nice contented pig[...]

Olga spoke quite a lot of Yiddish as well as fluent German. 'Alter Tata' is 'old Father' and 'schlepps' is 'drags'.

October 1938
c/o Metal Supplies Ltd
Australia House, Strand, London WC2

Dear B,

Little Herr Berlinger has been in the office to see me several times today, to follow up our talk at the Strand Palace. He waits until the office is empty, then he sits down at the next desk and says 'I will dictate'. He dictated several letters quoting the rock-bottom world market price for Copper Wire and after I wrote Hochachtungsvoll* at the end of each he suddenly says he wants a wife. She must be Very Beautiful, Very Very Religious (fromm) and Very Rich Indeed.

He looks at me with those round blue eyes so I put on some more lipstick and exposing my good sound teeth in a glamorous grin, I say, 'I can cook'.....

The blue eyes wear the expression suddenly of a startled faun. He glances at me sheepishly but fearfully and says, 'Ha! Ha! You English girls, you make always good jokes yes?! Ha Ha!' So I say Ha Ha yourself, but when the other girls come back from lunch I make them all nearly sick with laughter so no work gets done, not from any of us.

Michael, my rather elderly boyfriend, is calling for me at seven on Sunday and we are going out to Cockfosters, so I'll be able to let you know as soon as I can when we hope to come over to Birmingham.

Rosalie has gone to Paris, I think. Her job is now finished. I wish you wouldn't keep sending me Income Tax Demand notes you know perfectly well I can't pay. I refuse to pay anyway until Sir John Anderson stops skating in Switzerland and comes back to work and builds a proper bomb-proof shelter for me.

I am so sorry that Betty did not enjoy the party and I hope the others will be better. Didn't she have a Boy at all? Did Cousin Valerie look like Snow-White?

Love, Olga

P.S. Herr Berlinger asked me to go out with him on Sunday but I said sorry I already have an engagement. He says I am Very Beautiful and it is a great pity that I am not Good Jewess and not Rich. I think perhaps I will buy a Scheitel [a wig] and then I will borrow five pounds off your Frank, then I will cook a good Borsht from beetroot and perhaps one pound shin of beef and I think Herr Berlinger will take me.

Yours faithfully

October 1938
c/o Metal Supplies Ltd
Australia House, Strand, London WC2

Dear B,

Did you receive the chocs? On Tuesday night, Fraulein Behrend and I went to the House of Commons to hear the debate but we found the Unemployed with their Coffin had got there first and there had been so much rioting that the whole of Parliament Square was full of gendarmerie and they had closed the Strangers' Gallery and would not let us in. It was very disappointing.

We went to see Bergner in 'Stolen Life'. Very good. In Piccadilly Circus, however, on the way back we got involved in more rioting round about Eros. Everybody was screaming 'Arms for Spain' ..... and the police were charging about on horseback like there was a war on.

Frl. Behrend listened in to Hitler's speech (his own version) in German and what she told me she heard didn't sound much like the translation in the newspapers. Herr Suss (thank God) goes on holiday to Switzerland today, for a month. Miss Pinkus goes to Switzerland for the ski-ing for her holidays next week. Oh God I want a holiday too.

Everybody here has got the 'flu.

Love, O.

October 1938,
c/o Metal Supplies Ltd
Australia House, Strand, London WC2

Dear B,

Now with the Munich crisis over, what next? It broke out here quite soon. Iris Campbell, the beautiful blonde telephonist is the only other 'English' person in this office, except for the nice bookkeeping man and the dreadful office-boy. Iris is sometimes half-an-hour late in the morning! Herr Doktor Mayer famous for his technique for rushing in where others fear to tread sometimes looks up meaningfully at the clock when Miss C strolls in on very high heels, her bright gold hair and flawless complexion gleaming in the office gloom.

She speaks almost perfect German as her Father served with the occupation army in Germany after the Great War where she went to school as a child. She understands everything said to her which is a lot more than I do! But she refuses to SPEAK it. Her voice is rather refined. She says: 'I would like to catch some bloody German ticking ME off, late or not late.' Of course, her refusing to speak it makes a strong impression as it is thought, she refuses from choice or on principle. The top Director, Herr Suss who has a German Catholic wife he adores, makes a great thing of never ticking Iris off. He prefers to pretend to do things in 'the English way' as he says, 'only the English have good manners'. I think he'd see our

35

Iris set fire to the office and would smile sweetly and suggest 'yes, it is a bit chilly.' So when Miss C comes tripping in 30 minutes late (Which is something that none of us would dare to do), Herr Suss bestows upon her his sweetest and most artificial smile and remarks, 'What a beautiful weather we are having today!' or 'Do you think it will rain, Miss Campbell?' Then he goes to his own room, beaming with satisfaction still because he feels he has shown true English poise in dealing with the crisis which her absence has created. In fact he even ignores the sight of Herr Berlinger, hands clutching his curly fair head, totally abandoned to grief after being 'cut up' in the middle of an important telephone call which Miss C was not there to deal with. Herr B meanwhile has several genuine tears of frustration in his childlike blue eyes.

Those of us who are less obviously British to the backbone find our own shortcomings are received less cordially. When it was discovered (by some third-degree interrogation by the Herr Doktor) that I was not of purest English stock, some of my 'glamour' faded away in the eyes of the management. Herr Berlinger who engaged me on the strength of my being 'English lady with weak German grammar' no longer introduces me to newcomers as 'our English lady.'

As the international situation gets worse, the Herr Doktor whom we call 'The Brain' increases his attentions on remaining markets. One of his favourite customers is Holland where he was once entertained most royally with about 5 good meals a day, and Refreshments in between.

Suddenly ..... this week his Dutch files go missing. They contain all his beloved documents relating to his favourite Buyers, a firm named 'Invincinas'. He came in, screaming with rage; he has a high voice. We all have to turn out our cupboards, drawers, files, hatboxes, everything; no tiny crevice is overlooked.

Only Iris sits unmoved, philosophical at her switchboard while the storm rages around her. The Herr Doktor stands tall in the middle of the wreckage, his few remaining dark hairs upright, sweaty with his emotion. 'I will have Invincinas,' said the HD at last. No response from us exhausted staff, but a suppressed giggle from the switchboard. The Herr Doktor points at Mr. Mincer, the chief clerk whom we call Minnie. 'You shall seek,' says the HD, 'I will have Invincinas. You shall seek in the drawers of the ladies.' 'You can't say that,' says Minnie piously, 'it's rude.'

'It makes nothing,' shouts the Herr Doktor wildly with a baleful glance at us ladies, 'you shall seek,' catching Minnie's stony expression, 'from the gentlemen. Then you shall descend to the basement and you will seek among the old files, until 1925 no till 1920. There must be Invincinas.'

While all this was going on, little Herr Berlinger was watching calmly. He too was keenly anxious to investigate the Dutch files, but he was enjoying the storm. His little boy's face was peaceful and relaxed as he sucked his pencil.

Miss Campbell said coldly: 'Herr Doktor, stop yelling. If it's there we shall find it.'

'All must help in seeking,' said the Brain more calmly.

We had no lunch that day, any of us. Even Miss Campbell did not go out. But she was on a strict slimming diet and rather welcomed the opportunity of avoiding temptation.

We toiled in the darkness of the basement of Australia House. We lifted down files thick with dust and yellow with age. When we were all black with it, we at last found the missing file.

The whole team of us marched upstairs; we were hungry and tired. Minnie led the way into the office and brandished the file in front of the doctor's spectacles. 'We have found Invincinas,' said Minnie dramatically. The Herr Doktor did not look up.

'Is good,' he said, 'let it.'

Please write me all your news, love, Ogg

October 1938
c/o Metal Supplies Ltd
Australia House, Strand, London WC2

Dear B,

On the Tube this morning I bumped into Sally Genyon, an old friend of Aunt Sally's whom I once visited on the occasion of a Left Book Club meeting at Wembley. She asked me did I know that Rita had been dropped from the Alpine Hut? (Apparently this is a sort of BBC repertory company, radio shows etc.); And did I also know that Rita had been dropped by the B.B.C? It appears that during the last few months Rita has gone around saying to everyone, isn't the BBC just too BBB* for dropping me out of the 'Hut'?!

Exerting her magnetic influence over them, she managed to prevail upon a good many of her friends (not relatives of course obviously) to write to the B.B.C. complaining of their action in dropping one of their most talented members of the Cast.

Finally .... the correspondence assumed such alarming proportions that the B.B.C. hauled the luckless Rita before the BOARD and demanded to know why the Public en masse were outraged at Rita's absence from the show ... to the extent of writing letters by almost every post to demand 'What has been done to Rita Cave?'

As you can imagine ....sharp words were exchanged and finally Rita finds herself pitched out of the B.B.C. door forever. Just like the footprints of Lucy Grey in the snow 'and further there were none'. That is ALL. Well not quite .... it appears that the Producer of the show was of the opinion that Rita could not YODEL. All members of the Alpine Cast were expected fluently and musically to be able to yodel.

Much love to all, Olga

* *Bloody Boring British.*

14th October 1938
c/o Metal Supplies Ltd
Australia House, Strand, London WC2

Dear B,

The dance on Thursday so knocked me up I haven't been able to catch up on my sleep. I wish you could have seen me all got up in my borrowed plumes. I looked quite super. Even Rita and Ros said 'What a smashing dress;' it does have a classic beauty due to its simplicity.

I had to change the shoulder straps, putting looped velvet ones on instead because the thin sequin straps look too much (on me) like the top of a petticoat on my broad and bony shoulders. I had a spray of lilies of the valley and wore my hair a la Mozart. There were thousands of people there and I was in a big party with the Deutscher* hosts giving a big cocktail party first. I'll tell you all about it when I see you. Somebody said I looked like Kay Francis!** The tragic look, they said. Awful.

Saturday I went to see the Flashing Stream with some girl friends, Eve and Letty Dejong and Sunday I slept nearly all day and then joined a party at Rita and Rosalie Cave's. Cousin Jane Davis was there.

Tonight, bad throat and all, am going to Fraulein Pinkas' flat at Swiss Cottage to meet a Deutscher who has been brought to England by the Pen Club, a Writer. Did I tell you that Frl. Pinkas who is a typist at the office and does all the difficult maths calculations I can't even begin to do, turning Marks into Dollars etc., was a Judge in Berlin, just qualified when Hitler came and she had to leave. She has red hair[...]

There had been a large influx of German Jewish refugees into England and Olga and others referred to them as Deutschers in a slightly derogatory way.
**Kay Francis was a major Hollywood star of the 1930s and 1940s.*

15th October 1938

Dear B,

I made a last despairing effort to get into Fleet Street this week via four circular letters. Two replies I enclose herewith which show how hopeless it is. The Evening Standard just a snooty thanks for letter, no vacancy; from the Evening News nothing yet. All my attempts to extricate myself from the deadlock of the Financial Market seem so far abortive.

A reporting job would have been a solution to my problems, with the possibility of rising to a journalist's in the future. I thought the reply from the 'Star's' editor was very nice. Totally discouraged therefore ... I am still selling Scrap Metal to Poland and getting corns on my bottom from the office chair.

His Majesty's Revenue officers have the most delightful sense of humour. They have sent me another income tax demand note for another 30 bob! I paid them 30 bob [£1.50] only about a month ago .... and if they think I can raise another sum like that, they've got another think coming. 30 bob heh?! All I can say is, weakly, ha ha!

Last weekend I came home and found the flat had been burgled. I promptly dialled 999 and six (6) of the best-looking men in the C.I.D. rushed to the scene and hunted for clues, finger-prints; you know their stuff. If they'd asked me to strip in the Japanese fashion, I'd never have been able to refuse such a bevy of charm. Nothing of value was taken but drawers had been turned inside out and the flat was a riot of empty disused handbags. A poor haul. I blushed in a pretty confusion when my own drawers, untidy I confess, were thus brutally exposed to six pairs of attractive eyes representing the Law. They didn't seem surprised though, even at the sight of my pile of knickers nestling intimately with newspaper cuttings, hair-pins, hair-ribbons, Income-tax Demand notes, passport and House of Commons programme. Not a very enterprising burglar I think;

there were enough warm woolly knickers there to keep his buttocks warm these cool October days.

When the excitement had died down a little, I wrote an explanatory note and pinned it to the hallstand for Mrs. Mann's guidance when she should return. I decided not to wait in for her, the excitement being intense and I felt my arms could scarce support her, being a well-built lady[...]

20th October 1938
5, Park Mansions, Henry St
St John's Wood, London NW8

Dear B,

Simcox came up to town again from Birmetals this week and telephoned to take me out, but I refused of course. What does he think I am?

Christ, how boring these silly men are. I'm learning such a lot about men; if you treat them like dirt ... like you wouldn't touch with a barge-pole, they 'phone you three times a day and if you kick them well & truly in the pants, they 'phone you six times a day. So remember Auntie Ogg's advice for the future.

In the midst of one evening spent with some lousy-rich German Jew whom I'd met ages ago at the Cave's flat, I got so howling bored that I said excuse me and went to the lavatory and didn't come back. I came out of the lavatory eventually, naturally. Next day the silly bugger phoned me at the office, smarmy apologies etc. and wanted to know what he had done to offend me. I said, nothing of course I just got a bit bored. He said dear girl can I see you again tonight! I said No. He said can I phone you. I said if you like. He's been phoning ever since. My dressing-table is strewn with little notes from Mrs. Mann, the landlady. Mr. Horner phoned at six, at seven, at nine and at 10.30, on Wed, Thurs, Fri, Sat and Sunday.

Now ... if I'd been nice to that man I'd probably never have heard from him for six weeks, if ever. Sam phoned to take me out on Saturday night and I said I'd got a date already although I hadn't.

Och, mavourneen they make me sick these boring silly men, if you liquidated the lot they wouldn't even make a jelly.

Miss C in the office has been having trouble with her beau and the last two weeks was Intense Suffering, a Crisis, now safely over and they're going to Heyst-sur-Mer for their holiday week. At first it appeared he didn't want to take her but only to spend the August bank-holiday weekend with her in London but she was so disappointed that he weakened. He's taking the other week in Paris with a boy friend. I had an awful time consoling her. I said to her, look at my poor married sister, with child an' all, and HER husband goes off and leaves her in Wales, while he trips to the Casinos of France.

Met Aunt Sally by accident in a teashop in Baker Street. Aunt Phoebe had handbag stolen, the £4 in it removed, bag returned. Ha ha I said with an evil laugh. Sally says Cousin Rita is having a Magnificent time. With such a lot of introductions. Shouldn't have thought THOSE would be necessary I thought cattily. Sally reports Rita is meeting simply EVERYbody in Hollywood, going Everywhere, having a smashing time. Perhaps she won't come back I put in, hopefully. Perhaps they will forcibly compel her to stay in Hollywood and twinkle twinkle like a little star? No, said Sally staring at despised niece's white coat that still needs cleaning, Rita's booked her passage already.

The armchair in my room has just collapsed, leaving me sitting on the springs which have become embossed on my bottom. By the way I left my black beret hat on a bus (MY God that girl …. etc.) but I'm keeping my weather eye open for a tricky-looking bus-conductor with my black bow on him. It hasn't stopped raining in London for weeks; and beastly cold too[…]

Olga's cousin Rita Cave went to Hollywood as a member of the J. Arthur Rank Film Corporation. She later formed her own talent-spotting agency.

1st November 1938
5, Park Mansions, Henry St
St John's Wood, London NW8

Dear B,

Don't be too cross with me, though I expect you will be, for not writing for such a long time. I have no excuse so I won't make one. There was not much to write actually and I waited until I was able to scrape together the necessary which I enclose herewith

Making ends meet in London on 4 smackers [pounds] per week is no easy matter I am discovering, or rather did discover some time ago. It is probably due to lack of organisation, though even then….However,

41

it was really very naughty of me. Now you have two bad sisters instead of one. In fact how is the other bad one getting on? I'm afraid I never hear from her at all. She may think I'm dead, so it doesn't matter.

What is the provincial news, if any? The political situation is looking very nasty. I have been to the House of Commons several times and sat for hours listening to our worthy Ministers. Last Thursday I attended the Protest meeting in the Albert Hall along with 7,000 other Jews. I heard some fine speakers. It was as the papers rightly said one of the most remarkable platforms seen in our generation.

Sitting on the platform in one row, with Neville Laski my friend who likes to be kissed, sitting sulkily at one end, there were:- His Eminence The Cardinal Archbishop of Westminster, the Most Reverend Arthur Hinsley D.D. in his scarlet robes, the Right Hon. L.S. Amery M.P. representing the Tories, the Moderator of the Federal Council of Evangelical Free Churches of England, the Rev. Dr. Robert Bond; Lady Violet Bonham-Carter who is marvellous and drew tears with her passionate oratory, the Right Hon. Herbert Morrison M.P. LCC for Labour; the Very Rev. The Chief Rabbi Dr. Hertz Ph.D., Major Rt.Hon. Sir Archibald Sinclair Bt.CMG MP, Leader of the Liberal Party who is also marvellous and ought to be our Prime Minister and p'raps he will be one day, His Grace the Archbishop of York, the Most Rev. William Temple D.D. and sitting in the Grand Tier there was me.

In the House of Commons I heard the debate on the outrages in Germany. I heard Henry Samuel spouting for a trifle of two to three hours and I heard Mr. Grenfell for the Opposition who was good, and he told the story of how Walther Rathenau* was murdered in Germany and it was all very moving. I got the impression that Parliament was all very sympathetic and all that but that they didn't rightly see they could do much about the problem, what with all the troubles they got.**

Later in the week I attended the debate on Palestine though I had to wait some time before I could get in and then the Visitors' Gallery (which is quite small) was packed with tense Jewish faces which grew steadily more and more tense. I heard Lord Winterton wind up the debate and as he rubbed his hands a la Uriah Heap and turned his bent figure to the Right, he called upon 'my Committee to support me', I ground my teeth in my inimitable fashun [sic...]

---

* *Walter Rathenau was a Jew and leading industrialist who became Foreign Minister of Germany during the Weimar Republic. He was assassinated in 1922.*
** *There was a further protest meeting following Kristallnacht on 9th November 1938.*

November 1938
5, Park Mansions, Henry St
St John's Wood, London NW8

Dear Beryl,

I shall really have to buy some woolly knicks now. However, I feel much better. Am now proceeding to spread my 'flu germs all around Australia House to everyone's dismay.

That girl Hetty Metz you met in France phoned me yesterday and though I felt bad I did not want to offend her so I went out there, ghastly trek to Clapham South and quite an exhausting party, what with Mitzi and her brother Phil quarrelling like mad about how to get the 'Best out of Life' and arguing fiercely about the advantages and disadvantages of being a lady of the Mayfair salons (like our Rita Cave) and being an overworked mother-of-four in a tenement. Phil was all for being the overworked Mother and the argument grew so heated that eventually they parted and refused to go home together. Mitzi of course is both potty and pathetic. Hetty said to me 'how sweet your sister Beryl is; hasn't she got the sweeeeeeeetest nature and isn't she just too sweeeeeeet:' Whatever did you do to her?

Received last night a rather frantic sort of letter from Rudolf.* He says I cannot imagine what they all went through during the crisis. He does not think that peace can last very much longer and he said they were all ready set to leave Paris. He is coming over to London the weekend. I'm not quite sure what for. Is Frank any better? Please let me know what news.**

Did you know Michael used to be Rita Cave's 'escort'? He tells the story of how Rita once prevailed upon him to take her to Birmingham to stay with her brother Harold and Aunt Phoebe in the Stratford Road furniture shop and then tried to turn him into deluxe chauffeur and lap-dog; he became increasingly disgruntled and finally deserted, leaving her to come back by the L.M.S.*** However, Rita really does belong to the Upper Ten. Our New Year was very tame compared with hers, which was spent amongst the Very Best People at the Very Best Party thrown in Park Lane. She was very disappointed to find I had no natural aptitude for curling her unruly blonde hair as she had had to cancel her appointment with the hairdresser. Apart from her chosen 'buddies' J. Arthur Rank and Oscar Deutsch, the big cinema man, she wines and dines most nights at Quaglino's with the 'stars' ..... but more of these anon. She showed me the card from Harold who is ski-ing in Swisserland [sic], sending fondest love and another from our Cousins Agnes and Cyril**** also there, in a hotel so classy and stiff that Agnes has nearly ruptured her spine in trying to compete. It all sounds very expensive. D'you remember that story 'Trees Die at the Top'!

Please tell Betty the jumper she knitted for me has been tremendously admired. Write me a few lines old girl, don't forget. Gosh I'm sleepy[...]

Rudolf Frenkel, Olga's brother-in-law, was later captured by the Gestapo in Paris and managed to escape via Marseille to America.
**Frank Jaffa, Beryl's husband, was diagnosed with a serious thyroid problem which necessitated major surgery and lengthy convalescence.*
***London, Midland & Scottish Railway controlled the Euston to New Street, B'ham route prior to nationalisation.*
****By coincidence, Agnes and Cyril's daughter, Jill, married Oscar Deutsch's son, Ronnie. Oscar was, of course, another Brummie.*

3rd November 1938
5, Park Mansions, Henry St
St John's Wood, London NW8

Dear B,

In Hyde Park today I heard such a funny black man wearing a silver crown holding coloured feathers which waved and streamed in the wind.

'Underneath this British flag,' he howled, 'upon which the sun never sets and the wages never rise .... what is it makes Britain what it is today?' .... and the crowd yelled with one accord 'Littlewoods'....

'What is the cornerstone of Democracy?' he cried. 'Free Beer,' screamed the crowd.

I saw Anthony Eden in the House; he is the most beautiful creature I have ever seen and his hair, strange to note, is not black but a very light brown almost a thick shining yellow where the light falls.

I was invited by the Cave sisters to cook their dinner last Sunday. There were five of us (including Cousin Jane Davis) and the chicken weighed exactly 1¾ lbs. However, there were a few sausages and a little later we had tea.

They wanted me to go to a hop on Dec.15th but I had no dress and to another dance last week but I still had no dress so I wasn't keen but they nag so and they say why not borrow one and I don't know[...]

6th November 1938
c/o Metal Supplies Ltd
Australia House, Strand, London WC2

Dear Beryl,

Many thanks for the huge parcel. The stew certainly keeps intact in the glass jars but I cannot use either of those two boxes to return the jars to you as both arrived with the bottoms knocked almost out. The contents, however, were intact and in perfect condition. The stew was gorgeous!

And thank you for the bread and butter and oranges which were much appreciated. Why do you and Betty never write to me?

Michael has at last I think got tired of me for he did not ring at all last week, so I spent the weekend in lonely solitude and wrote a story. I wanted to buy the Writer's and Artists' Year Book to find out the best magazine to send stories to but I went to the Writing Class and my essay was chosen as the best again. But if you saw the rest of the class you wouldn't think that was much to write home about.

I've got to go and see Rene tonight; she is peeved with me for not phoning. I think she's getting married in April and wants to talk about it; Lee or Bernard, or Bernard or Lee and so on. Please read that delightful new book 'The Young Melbourne', also Norman Collins' new book 'Love in our Time'[…]

25th November 1938

Dear B,

My lovely jumper arrived rather spattered with stew and I'm afraid I had to wash it but I don't think it is in any way injured for it came up as fluffy as ever. Is it possible that you MADE it? Surely no human hand could weave anything so gossamer?!

This morning I received another parcel (Saturday) from you but did not have time to open it before leaving. However, I am going home direct at lunch time to make hay with the contents!

Why do you keep showering gifts upon me? Does it ever occur to you, my dear sister, that I do not deserve so much goodness? […]

28th November 1938
c/o Metal Supplies Ltd
Australia House, Strand, London WC2

Dear B,

It is a month this weekend since I saw you all but it seems much longer. Did you miss me at all?

This is a nerve-racking office and the girls keep getting breakdowns from overwork. Hardly a day passes without somebody dissolving into floods of tears. For my part I am no longer the bonny girl you used to know – though I drink a glass of hot milk in the mornings. The weather is wet.

This Sunday Michael and Lee and Rene and I are going down to Brighton for the day in Lee's car and if the weather improves, the air may do us some good. Tell me about my sisters Cora and Betty; will they be assembling at New Street station today when Neville Chamberlain arrives, waving little flags? [...]

30th November 1938
5, Park Mansions, Henry St
St John's Wood, London NW8

Dear Beryl,

The long day tapers off into a frost-flavoured darkness as I sit down to write to you.

Last night I was at the Caves. Ros & Rita were very gracious to'ards me and we chatted amiably about all and sundry. I wish I didn't find them both so pathetic but I do.

There was a dissipated blond Austrian from Paris, a friend of Rosalie's and a tall blond young man named Albert who was rather dull but he works at Woburn House and knows all the right people. Every now and then he made his contribution to the general talk by emitting disconnected sounds in the shape of 'Curious!' or 'Extraordinary' etc. from time to time. A curious bird.

The post has just come. Curious mixture. Dam that word! Box, square, looking like it holds an Easter egg turns out to be my belated Gas-mask. The Government obviously in no particular hurry to save my life, evidently do not think it worth preserving. How right they are.

Now ... for the other parcel, flat and square, No, not stew: You're wrong this time. Behold two pairs of silk stockings, sheer!... which Michael must have sent me from the shop because I complained of a ladder over the 'phone.

Do not yet allow Betty to read 'Wuthering Heights' as she wishes to do. I remember how, much more than a decade ago, my 12-year-old mind suffered in acutest sympathy with the agony of Heathcliff after the death of his Catherine. I recall my bleak misery at the thought of Heathcliff crashing his head against the tree-trunk until the blood matted his black hair and calling hopelessly at nights through the open window of her room at Wuthering Heights across the wind-swept moors, for Catherine. The 12-year-old schoolgirl wondered if Emily Bronte had perhaps exaggerated that account of torment, but the woman knows better.

Aunt Phoebe is at Smedleys in Matlock* until further notice. The Caves have a refugee girl to work in the flat for them. Her name is Gertie.

Rosalie returned from a trip to Paris. She had supper one night at my brother-in-law's flat in Boulevard Richard le Noir. Her French is jolly good so she got on well with Rudolf. She thought Marcel a wonderful child and Ruthchen very intelligent[...]

Smedley's Hydro.

4th December 1938
5, Park Mansions, Henry St
St John's Wood, London NW8

Dear B,

I am a bit bored with London; getting restless again. I am bored with the people and bored with my job and with myself.

With only one word of encouragement I shall chuck all UP and roam round the world. I could work my passage and write articles and so on.

I gotta be on the move all the time. The poor goddam Jews in Germany are having the bloodiest time but after all they're only refugees from Hitler and I'm a refugee from myself, which is worse.

MY bosses are working all they know to get their friends out of Germany; really they are marvellous what they do; friends, relatives, acquaintances, strangers, it's all the same to Suess and Friedmann; we're all of us staff occupied with refugee work and all day long it's Affidavits and Visas and Permits and Guarantee Forms and calling the Home Office and Woburn House and getting the low down on prospects in Brazil and Australia and Paraguay. Now the British Government are talking about Alaska, or the furthest coast of Queensland where the climate is sub-tropical. Better to die in Germany ...... it's quicker.

I love Low's cartoons in the Evening Standard. Last night he had a sketch of Sir John Anderson depicted as an angel with wings and holding a harp and singing 'You gotta ARP. I gotta ARP, all God's children gotta ARP.

What with Anthony Eden making mysterious trips to the States and gosh how they love him over there .... and what with the Italian Deputies yelling 'Tunis, Corsica, Nice!...' what with Hitler being rude and the Jews on the Front Page again ..... what with Franco borrowing British grain and commandeering ships .... what with Japan giggling all over their silly yellow faces at British PROtests .... what with the Pope nearly going and dying on our hands and Daladier bringing out machine guns for French strikers .... what with the naughty questions Geoffrey Mander is goin' to ask Neville Chamberlain in the House tomorrow about censorship of newsreels and the Press .... and the even naughtier questions old Attlee is going to ask about the visit to Rome in Jan, that is if the war doesn't start before then.... well it just doesn't leave poor old Nevv any time at the weekends to do any real fishing; guess the Chamberlain family have to live on tinned sardines meanwhile.

You will have seen the date above, Dec.4th when Mother died, still a young woman. Why does everyone who matters have to die and so young .... this is what I think about a lot and shall never understand.

How is Betty and why doesn't she ever write and how is Frank and all?

Love, Og

2

Lost in London (Part II)

The run up to the War begins in earnest and Olga combines her work at Metal Supplies while still managing to have some fun. She describes the growing tension in London as war preparations get underway.

2nd January 1939
5, Park Mansions, Henry St
St John's Wood, London NW8

Dear Beryl,

Thank you more than I can say for all the attractive food. I heartily enjoyed it all. Everything arrived intact and in perfect condition. I have not had to spend a cent on food for days and although this is marvellous for me, I do not like to think of all the trouble you have to go to in order to prepare and pack these delicious parcels.

How did you celebrate New Year? London went completely berserk. Rosalie and her young boyfriend Mark and myself and a few other people got trapped in that melee in Piccadilly Circus at midnight which you saw illustrated on the front page of the Sunday Express.

Ros got quite annoyed when drunken rowdies tried to kiss us and burst balloons in our faces, and there were people being sick everywhere and the noise and the mounted police and Eros all boarded up. I felt a bit sick too though I had drunk nothing but whisky but we had eaten Chinese and I thought it was awful but it would have been impolite not to. But I had envied the one man who sat in that Chinese restaurant and had the strength of character to use a knife and fork on a good steak and chips while everyone else struggled with chopsticks and chop suey. We had that; it consisted of about five different dishes. Boiled rice, a sauté of chicken and pineapple revoltingly sweet, weird sort of pancakes, a dish of unknown vegetables and onions, and another of unrecognisable ones with bamboo shoots floating about. I hated it but managed to swallow all without complaint. We went on for a little while to the A.P. Club in Windmill Street, where there was a dinner dance for ten bob [50p]. It all looked very rowdy and scruffy and unattractive and we did not stay long. As we left, more people poured in who had come on from the Arts and Tarts Club.

I enjoyed Sunday night much better. I expect you will be pleased to hear I am no longer alone and have made some nice new friends of whom you would probably approve. They are the same party I met at a dance in Seymour Hall and who I thought had at the time taken quite a fancy to me but presumed they must have forgotten me, as people do in London, as I had not heard from them again.

However, it appears they'd phoned the Caves flat at No.6, Grove End Gardens just before Christmas to ask for my 'phone number as they wanted me to make up a foursome to go down to Westgate for the Christmas holiday. However, it was Aunt Phoebe who answered the 'phone and she replied that I had no 'phone number and she did not know where I lived. Aunt Phoebe went herself to Westgate with Rosalie and Rita and was successful in securing FIRST PRIZE at the Fancy Dress Ball: a Japanese dressing-gown. Anyway the same party did phone at last and we drove out to Ye Olde Thatched Barn on the Barnet-By-Pass and ate richly but thank God Englishly of thick steaks swimming obscenely in parsley'd butter and then drank beer and gossiped in front of a huge old-fashioned log fire and afterwards walked on Hampstead Heath and I saw all the lights o'London, but it all ended very late, and having had only about four hours sleep this weekend, I was an hour late for work and the new regulations are we have got to go in to Herr Suss and apologise. It was sticky. I shall not be late again.

Michael Steen who was my share of the party is middle-aged, very nice.

It is quite extraordinarily attractive to have a few friends to be nice to one when one has been so very much alone as I have been, actually for months, except for the odd deutscher or refugee encountered who always ring up at the wrong times and avoid even buying one a cup of tea in the Corner House, and not from lack of money either. My landlady said one of these spent the whole weekend phoning in vain to see if I had returned; he had a bad cold and I suppose wanted coddling. I would have hated the rowdy Christmas parties at Westgate anyway and their infantile antics. I liked better always our spelling and quotation bees and watching the dawning of Betty's pretty little wit.

Best of all ... Michael is driving to Birmingham in about 3 weeks' time and will take me along, so I can see you all.

I also have an invitation from a nice man named Bernard S who I think once belonged to Rosalie and on Friday the De Jong sisters have invited me to supper in their house at Swiss Cottage ... so I have a busy time ahead.

Love, Ogg

January 1939
5, Park Mansions, Henry St
St John's Wood, London NW8

Dear Beryl,

Received tonight the stew with grateful thanks. The parcel looked rather as though it had been detained a while in Rugby for a game of rugger. However, I carefully licked the diced carrot out of the sodden envelope and just managed to decipher your handwriting.

It's all right there will only be me at the weekend thank God as the others will not be coming. So you will have my girlish chatter solo, won't that be nice.

I just saw Rita Cave on the bus and she looked like a Russian princess and she says I am a low bitch because I have not been round since New Year's Eve.

I am going to another goddam party tomorrow night and the theatre on Thursday so tonight I am going to bed.

It was like Spring in the Strand today; it made me think with nostalgia of Woodgate* and the good green grass.

Dr. Mayer thinks of nothing but food; he eats sandwiches from 10-30 until 1-30, then goes out for a smacking lunch; then at 3-30 eats 3 party buns and starts on some more sandwiches at five.

Miss Campbell has been away a week with flu; she looks goodgreen and she says her mother and father and three sisters have all been on their backs all week with temperatures varying from 102° to 104°. Dr.

Mayer was quite shocked when he heard. 'But who did the cooking?' he wailed in horror.

Love, Og

* *Birmetals factory, like many for aircraft construction, was built in 1937 in the then rural district of Quinton near Birmingham, near the village of Woodgate.*

February 1939
c/o Metal Supplies Ltd
Australia House, Strand, London WC2

Dear Beryl,

Thanks for your short note and TWO recent parcels. The weekend parcel was simply marvellous. The surprise chicken in the delectable soup, the incomparable flavour of the oxtail, and in last night's stew were surely included many expensive spring vegetables (naughty girl!) but how delicious.

I still don't know definitely whether I shall be coming on Sunday but if I do, it will be by train. I much prefer to do that. I am really getting rather tired of my 'friends' and I am looking forward to spending a 'quiet time' with you.

Lee and Rene got engaged last week so they want to do a spot of celebrating this weekend I expect. They are all right, these people and I'm afraid I make wicked use of them, but I find them all so silly. They think all their petty silly little doings and 'thinkings' are so important and sometimes my patience wears a bit thin. But it works out so much cheaper! Crude? oh yes!

Saturday last for instance I had your chicken for lunch, tea at the Cumberland with Bernard and supper with him at the Cafe de l'Europe in Leicester Square. Sunday I had your oxtail in the morning, went to hear Tchaikovsky's Fifth Symphony played at the People's Palace by the New Metropolitan Symphony Orchestra, tea at the Cumberland where we met Dr. Holdman and his wife on a lightning visit, then a News Theatre, then a ride in the country and dinner. It was too cold to go to Brighton.

Yours, Ogg

April 1939
5, Park Mansions, Henry St
St John's Wood, London NW8

Dear B,

Funniest sight of the week:-

Herr Doktor Erich Mayer, coat-and hatted, gliding downwards in the lift to the pillared hall of Australia House and holding with both hands to his grotesquely-masticating mouth, two large square sheets of Rakusen's motzas.* The Motzas lie sandwich-wise, one upon the other and from each end protrude two slender pink tongues of Salt Beef. It is the Herr Doktor himself, celebrating the Passover with all due ceremony.

As the lift sank below floor level, I caught, silhouetted against a shower of Motza crumbs, a glimpse of the astonished lift-girl's face.

Most interesting event of the week:-

The Foreign Affairs debate at the House of Commons last night.** To which I will return at the end of this letter so that if it bores you too much, there is no need to wade through it.

Most annoying fact of the week:-

That I have not heard either from you or from Betty. Is it possible that I have incurred your displeasure?

Lee phoned me today and said I must make up my mind whether I go to Westgate with him at the weekend as Rene and his mother and her mother are already there. I find it always more exhausting to have to make up one's mind about trivial things that do not matter a great deal. He says it will be approx. 3 guineas or less. I want neither to go nor not to go only feel I ought to go. God what a tangle of negatives. I find increasingly that I have such a taste for my own solitary company that against my will I have almost to force myself to go among people. I do not mind, I even like, meeting people for the first time but I never have any wish to see them for a second time, and if I have to, I am always bored. The fault of course lies only in myself, but to try and illustrate to you what I mean I will quote you a few lines from a book I read a few days ago, which is what I mean, only this man puts it so much better than I could.....

'But loneliness is as insidious as a drug, the more you indulge the more you require – a drug habit for which a little extra money cannot buy the cure, and which leisure only aggravates....'

So perhaps I should take this holiday by way of punishment. I know

I shall be bored to tears. But if I do go I shall take my machine and amuse myself writing to you my rancid rantings and criticisms of my fellow victims. I do not expect Michael will be going; I think he is going to Bournemouth with Bernard. We have not exactly quarrelled but we have I think ceased to like one another. Eccentric as I am myself, I found him even more eccentric so no wonder he got on my nerves so much.

Miss C at Metal Supplies is going sailing with her boyfriend on the Norfolk Broads. She is looking forward to days of leisured lust drifting about the pale cool waters. It is to be hoped the weather will be kind to them[...]

* *Unleavened bread, eaten by Jews during the eight days of Passover.*
** *Olga seems to have gone to the House of Commons in preference to attending the Passover Seder (service).*

7th April 1939
Westgate-on-Sea

Dear Beryl,

What do you mean by not telling me before?! Did you imagine I would be anything less than delighted? And happy. And pleased. I expect Betty is thrilled to bits at the prospect of a baby nephew or niece. Well, I suppose it is about time our Family started to do something about posterity. And now you and Corrie will have something in common, and you will be able to wheel your babies out together.*

It will be delightful though I expect I shall find myself left outside in the cold, which is of course to an extent inevitable. I enclose letter addressed to Cora but as I do not know her new address, will you kindly pass same on to her.

I wish you could be down here on the East Coast enjoying the sunshine. Above me at this moment is blue sky, strong sunshine and before me a placid sea, only flecked with white dots as the white horses ride home.

There was the usual 'performance' to get away from the office last night. I worked until 7 o'clock and then came on down here in Lee's car. I think it torments Mr. Suss to think we have so many free days' holiday that he makes our lives a misery both before and afterwards. When Dr. Mayer called me in at 5-30 and gave me another whole batch

54

of work to do last night, I marched back to our office and started on it, but it was complicated work and none of it so vital that it could not have waited until after the holiday. I felt hysterical a little. Frl. Behrend was cursing bitterly in German. Just before 7 I told Dr. M venomously, 'I was sick of it.' Although none of us can afford to lose our jobs, we sometimes cannot contain our feelings and we are always 'telling' them, but it makes no difference.

I was not pleased therefore on waking this morning to hear the throaty prattle of German voices. Next door is the large dining-room where there are some 30 odd refugee boys, stationed in this hotel because they are all very orthodox. When the Passover arrived, the Proprietress tried to get away with it by soaking their crockery in soda water, but they would not have it and she was compelled to purchase new crocks.** They are nice lads but all of them quite painfully religious.

In the garden there are narcissi and daffodils and grape hyacinths. This is an attractive bay and very quiet.

Now that Betty has started a banking account I shall send her a remittance from time to time for her to deposit. She will feel happier with her own little banking-account and feel just a little bit independent. Is she busy knitting already? Who is to be your doctor? And you don't say … when?

I feel very sorry for Cousin Rita Rainbow. I am afraid that, surrounded by expectant mothers, she will in her jealousy be driven to add her quota to the impending assembly.

Our Miss Shaer worked at Metal Supplies right up to the end of the 9th month; her son duly arrived after another 4 weeks of waiting, in the Mile End Road. Mr. Suss and Mr. Friedmann both sent her presents and she wrote thanking them and said she fully expected her son would one day become Prime Minister and set our toppling world to rights. Actually she'd been knitting away for a daughter Antoinette who has now turned into Anthony Paul.

I hate springtime, particularly April and May time. As the sun warms the earth from brown to green, the purple aubrietia and the golden alyssum come out and make too bright a show. I am glad that aubrietia does not grow in London. At Lordswood Road, Harborne it used to billow right out into the road.

I suggest that in view of the forthcoming happy event, you should discontinue sending great hampers of food to me at the weekend. Firstly, I am fat enough now and have gained considerable weight. Secondly it is too expensive. Save the money instead for you will surely need it later.

Thirdly in your delicate state of health, I do not think it right for you to stand cleaning masses of vegetables and fussing with extra cooking and making up parcels. I can manage very well, I shall not starve.

Love, Og

The babies referred to in this letter were Vivienne, Cora's daughter, born on 28th October 1939, and Richard, Beryl's son, born on 20th November 1939. Rita Rainbow (who became Rita Thomas) had a daughter called Rosemary the following year.
**Orthodox Jews change all their crockery and cutlery for the eight days of the Passover Festival.*

15th April 1939
5, Park Mansions, Henry St
St John's Wood, London NW8

Dear Beryl,

I hope you are looking and feeling better. Are you? Mind you reply. My supply of food is lasting well. I have still eggs and butter and half a loaf. All of it was and is delicious.

We expect to see Herr Hitler in the Strand any day now. I am wondering which hat I shall wear when he COMES. Do you think he would like me best in the brown one; nice military shape like in an Ivor Novello romance.

Last night I was invited to Michael's place. His sister wanted to congratulate Lee and Rene in person. It was a bit of a flop, however, because we all expected supper and we didn't get, except me, having come straight from work. Lee and Rene were starving so that Rene ate the piece of bread off my plate. Isn't it an extraordinary thing that those people who think they are really wonderful cooks, can't.... I was placed in lonely state at the table and told to eat but I looked from my plate to R & L's hungry faces with envy. They didn't miss anything. I was given a plate of bones, attached to which were some greyish rags of meat whilst large slivers of greyish fat swam delicately in a pale unknown liquid. The question occupying me all day is, what was it? Could it have been Oxtail? The bones seemed similar but the flavour was not that of the oxtail family. Lamb I dismiss, veal impossible, beef remote, mutton out of the question, then what? They probably thought it made it more exciting to leave the guest to guess what it was. And if any guest can in ten guesses, then you can shove Mr. Chamberlain's Gamp down my Ungrateful Gullet.

The evening was further imperilled by Michael making a most unfortunate and ill-chosen remark, when being shown Rene's sapphire engagement ring, he said childishly, 'personally I prefer white stones.' After this the evening lapsed into gloom.

Michael who owns some stores complains that Business is very bad but the windows of his biggest store do not attract. One window carries a ghostly burden of thick white woollen combinations with long legs to them and there are many thick woolly garments described as 'Interlock Nights' which sounds very rude but are nevertheless billed as an Indisputable Offer.

Everything happens to us non-Aryan foreigners at Metal Supplies Ltd., as though we were not already sufficiently disliked in Australia House already. Not only do we stick bayonets in babies' bellies, use Christian blood for our Passover cakes, swindle good Aryan money out of perfectly good Aryan pockets, but we are also sick all over Lift Girls in Lifts.

I can just imagine the High Commissioner saying, as we so often do ourselves, 'those bloody deutschers again,' when they scouted round Australia House on Monday to find out who was the young lad who vomited in the lift, thereby desecrating the complete and entire person of the Lift Girl in front of him, from her blond hair, to the hem of her smart black and white uniform.

Our new young office boy, a Jewish lad named Lavender, smoked his first pipe on Monday and in the lift after lunch his stomach rejected it. I shall have to recommend Baby's Bottom. I tell you everything happens to us.

Oh I wonder what poor Aunt Becky will say when she sees Hitler strutting round her beloved Pilsen and swilling their beloved Pilsener Lager.

Is it very costly for a girl to take agricultural training these days? I notice that Studley College, Warwickshire offer a 60-guinea scholarship and Bursaries to girls entering for Horticulture, Dairying or Poultry Husbandry. I'm sure our Betty would be very good with chickens. What a nice life for a girl, don't you think, ah me!

How is our old-fashioned sister Coralie? Everyone has gone to the Three C's Ball tonight. I didn't because I hadn't a dress and anyway I wasn't keen.

I walked in the gardens of Savoy Place today, sandwiched in between the river and the Strand from Charing Cross to Temple Bar. The gardens are abloom in the sun with blue and purple crocuses. I noticed the large bronze statue of Robert Burns, who is very goodlooking, and there is a nice statue to Arthur Sullivan who is being embraced by a very nice looking woman who is losing her gown. There are angels on the top of Shell-Mex House. You go up the steps and you are back in the Strand again. I like London. I can still taste the strange pungent unknown flavour of that rag stew from yesternight. I wonder what it was. Perhaps she opened the wrong parcel and stewed some Interlock Nighties by mistake.

Love Olga.

April 1939
5, Park Mansions, Henry St
St John's Wood, London NW8

Dear Beryl,

Yes, I enjoyed my holiday. Terribly sorry to hear that Frank has lost weight. Does he need a holiday do you think? Else what is the reason?

No, I haven't seen Aunt Becky yet; I didn't know she was in London until I got Betty's letter tonight. As for the Caves I haven't seen them since about January. I expect they hate me. I can't help it. So do a lot of people.

I am always breaking appointments or forgetting them or something. I never seem to find time to visit people with any rational sort of regularity and I am always meeting new people. However, I wrote Rosalie a little note asking for forgiveness. I always seem to be asking for her forgiveness for something.

I don't think I can possibly manage a whole weekend as I simply have not got the money, but I am determined to come over on the Sunday. I want to see you (it seems ages) and I want to see how Frank looks.

I have rather a lot of dates and whatnots. I want to write you a long, long letter about everyone I have met and all I have been doing. But if I come on Sunday I can just talk which will be nice for you, won't it?? I seem to talk such a lot lately, people think I'm an orator or something. Public Driveller No.1 that's me. Still, some of the nicest people think I'm a pain in the neck.

I am very brown, like a red indian squaw. At Westgate I had to share a room with Lee's sister. She has discovered the eighth wonder of the world. She used to lay swooning in her bed of a morning because my curls rose up from the pillow in their great strength intact and did not even need combing. She used to wear curlers and a net and it took one hour each night. Apart from that she was a nice girl.

Herr Doktor Mayer knows I visit the House of Commons rather a lot. Today when I spent rather a long visit in the lavatory, he phoned through to Miss Campbell and all unwittingly asked with impatience, 'Where is Mrs. Franklin? Is she gone to Parliament?'

I could write reams about the delightful refugee boys at Westgate and the concert they gave us. I would like to adopt them all. But I am nearly asleep already so it will have to keep till I see you unless I get a chance to write again between now and Friday. The food in the hotel was uniformly bad. If I couldn't cook any better than that I would lose myself in the snow like little Lucy.

Is it not pitiful and terrible about poor Queen Geraldine?* No wonder Chamberlain likes Mussolini, he is such a gentleman[...]

PS. I had a two page letter from the American I met in the House of Commons I told you about. He asks: 'What is the matter with England?'

It is so breathlessly hot in London. We are having a heatwave, are you?

* *Geraldine was the wife of King Zog of Albania. Mussolini annexed Albania in April 1939. Olga would meet them after the war (see later).*

April 1939
5, Park Mansions, Henry St
St John's Wood, London NW8

Dear B

On Saturday afternoon I walked in Hyde Park to look at the guns and all the paraphernalia of war which was there displayed.

Two balloons, bright silver, sailed in the rain-swept sky. Lower and lower they came. Like the heads of great elephants with the trunks curled round their heads.

Elderly ladies squealed in fright. It was difficult to convince them there was no one in the balloons. As the silvery mass collapsed upon the grass, the crowds surged forward to investigate the prostrated body.

Trim nurses demonstrated first-aid; sirens hooted and ambulances dashed backwards and forwards. When the first guns went off, I jumped three feet in the air, heart pounding. I soon became accustomed, however, and marched about bravely. Tin-helmeted soldiers perched and pirouetted on the tops of tanks and armoured cars and wise-cracked to the admiring crowds milling around them.

A large white tent dedicated to the recruiting of new members for the Territorial Army stood invitingly open. As dusk fell, a drizzling rain set in but the crowds remained. Parents wandered hither and thither and in their wake the eager, interested faces of their children.

It was soon quite dark and the searchlights operated by soldiers in khaki and tin-helmets and cordoned off in a great space, threw an eerie light over the park. The lights were swivelled, hunting the sky. Someone screamed. The rain fell faster.

An hour later, Hitler's speech was on the placards and the crowds went home.

Last night I sat in the House of Commons for three hours and listened to British history being made. History which, according to Chamberlain, will when written be worthy of a chapter all to itself. He should know. I got in easily. That is after sitting 1½ hours in the great hall reading 'Fallen Bastions'.* My Australian escort soon got on my nerves and I decided to lose him as quickly as possible.

Once inside, however, my patience was rewarded. The House was packed, every bench crowded, the atmosphere tense and dramatic.

I was thrilled with excitement when Mr. Chamberlain came in and with slow steps walked to his seat where he sat with arms folded and head down the whole evening. I admired the thick beautifully-iron-grey hair and the elasticity of his well-dressed figure. Winston Churchill sat a few feet away, sporting only a few wisps of hair upon his noble head. Lloyd George sat opposite him and his hair was long and straight and snowy-white.

The two pink bald heads of Hoary Samuel** and Sir John Simon clustered affectionately together close to the Prime Minister. I studied them all, the quiet dignity of Anthony Eden, the picturesque beauty of Sir Archibald Sinclair, the charm of Dr. Summerskill's smartly curled auburn head, the sturdy figure of my own precious Lieut. Commander Fletcher, Stafford Cripps, Herbert Morrison, Mr. Dalton, Greenwood, old Uncle Tom Cobley and all.

The debate was absorbing, noisy, dramatic. I sat without moving, though my bottom ached and my eyes burned. I went home at any rate with the conviction that this time the Government are really sincere. They are not going to do a diddle this time. And if they play their cards right I don't think there is much danger of war, for years to come.

Have you any news? Have you your new Spring costume? Is it nice?

Everyone has been showing off their sisters at the office this week. Miss Campbell's sister Vera was presented and inspected. Frl. Behrend's sister arrived from Germany and came to the office to see us. Frl. Pinkas presented us also with her sister. So I think it is high time you and Betty came over and showed yourselves, especially if you have a new spring costume and Betty of course has her Deanna Durbin on.

Much love, Olga

*Fallen Bastions *was a major work by journalist G.E.R. Gedye where he strongly* *attacked appeasement.*
**Sir Samuel Hoare.*

8th May 1939
c/o Metal Supplies Ltd
Australia House, Strand, London WC2

Dear Beryl,

Forgive for not writing for so long. How are you all and why doesn't Betty write?

I had so many late nights last week, was washed out completely on Friday when Henry Rose came up to town for the Cup Final, so that I was certainly not looking my best and I felt so shabby that I have since purchased new gloves and shoes and I am just about broke.

He had a lot of trouble getting my address; he first phoned Aunt Ray and she didn't know and then he phoned Birmingham and he said 'a nice little maid replied and gave him the address right away.' After the show we went to the Hungaria and I wished I had not put my blue frock on. There we met Michael Carr and his wife. Michael Carr is the world-famous song-writer, son of a Jewish father and an Irish mother, he is a little mad. We had a smashing supper of smoked salmon, chicken and rice, a dish of asparagus tips in butter, fresh strawberries and cream, champagne, coffee and liqueur kummel or something. Later we went back to the Carr's flat in Kensington for more drinks. I felt a bit sozzled but oh so tired. Henry is just the same, a good bit more sensible but gosh how fat: He now has two chins; it is such a shame. It simply WRECKS his beauty. He had the usual stream of funny stories to tell.

I saw Aunt Becky and Uncle Ernest again on Sunday afternoon. Becky is really quite nice when you get to know her; I don't see why Father hated her so much. They feel terribly hurt that not ONE member of the family has invited them to Birmingham even for a day. Uncle Mo has written to Sally (in confidence) that he does not intend to do anything for them. Not a word, not a sausage from nephews Cyril, David or anyone. They are keeping their chins up but they feel terribly hurt. I think Harold is coming up to see them but he is the only one. Actually it is rather bad, after 25 years; that was when Becky married Ernest and they went to live in Pilsen which is in poor old Czechoslovakia. Now they are homeless refugees and the rich relations don't want to know... Besides it is not very nice for them living with Rita and Ros who, so they say, are still fighting like dog and cat, which drives them nearly mad.

The Communist May-Day celebrations took place in the rain yesterday but it provided us with a change in Australia House. I love processions especially when there are very loud bands. I bought a black straw hat tonight: From now until Friday I shall live on air. Thank God, I have a dinner invitation for tomorrow night. My Saturday off is on May 13th so I shall be coming over weekend after next if I am invited.

Dear Betty, please write, best love, Ogg.

17th May 1939
c/o Metal Supplies Ltd
Australia House, Strand, London WC2

Dear Beryl,

You had me sobbing into my morning coffee. Such goodness. You will end up by restoring my faith in human nature. The remittance I swear will be refunded at the end of the week, so help me. And thanks a million.

Yes I will take your advice about the suitcase; you are a clever girl. If the rain doesn't stop soon, we shall have to leave our Gas Masks at home and bring our water-wings instead, for the river Thames will flood its banks.

You bet when the river calls at our door in the Strand, the Herr

Doktor Mayer will howl as he does when he sees my bad German grammar ..... 'Zis CANNOT BE!'

Much love to orl, Ol

May 1939
c/o Metal Supplies Ltd
Australia House, Strand, London WC2

Dear B,

What do you think of Chamberlain's 'change of heart'? Personally I think he is an actor of no mean merit. He knew that Hitler was going to take Czechoslovakia on March 10th. In the House on Wednesday, he says weakly it was not 'in accordance with the spirit of Munich' but 'we must not desist from our policy of appeasement' and then on the Friday (driven by the force of public opinion and the fear of losing his job) he rallies the gullible public of this country behind him by suddenly bursting out into impotent fury against the man who has betrayed him .... etc. Notice that his stern and angry words have not in any way been followed up by action; his speech was simply full of sound and fury signifying nothing.*

I take a quite eccentric interest in politics. I am almost completely wrapped up in it, which is silly. Politics, however, has that human and personal interest which appeals to me and which commerce sadly lacks.

I never get time to finish my letters to you. Have been rushed off my feet the last two days. It is hateful at the office. Everyone shouts and shouts and rushes about like mad. Nobody knows why. Herr Dr. Mayer's voice is like a machine-gun; it rattles all day long and the walls of Australia House tremble with the noise of it. We are all a bundle of nerves because of it and we have to keep taking Aspros because of the headaches we get in consequence. Today when he nearly knocked me over (which is nothing) I just got mad and I said, Dr. Mayer you are so rude, you have no manners at all, no Englishman would dare behave like that. He laughed.

I am going out with Michael for a cup o' tea and a chat about nine tonight. .

Wish I didn't feel so exhausted. But he has had 'flu and I haven't seen him for some time. Rosalie phoned me last night; she also has a job with a bloody Deutscher**; it is in the City and she has to work like mad and she says it's awful and she doesn't know how long she'll stick, but he's a bachelor! With brothers!

Tomorrow night I am being taken to dinner and the opera. Don't laugh.

He's a young kid I met at the Left Book Club and he phoned the Genyons and asked for my phone number. I didn't like to offend him by saying no for he's a bright amusing intelligent lad with gobs of personality. And he makes me laugh and laugh and I get to feel so infantile I forget I'm nearly old enough to be his mother, almost, he's only 25 .... and I'm 27 in two months' time.

Tonight Madrid falls, Poland trembles and Time marches on. England still dithers. I'm sure if only Frank and Alec would rush to join up and you started to knit socks and Betty learned how to use a hosepipe, we would have no need of conscription. There's the bell, that's Michael.

Best love, Ogg

Hitler, who was supposed to confine himself to the Sudetenland, broke his agreement.
**Derogatory term for a German refugee.*

2nd July 1939
c/o Metal Supplies Ltd
Australia House, Strand, London WC2

Dear Beryl,

You beautiful sweet girl. Pearl without price. Beautiful even if you are a bit fat and heavy with child.

How did you KNOW that I was in urgent need of a) a nightdress and b) stockings. What intuition. What cleverness. But let me explain.

The next time you hear from me (Which will be I hope about Monday or Tuesday) I shall be in Copenhagen. From there I go by aeroplane to Warsaw, that is to say I arrive in Poland about Thursday approx.

Our Director Mr. Friedmann (the nice one) is to make another business trip to Poland and this time he wants to take a secretary with him because there is a lot of work to be done, and he is taking me! Yesterday I was at the Polish Consulate and obtained my visa, valid for one year, @ £1.13.4. (Golly!) I shall of course travel 1st class.

If you know me, (and you should know me by now) you will well know that there is nothing I would sooner do just now than go to

Poland. I am so excited that I haven't eaten anything since Thursday. Of course it will be hard work. He was doubtful at first about taking me because my German he thought may not be good enough. The Polish people speak no English; all dictation, conversation and correspondence will be in German, my God. And although I myself have my doubts about my ability to come up to scratch, I wasn't going to let anything stand in my way so I puffed out my little chest and tried to look like Perfect Secretary No.1. The only trouble is that the other girls are so wildly jealous and I just hate to have anyone jealous of me for any reason whatever.

Anyway I guess it's those dam shmoozy ways of mine that I can't even help, taking me this time as far as Poland. Christ knows where they'll land me eventually. Miss C says though, and I know she's right, that I'm the only one he could take on this mission (which is to sell arms to Poland) simply-because I'm the only one in the office who has a British passport!

Will write soon as possible. Mum's the word! Am breaking all the rules in mentioning Poland, so please NOT A SINGLE WORD to anyone. Mr. F says I am allowed to tell my family only that I'm going on a trip to do some business in Denmark. He says it's deadly secret, and afterwards we may be sent on the same mission to Greece and Yugoslavia .... the places on Hitler's threat list. love, Og.

The Warsaw that Olga describes in the following letters, ceased to exist a month later when the Germans invaded.

28th July 1939
Hotel Europejski
Warszawa
(I think it's Friday, isn't it?)

Dear Beryl,

Many thanks for your letter which arrived safely via Metal Supplies. Please do not write me at the above hotel but if you write, do so again in the same manner exactly via Metal Supplies, for reasons afore-mentioned. Herr F. says secrecy 'essential'; all our 'competition' i.e. France, Switzerland, Sweden etc., all Big Industry is after the business. However, no one but US has the key to open the door. He has a secret contact inside Poland.

For same reason I may not write to Frank either, but perhaps you will give him my love when you write.

It is unbearably hot in Warsaw and I have no cool clothes. It is a positively African heat and sun. Warsaw is entirely beautiful and not at all as I had imagined. It is a city of flowers, looking more like say Marienbad or Salzburg than a big city. This hotel and my window faces a huge white square built in the Russian style, at the time when Poland was under the Russian heel; each tall lamp-post carries an enormous tray of flowers round its middle, a sort of scarlet quadruple gladioli and the smashing dahlias are magnificent.

At 12 noon I can watch the changing of the guard in the square from my window; the soldiers are picturesque in their khaki uniforms and top-boots. But all the time there is the clatter of horses' hooves as the droschkys go round and round the squares; in this weather it is much more pleasant to ride in a droschky than in a taxi, and so we do. Every hotel window, every shop window, every house and flat, even in the meanest streets, and from ground floor to the topmost storey has its own window-box of carefully-tended flowers, and these window-boxes are so huge that you can hardly see any window but only masses of flowers.

It is a fascinating city; last night we made a grand Rundfahrt (round tour) for my benefit, in a friend's car, travelling along miles of great, wide, tree-lined avenues on either side the River Vistula. We heard the soldiers singing as they crossed the bridge in mass formation and marched off into the darkness; we went through the enormous Jewish quarter (the ghetto), slowly through the hot crowded streets and saw only Jews on the streets which were so crowded that the car could scarcely pass through brightly lit wide streets and mile upon mile, it seemed, of busy shops; bearded Jews with round black hats and black cloaks are there, young and old. It was fascinating.

The Polish food is the best in the world, next to yours. Magnificent: Today I had cold borsht with thin sliced cucumber and strings of greenest parsley. Chicken with sweet carrots, sweet beer and compote, and thank God the finest (Herbata) Tea in the world.

The grand white new airport at Copenhagen was like something out of the film 'Things to Come'. I was not at all nervous. We were three and a half hours in the air. Arriving at the Polish coast, we landed at Gdynia which is half-an-hour from Danzig, our luggage was taken out and examined, money declared, passports examined, and back we climbed into the plane. It is a very luxurious way of travelling, so restful, but I forgot to keep on 'schlucken' (swallowing) like Mr. Friedmann told me so I got a dreadful pain in my ear. Then he gave me some chewing-gum and watched that I schluckened properly.

There was a nice little lavatory at the back so I incurred the undying hatred of the man in the back seat by making him get up and down so I could enjoy the novelty of wee-ing in the air. There were ten people in the plane including us but without the two pilots and they were all different nationalities. Flying is the finest way of learning geography; you can see from high up which way the rivers run, where the hills are, where the little towns begin and finish. We flew for about an hour across the Baltic Sea. It is horribly expensive. It cost £3 to pay on excess luggage alone.

Polish people are lovely but I can't understand a dam word they say. It all sounds like chick chick chicken. So far I am having a soft time as the work has hardly begun. I spent a lot of time sitting in the beautiful parks or outside the cafes. It is much more beautiful and exciting than Paris, but unfortunately much hotter.

Mr. F went out at 2. I am waiting in until 3 in case there are any cables from Metal Supplies or from our Suppliers I.C.I. or Bethlehem Steel ... then I can go out until about 5.30. What a soft life! I am looking very well. Oh for a drop of rain. Every few hours they swill the streets with water to freshen them...

Much love, Olga

9th August 1939
Hotel Europejski
Warszawa

Dear Beryl,

I am having a delightful time. The heat, however, has been terrific and in spite of working in a great vast high-ceilinged hotel suite, we have 'geschwizt' (sweated) like in a Turkish bath.

Sunday was an impossible day, the blazing sun hurt the air ... yet outside throughout the morning in the great square facing our hotel, there were parades to commemorate the 25th anniversary of something military or other. I think it was Marshal Pilsudski's victory over the Russians near Brest-Litovsk ... As though there were not enough light and heat, they lit two great stone torches (!) and the people sang, and the loud-speakers howled and we tried to work in a heat and noise excruciating.

We are having a very gay time socially. We have been out every night and have met a great many charming Polish engineers, their girl-friends and a number of half-German, half-Polish citizens and refugees who are also, ... to make it even more complicated, half-jewish and half-catholic! Sunday afternoon we were taken to a large gay bathing-pool in Warsaw; I swam twice with three young men who could speak only Polish and French; then we sunbathed. After tea we went back to the hotel and did some more work ... me typing page after page of Specifications for brass and copper semi-manufactured materials to be made into heavy Tanks and Guns for the Polish Govt arms factories....

At 9 o'clock we joined the same party again at the Cafe Royal, where we drank wine under the trees and danced in the open until midnight. We were very gay. The girls in our party are very beautiful; all the girls in Poland are; you must never allow Frank to come to Warsaw, for there are more genuinely beautiful girls here than I have ever seen. Every evening a charming young Polish/German blond young engineer comes to call for us and takes us out to dine, to sit outside the cafes among the trees or drive through the cool night air in a droschky.

One evening we had vodka which was my undoing. Never again! It is about ten times as strong as whisky. We enjoy the choice Polish cooking. We start always with the wonderful iced borsht and then we have iced jellied Carp or mushrooms sauteed in cheese sauce, or jellied Salmon. If Herr Friedmann wants to have meat (must be kosher for him) we go to the open-air Jewish restaurant and have noodle soup and kalbsbraten* with gurken and peas and compote of many fruits.

He is very pleased with me because he says I get on so well with everybody, in spite of language difficulties. Here they prefer to speak French, and if you can speak only German, then you have to do it in hushed tones. I should like to think that the charming young man who calls for us (he is called Pan (Mister) Tadeusz Wdowinski) does so because he likes our company. I fear, however, it must be for business reasons, as he holds a high position in one of the firms with whom we are or hope to be connected, especially Panstwowe Witwornie Uzbrojenie TISSA which is a huge arms factory. This young man has all that sweet-ness and fineness and nobility of character which Mr. Friedmann also has, and with which qualities I am familiar, having once been married to them. I find also that many of the Polish Jews in Warsaw are of a very fine type, having all the culture and education of the Germans, without the German-Jewish aggressiveness and hardness. I was taken for a drive through the Ghetto one day but it was much too big to get any impression in that way. It looked very prosperous, even elegant I thought.

This hotel is very expensive and Mr. F advised me not to lunch in the hotel garden with the fountain, orchestra etc. for this reason. One day I did, however, and having chosen what I thought would be most reasonable, Spaghetti au Gratin and a glass of Tea, I was astonished to be presented with a bill for more than 6 Zloty, about six shillings [equivalent to more than £17 now].

Although I promised not to write home for reasons afore-mentioned, I just have to write you a little from time to time, because I know, being conscious always of your loving care for my unworthy person, how pleased you will be that I am having such a good time. I hope you are getting benefit from your holiday. Perhaps you will drop me a line via Metal Supplies. Mr. F says there are spies everywhere, listening-in; he talks French in whispers too; when I told him I thought it unlikely that my little sister Betty who is only 13 would be likely to 'betray' us to her school friends ... he said she might prattle to them about Big sister working in Poland ... and we might Lose the Business to wicked Competitors in France or Sweden!

Much love, Olga

* *Roast veal*

20th August 1939
Hotel Europejski
Warsaw

Dear Beryl,

It is impossible to say definitely what our plans are, in reply to your question as to when I expect to be back in England. There is a great deal of delay in everything, and Monday and Tuesday are Bank holidays next week in Poland, which means more delay, because everything will be slack if not closed up. Of course we did not know until yesterday about this holiday.

Mr. F is in any case anxious to leave as soon as possible, as he has to go to Sweden, and he is also a little anxious about the political situation which grows as hot as the weather, if anything COULD be as hot as this blazing Polish sun.

It appears that over the weekend there was nearly war, but everything has now blown over and I do not think there is any danger. If war came suddenly ... Mr. F has only his German passport and would be arrested by the Gestapo if he tried to go home across Germany. He showed me his 'souvenir', his Iron Cross for service as an Officer in the last war and said 'this would not help me much' and put it back in his wallet. Pan Wdowinski warned us that all flights and all boats for us to go back via Scandinavia or Russia are booked solid, and not a seat to be had on a plane.

We are about 10 hours from Gdynia and the sea by rail, but the last steamer for Copenhagen left yesterday and there is no other for nearly a week. For my part, I hope our departure will be postponed for I do not want to go back to London, at all, at all. We hear from London (Herr Berlinger or Herr Doktor Mayer telephone us about once every hour) that the weather there is terrible; it is impossible to imagine because we are sweltering all the day and have to have the blinds drawn in order to work; if you held an egg in your hand in the sun, it would be hardboiled in a minute.

If it is not possible to go by air via Gdynia we may have to go via Kaunas, Riga and Tallinn (which would be a grand thrill for me to see the place where our grandparents lived and the very port from which they sailed) but in any case Mr. F has no need of me in Stockholm, so I have to wait for him at the Hotel Terminus in Copenhagen.

I did not receive Betty's birthday present so perhaps it is lying waiting for me at home. I detest the idea of leaving this heavenly place and going back to Ldn. Tomorrow is another holiday festival in Poland and all morning they have been once again putting up the flags in the great square and I shan't be here to watch the soldiers marching and the brass bands blaring. (I go with Mr. F to Konstantin to 'celebrate' the signing of the contracts at long last, with a big luncheon party ... with more Chopin and more vodka and more iced borsht.)

Still I can watch the preparations from my balcony. Opposite the Europejski is the military headquarters and every day I can watch the changing of the guard and see the khaki ranks with their blue-peaked caps march across the white flower-ringed square. There is martial music and drill all day long. Mr. F and I have learned about a dozen words apiece of Polish and we shall pretend to speak it together back in the office as the poor mutts won't know the difference anyway.

Love, Og

31st August 1939
Hotel Terminus, Copenhagen

Dear Beryl,

We hope with luck to be back in London by September 1st. From the 'plane I shed copious pearly tears into the Baltic ocean because I did not want to leave Poland. It was a smooth swift flight above the clouds, but too high and for a little while I was dreadfully cold. Till Mr. F covered me with his coat. We landed, then there was a mad rush, to have lunch, get him shaved in the hotel, park our luggage and rush like mad back to the airport, nearly missing the plane to Stockholm. He left me £25 in case I should run short of a cup of tea or something:

I spent the morning sunning on the white-sanded beach yesterday. They are sure to make nasty cracks when I get back to the office about my having had more holiday than work, when they see my sunny mug, for I'm brown as a berry. Mr. F just wired me to say he will be back on Friday but I could get no berths on the steamer, so have reserved two 1st-class berths from Esbjerg to Harwich on Saturday night; presumably therefore will arrive London Sunday night. However, it will mean spending many hours in Esbjerg, so Mr. F will not be pleased; but the steamers here are fearfully full, it being holiday-time and so many people visiting Scandinavia this year … in preference to the Axis countries.

There is no doubt, having once visited Denmark and Sweden, people will come again, and again. The only fault I have to find is that this country is almost too contented. Everyone wears that comfortable well-fed look and everyone is so blazingly blond that all the people lookalike. The Danes are an extremely beautiful race, the girls all pretty, the men all handsome, but the continual blondness is boring. The food in shops and cafes is considerably better in quality than that in England; no wonder the children look so beautiful when eggs and butter and milk are so plentiful; in any cafe you have to scrape masses of butter off your bread before you can eat it, they spread it so disproportionately thickly. Their vegetable soup is a dream and they bring you a whole tureen of it. No wonder their cooking is so good when there is so much to choose from.

Copenhagen itself is a glorious city of wide streets, with special cyclist tracks; everyone cycles and mothers carry tiny infants in baskets strapped to the front of their bikes as they spin through the busy streets of the centre. The flats are unbelievable dwellings with wide windows and

71

balconies massed with flowers; nursery gardens everywhere stacked with blooms; flower-laden parks and gardens. There are no slums. I have searched. It is a dream town, almost too good to be true.

A few minutes from the city, a great park, more trees, more flowers, and on the other side, the SEA, very blue against the white sand and the craft of sailing-boats with great Viking masts and the fat, rosy blond people, stacking their bicycles on the seashore and splashing laughing in the water. Only their voices repel me, such clacky sounds they make. Thank you is 'Tak' and all Danish has that click-clack sound about it, high-pitched and not soothing. At night Copenhagen becomes fairy-land; the flashing lights of the Tivoli Gardens makes Piccadilly Circus look like someone left a candle burning. Copenhagen and Warsaw make me a bit ashamed of London. Can it be the climate that made England build its cities so drably, meanly? Is England rich? Impossible to believe. Warsaw is the Capital of a poor country and you should see its flats and flowers and gardens, gay open-air cafes, bathing-pools bang in the city for the poor thin underfed children, so they can at least get some sunshine.

I went and had my hair washed, much needed. The young man who did me could not speak one word of English, German or French, like so many of the people over here. I always start off, Sprechen Sie Englisch oder Deutsch? but one is not often lucky; but on a tram-car someone always pipes up and tries to help you with bad German or worse English. I told the young man to rub my head 'hart' and that seemed to sink home (with actions) for light suddenly broke over his charming face and he beamed, saying 'Hort! Ja. ha!' and proceeded with great vigour almost to remove my head from the rest of my person. However, I now gleam with bright curls. Am faced with incomprehensible menu:

Hefrossenen Styvesjekborgford (or something like that)
Able bonne femme
Eller
Melon
Eller
Is

If you know what that is, let me know, there's an able bonne femme. I think the last bit is ice-cream[…]

Too exasperating to get a stomach-ache all day yesterday. With money

to spend and glorious food to choose from, and nothing else to do but
eat it. And I could not. There's a situation tragique for you. Why do I
get chills on the tummy, when I would much prefer to have a cold in
the head? Can you explain it? I admit it is rather cooler here than in
Poland, but then in Warsaw I wore a strip of lace no wider than this
————————————— around my middle, but upon leaving I donned my
proper suspender belt again. So why? Well, you've no idea how cool it
can be 1000 metres above the earth.

Mr. F always sends us a postcard with a little poem on it to the office
when he is away travelling. This time I provided the poem, which is very
poor but seemed to please him. I wrote it whilst eating Gefillte fish in
a Warsaw restaurant and next door (this was in the Ghetto) there is a
shiel* and somebody is davaning** like mad.

> The sun shines on the flowers in Lovely Old Warsaw,
> And though we kukked an alles,*** we couldn't see no War,
> The droschkies clatter through the streets. Tlot! Tlot!
> And Mr. Friedmann sings an awful lot.
> While I go shopping in the Marshalkovska,****
> And seeing the prices, cry out 'Doppscha Doppscha:'*****

It is lonely here without Mr. F, but I am having a good time, now my
tummy is on the mend. The whole month has been just like holidays
and I haven't enjoyed myself so much in years. I am no end grateful to
Mr. F for taking me; he is an angel of a man, the finest humorous
company; we laughed at everything; he sings and is cheerful the whole
time. Working hard as he did in the heat was no joke; poor lamb he
nearly melted away; used to bathe in Eau de Cologne to cool himself.
He sent for a young fellow named Kraftlos, an ex-employee from the
old Berlin office, ausgewiesen from Germany and starving in Krakow.
He put him in a room in our expensive hotel; plied him with money
and food and clothes, found him a job and someone to look after him.
You should have seen the fellow's face when our plane took off from
Warsaw airport; I wondered if we'd get off the ground before poor
Kraftlos broke into tears. He was one solid mass of worship for Mr. F.
Mr. F told him I was a 'goldenes Madel' [golden girl].

Oh dear I didn't even have time to buy you anything very much; I
had no time for shopping and had to rush the last minute trying to buy
a dressing-gown for Mr. F's daughter Hilda which was some job and I
hope she'll like it but I could have got something heaps nicer in London

for half the price; everything is madly dear here. Will you write and tell me if you would like to see me; that is just me in spite of my giftlessness.

Love to Betty & Frank and all, Olga.

Olga got this wrong; the word is 'stiebl' – a small synagogue.
**Praying.*
***Looked everywhere.*
****Warsaw's 'Regent Street'.*
*****Good, splendid.*

The Nazis invaded Poland on September 1st and war was declared two days later, on 3rd September.

September 1939
5, Park Mansions, Henry St
St John's Wood, London NW8

Dear Beryl,

Have just written to Betty. Let me know how she got on at the Specialist. I didn't get to the office until noon, but nobody minded...

I've just had Cyril pounding furiously on my door because I haven't blacked out.

I reported my loss at the office and discovered that my registered letter is the third case from our firm and that so far as one can say it was the Office boy who handled the letters. Herr Suess had him in the office tonight and I think was dismissing him, but nothing was said about the registered letters and some quite minor excuse was found for tackling him. They preferred to do it this way... I feel a bit miserable now having got the fellow into trouble and probably the sack, but it seems such a daring thing for him to have done and since he is really lucky to get away with it without being brought before the police I suppose one oughtn't to feel sorry for him.

Anyway Mr. Friedmann refunded the £1 to me right away as he said he felt the firm was responsible under the circumstances. So he gave me a note for the cashier and I have my pound back again. (We still have the nice boy Lavender anyway).

Not much more news. Miss Campbell took the day off to join the Army or the RAF as a clerk or something; she wants to go somewhere

where they'll have fun and she can be the Regiment's Pet or something like that. She has visions .... tripping smartly about in a glamorous uniform being feted by handsome officers and stunning the old contemptibles with her blonde beauty, which she surely will. All this because she is again having Boy Friend trouble; he having taken the opportunity of a World War to say Goodbye. One feels sorry for her though she is a bit silly really.

I notice a paragraph in the paper tonight about 7,000 ARP wardens getting the sack through being inefficient and through having picked the best jobs indiscriminately. So Rita Thomas and Gerald should look out.... Cousin Rita would be the best Organiser I reckon they could find.

Did you notice that William Forrest, Foreign Correspondent of the News Chronicle is sending his Warsaw dispatches from the Hotel Europejski where he is staying. Good old Warsaw is holding out...

Take care of your sweet self. Don't forget your gas mask and don't forget your Identity Card otherwise one of these blacked-out nights, you might find yourself going to bed with Gerald Thomas* by mistake. Horrors:

Love to Frank and you, Og

*Gerald Thomas was married to (and later divorced from) Olga's cousin Rita Rainbow.

10th September 1939
5, Park Mansions, Henry St
St John's Wood, London NW8

Dear Beryl,

Just got your letter. I am sending off £1 towards Betty's fees by registered post in the morning. Let me know if it is not enough and I will try and raise some more somehow.

I received only last night a very sweet letter from Betty, but she doesn't say very much. I should also like to go and see her, but I learn it costs 20/8d to travel to Gloucester and then by bus to Cinderford. I shall have to see.*

Let me know your plans and also how you are. Don't take any notice of those air-raid warnings; they are too silly. They only have to sight a speck way over the North Sea and they turn on the noise. St John's Wood is so close to the centre that we get the full blast of it bang in the face; it nearly lays you flat. We have had 3 warnings to date, one at 3 o'clock in the morning. Personally I think that hideous wailing crescendo of sound is almost worse than the bombs. I was very glad to hear from Frank over the 'phone that you are 'as cool as a cucumber'; hope you will continue to be.

I swelled with pride when he told me you were the toast of Manor Road North, Edgbaston because of your cool toughness and that you are in fact the answer to an A.R.P. Warden's prayer. But I worry awfully about you and Betty when I wake up to hear that awful wail, 'cos I wonder if you've been woken up by it too and if you are nervous. But Betty doesn't sound very scared either, from her letter, but it is dated Sunday. So thank God, I have two tough plucky sisters. I'd go mad if you were like one of the frauleins in our office who swoons every time a motorcar hoots and carts her blasted gas-mask with her to the lavatory.

And Mrs. Mann, my landlady, shakes like a jelly and moans 'Cyril:' at one-minute intervals. 'Cyril' stalks through Henry Street and Circus Road and around St John's Wood tube station, clutching his gas-mask with a tin-helmet jammed flat on his head. Mostly I see the funny side, but when I get woken up at 3am in the night from a so much-needed sleep, I stamp my little feet with temper, bang bang.

I can tell you life in London is pretty grim. The blackness is thick, and in the heat like a choking blanket. When the air-raid sirens scream, 'Cyril' rushes in and closes my window and I get claustrophobia – I make for the street-door and grim-looking tin-helmeted ARPS order me sternly back.

At 6-30pm restaurants close up, milk-bars, tea-shops, everything, but you may be sure in Metal Supplies we're still working each night till they turn us out and turn off the lights. There's nothing to do but go home in the blackness and get what sleep is possible. So I go, boarding the unlighted buses swishing my little torch importantly. I'm so sick and bored with the beastly war and it hasn't even started yet.

Rosalie will have to go back to Brum to look after the furniture shop in the Stratford Road. She is not pleased. P'raps she will come and see you. She has a spot on her face. It seems silly to buy clothes so I haven't got anything. I haven't much money and I don't know whether my job will dissolve under me, but I think I still have about £25 in the world and Nobby's gold watch and my engagement ring which I keep in the B'ham Municipal Bank.

There's an awful lot of people been thrown out of work, and until a few soldiers are killed off I don't suppose there'll be any work to be had. What a bloody world: I might come to Brum the weekend; write back quickly and say if you are being evacuated in your condition too. And tell me all you know about Betty.

My colleagues get cross with me because they say I'm FOOLhardy.

Guess the first part is right. Herr Friedmann ordered me summarily back to the office at lunchtime for going out of Australia House without my gas-mask. Not much news. Rene phoned me whilst in London a few hours; their air-raid shelter in Westgate is the beach. She is very annoyed about the war; thinks Lee will certainly be called up. A fellow named Henry Adler phoned last week to make a date, then war broke out and he flew down to the sea; hasn't been heard of since. He phoned me at the office and said he was going.

Sam phoned, took me for a run in the country, made a date for Sunday but World War broke out and he has to move his mother down to Devon. Devon and Cornwall by the way are the really only safe places. If only I knew definitely and comfortably that you and Betty were safe and comfortable and not being upset with those filthy sirens all night, I could face anything, even the windows being closed in the heat, bathing in the dark and hearing 'Cyril' all the blasted time. Did you get any food stores at all? I bought a dozen lemons. I'll send the dough off in the morning. This morning at 7 o'clock during the 'air-raid', I went in Regent's Park to look for the war, couldn't see anything.

Mr. Friedmann and I get awful sick when we read the sticky news from Warsaw where we were only a few days ago and we think about our nice friends going through it.

All my love, Olga

Betty, now sixteen, had been evacuated from Birmingham to the Forest of Dean.

15th September 1939
5, Park Mansions, Henry St
St John's Wood, London NW8

Dear B,

Received this morning your nice chatty letter. Am always so pleased to hear all the fruity gossip. Am longing to come over to see you. I ought to go over to see Betty as they have gotten in a camp-bed for me, but I cannot go there empty-handed and after paying my fare that is how I would be. I am sending her off 5/- pocket-money today as I daresay she must be broke. I am worried to death to hear about her nettlerash again; I thought they must be quite better by now. What did Aunt Ray say about it? What did she expect we should do or did she offer to educate Betty herself? After what you tell me about the evacuation of children, it does make my blood run a bit cold.

I suppose we can think ourselves very lucky then that Betty is settling down with those nice people in the Forest of Dean and her schoolfriends. Certainly her letters sound very gay, but you never can tell with Betty. I never knew a child to be so reserved.

I find it hard to believe all your stories though about children being whipped and so on. Surely the child evacuees can complain to their teachers and in that case what are the teachers there for but to pass on the complaints?

Your neighbour Annie is a silly ass; what makes her think that Leeds is any safer than Birmingham; I should say if anything it is less safe, because Scarborough was bombed and shelled several times in the last war, and that coast is far more likely to be attacked than any other. Isn't she desperately ashamed of herself, when she knows you are still bravely sticking to your post, and in your pregnant condition. Is her face red?

Well, it looks like you were right and we're in for a long and a sticky war. What if those Russkies are after 'our India' too? Cor luv-a-duck:

Last Sunday I spent with the nice Friedmanns, Saturday with my 'low' friends. They are not low, merely intelligent, which may be the same thing; I wouldn't know. Tonight I've got to go out with Sam who has phoned umpteen times during the past couple of weeks. He is a bit boring but has a car which means a ride in the country. Lovely! He says he has fallen for me. Cor! What fellows can see in some sloppy girls. I told him that in spite of his good looks he wasn't book-larned [sic] enough for my taste. Now he says he is taking 'Mein Kampf' to read on the three whole nights a week when he is on ARP duty all night.

Well the job is still going, though I can't see how they can carry on for long with such a big staff. I guess some firms would have sacked off a few long before this, but they haven't removed anyone except our English-Jewish office boy on account of his having taken £1 note intended for our Betty out of my registered letter. A man came from the Post Office and said there would be no compensation because the money was not enclosed in one of their registered envelopes. Also he pointed out as delicately as possible that it was the THIRD case from our office.

I wrote after a couple of jobs but I expect there will be hundreds of replies to any job because there are so many out of work.

When you see Cora, please give her my good wishes and felicitations on account of her birthday. I hope she did not mind too much my not sending her a present (I keep forgetting her address so I did not write either) but any spare cash I have which is not much I prefer to send to Betty for pocket-money. What do you think of the Inc.Tax; what with food going up like mad it's a fair struggle to live. Mrs. Mann watches my gas-fire like a hawk instead of being glad to have a lodger which is a good deal more than most people have got. She is a pain. I hope to Christ they evacuate her when the bombs start dropping; she chortles and gurgles enough in peace-time Cor-strike-a-match. You oughta have heard the pantomime about her and her old woman paltie (friend) having to put their ages down on the Registration Bureau .... you'd have thought she'd had a proposal of marriage from the Government[...]

I liked your story about Frank and his activities in the Air Raid Precautions group. Fraulein Behrend tells the story from her own Hampstead branch that at Stretcher-party first-aid practice, the victim turned up to be rescued and operated upon, but the Stretcher-party didn't. They arrived an hour later, however, to find a note from the victim saying, 'Bled to Death, gone Home.'

Had beastly cold and throat-ache all week, tis going slowly. Did you notice that the Hotel Europejski, the fashionable hotel of Warsaw, has been partly burnt to the ground by incendiary bombs and the Gestapo have set up their headquarters in the part still standing.

Mr. F. says doesn't it give you a creepy feeling to think we saw Warsaw just before she died, and that THAT Warsaw as it then was will never be seen again. It makes me weep with helpless fury; it was such a beautiful city. I keep wondering what has happened to our friend Mr. Wdowinski and to other friends. And also I wonder what is happening to all Nobby's relations in Lodz, now in German hands. His only sister Lori has six little girls, all under 15.

I suppose Paris will get it next and then us. But don't worry sweetie, when things get really bad I'm going to see you get evacuated,* all of you, down to the furthest village in Cornwall. Why not? You could make Frank and Ivan sell their businesses and buy a little farm down there and raise pigs. I think it's a grand idea. Don't say it's impossible.

People will begin to learn during the next few months, that all things are possible if necessity makes them so. As the newspapers are rightly saying, one little bomb, ever such a little one would settle once and for all, all the niggling little problems and dissatisfactions of Evacuation. Flighty young mothers would discover they actually liked the country after all.

I went to the Liberal shool** in St John's Wood on Yom Kippur; very nice place and I like the clever Reverend Mattuck, also the organ and the singing. Many shools in the West End are closed and Services which did take place only lasted a couple of hours instead of all day[...]

In fact Beryl and Cora, both heavily pregnant, were evacuated to Tamworth in Staffordshire about twelve miles out of Birmingham where Cora's husband had a business.
**Synagogue.*

October 1939
c/o Metal Supplies Ltd
Australia House, Strand, London WC2

Dear Beryl,

Many thanks for informative letter, much appreciated.

Glad to hear you are going to be settled in Tamworth for the confinement together with Cora and hope you will like it. Shall have to come over and inspect arrangements, but I am broke:

However, I think the war will be over this week. I may be wrong of course! Even I am not infallible ... But it is my considered opinion that when Hitler appears with his pretty little truce all pinned up in pink ribbon, it will be accepted. Indeed they would be fools not to accept it. The alternative is to go on battering away at the Siegfried Line which might take years & years even to damage ... and cost millions of British and French lives, and then what?

And nobody knows whether Russia might not lend her aid to Germany. Japan will take care of America; Italy and Spain will take care of France and we will train a few more schoolboys how to drop leaflets.

Much as it goes against the grain, one has these days to be a realist, which means old Neville going to Adolf and saying simply: 'You're a better man than I am Gunga Din.' Easy enough for England to stop the war she hasn't even yet started. By the time Britain has trained enough soldiers, all the French will be dead.

Easy enough for Lords Beaverbrook and Baldwin and Vicky Castlerosse*
to rant & talk about 'Duty' whilst they sit nice and cosy in Canada and
the U.S.A. I don't notice any of them hurrying back to join up but you
can note plenty of them booking passages as fast as they can for the
New and Safer World. No, I think the war will be over either this week
or next and then watch out for some fast changes. It is a great satisfaction
to live in an age when such vast and vital changes will take place before
my very eyes; we are on the threshold of a new era and I have my
eyes on the horizon scanning for the pink dawn of a new and better
socialism....

I bought a nice book seven and a tanner [7/6d] of short stories for
Betty, and sent it on to her. It is Selected stories by famous authors for
girls up to 16 years of age. Sent a three bob box of chocs to Mrs. G,
her evacuee 'mum'. Mrs. G sent me a nice letter too and I heard from
Betty all about her rich blood and the castor oil, poor kid:

It would seem as though the specialist was right. The dentist cost me
half-a-guinea, then I bought a hat and a five-bob jumper. I feel nearly
new.

Business is very bad with us, for obvious reasons. Am wondering what
will happen to us all.

Betty has probably not got rich blood but acid blood like me ... now
you know why I'm a sour bitch; the dentist said I ought to go on the
Hay diet but I didn't care for the sound of it; the only thing you get
left to eat is the front lawn.

Sat in Hyde Park in the sunshine nearly all day developing a solution
to all world problems with two socialist chums of mine. One is a beautiful
broken-down aristocrat named Tony Smith-Cullen (Irish) and the other
a brilliantly clever tub-thumper (Scottish) who can knock spots off Adolf
Hitler and has been all round the world including a visit to jail (nice
company your sister keeps). Tony is so beautiful, over 6 feet high with
a blond military moustache, he really ought to be on the fillums [sic].
Once he was a pal of the crooked financier Clarence Hatry** late of
Maidstone, so I daresay he has also seen slices of 'life'. However, both
the Irishman and the Scotsman have now found Jesus; apart from this
had a most entertaining day and a nice tea provided.

Our Miss Campbell (Cammie) has already been called up for the WAAF,
so too late to warn her about the uniform. Anyway she has joined it
because it is the best uniform going. So she left last Friday taking her
holiday money with her. It makes Herr Suess feel he is doing his 'bit'
... to lose our much-loved German-speaking telephonist to the Forces.

Just as well you are moving out of town in case the big stiffs are going to carry on with the war. Papers tonight say 'Courageous, 579 not accounted for.'

Great God: Now Winnie Churchill, what are you going to do about it?

Write to me fully about everything and about yourself. But no more please about Cousin Rita or Cousin Gerald or Frank's ARP activities, because it gives me a pain. They are all treating war as though it were a joke. They forget it hasn't yet started by a long shot and if and when it does, I guarantee you'll not see Rita or Gerald & Co. for dust. I'm not saying I'd exactly play hopscotch in the streets myself when bombs and shells were falling, but then I'm not parading round in a tin helmet and policeman's boots looking like Firefighter No.1.

You should see the incongruity of some of our London lovelies stalking the streets nowadays with tin helmets balanced carefully on immaculate perms; the awfulness of a tin helmet or even a military cap on top of a rouged and lipsticked face.

Do write; think of my disappointment when the postman calls of a morning and there's no letter from you. Had a pathetic letter from poor Mario whom I met in Askona (remember I came home with Tonsillitis after spending a night with him out on Lake Lugano and Dr. Margolin was furious and shouted) ... well Mario has now been mobilised along with the rest of the Swiss Army and writes of bad-eating, bad-sleeping (on straw) no sanitation to speak of, and their longing to get back to the civil-life. Guess they'll be lucky if Stalin and Hitler & Co. leave them any life at all to get back too.

I went with the Friedmann family to their Hendon shool. It was like a tiny picture palace, with factory windows, bright hard seats of golden wood.

Much love, Og

* *Viscount Castlerosse (1891–1943) was a prominent writer on the* Sunday Express.
** *Clarence Hatry was the biggest fraudster of his generation. In 1929 his businesses collapsed with debts of $145 million, the biggest ever commercial collapse at that time. Hatry, who was sentenced to fourteen years, was said to have contributed to the Wall Street Crash which followed very shortly after.*

3

Shelters and Lovers

The war is a month old and Olga is struggling at Metal Supplies where the future of the business is pretty bleak. Her sisters' babies are imminent, while evacuated sister, Betty, gives some cause for concern. Olga's love-life seems to be taking the idea of the Merry Widow to excess.

October 1939
5, Park Mansions, Henry St
St John's Wood, London NW8

Darling,

I wish you could have seen my delight at receiving your parcel and my intense gratitude at ALL its contents. You know what I mean! I sat down to the fried fish immediately, having just returned from the office very empty at noon on Saturday, and having just a few moments to wash and change, there was no time to buy or cook anything to eat and I thought I would have to go for a walk in the wind on Hampstead Heath with Natey* with empty stomach, when lo and behold, the fish, and I ate all three at one go! Very sincere thanks for my clean scarf & vest and for the jumper. I will pay in due course but I hope you won't mind waiting just a little, having this week paid half my income tax and have been given grace until the 17th inst., to pay the rest, another two quid.

I saw Desire under the Elms with Rene last Thursday but it was rather a disappointment. So much unnecessary suffering, it seemed. O'Neill hasn't the art of a Chekhov or an Ibsen for making self-inflicted torment and mental suffering seem inevitable and unavoidable. On Saturday night with Natey I saw the Stars Look Down – more suffering; it was a good effort by Rene Clair but just misses the mark like most English pictures somehow. The appeal to one's pity and emotion is done too crudely and obviously, but in parts it is a good picture. Margaret Lockwood is very beautiful and Michael Redgrave always a pleasure to watch.

Sunday evening I spent again with Natey. I have, however, the feeling, but more than a feeling, almost the conviction that he is making use of my company much more because he is lonely than because he likes <u>me</u> particularly. It has taken me a long time to arrive at that conclusion on account of my colossal conceit, but nevertheless I am slowly arriving at it.

Perhaps he will end up by liking me in the end and forgetting the blonde who turned him down; on the other hand he might not but might even fall for another girl instead, you never know. He is obviously susceptible to female beauty, of which I have not a jot. Rene told me the blonde turned him down and married someone else.

In the meantime I am quite happy going about with him and do enjoy his very talkative company. With him you have to make up your mind to listen, for you don't get much chance to do anything else.

I can just see Frank shaking his head meaningly [sic] over this, and mournfully. But he need not. I know (I think) what I am doing. Natey is sweet and good, but he doesn't change quickly. Maybe he will love me in the end when I would be happy, happier certainly than I ever expected I could be: but if he doesn't and I lose him eventually why then I don't think I should grieve too much because of the rather rooted conviction that I have that the man who doesn't know how to appreciate little me is not worth having. God, what a conceit! I did a few days ago rather toy with the idea (it was after one evening listening to rather a lot of reminiscing about the blonde) of telling him to stay away and giving him thus a chance to miss me a bit and to make up his mind whether he liked me or not; but after wrestling 24 hours with my will-power – always rather a feeble little plant – I gave up the idea; because the prospect of going back to rediscover loneliness again and the awful paralysing boredom of meaningless friends, was too chilling, quite apart from the gap which would be left by the loss of his nice wholesome boyish charm.

Thus do we old women get made fools of eventually by these young boys; mark my words sister mine and never let your wise old head be turned, as my senile one has been softened, at the sight of the glossy apple glow on a boy's round cheek! Enough of this drivel; I would be most glad to have a word from you with all the local (and baby-land) news; how are the Thomas's, the Rainbows, the Jaffas, the Livingstones?

I have enjoyed Elizabeth's** 'Mr. Skeffington'; tell Annie, you know Elizabeth & Her German Garden; ... probably because it is all about a woman who wakes up to find herself one morning 50, with her looks and lovers gone and spends the rest of the book wondering how she will fill in her time. It is quite amusing. Annie (and you also of course) might also like Morchard Bishop's 'The Green Tree & the Dry' – I could mention others if you are interested and have a book list, so let me know.

I had a letter at long last from Betty, asking what she should do with the ten bob. She appears to be enjoying school fine.

I am going to a dressmaker this week. I am depressed at the thought of meat rationing; what will one be able to buy? Have you any further news of our brother George? Do WRITE me old girl.

Very much luv, Olga. Luv to Frank.

*Natey Zamet owned a pharmacy business, N. Zamet (Chemist) Ltd.
**Elizabeth was Elizabeth von Arnim (1866–1941), Australian-born novelist married to a Prussian noble, who after the success of her book, Elizabeth and Her German Garden, used that as her name for her subsequent books.

1st November 1939
5, Park Mansions, Henry St
St John's Wood, London NW8

Dearest Beryl,

How are you? Am waiting anxiously for news.

Betty could not come, having a cold. I expect her next weekend if she gets permission from Dr. Flack. Mrs. G says she needs new shoes; she wants her to come by coach from Cinderford but I have written asking her to let her travel by train if possible.

Do hurry up luv. I know you'll get cross in a minnit [sic]. I am very well.

I am saving money by cooking ALL my own food. Surprising what a difference it makes. I have to have it rather late but at least I can have the kitchen to myself after Mr. Mann has washed-up after Cyril.

How is Cora and her babe?* Why not ask her to contribute towards the new shoes for Betty; I'm sure she will if you ask her.

By the way when rationing starts, don't worry; I shall send you my ration of butter because I don't care for butter all that much and you will have two to feed. How's Frank?

Best love to all, Olga

Vivienne Lieberman (Cora's daughter) was born on 28th October and Richard Jaffa (Beryl's son) on 20th November (incidentally in the same room in Tamworth, Staffordshire).

November 1939
5, Park Mansions, Henry St
St John's Wood, London NW8

The telegraph from Frank which arrived at 11-35 caused me so much excitement that I haven't been able to do an honest stroke of work. The telegram has now gone through in the outgoing Metal Supplies Ltd. mail so that Herr Suess can see it's a BOY and it's come and will stop asking me every morning an' grinning all over his silly face. The staff all send their heartiest congratulations.

Was Frank very excited? I would like to have all details, but if you don't feel strong enough, p'raps Corrie will write me at fullest length and tell what kind of a time you had. I myself am tickled to death it's a boy so I hope you're pleased too. Now .....what about names? What does Junior look like? Hope Corrie and Ivan aren't too jealous.

I am a bit worried about Betty. Mrs. G writes she is very temperamental also she has her bad nettlerash again. Anyway don't worry, she is better now and very excited at the prospect of a change. I'll see what she looks like. I'd love to have seen Frank's face when he heard it was a boy.

Remember me to Nurse and to Mrs. Lieberman.

Best love to all, Olga

November 1939,
5, Park Mansions, Henry St
St John's Wood, London NW8

Dear Beryl,

Have you received my earlier letter which would have gone to Tamworth? I hope Richard has now been trimmed.* And you settling down all right. I am pleased to hear you have a good girl. Don't worry about being fat; you'll soon get that down at home. But you'll have your work cut out now if you have got to start nursing Frank as well. I hope he will start to put some weight on now.

He should do now he can have your inimitable cooking again. I am sorry to hear poor little Vivienne has been overfed; this is surely as unwise as the opposite extreme. How do you manage about having all your sheets and blankets and things aired before you can use them? I hope your brother-in-law and his car are at your disposal.

We are going through the agonising process of choosing Herr Suess' Christmas cards. He insists on having typically English Tudor fireplaces etc., and there are none to be had. The office is in an uproar. Either Tudor fireplaces are produced or else... Now you know how it is that Deutschers get things done.

Sorry to tell you my cough is back again, a real beauty this time. But don't worry ole girl. I feel fit as a fiddle and everyone says I look very well. My handkerchiefs look like the Communist red flag but I am full of beans!

I sent Betty's shoes off last Friday so I hope she has got them by now.

Mrs. Mann (who has been terribly constipated all week and had to have castor oil last night) got a bit of a shock on Sunday evening when a Commissioned Officer wearing His Majesty's full-dress uniform (and very handsome it is too) marched into Frankie's little room. It was only our Brummagem dentist, Jerry Simons, but it might have been (judging by the get-up) at least Lord Gort come to arrest me ....for speaking agin the Government.

(In my last letter which you may not have received, I told the sad story of Aircraftwoman Campbell of the W.A.A.F.S......) well, whilst I was entertaining the big blond Walter to supper on Saturday evening, Sam telephoned and told me whilst my supper got cold, the long sad story of his experiences with the Royal Navy. I think I forgot to tell you the end of the story of Sam Lansman. He got a crush on me and when I remained deaf to all his entreaties, he phoned me at the office one day and said darkly: 'Now you've done it, you've missed your chance now. I've joined the ARMY, or rather the NAVY.'

And that, apparently, is the end of Sam. He hates it as much as poor Campbell. So it just goes to show. If Cousin Rita Thomas is attracted by the uniform as you say and decides to join the Forces, you must do your best to dissuade her. Of course, Major-Lieutenant 'General' Simons had quite a different story. He is ENJOYING the Army and feels like a bleeding Viscount at least.

The big, blond Walter is a sort of Austrian refugee protégé of the Friedmann's. He seemed even bigger inside my little room. And when he came in I had to go out. Finally we managed to squeeze me back in again but I had to sit on the window-sill otherwise suffocation would have set in.

I gave him chicken soup (from which he piously removed the scraps of onion), fried chicken and mushrooms. I had hoped, albeit faintly, there might be a scrap of my 1¾ lbs chicken left, but no not even a hair of its sparrow-sized form was remaining. Walter, I discovered, had an appetite in proportion to his size. So I had nothing left but a cup o' tea to give Major Simons, and whilst we had tea, Sam (who is rather persistent) phoned twice. 'Boys' as Frank would call them, come, like troubles, altogether. Though they are hardly boys, Blond Walter is 33, Sam 34 and Jerry is ageing rapidly, a trifle I thought, too rapidly.

Isn't it ruddy cold today? I'm going to finish off my soup tonight. I got a marvellous veal knuckle bone for 4d and added it to the infinitesimal remains of the chuckie. The result is 'a solid jelly'. I wrote a note to the Doc Margolin about my cough so p'raps he'll write back and say what to do, if anything. Otherwise I won't come within half-a-mile of baby Richard. But I'm dying to see him.

Write back ole gel. Why does Corrie never write me now? How are all the liebe Liebermans? I was tickled to hear that Miriam couldn't come to see you on account of indigestion. Why don't they rig up an ambulance and then she could go around everywhere, like a perambulating dispensary and hospital. Cor!

Love, (Frankie) O.

* *Circumcised.*

November 1939
5, Park Mansions, Henry St
St John's Wood, London NW8

Dear Beryl,

I hope everything went off all right yesterday and that little Richard has got over his ordeal.* Did your mother-in-law come to see you .... is she pleased with you?

I had to 'phone the other night for my anxiety had been mounting to a climax; the reason being that Frank was so anxious on the 'phone not to worry me when he was in London that he would not explain the reason hardly why the 'event' had been postponed which made it all sound as though he 'were keeping something from me.'

I was very glad to hear Nurse's placid words of commonsense; she must be a great kid to have around the house.

Well, how are you feeling? How can you go home without having made any arrangements to get someone in to help you? How is little Vivvie, is she putting on weight yet?

Betty sent me back the vest but didn't say a word as usual as to whether her spots were getting any better or not. It seems useless to ask as she will never tell the truth about it. Has she written to you?

Business is not awful; it just doesn't exist anymore. Not a sausage. God knows what we shall do, but we expect to go bankrupt any minnit [sic].

Every time we get a decent order, either Hitler or Stalin go and blow it to high heaven, as witness first Poland, now Finland.

What news have you of any of our jolly ole relations? Have any of the more stalwart ones come creeping back to town?

When your Daily Express, bless it, tells you about Stalin the red butcher and babies in the snow etc., remember that your old wise arnty [sic] told you to take 80% of it with one or two handfuls of salt to taste. I am not going to cry the communist wares for I differ with them on more than 60% of their arguments. I belong to no party and support no creed but that of Truth. But you will find that even the Times admits quite unblushingly that England interfered in the Russo-Finnish talks when they were really going along rather nicely and looked rather threateningly as though they would end in a nice peaceable pact.

'England,' says the Evening Standard boldly, 'could not advise the Finns to agree to concessions which threatened their independence.'** Now that sounds funny to me, considering that the Finnish delegate at Moscow frankly admitted that none of the Russian proposals threatened Finnish integrity or independence.

Someone therefore is lying. Russia was not afraid of Finland obviously, but she was afraid of either a German invasion of Russia through Finland which is within shooting-distance of exposed Leningrad, or of an English invasion through the same opening, or if you laugh that one off then (perhaps more likely) an allied German/English invasion of Russia at this point. So we arrive at the conclusion that Stalin had a right to act in self-defence. Still I admit that's no excuse for bombing women and children ... but the war reports were conflicting. First one out of Finland gave 200 dead which calmed down that same evening by degrees to 20. I am not suggesting the Moscow communiques were correct, but then neither were the others and it seems most casualties were caused by anti-aircraft fall-out and shells.

Finland, which enjoyed many fine democratic institutions, was for the most part run on British capital, notably that of the Eng. Jew Lord Bearsted*** who owns the Mond-Nickel mines, now reported to be on fire, and it was obviously therefore English voices, which means the Eng. press, which means the English money which had the last word. I am not trying to defend Russia's action but in a world gone mad where dog eats dog, it is the dog whose bite is as fierce as his bark who survives.

Surely it's just the mighty avalanche which is Capitalism and which started to crumble with a mighty roar in 1914 and has been still slithering down the slippery slope grumblingly ever since .... may bring down with it all the other 'rackets' such as Communism and Pseudo Communism, Stalinism, Fascism, Imperialism and all the other isms. God knows what they'll put in its place but that, said Stanley Baldwin to a friend (when questioned as to whether his reluctant and retarded rearmament programme might not put Britain in the danger of future war) will be a problem 'for my successor.' P'raps I'll start some Olgarism, but I'm going to have only the best-looking boys in my gang.

All this apropos of what? Don't quite know ... except we now have our boy Richard to become one of the leading lights of the future generation, with an ambitious Arntie behind him....

I am going to cook a nice dinner Saturday for a nice refugee boyfriend of mine who's been living on bread & sardines & losing weight. The dear boy has no great or profound intelligence (but then who else has got a brain like Arnty's thank God) but he is very beautiful, tall & strong, blue-eyed, flashing white teeth and hair of spun gold which you must run your fingers through or else your hand will tickle. And if that doesn't make your mouth water, it's because you're holding pink gold haired Richard in his bath. Funny how much one's thoughts are occupied with food, at least mine are... due perhaps to war, rising prices; at the office we talk of little else, but how to make the biggest dinner for 3½d.

Love Og

The circumcision which was actually postponed.
**Russia invaded Finland on 30th November 1939.*
***Olga is referring to Lord Bearsted who founded Shell, but probably meant Alfred Mond (Lord Melchett) who had extensive interests in Finland and its nickel deposits.*

October or November 1939
c/o Metal Supplies Ltd
Australia House, Strand, London WC2

Dear B,

I wonder if you or Cora could use a refugee woman for your household, a good cook and a real hardworker whom I can recommend and whom I am trying to find a home for on Herr Friedmann's urgent request. Her husband is in the Richborough Camp*, one of the last to get out of Germany, and she has a baby of nearly two which could be placed in a children's institution somewhere near. The child is at the moment at Miss Gaster's Nursing Home for children at Watford, but according to reliable reports is receiving very bad treatment so they are anxious to get it out and into another place. If you don't need any help or Cora, perhaps Melie and Madge could use some. Of course I realise Cora already looks after the little refugee boy Walter Schott but she might need help perhaps.

My job is still going but very weakly. I wrote after a job in the Telegraph today but I expect there will be hundreds after it; the unemployment here is terrible.

Have a bad cold ... the winter here has already started and Australia House is icy. I'm so sick of the blinking war and the blackout and the BBC and the unreadable papers. I swooned straight off when I saw the income tax up to 7/6d, almost double the amount I broke my neck to pay a few weeks ago. The House of Commons, I hear, chortled with glee. It was only with great difficulty that our fully-trained A.R.P.-trained sick bay were able to revive me, after sniffing the bottle of Iodine.

I ask you ... is it a life at all? Write to me awlduns as Betty calls it.
Og

* *The Kitchener Camp at Richborough in Kent accommodated 4,000 male refugees from Nazi Germany.*

30th November 1939
c/o Metal Supplies Ltd
Australia House, Strand, London WC2

Dear Beryl,

Forgive me for not writing before. I hope you and baby are very well
and that Richard will get over today all right. Are you feeding him without
difficulty? I expect by now he has turned into a beautiful child. What
rot you and Frank do talk about the pore[sic] little thing. Did you ever
see a day-old infant which was beautiful? I admit Betty was a beautiful
baby, but then I was almost 14 when our youngest sister was born ...a
time when all babies look pretty. Betty was avid to hear all about the
babies, but I had news for her only about Richard. So ... how is little
Vivvie and Cora and all the liebe Liebermans?

Frank just phoned. It is now 5 o'clock so I presume he will now not
be coming to see me. I think he is very mean not to come. I talked his
head off over the phone so that he couldn't get a word in, poor lamb.
He says Richard's little operation is postponed until next Sunday. Is your
feed disagreeing with him, do you think? Let me know please by return.

I think Betty enjoyed her weekend. I am quite exhausted from dashing
about. Also I have spent more than £2. Thank you for the 15 bob for
the shoes; I hope you don't mind, but I spent 16/11d on them; they
are calf-skin with crepe soles, very strong and comfortable and they are
the ones she wanted, so I do hope you won't be angry; (also Size 4 is
Ladies' size; there's no selection in children's sizes at all). They had nothing
like she'd got on in Dolcis; they don't make brogues any more. I left
her old pair there to be re-soled with entire new soles. Saturday morning
after brekk, we bought some stockings 2 pairs of sheer silk for Mrs.
Griffiths which she wanted, and then Betty's shoes and then we had
lunch and then I took Betty to have her awful hair shampooed and set,
which cost 4/- but it was worth it. Unfortunately it looks nice only for
one day. Poor kid was in absolute despair at the horrible ignominy of it
all; I'm afraid she thought it was all too frightfully sissy, but you oughta
see the difference it makes to her hair. When Miss Lydia finally sprayed
some scented lotion on her curls it was really the last degrading blow.
However, she was quite pleased when it was done and nearly wept when
we got caught in the rain and most of the glamorous curls came out.
After that we went to Madame Tussauds and she proved quite good at
History but was furious with the Chamber of Horrors. After this we

went to the pictures with Hilda Friedmann and saw Nurse Cavell which she enjoyed; also a funny film. Then we had a rather late supper and so to bed; Sunday we spent the afternoon with Rosalie in Anne Trilnick's* flat and saw another flick. The weather rather spoilt things.

I found Betty just a trifle improved in temperament, though I understand she has caused the Griffiths family no little trouble, which you can well imagine if you recall her fits of sulks and so on. Actually you know she is dying to come home to you and Frank, but is grimly determined to stick it and stick to her school. But what is the school worth do you think with half the teachers run home because they are tired of being evacuated. The Griffiths are wonderfully kind to her and she appreciates it, but the child has an almost abnormal love of and loyalty to the 'Family'. I suppose that's what being an orphan in early childhood has done to her. Family relationship is to her Everything. A tiny example of this: She actually thought Anne Trilnick the nicest of the two of our 'hostesses' but she said of course she liked Rosalie best because of her being a Cousin! She is quite passionately devoted to Frank, but Ivan she somehow doesn't include in the Family because she says bitterly, he has made Corrie quite 'different'.

Tuesday morning; I couldn't send this off last night; went to bed early to get some rest. Betty's nettle rash has come back .... only worse than she ever had it before, though she had it ever since being evacuated. Only I've never seen anything like this; I think the poor kid even scratches in her sleep. Could it be the water in the Forest of Dean area or what? Her spots simply never got better at all; they have all been deceiving us. She must have suffered terribly. From head to foot down to her little toes there is not one millimetre of her that is not disfigures with scars and on her back two huge boils. I had to lend her my vest to wear to go back because her own was covered with blood and poison where the cotton wool had come away.

Mrs. Griffiths had doctored one for her the same day and nearly fainted in the process, but until it burst, the child said she was almost paralysed with it from the pain. I can only say that few people would have kept her in the house under the circumstances and there is no doubt in my mind at all about the kindness and goodness of the Griffiths family and how good they've been to her.

I don't know whether it is right for me to tell you all these details, but I hope you won't be upset because the amazing thing is that, apart from the nettle rash spots (and she is by now so used to them that says herself she has even got past minding them) she looks very well. I think actually she is very strong and if it had not been for the spots, I would say she looks quite well.

The Griffiths are very kind to her (particularly Mr. G) but I think she would jump at the idea of coming home. I don't know what you will think about it. But if the spots simply go on and on, it is obvious she will never get used to living there and being 'evacuated' because if it were simply due to the Change, it should not have lasted nearly three months. Three specialists she has had, described it as 'peulier populosis'; Christ knows what that is. She seemed to be a little better in London; there were no new spots and fortunately they cleared off her face completely which she says was very disfigured a week ago. I don't know what to make of her.

She seems a trifle improved in character but is as touchy as ever. She is sensitive to the nth degree and I only hope to God she will grow out of it. If you are even too kind to her she weeps, so you have to handle her with a brisk common-sense; I managed with a big effort and by using the utmost tact to get through the weekend without any scenes, and when she forgets about herself for a bit there is no doubt she is a most lovable child. But so much will depend on how she gets through the next few years; otherwise she will surely develop into a problem. The Griffiths daughter Jean is apparently an angel to her, 'like a sister,' Betty says, as though this were the highest praise possible. Jean kisses her and Betty says – don't you'll get my spots – and Jean says I baint get no spots and anyway I'd rather have them than you should have them. But apparently the other evacuee Margaret, with whom she has to sleep, is rather more particular.

She still doesn't know how to hold a knife & fork so without you to nag her, she won't learn much in that line at Cinderford. I said why didn't you tell me at least about the spots. She said because I knew you'd tell Beryl and I was frightened for her and the baby. I said you won't hurt Beryl & the baby; they're strong as lions. She said, yes it might hurt the baby and then she started to weep and get in such a state I had to promise not to say anything, but she wouldn't stop crying so I showed her your letter and then she was pacified.

She has had no taste of an egg these three months; milk is not allowed and apples also are forbidden. I think it possible the worst may be over and she will start to get better. It may have been something Mrs. G gave her last week because she had a pain right round her throat that started the spots off again so terribly. All her clothes and underclothes were spotlessly clean. I don't think she has been neglected by any means, though her stockings could do with replacing later on, not just yet.

It seems that your Frank is her favourite out of all the family, as we represent rather too much correction and discipline. She has learned in Cinderford that she is 'difficult' and to some small extent they have taught her to laugh at herself, which at any rate is no small beginning.

A good percentage of the evacuated schoolchildren have come home; all suffered more or less from the change, and there have been outbreaks of almost every kind of illness. It is recognised, however, that Margaret and Betty have the best billet there, in the Forest of Dean, even though some children have been billeted at better and bigger houses; only the Griffiths family seem to take their responsibilities really seriously.

When I thought it best to tell you all I know and see that you think about it. I don't think there is any cause for worry about her; Mrs. G is doing probably more than we ourselves would do to get to know the cause & cure of the spots and the child must be strong and in good health otherwise the awful and continual outbreak would have had some effect on her health, which I think it definitely has not. There is a form waiting at Manor Road North to be filled up, so if you want to have her for a fortnight at Christmas, you have to fill up this form and send to Dr. Flack. These forms have been sent to all parents. You will never know really how she is until you see her because in her letters she will never tell YOU the truth for fear of upsetting you.

But I can assure you there is no need for worry; if only she gets over these spots I would advise leaving her where she is. Even YOU could not possibly give her better attention.

I'll be glad if you find time to write and tell me what arrangements you are making for going home with the baby. Are you going to have a maid? Of course if you were to have Betty back, you could possibly manage with a girl coming in each day; Betty is both capable and willing.

We had to buy my landlady Mrs. Mann a box of chocolates and also a box for her to take home to the family Griffiths, which I hope will serve partly at any rate as Christmas gifts. Any pocket-money you send her is being saved up for presents (you can't argue with Betty) but most of her p.c. (petty cash) has gone on shoe-repairs and toothpaste and so on.

The office has been exhausting, nervously exhausting the past week or ten days. I shall not send a gift for Richard until Xmas, so please don't think I've forgotten him. Quite the contrary; he is the only bright spot in my life. Write me your plans & news.

Best love, Og.

Annie Trilnick (1899–1970) was an actress better known as Ann Trevor.

10th December 1939
5, Park Mansions, Henry St
St John's Wood, London NW8

Dear Bailkie,

The journey back was long and slow, after a late start ... How is my luvly Richard; I can just see his divine smile and golden head.

Not a word from Betty; perhaps I didn't send her enough. I left behind me (of course) one pink vest and one soiled blue scarf. Ah well.

Natey enjoyed his steak last night. I forgot that fillet steak is quite a thrill to people who can't get such fare nowadays. I did it for him with a lamb's kidney, tomato, mushroom and a little lettuce heart. Lettuce is now 8d and cucumber (which I did not buy) is 2 shillings!! Anyway he was surprisingly impressed.

I made myself barley water from your barley; didn't you say juice of 1 lemon, or did you say ½ a lemon. Lemons by the way are 1½d each.

Hope you aren't too lonely without Frank. Give my luv to Anna.

Went round to Rene's after supper to hear some music, but there was only Lee there; Rene having gone upstairs to the next floor to a Knitting Bee where all the Ladies of Grove End Gardens are knitting for the troops. They are going to try and rope Rosalie in.

Keep well, look after your hair, take plenty of exercise and decrease the waistline. I shall expect a vast improvement next time I see you.

By the way if you really want to get rid of the yellow jumper I will give you the price of it, or 5/- if acceptable.

Best luv, Og

December 1939
c/o Metal Supplies Ltd
Australia House, Strand, London WC2

Dear B,

That chappie I met in the queue for the House of Commons debates, who lives in New York and used to write me, visited William Wolf of 120, Broadway who is our New York agent for Suess & Friedmann etc., and asked if Mrs. Franklin of Metal Supplies 'was still alive or had she been (not a chance!) bombed out of existence.' So W.W wrote me to write him and set his mind at rest.

Sylvia gave a wild party last Sunday and invited a whole crowd of what looked like Dagoes to me. Rosalie and Sally and I have got quite thick and pally chewing over the more lurid details.

I don't get a chance to write anybody these days. Sally had a letter from Becky in Palestine and it took 3 months to arrive. Becky said she'd had all news from Major Gerry Simons* who was stationed out there.

Love, Og

*Gerry Simons had been best man at Beryl's wedding.

December 1939
c/o Metal Supplies Ltd
Australia House, Strand, London WC2

Dear Beryl,

Still no letters from you, oh yes one, but nothing since. You sound as though you are having a rotten time. Is it really so difficult to get a good girl? You cannot go on like this surely? And the weather is still ghastly here, raw cold. I am sorry you are having it so hard, I do hope they will open the school in Brum soon and you can have Betty home, for your sake and for Betty's. It would certainly be an ideal arrangement. I have not yet replied to Mrs. G's letter, nor I regret to say have I been able to send Betty any pocket-money as yet, nor have I paid my ink-tax [sic]. Last week I had to buy some new panties, some flowers for someone, a book for Hilda Friedmann who has German measles, and a birthday-present for Miss Pinkas. Now I am broken. I don't much like what you write about Betty and Mrs. G. I hope they won't make Betty sloppy; it seems once we get rid of one problem with her she finds another. Mrs. G is inclined to be a bit melodramatic; she must not be encouraged.

I am still seeing Natey. We had a little tiff last week whereupon I wrote you in disillusioned strain. I enjoy being with him; whether our liking for each other is real and enduring or not is absolutely impossible to say; on my part I think I like him with more sex than sense. Actually he is an ugly bugger but has that very masculine, he-mannish dominating quality that always gets me. He is blond, red-faced, with ears that would reconcile you entirely to your husband's; ugly hands, with an aggressive-looking pipe stuck in one corner of his mouth and he talks out of the other side like Bill Sykes, and wears (usually) a CAP! (Just like our Dad)

97

Can you imagine anything more unprepossessing? He talks <u>all the time</u>, is powerful, strong, tough and dogmatic and a woman of my type would gravitate towards him like a pebble rolling down a hill.

Certainly he has made more impression upon my slightly-silly mind than any other has been successful in doing to date. You know (or perhaps you don't know) how many boy-friends I have had in the past two years and have had more than several lovers. I cared about each and every one of them so little that I could never have squeezed even a tear if they'd been run over by a bus any day. I'm a tough littel [sic] bitch as you know. It is possible that within the course of the next week or so, NZ (Natey) will also be relegated to the ranks of Forgotten Men, but I hope not, for at the moment he certainly makes an interest in life. He (perhaps this is the reason why I like him) is by no means hopelessly enmeshed in my charms; he sees through my little pranks very plainly, debunks me upon every occasion and treats me rough. However, don't be too sorry for me, will you?

We went round to Rene's last night to hear some Schumann but we didn't actually hear any Schumann because Rene wanted advice about reliable contraceptives so chemist N had to advise. Rene is terrified of having a baby; she was 3 days late last month and was brought to the point almost of collapse!

Do you think Frank could let me have a black costume or coat fairly cheap? Selfridges have some gorgeous ones but they are all 5½ and 6 guineas!

We may be going to N's house again on Saturday but I hope not; his Momma scares the daylights out of me.

Selfridges had some gorgeous little romper suits, at 39/6d [£1.97 then but with inflation would cost £80 now] if you please, in red and white silk but oh how heavenly. I wish to God I had some money; cannot bear to think of Richard growing big without my seeing him grow.

Cousin Julian (Rainbow) on leave from his Regiment is coming to see me in town this weekend; what shall I do with him? Sorry this letter is so staccato, I have to try and write this while Frank-Josef Berlinger is looking the other way which isn't often.

Love, Og

December 1939
5, Park Mansions, Henry St
St John's Wood, London NW8

Dear Beryl,

Had a pleased letter from Betty saying that she is going home to you for the Christmas holidays. Also a very nice letter from Mrs. G. I only hope all Evacuees have such a lovely 'mum' as Mrs. G. She tells me that Betty has now got a new worry. She is 'worrying' about me, living' all by myself in one room. It appears she has painted such a sorry picture of me that all sunrays have been melted into one river of pity on my account. So, after writing to you a few lines, I must tap out a few words of comfort for the kind Griffithses and warn them not to waste their tears upon such a ridiculously undeserving cause.

Betty, I think, always feels too much pity both for herself and for others; we shall have to give her the Stefan Zweig* wonderful book 'Beware of Pity' for a Christmas present.

Talking of presents, we all had ours yesterday in the office at which we were as much surprised as gratified. Upon being handed a whole week's salary as a Christmas box we couldn't help showing our astonishment in view of the ruinous conditions we have been working under for so many months, with absolutely NO business at all coming in, and we all gave our thanks with the remark that we really hadn't expected a present this year. That said, Herr Friedmann, is just the reason why we have strained every sinew in-order to be able to fix somehow to give you one.

He explained that he and Herr Suess have absolutely no idea whether they will be able to carry on the business after the New Year, and they want to be able to give us what they can while they are still able. Certainly the outlook seems black at the moment; we haven't done a stroke of business for goodness knows how long, but we all hope that some of the restrictions upon export and upon the Metal Market will be lifted, so there you are, that's the position; we just have to hope. Up to date we have arranged to carry on, with full staff, but to give up the posher part of our offices and all try and crowd into Josie Berlinger's and Dr. Mayer's offices after new year.

They are frightfully decent people and personally I should hate to work anywhere else, in spite of all their faults, which are comic more than anything when they are not exhausting. Moreover, half the work was always trying to organise financial help to save more refugees, to arrange affidavits by good, kind English people to accept refugee workers in their homes as domestics or gardeners or whatever, giving advice and help to any and every person who came and they called in droves at our offices in Australia House every blinking day.

Of course, I, being the general favourite, and so petted and fussed over and made much of, would not half feel the cold draught if I had to go out and get another job amongst cold strangers 'who know not me', quite apart from the cold hard fact that there is not one member of the staff who could hope to get anything approaching the sort of salary they are getting at Metal Supplies, which was once Firma Suss & Friedmann G.m.b.H., of Berlin and Cologne!

Mr. Friedmann who has been too awfully gloomy the past week, was beaming like anything today on account of giving us the Christmas boxes, and when I said to him that he was really only happy when he was making other people happy, his beams spread around his whole stout person as he replied tenderly that I was the only one who understood him properly. He always calls me his 'liebes Kind'.

Unfortunately, the cruel fact is that I shall have to put the £4 on one side because it is the exact amount which has to be remitted to His Majesty's intolerable Inspector of Intolerable Taxes on January 1st, and on July 1st there will be another £4 to find, always supposing that anyone has work by that time.

Fraulein Behrend and I were infinitely depressed by the evening we spent this week with our old colleague Miss Campbell… remember the blonde? Flight-Lieutenant 'Commodore' Campbell of the W.A.A.F.s is today one of the unhappiest girls in England. She joined the Forces as you know, rather thinking she was going to have a 'good time.' The full account of her sufferings, which came out in the Strand Corner House, bit by bit, but rising towards the end into a positive crescendo of misery…. At Metal Supplies she had of course the softest job, as telephonist at £3.10s per week; she strolled in nonchalantly every morning at 10 o'clock and often later. If ever a gentle word of protest was tentatively and embarrassedly made to her, she stormed with wrath; how dared these Germans, these foreigners reprimand her? Not that she WAS EVER reprimanded; but about once in 4 months, Herr Suss, scarlet with blushes and trembling all over, would implore her to make a special effort for his sake and then would make a great fuss of her all day in case he had been too harsh. But NOW! life in the army is a nightmare for poor Cammie…..

Cammie's day starts at 7-45 and drill in the cold damp Essex air lasts until 9.00. The first offence of being late is overlooked, the second offence which occurred this week is punished with fatigue duty. Campbell, as she is now called, being just a ranker, was actually only TWO minutes late; that is to say even just in time for when her name was called, but she entered the room when the roll-call had already commenced; was spotted and reported.

Her fatigue duty consists of spending this weekend (which should normally be her free time) scrubbing floors and cleaning-out flues!... Cammie! who never had to do anything harder than laundering her nylon nighties. Any third offence means 4 weekends spent in this way.....! A 4th offence is too awful to be contemplated. The discipline is not strict; it is unbearable; any complaint is received coldly with the reminder 'you are in the ARMY now, you know'. The girls are treated like men. They work 3 nights a week until 7, but this is often prolonged until 8 or 9, according to the wish of the snobby Assistant-Commander. They have to put in many hours of overtime because there is so much to do, but this is not paid for. They get 2/2d per day, but the food is so poor, that this goes on filling-up. They suffer miserably from the cold; some girls having to work in icy aircraft hangars, quite unheated. The promised uniforms have not yet arrived (after 3 months of war!) ... and they wear merely shirt-blouses and skirts, and a blue coat which is the weight and warmth of a mackintosh, with no proper lining to it.

She asked to be allowed to wear her own navy-blue sporty coat as it is at least warm and heavy. Her request was refused. She is not allowed to wear the blonde curls of which she was so proud, hanging down at the back. It has to be worn pinned severely into a bun. The slightest offence against the strict discipline involves the dreaded fatigue duty.

The discipline and in fact the whole racket is run on the lines of prison routine. Her spirit is not yet broken, but she nearly broke down, telling us the whole story with tears in her eyes. I think she had never dreamt it would be like this. Most of the girls, less spirited than she, are utterly cowed and only too ready to split on the others. The class distinction, she says, is hard to bear. Actually it is forbidden that they speak or associate with an Officer, but she and a chum have managed to evade this rule and have gone out drinking & car-rides at night with one or two Officers.

This, she says, has been the only compensation but it is short-lived because the Officers move on to another depot every other week or so.

Finally, the truth came out and she begged me to put in a word for her with Herr Friedmann. It is possible that she will not be allowed to leave the Army, having signed on for 3 years, but she says that if there were any prospect of being able to come back to Metal Supplies, she would try and plead ill-health and resign. If any girl were to fail to turn up after an evening at home, say or elsewhere, soldiers would be immediately dispatched to arrest the girl and she would be confined to barracks on bread and water. Absolutely no difference is made between these poor wretched girls attached as clerks to the Army and the actual fighting forces. We were livid with anger as we listened.

Of course, women (suddenly in possession of too much power) are responsible for many of these abuses. There is often little to choose between the Army-Commander type of women to be found bullying these pathetic female battalions and any storm-trooper from a concentration camp. As Cammie told her story, we felt ashamed of our own sex. To poor Cammie, the thought of Metal Supplies, with the little electric fire we wangled out of my pal the chief electrician, our gossips and our tea and biscuits and all our little privileges and comforts, even the noisy foreigners she had despised, seems to her now like an unattainable paradise. Not to mention the £3/10s a week.

I can't tell you all the things she told us, for it would take too long but the atmosphere sounds rather like that of Lowood school, the charitable institution where Jane Eyre was brought up; our Betty would remember. It seems rather hard that girls, many who have come from good homes and have given up good jobs to do their bit for their country, should be treated like inmates of a Borstal institution or reformatory.

Rene & Lee (Who got married last Easter) remember them? ... have de-evacuated themselves from Westgate and taken a tiny flat in Grove End Gardens around the corner from Flat No.6. (The Cave's flat) I have been trying to give her lessons in Simple Cooking but she has an electric stove which is awful to handle. I should hate to have to cook on an electric stove. She says Life is just the same except that she is just a little more unhappy than before. Strange girl! This type ought to have a little army-training, it might benefit.

How are you? Please don't get out of bed until you feel really strong. I am longing to see my little Richard and to hold him.

Love, Frankie.

P.S. No one calls me Olga; no one likes the name. Must be the intolerable russians.

Stefan Zweig, a brilliant young novelist driven into exile by the Nazis, committed suicide in 1942. Olga went to hear him speak in London.

December 1939
c/o Metal Supplies Ltd
Australia House, Strand, London WC2

Dear Beryl,

The Hamper was particularly delicious this week. I enjoyed the fish immensely, likewise the stew with those delectable vegetables, the tomatoes were so tasty (what kind are they?) and with an egg and that very good smoked beef, went down very well. The bread and butter were both awfully much appreciated. You are too good to me. Which you know already.

Why no news of you? How is your flu now? Everybody's got 'flu or worse over here.

This b...y cold weather, there seems to be no end to it. You can't imagine how cold it is in our office. We sit in our coats nearly all day, our hands and feet like ice. We are all ailing. At least all the others are. I have your stew to keep me warm. My innards are affected, however, for I have to visit my aunt* on an average once every quarter of an hour. The girls think it is funny but I don't. I've probably got Dysuria like Napoleon had. Poor old Bony used to be attacked by his Dysuria on the battlefield; in later life. It got so bad that it used to upset all his plans; the result was the Retreat from Moscow and humiliation and ignominy.

I was taken to a meeting of the Left Book Club last night, right out at Sudbury. I was taken by Sally's friends, the Genyons who live at Wembley Park. It was quite interesting, consisting of people from all classes and all parties. A few Communists, a few Socialists, some Liberals, some S.P.G.B.'s (Socialist Party of Great Britain), some Labour Party members, some I.L.P.'s and many Independents like myself. Doctors, architects, printers, clerks, working class men. There was a discussion about the international situation, in which I took part and then Louis Genyon showed films produced by the Gas Light & Coke Company (later North Thames Gas) showing the insides of slums and then the insides of the new working class flats at Kensal Green.

I was made quite a fuss of which I duly enjoyed. I recognise it as one of the chief and inherent weaknesses of my already weak character that I like to be made a fuss of. I thrive on fuss, without it I wither and atrophy. In another station of life I should probably take to my bed like Mirrie Segal and hold court there. But you can't very well go to bed with Dysuria; I mean you'd have to keep getting out so what's the use.

Business is very bad; I wonder if we shall all get the sack one of the days. There is loads of work as usual but no business.

You and Cora seem to be absolute Greeners when it comes to feeding the little ones (says the Expert). Blimey I thought you'd both devoured the Motherhood book from cover to cover and now look at you! Take this all in good part please. I would probably spill the milk I put down for pussy.

The doc wrote me to go have an examination at the Brompton hospital. No thanks. When I pass out it's going to be beneath my own little roof. Don't worry. I feel fine. To discourage my cough I ate a whole chicken over the weekend; at least I'm going to finish it off tonight. It weighed 2½ lbs and it cost three shillings! But it was worth it; I made 5 lots of jellied soup and the rest I fried piping hot in fat and had with sweet hot mustard served as a sauce with tomaters [sic].

Of course I'll do the cooking when I come over old girl. If Frank can stand it.

luv, O

* *This seems rather dated now but it was a ladylike euphemism for going to the loo.*

1940

January 1940
5, Park Mansions, Henry St
St John's Wood, London NW8

Dear Beryl,

Thanks for your telegram; sorry you were put to the trouble and expense of wiring. I ought to have written you before of course but why didn't you also write? I know you're pretty fully occupied with Richard, but I wish you'd drop me a line now and then just saying how you all are.

What is your news of Betty? I am a bit anxious about her, as the last letter from Mrs. Griffiths said that she (Mrs. G) was ill with heart trouble and might have to lose her two evacuees in consequence. She said if she had to part with only one, she would part with Margaret and keep Betty. But when I got her letter, beginning of last week, nothing had been decided and she did not want to send either child away unless she had to, she said.

Now as to me. Been very well up till now. No cough or cold and putting on weight rapidly. Yesterday, however, for no reason at all I cleared my throat and spat out a tiny clot of scarlet. Can't imagine why, though it always seems to happen round about the time I am expecting the period. Hope it won't happen again; it is the first time for ages. If I have got a littel hole somewhere I suppose I shall always spit blood, but as it doesn't seem to affect my general health much, I don't see why I should worry. I haven't written the old doc, suppose I'd better soon. Betty must be hard-up. Must send her a bit of pocket-money, pore [sic] kid.

How is my lovely Richard? He must be getting quite a big boy now the luvly. How also does little Viv look, and how are Corrie and Ivan? I heard she was very upset when he volunteered for the RAF in the very first week. I had a long letter from, of all people, Cousin Julian Rainbow, full of military detail. Funny how the boys all like writing letters once they're in the Army.

Had a letter from Miss Campbell too. She was supposed to come out with us on Thursday but she had to work overtime; she was recommended along with 4 other girls for a Commission and is very fed up because the others got it and she didn't. Also her mother has been operated on for cancer of the stomach.

Business continues bad and the crazy Leute get crazier than ever.

The expensive suite of rooms we evacuated at Christmas for economy's sake, they hired again this week because they were expecting important visitors for a conference. The conference lasted about two hours but they had to hire the room for two months! I think some of the guests were important Polish Officers, including from the Polish-Government-in-exile who have come over from Paris; the Conference was to return most of the money which Mr. Friedmann and I earned in Warsaw, on behalf of I.C.I. Enfield Motors and Bethlehem Steel. The money for arms was paid over about 2 days before war broke out. Isn't it sad? ... and sorry.... to be so late.

A bit of news to make you larf and larf though it's not specially funny. Of all the ridiculous and unbecoming things to happen to me in my old age, my autumn .... with all the garnered wisdom of years on my battered shoulders. I think I have fallen (a bit) in love. I mean of course Natey. His name is Nathan Zamet; some call him Nachman. My friend Rene is to blame. She takes an interest, which you must admit is very nice of her, in other people's romantic doings. She invited me round to meet an old friend of hers, to whose house we then went where there was a party for the purpose of listening to music. Since then it's been all Brahms, Bach, Schumann, Tchaikovsky and Grieg and Mozart .... to make my head go round, so maybe this has something to do with it. Also War, so the papers say, tends to produce an 'erotic' atmosphere. I wouldn't know. He is 33, qualified chemist, parents are or were poor tailors. I find him attractive, in spite of a sniff which is worse than Rita Cave's.

Talking of Caves I've not seen any for ages. I'm always nervous I'll tumble into one when I go several times a week to Rene's flat, but so far, tripping furtively along the corridors of Grove End Gardens, I haven't seen any Caves.

I think Herr Suess is highly displeased with my obvious absent-mindedness the past fortnight. Two important appointments I clean forgot. 'In case,' he remarked mildly, 'I am not always good speaking, I ask you tell it.'

'Yes sir,' I said weakly, 'I tell it.'

But how can you blurt out – please sir I think I'm in lerv [sic]; they'd send me back to that hospital for examination. I know you'll write back saying don't be a bloody fool, pull yourself together and act your age, at your time of life you oughta be ashamed and so on. Don't worry, by the time you write I'll be together, you bet. With luv to Richard especially from old Arnty who is so old she's got softening of the brain.

O.F.

January 1940
c/o 328, Bush House
London WC2

Darling,

Sorry I didn't write before. Hope you liked the cucumbers. It was sweet (and typical) of you to have the shoes mended. Many, many thanks. I clean forgot them of course, going off in a hurry like that – be cos of talking too much as usual.

It's so bloody cold – I've come in here out of the cold. Had a chill on my tummy this week and couldn't keep my food down. Feel better now though tummy still uncertain, p'raps not warm enough.

I hope my loved Richard-Dick is all right, also you? I feel rather bloody. Bad a row with Natey on New Year's eve and have parted. I wrote in fact to tell him that I was leaving London. Don't laugh. (Funny the way you're always right about people – you're uncanny – even those you haven't met). Mr. Friedmann says Natey is the Compleat Egoist. So what? What men are not? When I feel a bit better in the tum I am going to look out with some keenness for another job. I wrote about a dozen Press Agencies last week asking whether they could use a woman reporter. Don't suppose anything will come of it. But I'll keep trying. They're sure to need someone soon when more men are called up. Must try and find a room. It's bloody being without a roof over one's head in this weather.

But don't be too sorry for me. I'm such a complete ass. Oh to be methodical like Rosalie who is even better at it than Cousin Melie* in Brum.

Love, Og

*Amelie Rainbow, married to Olga's first cousin Bertram Rainbow.

January 1940
c/o Metal Supplies Ltd
Australia House, Strand, London WC2

Dear Berylline,

It is snowing today after days of lovely spring weather. Forgive darlint [sic] my not having written for so many days; have also a pile of washing rolled up under the bed which has been there now for 10 days probably going mouldy and no time to do it.

I would be glad to have one or two ration-cookery suggestions from you as I don't know what to get these days. Yesterday I went very rash and bought a tiny steak of scotch salmon for ¼d for Natey's supper. Rene is mad, very mad with me for cooking him meals but it has only happened twice and I enjoy doing it. However, she made me promise not to do it again otherwise she said she would 'speak to him' so I promised.

I have not been able to find a dressmaker or anyone to recommend one except someone who will charge about 3gns for making. This is very annoying because I have chosen a style as per enclosed. This week I have got to pay the two remaining pounds for my income tax and must buy some walking shoes, so I shall not be able to come to Brum this weekend, much as I would love to be with you and little Richard who is getting bigger and more beautiful every day.

Saturday night Natey took me to see Emlyn Williams and Sybil Thorndike in Williams' play 'The Corn is Green', which was very good. Afterwards we went to see some other friends of his; one is an old friend of my friend Henry Rose. Sunday Natey went hiking with some boyfriends, would not take me in any case as I have no shoes.

Tuesday we went to hear H.G. Wells, Professor Joad, Middleton Murry and Senor Madariaga* speak on The New World Order.

H.G.W. has a disappointing high pitched voice, is small & fat. Fascists nearly broke up the meeting altogether when there was a fight and much shouting for Mosley to come and stop the Jewish war and hypocrites like H.G.

Just our luck, we had a gang of them in the row behind us and they kicked up such a noise that Natey got all pugnacious & wanted to go for them. I held on to his trousers for dear life, could see such a brawl coming, but luckily the ringleaders got thrown out by a whole army of earnest-looking spectacled students, so the others had to shut up or be thrown out too.

Last night Natey took me to see Irene Dunne & Charles Boyer in 'Love Affair' and 'Prisons des Femmes'. Love Affair was a smashing picture. Afterwards I had to go round to Rene's as promised, which unfortunately meant another late night. She had one or two musical boy-friends there and we listened to Cesar Franck's symphony (the 4th) but in the last movement to everyone's horror I fell asleep. They even said I snored.

We are in great trouble, as we are being turfed out of Australia House; the Australian Government want our offices and our lease is up and they will not renew it. We have got about a week to find new offices and get moved.

Everyone is running around like mad, looking at South Africa House and Aldwych House and Shell-Mex House but I think Herr Suess is keen to move down into the City. We all hope not, but he's apparently got his eye on some place in King William Street near London Bridge. So it looks as though we're goin' East. There'll be some fireworks I expect before we finally get settled down. Everyone is corning in from lunch just now and everyone has seen 'a very nice place' somewhere else; locations vary anywhere between Euston and Liverpool street.

Write me all your news, lamb. Very best luv to all and luv to Corrie and Ivan and Vivvie also.

Og

*Joad would later become a leading member of the Brains Trust on the BBC; John

Middleton Murry (1889–1957) was married to writer Katherine Mansfield and a friend of D.H. Lawrence; Salvador de Madariaga (1886–1978) was a journalist, essayist, academic and opponent of General Franco.

January 1940
40, Chancery Lane
London WC2

Dear Bella,

Forgive me not writing ... what with moving office, flat-hunting and trying to get better; altogether don't have a moment to live, and certainly not to get better.

Just like you said (and serve me right of course) have been awfully ill. Was in bed until Saturday, with no one to look after me, managed to get out of bed just enough to make tea; no food in the house and no money. Oh, it was lovely, thought I should die finally, but pulled self together eventually. T'will take me weeks to get over it; cannot get rid of all the fluid in head and on chest. Gotta river inside me. Blood-streaked cough but nose bleed also frequent so am hopeful it all came from same source. Everyone says I look like hell. I got my feet soaking wet on the Tuesday going to the bank for Mr. Suess so that's what started it, goddam. Wednesday Mr. Friedmann sent me home to bed. Thursday I tried again, felt so bloody in bed, but Mr. F sent me home again, so stayed in bed feeling sorry for myself until Saturday. (Not a single cup of tea did my dear landlady Mrs. Mann bring me, blast her.) I came back to the office Monday, Mr. Suess said go home, and then proceeded to give me three weeks' work, so here I still am, sitting up to my tummy in filth, plaster, bits of brick and bits of ceiling. The place is being decorated round our wincing bodies. I got a lil' table and sat crouched near as I could get to the gas-fire when all of a sudden, wall on my left disappears with loud crash and two faces appear, which ask me respectfully if I would mind moving on.

I've moved seven times with desk, papers etc., in two days, but each time I get settled with all my work, someone comes along and removes a wall or a roof. I expect t'ground unter me to go next.

I am also flat-hunting; it hurts too much to go on paying out to Mrs. M whom I abhor; she has not only put up the price but has also wangled the gas so I can't use it the same way anymore. When I turn on t'fire,

I can't use the gas-stove; fire goes nearly out or vice versa. In any case Natey despises my little room and says why don't I get a flat and share with another girl and live like a human being and entertain! I looked at some in Southampton Row, Bloomsbury but they were no good.

Tonight I'm going to have supper with Cecil Asbridge (remember the girl I was in Switzerland with) her flat is full up but she says there's one going next door to her at 25 bob a week and I'm going to have a look at it. I can get bits of furniture as I go along and I would like to have all my bits and humble chattels if I may as soon as I get settled. To get a furnished place in modern style is silly, for they ask 30 bob a week [£1.50] for tiny cells you can't move or swing cat in.

Funny story: Rene said why don't you go and live with your Cousin Rosalie; she lives now quite alone and she is going into the millinery business (her own) and would probably be glad of a bit of financial help. Offer her, said Rene, 15 bob, she will probably ask you for a guinea, but try it. Well I went round and tried it. Rosalie said of course I am not willing to give up my freedom and accommodate myself to someone in the flat for a paltry 25 bob a week.

I should expect you (as I told Cousin Jane the same, said she) to share the expenses of the flat; particularly, said she, such a peculiar person as you are with queer vague unreliable habits etc. etc. And what, said I, will half the expenses be? Half the rent, said she (which by the way Phoebe her mother pays and the other exes also) will be half £2.12.6, i.e. 26/-, then half the other exes such as 'phone, electricity, food and so on, will bring it up to £3 per week. On any other terms, she said, I would not consider it. Then she gave me lunch; we had a herring and turnips.

I'd better get on with my mountain of work; everyone keeps away from me as I spit such a lot. I look 90.

Best love to all, Og

PS. I will send 10 bob for Betty's birthday. Could you ask Frank if he would very kindly have Nobby's gold watch valued for me which possibly might cover my expenses for moving into and starting a flat.

Olga's continual chest problems appear to be related to the damage she suffered as a result of her suicide attempt after the death of her husband, Norbert.

March 1940
c/o Metal Supplies Ltd
40, Chancery Lane
London WC2

Dear Berylline,

Many many thanks for your letter and all advices. I am sure putting you and Corrie to a helluva lot of trubble [sic]. I shall be glad when I'm in an' settled and you'll be still gladder.

As I aim to move in on Friday to my Chalk Farm flat, will it be humanly possible to have my curtains by then? If not, what do you suggest I do, as I have duly given notice to Mrs. Mann, telling her I am moving out on Saturday next? P'raps it would be best if I sleep at the Royal for a night and do my moving in over the weekend. Can you possibly come over? I shall be thrilled to bits if you can possibly make it, but if you can't or if you don't want to leave Richard or any other reason you know I'll understand.

You are quite right; the flat was the best I could get for the money and honestly even WITH my rise, £1 a week is as much as I could go to: for I'm a wasteful bugger and even if I'm careful it will be months before I need stop buying initial things I shall need. Just take a look at this list.

Carpet: don't howl please. I bought a second hand green plain carpet faded and slightly worn, 14' x 6' for £3/10 including felt underlay. I wanted something bright like green; it's got to look cheerful else God help me. Then my Birmetals gift chair is green & beige, electric fire is green and I hope you & Cork will get me curtains with some green in it.

Bed: This is a £5 divan couch, a good one. Price has gone up. The very cheapest single divan bed is now £3/10; I am told this is a bargain. However, will have another look at it. It serves as proper couch in the daytime; does not have to be covered up with counterpane at all.

Curtains: Sounds expensive; will try & get estimate from our office carpenter for two wooden pelmets, though would have preferred a frill. Will also have to ask him for estimate for a 3-ply wooden wardrobe-cupboard with shelves; as I have no wardrobe or place to put my clothes. God knows what this will cost.

Kitchen: I shall have to wait a bit then buy some lino for the wooden-plank floor, otherwise it will look ghastly; then must buy pots & pans and a thousand & one things.

Have bought brush & varnish from Woolworths and am going to stain the surround not too dark a brown on Friday night. Natey has promised to do it for me, so perhaps I will get a chance to attend to something else. He will also cart my two little bags with all my small worldly possessions round in the car on Friday night.

I can have Cecil's char for one shilling an hour. Will have to buy a coal-bucket and a sack of coal. Do you think I could also have the electric fire and one gas-fire stored in Brum, the chair etc. and a few things posted this week so I can try to make the room a bit fit for human habitation? I'm horribly afraid for you to see it in its naked grim condition.

Money: My total capital amounts to rather less than £30 which have been saving up since 1937. Drawing a few pounds to meet present crisis but it occurs to me the time has come to sell N's gold watch which, with Daddy's old typewriter, represent my total sum of worldly goods (oh and the Birmetals linen basket etc., plus one elec. fire, one gas-fire, one hat-box) Would it be wrong to ask Frank to try and sell it for me now? Or should it be kept for dire emergency? Also I owe Frank a pound; hope he will be a little patient until the worst of moving is over. Will you let me know soon how much you want for the curtains and how much for the luggage removal?

Also could do with a step-ladder and must get window-fittings from Woolworths. Who would think it so much work & expense to fit & furnish one room; the kitchen in any case must wait.

Mrs. Mann has not spoken one word to me since I gave her my notice. Am going out with Cecil and Mary this afternoon.

All love & thanks, Og

March 1940
160, Regent's Park Road
Chalk Farm, London NW1

Dear Beryl,

I changed my mind about the green carpet as it looked so faded on second glance; bought an Indian carpet second hand 10'x9', light beige, green blue and so on, for £2-13-6d including cost of cleaning & delivery; I sure don't think I could have got anything much cheaper; cost of EVERYthing has gone up like mad.

I am still dead scared of mouses and shall go hunting around for holes; there are plenty of 'em. Is it possible do you think to have a cat if you are out all day and would I get a grown-up cat to stay at all?

Did Frank make any more enquiries about my watch? Suppose he forgot or didn't have time?

Yes I sure wish you were coming over, for you know my taste is funny & what is going to be the nett result, don't ask me.

Why did Betty leave the Griffithses? D'you think she's all right?

Best love, Og.

March 1940,
c/o Metal Supplies Ltd
40, Chancery Lane
London WC2

Dear Beryl,

How are you? Hope you're not too exhausted and knocked up after nursing me? Any more news of Betty? Do write if you get a chance. I am quite well again. Went to the Freier Deutscher Kulturbund last night. Heard Stefan Zweig speak, also Wickham Steed and Kingsley Martin.*

Just saw Kingy & Queeny. Got a very close view. They both look tired and so old. His face is lined and grim. She looks exhausted but with her usual determined animation. The crowd cheered feebly in their usual self-conscious manner.

Had several letters more from Mario. The last one I thought was a bit silly so I didn't answer it. People, especially men, always manage to disappoint me after about a week. You are the only person who never disappoints me.

I have to forfeit my Saturday this week 'cos Nellie is away with a bad throat, larynx not tonsils. Fraulein Wahl has a bad throat too.

Miss Wahl says we ought to do something about Mr. Suess's terrible English. She says, 'he always says 'zis' and 'zat' instead of 'dis' and 'datto'.'

I enclose herewith my debt of honour to you, being 10/0. I enjoyed the stew. I went home specially last night to have it before going to the Kulturbund.

Let me have a line old girl.

Much love, Og.

* Freier Deutsche Kulturbund was founded in London 1939 to represent anti-Nazi

opinion and was strongly supported by German exiles; Wickham Steed had been editor of The Times *in the 1920s; Kingsley Martin was editor of the* New Statesman.

May 1940
160, Regent's Park Road
Chalk Farm, London NW1

Sweetie,

Forgive me (if you can) for not writing before. I don't get a moment. At the office, driven & harried all the blasted day long & in the evening most always someone comes and when they don't I'm clearing up after myself or them.

I tried to 'phone you tonight (Friday) but I couldn't get through. Operator told me if I liked to try during the middle of the night I might make it! I am just a wee bit anxious; I would have liked to talk to you. I want to be reassured you're all all right and that Betty is with you. It's awful not knowing what is happening at your end. P'raps I'll try & get through again tomorrow night. When I rose at 6-30 this morning and turned on the radio I certainly didn't expect to hear at 7 o'clock the sickening news!*

By the time I'd recovered my breath it was 8 o'clock and it was all confirmed. Then followed a crazy day at the office; Mr. Suess, as usual, ignoring the news & general excitement completely and giving me a ton of work which I had to concentrate on whilst all round me everyone reading the papers and rushing around like mad. However, p'raps it's just as well it's started; it'll be over the sooner.

I just want very much tonight to be reassured you aren't worrying and that Frank is all right and feeling better.

After listening to the 7 o'clock news and then hearing it followed by the usual morning exercises (Let's try it again – shall we – head up, swing with your arms etc.) I just wanted to sit in the middle of my vast room and have hysterics....

Chalk Farm is a bit of an awkward spot, with the guns right on top of Primrose Hill where there is a garrison of soldiers among the luscious green-yellow trees and the green hills. So, if and when the guns go off, it's likely every window in the district will be shattered. Natey came rushing round tonight with sticky paper (he left his Pa in the car outside 'cos he didn't want his pa to know I lived alone) and plastered up my windows.

Haven't got to go to the office in the morning thank God, but Monday's holiday is cancelled. I'm among those who've got to come in. Sunday afternoon Natey is inviting me and the Friedmanns to his home to tea.

Tomorrow I shall probably go cycling with Mary, one of the girls living with Cecil Asbridge. Cecil has gone to the country to stay with E. Arnot Robertson and her husband. Rene has gone to the country with Lee. I did think of going down to Westgate (free of charge) with Michael and Bernard, but I noticed they'd been dropping bombs on Kent; in any case the holiday is off.

If the Germans crunch right through France to Paris, what will happen to my relations in the rue de Sommerard? It doesn't bear thinking about.

I wanted very much to come to Brum, but a pound (it's more now, isn't it?) is absolutely out of the question. I was rather disappointed to hear you wouldn't come to London yet awhile and I suppose now it's even more out of the question. Then when am I going to see you and Richard again? By the way could you spare Betty next week-end do you think? If you don't want to part with her, then please don't; and God knows what'll be by next weekend anyway, but it's rather bloody being separated for so long.

Don't you worry about me though; I'm all right, only missing you very much.

Give my love to Corrie and Ivan. I've still not written to Corrie; it is swinish of me, she's alone a lot now that Ivan's in the RAF; it's that swine Suess's fault; ever since he gave me that rise he's been driving me to death, determined evidently to get his money's worth. Mr. Friedmann is as sweet as ever & if it weren't for his protection I'd go completely potty at Mental Surprise Limited. I shall try & ring you Saturday eve if I can get through, but should you be going out, don't stay in on account of me, I can always try again. Please take care of yourself and Richard and Frank and don't let the bleeding Huns frighten you; but knowing you I know they won't.

All my luv, Og.

* *The news was the German advance, which outflanked the British Expeditionary Force and led to the evacuation at Dunkirk.*

May 1940
160, Regent's Park Road
Chalk Farm, London NW1

Dear Beryl,

Guess I owe you another letter, so here goes. Hope you are not still worrying about me; you should know by now I'm hard to kill. Also, what about my mystic-Cassandra-qualities? When one of us is going to get bumped off, I'll let you know in good time, if possible. I'm not saying it's not perfectly bloody in London now, seeing the streets of wreckage all round you, every day a new lot, even in your own street, listening to the long whine and whistle and thud of the bombs at night falling so close it seems to take the skin off your nose, heart in mouth, hair standing on end, thanking all the good fairies it didn't hit you – quite – and wondering whom it did hit – and if it's anyone you know. Lordy.

83 kids torpedoed and sunk, Christ! And Natey's sister Freda now can hardly make up her mind whether to take her two little boys to the U.S.A. But the three houses next door to her ... just around the corner from Natey's, collapsed so there's not one brick left upon another, what a sight, and in the house next door to her lived of all people, Leopold Harris,* who had an ear torn off and skull broken and subsequently died. So no wonder she's jumpy.

I slept last night (Sunday) with her and the two boys in their Anderson shelter whilst her husband (ARP warden out on duty every other night) was away. The shelter was more comfortable than Natey's with beds and bedding and lights and all but lying down in the ground I can't breathe, I suffer from claustrophobia; I choke, I claw the air and the sweat pours off me. I don't know how I stuck it through the night, only I couldn't move without waking Freda. In Natey's shelter I don't get that feeling, at least not so bad, because we all sit up on deck-chairs, I am near the door, there is more air and it is not quite so deep in the ground. But even then it's bad enough. So I still think it's best to stay in bed and take a chance. Rene has got a fierce cold from sleeping on the floor in her hall. Natey has really made a marvellous job of his shelter; he mixed the concrete himself and built a wall all round and reinforced the whole thing; no one showed him how; he worked like a nigger; he's really only happy when he's doing that kind of work or digging the soil, up to his knees in mud and covered with dirt from his mudspattered blond hair to his mud-caked ankles.

I spent all Sunday trying to clear up after his Ma; she is a dirty worker, a rotten cook and a worse manager; as fast as you clear up after her, she starts another mess. All she knows is Salt Beef and chips and Boiled and Fried Cod! And bread pudding! But she's a nice old girl, otherwise.

She came up behind me while I was washing-up at the kitchen sink and muttered: 'Why doesn't my Natey get married?' Was a bit taken aback and didn't reply. She went on: 'He's 35 ... he should. You've been unlucky ... it's not your fault.' (It seems she was discreetly referring to my widowhood.) 'Do me a favour ... try and catch Natey.' The way it sounded was 'ketch Natey'. I was a bit flabbergasted. Mind you she did catch us very nearly under the same blankets lying on the hall floor the night before because I just couldn't stand it in the Anderson shelter any longer ... but we were fully dressed. Besides, everyone nowadays sleeps on floors all mixed up with everyone else. But I do have a good giggle about ketching N ... feeling as I do now, I might ketch myself a good cold if nothing worse!

The old girl from over the road who shares their shelter with her hubby, has got B.O. and no one wants to be the one to tell her about it. But something has to be done. Still I quite like her, smell an' all because she told everyone she thought I was 19 years old. Ha Ha. I'm going back there now for another dose, blimey... when Archie and Leo (that's the two biggest guns) get going it's like all hell let loose. I can hardly hear me own teeth chattering. Every night you can't help wishing the buggers would stay away just ONE night, just ONE night's sleep would be such heaven. How is it at your end now?

Best love to all my loves, Olga

Love to Coralie also

Leopold Harris was a professional arsonist who in the 1930s was estimated to be making £500,000 a year out of burning down warehouses and collecting insurance. He was jailed for fourteen years.

10th June 1940
160, Regent's Park Road
Chalk Farm, London NW1

Dear B,

I'm already missing my beautiful child Richard. Is his tummy all right
again now? Was it a chill, do you think? Everyone said I looked like I'd
been on my holidays again. I certainly feel much better.

The flat looks a bit dirty and so far have not had a chance to clean
it. Last night my No.2 boyfriend Sam came over and I took him to see
Cecil and Mary and Margaret who had some visitors and we drank beer
and torked [sic]. I keep putting off the cleaning. Hope you have Betty
back with you now. Don't forget to remind her to let her hair grow.

Everyone thinks the war will take a decisive turn or at least reach a
decisive stage during the coming fortnight. I am glad you have a decent
shelter to go to, but I shall worry just the same. It seems to me a long
walk up the road to it ... especially carrying Richard in his carry-cot.

Had a bad night on Tuesday; not bombs this time. Your un-favourite,
the one you call Noxious Natey came round. Of course you were right
as usual. Probably you must know more about the 'wickednesses' of men
than I do; I think the pore [sic] fellow is a bit potty too. Tells me a
different story each time. Tells me now he likes me very much but he
does not want to marry, partly because he cannot be tied and partly on
account of the war and consequent insecurity of everything. I cried a
lot (ha ha) and told him to get out and not come back. He said, don't
be silly, there is no reason why we can't carry on like this forever. Says
he won't hear of it being ended; said he might change his mind about
marrying me in about three or four months when the war situation might
be entirely different. I think he first wants to see if he can't find himself
something better in the meantime. Clearly, I do absolutely nothing for
his ego. However, c'est l'amour, c'est la vie, ca va and what have you.

I hope you will not join up with your neighbour Mrs. B and start
playing fun & games; probably she is smarter than you and you would
be left weeping. Or would you?

Cecil is very proud of having made 10 lbs of plum jam but the girls
are incensed because she has used up all their sugar ration. I have great
clots of your jam in my porridge at brekfast [sic]; it is very good. Not
much work at Metal Supplies the last few days and I am getting lazy.
Sorry to write you such a dull letter but I do not think any thorts [sic],

so cannot write any. And those I think would not be decent and the ole censor would scratch 'em out with his B.P.

Am now on my last egg, but if I go down the East End I might get given some. Please tell Cora I got her p.o [postal order] and thank her for this. Your photograph looks very nice on my mantelpiece and brightens the whole room. Everyone says wot a pretty girl you are. Best love to Richard and Frank and you. How is the royal divorce?

10th September 1940
c/o Metal Supplies Ltd.
40, Chancery Lane
London WC2

Dear Beryl,

So much love to my Beautiful Richard, bless him.

I started writing this postcard in an air-raid shelter. Today is Tuesday, the 10th September. You say in your letter, why don't I write, but until tonight I didn't know your address. Cora phoned me at the office, was worried about me. It certainly is bloody here. Top of Chancery Lane was on fire yesterday, today the bottom end is burning and we are in the middle somewhere but still intact.

The sirens have just gone and I ought to find some shelter for the night.

Don't worry about me ole girl – at long last Natey is taking care of me ... (must be due to the Blitzkrieg) I spent the whole weekend at his home – they have an Anderson shelter in the garden near Cricklewood. Weekend was terrible – the East End of London simply isn't there anymore. I really don't want to die, not now I think N really cares so I'll do my best to avoid a direct hit.

Best love, Og

23rd October 1940
Metal Supplies Ltd
Brettenham House, Lancaster Place
London WC2

Dear Beryl,

Thanks for your letter; I am fine so don't worry please. Yes, the bombing happened about 10 pm in the evening.*

Shall try to find somewhere to store some of my stuff. Rosalie is taking the electric fire to use in her showroom.

I wash up evenings in Flat No.6 Grove End Gardens in payment for taking a bath.

The worry is what to say as my regd. address as I have none. Nobody wants poor little orphan annie to live with them, but Rosalie is letting me sleep on the floor in the corridor outside her front door. She sleeps on her hall floor as it has no windows and is safe from flying glass.

I am glad Betty is well; she hasn't written me. Please find a house in the country, preferably Cinderford and take Frank there else I shall be worried sick about you. Very glad to hear Richard sleeps well in the shelter. I think Natey will help me with my stuff on Sat'dy. I meant to write you a letter but no time, try tomorrow.

Best luv, Og

* *The house in Chalk Farm was affected by bomb damage.*

2nd November 1940
Metal Supplies Ltd
Brettenham House, Lancaster Place
London WC2

Luvchicks,

I'd be glad to hear from you right away that you are all right. Am rather worried also about Corrie and Ivan. Have you news of them? I wish they would get out of Birmingham.*

We are having it quite quiet lately; although our office was bombed for the second time! Blasted to smithereens we found Wednesday morning was the Ministry of Supply Salvage Dept., bang opposite to us in

Brettenham House. All our windows are gone, the ceilings deeply cracked and the walls sagging inwards. So we are moving again on Monday, apparently to Bush House, which is also in the Strand.

The Strand Palace also got it TWICE, and the Savoy twice and Simpsons; and outside Brettenham House in Lancaster Place there WAS a Ladies', which is now a Very Deep Hole, very deep.

Tonight the plan is for all the dames to have their hair dyed and done, wot a row. Rosalie won't let me have a bath anymore; her girlfriend Freda is bombed out too and has come to stay at No. 6. However, I bath at Sylvia's three doors away along the corridor, which is also the accommodation address for a few bits of my underwear etc.

I'll write you a long letter, luvie, but at the moment gotta make tea for a round dozen of them. Please write me quickly pet, otherwise I shall worry. Kisses for Richard Dick.

Pity you're not here having your hair touched up & done like the other dames (all 4 of them) then Uncle Louis Rainbow could say you were a tart.

* *The Jaffa family did move out of Birmingham and Beryl took Richard to Malvern in Worcestershire.*

20th December 1940
c/o The Corridor, Grove End Gardens,
London NW8

Dear Beryl,

Thanks for your letter. I had to tell the whole office about Richard and his chamber pot which they enjoyed very much.

I knew you would be pleased to hear about Reuters, but please do not be too jubilant too much in advance. After all I've not started yet although there is every hope and prospect I will be 'called up' during the coming week.

I nearly didn't find out about it … the letter arrived from the Editor at the old Henry Street address and then sent on to my ruined room in Chalk Farm, now inhabited only by the mice so thick on the ground I'm scared ever to go in there. My fault; when I painted the surrounds all brown, I must have left sticky bits because I found one little mouse sort of impaled in it between the rickety floorboards. The letter said just

'Referring to your letter of two years ago ... please will you call next week for an interview, etc.' They must have a better filing system than we had at Metal Supplies. Remember the Grand Search for 'Invincinas'? It is rather sad to see the Herr Doktor sitting forlorn with not a darn thing to do in the office of Metal Supplies; just reading up old files of letters as though they were Love Letters or something. He didn't yell at me either when I went in to see him; all the fire has gone out of him; sometimes he looks too weary to take off his gas mask and there it hangs, all tangled round his long arms. Ever since the Chancery Lane bombing, little Herr B always puts his gas mask on to go to the lavatory which is on the floor below. (Metal Supplies are still paying us...and for doing nothing.)

With my usual pessimism I am not counting on getting a proper journalist's job until I am officially summoned and asked to begin. I was summoned to a second interview this week to see the Assistant to the Editor-in-chief who filled up a form with all my particulars and who asked if I would agree to start at £4.10s, to which I said yes, provided there were prospects of promotion for me. He seemed chiefly interested in the fact that I had worked in Poland and had been highly recommended by the first man who gave me the shorthand test. So of course I was a bit disappointed and discouraged that after all that I was not asked to start at once. However, when I do I hope finally get started ... at least on the very bottom rung of the ladder. I will do my level best to fulfil your expectations.

Rosalie is not <u>so</u> jealous ....after all her French and German are infinitely more fluent than mine and a lot of the work I'm told is in a terrible French, they called it 'cable-ese' which means that the News is cabled in from all the war-free places like Ankara and Rio de Janeiro in bad French with all the words stuck together for economy of course and you have to sort it all out into decent readable English for the newspapers. Rosalie says it sounds too much like hard work to her – 12-hour night shifts for one thing. Strangest thing of all, it is Rene who is uncommonly jealous and has been so nasty that we have practically quarrelled over it all. She said that of course if it were not for the fact that soldiers and men are being killed off and going to be killed off like flies, my application would never for a moment have been considered by Reuters.

Love, Ogg

1941

At the beginning of 1941 the war in North Africa is at its fiercest and the Nazis extend their control over much of Europe.

January 1941
6, Grove End Gardens
London NW8

Darling B,

[...]as I told Bob on the Phone, please do NOT wire people; telegrams take at least two days; besides giving me the jitters when I open 'em.

Moreover, as I have pointed out before, the raiders with their bombs do not maliciously seek out my non-valuable life; humble walk I always in my ways and feel that as a target they despise me. To carry my point further I can add, for your peace of mind, a reminder that we, in Grove End Gardens, already bear evidence to our (as one distraught lady put it) 'baptism of fire'. Popular feeling is confident that in consequence we can count on being happily neglected in future.

This being Sunday afternoon, and wet, and I carrying such a cold in my head, felt entitled to drop in to the local pub and treated myself to two ports; feel right warmer but if my hand slips you will know the reason. Have coughed a whole week now, heartily, and with the usual mysterious and bloodstained results; shadowy forms shrink fearfully to the wall as I pass by in the Corridor (where we all sleep on the blue carpet) scampering on my way to the Ladies.

Yesterday, being my Saturday morning, I lay abed till 9, until prodded in the bottom by dustman with bin. A Very Annoyed Dustman, because my sickly form barred his legitimate entry to the bin, against which I lay my head, for emptying. Dustman dismissed me summarily and could not, I found, be pacified by an exhibition of my almost naked charms.

The cold was contracted last Sunday, carrying groceries through the rain for Rosalie. I could not get at my rubber boots because they were being stored in Sylvia's flat, my belongings being almost evenly distributed amongst my neighbours here, since being 'bombed out' of my Chalk Farm flat.

Sylvia enjoys temporary possession of my underwear, such as it is, in a brown paper parcel; whilst Rosalie reigns over my assorted jumpers and one hat ... all these being secreted in a dark cupboard all unknown to her. Oft I awake sweating in the night, having dreamed that in one of her almost-nightly 'turnouts', she has come across their uninvited presence. This secret, known only to myself, weighs heavily upon me which probably accounts for my having a shifty shuffly look about me which everyone complains of. This opens up a chapter of my current sufferings I must unburden. Here there live only Very Smart Ladies. There are a lot of them and they are here every night, both inside and outside Flat No.6, in their best dressing-gowns, curls and the newest shade of lipstick. Everyone feels they must look their best in case another bomb drops on the Grove End Gardens block and the local, hopefully best looking members of the ARP on the roof – who include Cousin Harold by the way – come rushing in to save us from the wreckage.

There is Mrs. Hunter from three doors along the Corridor, in pink satin and Sylvia in pink velvet. There is Doris (with a 3-week's baby) in royal-blue velvet; Betty in green; Rosalie smart in navy with pale-blue piping; Sally in slacks; Phyllis in hand-woven jumpers in every shade. There is Letty & Freda and Rene and Rosa; finally there is me.

Sylvia (Who was before marriage a year ago, a Mayfair hairdresser from Simon's you know), has bought a hair-dryer for 16 guineas and everyone attends. Everyone has woken up to the fact that, of an evening, whilst the guns are booming and bombs dropping, their scalps still need attention; personality must be paid for, tired skins revived; coiffeurs brought, alluringly, within the mode.

Sylvia, who has winning ways and has won over everyone except me, to their cost, has altered everyone. She has given Rene ginger curls atop & black behind; Rosalie has become piquant with top curls; Sally's thinning hairs have been coaxed into waves; Phyllis goes to sleep vertically from the shoulders so as not to spoil the line. Whilst I remain adamant, to their combined fury. (if our little sister Betty is sometimes called obstinate, I am stone.) Each night when one female siren or another shrieks 'Sylvie darling! <u>When</u> are you going to do something about Olga's hair?' I, washing up at the sink the dishes and pans from a supper I have not eaten, wear, I know, an expression that George used to wear when the Old Man [her father] asked him how much change he had brought back from shopping. They despise me.

They despise my coarse unpainted face, my cheap and always laddering stockings, my worn jumpers which show, says Rosalie disgustedly, all your bust. They despise, and rightly, my 1936-model black claque jacket with its fraying cuffs and collar. Continued pressure has had its effect though:

I boast a pair of new (and sensible) shoes; a black woollen dress from C&A for 24/11d [just under £1.25], fitting well & in which I am trim to the point of disappearance. Great difficulty was the stockings for Rosalie will not allow me to leave mine overnight to dry on the hot-rail in the bathroom, perforce I have bought another pair.

Every night (and how grim this is) there is Company. I arrive with the coffee (black) to which I am invited and with which I provide for the company, chocolate peppermints. I then wash the dishes (otherwise I get no bath afterwards: 'go and ask Sylvia, perhaps she'll let you.') I then make tea for anything from 8 to a dozen people upwards. I then take a bath; after that I am forcibly dragged from one flat to another to entertain the Company, and then when all are deep in their cups or in a discussion of someone's inferior character or underwear, I sneak out & climb on to my mattress, shrinkingly for fear I shall be noticed and, undressing beneath the bedclothes (or rather the rug & eiderdown) I disappear all but the despised pigtail.

I can count it a lucky night if no wag, staggering up from the Bar, or chatty female wishing to unburden ('Darling, he simply AVOIDS marrying me').... will pass by my shrinking form and NOT pull the pigtail with joyous abandon, to show apparently I am not forgotten.

There are those who on leaving the Bar, feel amorously inclined and cannot be deflected from trafficking beside my mattress. Thank God I shall tomorrow have my own single; the double one I have been so far using, having called forth far too much in the way of ribald invitation; the drunks or half-drunks cannot pass it by without a leer and a snigger or a playful pinch for my bottom.

Rosalie now sends her boyfriend home right through the thunder and danger of the nightly gun barrage because she cannot stand the way he parks on my mattress and cannot be induced to budge.

Sally, who sleeps on the mattress just behind mine, just snorts, 'What do you expect when you uncover yourself like a whore!' Sally has the lowest possible opinion of my character. I think the Spirits at her weekly séances have informed her I am sexually untrustworthy. Also, as she often reminds me, our Father was not her best liked brother; unlike Brothers Abe and Moe whom she did like. Even Sam Davis sitting out the war in faraway Johannesburg was more popular with Sally than Izzy 'trouble-maker and woman-chaser.'* She does not understand that I cannot inform the whole Corridor that I uncover my shoulders because at night I sweat otherwise.

I am, however, indulged to the extent of being allowed a cup of the tea I have made of an evening. This is because each week I bring a full ration of Tea and Sugar also. I use the bath but I also bring of course my own soap and towels. If there is anything by way of an odd bit of vegetable or salad or sweet left over from the table I am invited to partake, but I have always 'had my supper thank you'.

Cousin Rosalie has all the legendary Cave meanness & almost it hurts to see how she stints and starves poor Phyllis who is a paying-guest & quite a nice girl. Rosalie herself also approves of her because as she informed me confidentially, 'Poor Phyllis has no sex-appeal.' Phyllis is a good sort and often sneaks out to help me with the drying-up. But she is rather tall & stands very high in her slacks.

Sylvia would require a chapter to herself to describe so I won't attempt; but she is a good sort & so is her husband Lionel who is an old friend of Natey's. Sylvia has had a week in Brighton & I have been cooking Lionel's breakfast & dinner in the evenings and likewise my own, which was very nice for me as otherwise I eat in the restaurant mostly.

Every Sunday afternoon there is a party, which will probably start soon & goes on until midnight. Sylvia invites all her boyfriends; I think she is trying to find a man for Rosalie. Ha ha. Natey came once but didn't like it and hasn't been since. He says we are all false & phoney and don't we realise there is a war on, please? He despised the sumptuous table of fruity cakes (from the Corner House) of petit-fours and sausages-on-sticks and savouries & salads. However, the dislike was mutual; they all said he was stuck-up and aggressive. Natey is busy digging for victory; he also broods for it a lot and cannot be deflected by petit-fours & the smug chatter of perfumed women.

Still I am sorry for Natey; something terrible happened to one of his Dispensers. You know he and his younger brother have chemists shops on railway stations like Kings Cross and Liverpool Street, called Zamet. In one shop in Grays Inn Road was a divinely good looking and very sweet young man with the bluest-bluest eyes you ever saw. He became engaged to a gorgeous redhead about a fortnight ago. After a late flick he went one night to sleep in the YMCA in Tottenham Court Road which got a direct hit from a bomb. Flying glass took out both the young man's blue eyes. His devoted fiancée is looking after him, but Natey his boss and friend is very nearly inconsolable. And probably very frightened for himself too.

Love, Ogg

* Olga's Aunt Sally had fallen out with her brother, Olga's father Izzy, some years earlier.

15th January 1941
86, Canfield Gardens
West Hampstead, London NW6

Dear B,

Thanks to Freda's good advice, I found a little room with full board
(except lunch) in a boarding-house in West Hampstead for 30/- a week
which you will admit is very cheap. I am moving in tomorrow night.
Have had enough of the corridor at Grove End Gardens.

The address is as above. It is not so very far past St John's Wood, being
somewhere between Swiss Cottage and Hampstead. The fare to Charing
Cross is one penny more than St John's Wood station ... so you can tell.

I told Mr. Friedmann about Reuters making me an offer of work and
he seemed quite taken aback and said no one had asked me to go; which
I thought funny in view of the fact that we all know they are making
preparations to leave for the U.S.A., and would leave tomorrow if there
were a boat.

I was obliged to give two references at Reuters, one a doctor and I had
to give Dr. Ilya Margolin, not knowing any other. Can you find out if he
still exists in Colebank Road. I do hope he won't let on that I tried to do
away with myself in May 1937 and ended up in ghastly awful Erdington
House in a police van, and that he saved my life by gate-crashing his way
into Dudley Road hospital and forcing Matron to 'fetch oxygen' etc. Hope
he won't mention it though I know, as he told me, he still thinks me a
wicked girl, not so much for THAT, but for 'trying to destroy' his career
by getting him in trouble.... I think he plans to go into the RAMC which
is fair enough in spite of his Russian/German background, because I do
think it was awful he had to take his degree all over again at Edinburgh
after having been years and years the top doctor in Berlin.

I need a new dress or costume badly – have you any advices? Also
Rosalie says my black hat is dowdy, but it wasn't a hint ... she knows
her prices are way out of reach. My Jaffa* coat you gave me second-
hand already looks a rag – Mr. Friedmann's nice daughter Hilda sewed
the buttons on for me, all of them needed it but now the hood is
coming off. I had my black coat shortened for the interview – cost me
6/6d – I had it done at the repeated request of Sally, Rosalie and Phyllis.

Did you like Bieklski's bitter chocolate marzipan? [...]

* *Olga's brother-in-law Frank Jaffa was a ladies coat manufacturer.*

19th January 1941
c/o Reuters
85, Fleet Street
London EC4

Dear B,

I hope the chocs arrived all right. I am all right.

The job is all right. I don't have to work too hard; on the contrary I could do with more work; there has to be always three on each job apparently and there are long hours of waiting for the News to come through. This could be monotonous, but you can read books or papers or do anything you like; all very free & easy which is one of the compensations of the job one girl told me. There is no supervision & you do as you like, provided you are there to take the news when it comes through ... and it seems slower just now owing to all the war restrictions & being cut off from the Continent.

I think also there seems very little chance of promotion to journalist status yet anyway; the other girls are old or have been here ages. There's a nice girl across the floor in the P.A. (Press Association) crowd, named Ellen Bayliss who works mostly in the House of Commons press lobby. When I read the news in the evening papers, I get cold shivers wondering if I have taken it down right.

Best love, Ogg

March 1941
6, Grove End Gardens
London NW8

Dear B,

I recently described what goes on inside Flat No.6 here in Grove End Gardens, St John's Wood. Outside is a different story. But unless the building rocks and the furniture climbs about, no one inside takes any notice. The great advantage of this type of big block of flats is that the noise of the guns is a little muffled, at least compared with sleeping in a house or a shelter.

Parts of London gape hollowly, notably Holborn & Bloomsbury and places like Leicester Square. I have gotten used, like so many other people, to journeying home during the barrage. One can hardly be expected to jump at bombs and guns, when they drop so often and bang so continuously. Even Rosalie is getting brave; at one time whenever a bomb fell, she sprang into the hall and prostrated herself on the floor with such violence, knocking me out of the way several times in her haste, with the result I was as banged about as if the bomb had actually hit us. This got to be such a habit with her, I always sensibly keep my distance when little Jerry is active overhead.

I guess I'd better do something about paying and seeing to my belongings still stored in some fearful cellar. If I leave them there much longer, it's over a year now, will they rot do you think? Do give me your advice.

I should love to have been at the tea party and eaten some of the chocolate cake made with cocoa. I must write to Coralie and send my good wishes for Vivie's birthday; alas it is all I can send. Do you think I am a swine? I am now so MEAN that I stay in bed and try to sleep rather than get up and have to have a meal. I can see myself arranging to walk to work eventually. It's not quite so bad at the bawdy house for me as I am apparently one of Mrs. Morley's favourites (in spite of my untidy ways) but she's a tough woman, hard as nails and it's not quite so good for some of the other women lodgers whom she doesn't care so much for. I can always get a second helping and a good one, which is more than they can get.

The rich old dame with the two late husbands burst into tears the other night when they'd all gone to bed and confided in me she'd never been so unhappy in her life. 'They all hurt me,' she wept, 'and I can't be hurt, I'm too tender. My husbands adored me; I never asked for such idolatry and now, ... such hardness, such coarseness, oh oh!' I patted her plump shoulder and said 'there, there' but she sobbed so hard that Mrs. Morley who sleeps downstairs came in in her dressing-gown to hear what all the row was about, and after saying to poor Mrs. G, 'Stuff and nonsense, woman, it's all chaff' etc., etc., in a voice like a gong striking, she duly and summarily dispatched the woman to bed. Mrs. G staggered off upstairs still moaning despairingly ... 'I can hear my darling saying to me, Beloved, they're not fit to wipe your boots, such coarseness, you're too good, a tender angel like you – and all your lovely flesh melting away' .... the Spirit husband is believed to have added, which I thought cast rather a nasty nasturtion* on Mrs. Morley's table.

But there ... that's life in a boarding-house; we certainly see it. I'm on duty again at 8 in the morning so I'll post this and go home to bed. I'm still bare-legged without stockings; it's a question of principle now;

I won't give in; besides I can't afford stockings and my legs are quite hardened to the cold by now; my little sniff apparently permanent more or less. I'm quite well love, never looked better, but would love you to write me all the news ... if you are not too fed up with me after waiting so long to hear and then getting such a basin full of jaw.

Love, Ogg

Aspertion. This misspelling is Olga's sort of rhyming slang.

March 1941
c/o Reuters
85, Fleet Street
London EC4

Dear Beryl,

Just starting my first night-duty and looks like being very quiet so far. Just my rotten luck I should not be feeling up to the mark. My flu attack culminated last night in another haemoptysis or whatever. Not quite so uncontrollable as last time but just as much bloody blood. I went to see the doctor at Hendon this afternoon and he prescribed go-to-bed immediately, with cold drinks only for food and to stop the coughing, of all things, some liquid drops of morph.hydrochloride. Said it might make me feel sleepy, he's telling me! However, I'll hold out until 5am tomorrow all right. Then I've got all day Sunday and all day Monday off so I can stay in bed. I'll be quite all right; he said it's absolutely certain I'm not t.b. but I've got probably a ruptured bronc tube near the old abscess scar and I orta stay in bed until the bleeding stops.

He says in cases like mine you can coff like mad if you've ruptured yourself and it doesn't mean there's anything wrong. I hope the dawn will see me snug in bed and I'll stay there till I'm ok. Next week I've got Night Duty Fri-Sat, that is 5pm till 6am, with Sat and Sun off. My week starts with an 8 till 4 shift on Tuesday.

Thanks for the dress; I'll get some white collars or jabots and it'll look fine; the sleeves are perhaps a little wide but no matter.

Had a beastly night last Wed: the buggers dropped all their bombs (7) in our district and there were 3 in our road in Canfield Gardens, West Hampstead and the others close by. It was filthy. I got under the bed and then smack all the lights went out (it was only 10pm); eventually we got to sleep. This morning saw, of all people, Wendy Lesser's mother and father on the bus; remember I was at school with her when we were both 8. Her whole family have come to live in London on account of his business; fetched up in the Swiss Cottage, West Hampstead district too … and didn't like Wednesday night much.

I'll be glad when this wee nicht is over; I can take two hours sleep in a bunk in the shelter in the basement if I want during the night. The noise of the teleprinters and ticker-tape down there is so great that it stops anyone from hearing the bombs falling even when they land on Fleet Street itself or in the City close by. I want to come to Malvern to see you and my Ricky-ticky* so I asked the man who fixes the weekly schedule if I could do some consecutive nights which means you get a week off. I think you do 4 nights and then 3 or something like that. The chappie said he thought I'd find it rather much, but if you stick to sleeping in the day I don't see why.

Rosalie is doing good biz with her hat shop in George Street just off Baker Street. She had a page in Vogue; Harold is coming over to see her on Sunday.

P.S. Don't want you to be worried by the foregoing so, in a lull, a few more lines, my pet. It's just striking 12 o'clock and I'm fresh as a daisy. Didn't cough once (so far) though I was terrified of it. I did more work in one hour tonight than I've done all week; seems like it comes through more in the evenings at least up till midnight. The time has simply flown; the phones didn't stop ringing and I've covered the communiques from Switzerland, Athens, Ankara, Cairo and several speeches reported in full from elsewhere. But I've a horrible thirst. I've drunk one pint of lemonade, two cups of tea and three cups of cold milk. I'm still thirsty. I'm on the job tonight with two men; one cup of milk was intended for us to make a pot of tea with later, and I was horrified to discover I'd drunk it. But that was a good tip from the doctor that something cold stops you from coughing.

*After 'Rikki-Tikki-Tavi' from Kipling's The Jungle Book.

March 1941
c/o Reuters
85, Fleet Street
London EC4

Dear B,

Surprised to find Aunt Phoebe back home with her daughters Ros and Rita at No. 6. Rosalie seemed quite pleased to see me but Riorita did not appear to care for me much.

I could not bear to look at Aunty who is a vacant pathetic figure, speaking now much as though she'd lately had a stroke; just a few short staccato words then a pause. Les Girls talk about her just as though she weren't there at all, which is awful. She is fairly deaf and altogether they treat her like she was a mendicant child without any faculties.

After lunch Rosalie had the job of uncorseting her great stomach which fell with a bang from the restraining steel; while Riorita fled shuddering into the hall … 'I can't bear doing that sort of thing; Rosalie understands how to do it.'

How ghastly to end up like that in that slow decaying way, but what is more awful still is that her daughters themselves look only slightly less decaying.

Rita looks at you through hanging wisps of pink and grey hair and says to me; 'Your hair is rather elaborate, isn't it?' It didn't seem to please her at all, …aren't I a bitch, teehee. Yes I am. Actually … making no attempt to conceal my vanity, I'd only just that day had it glamorously washed and set and had a wine-red scarf twined round it in a manner so fetching that all the girls at the office are sitting working in head scarves and bandeaux today and I have had so many appeals to 'show how I've got the scarf tied' that I haven't got much work done today. It's all right, darlint I'm not getting conceited. I just thought it would amuse you to hear. And all the girls are smugly contemplating the day when hairdressing is (as the newspapers threaten) going to be RATIONED too. Pins will be unobtainable and then they tell me delightedly, 'You'll have to have all your hair cut off, our Olga!'

Half an hour later Rita suddenly discovered I was there, just as though I'd only just come in. But she was very haughty … and the car and the Odeon and the Dorchester Hotel and an appointment at the BBC tripped off her tongue swiftly and vaguely so that I was well and truly put in my place all right.

'And I've simply got to have a new coat and costume and you've got to give me the coupons, Rosie' ... and Rosie (Who can't bear to be called Rosie) said she needed all the coupons for her own business and Rita began to threaten and I thought ... here's where I depart before the oaths start flying ... and after Aunty's stomach had been let down and inserted between the bedclothes for its afternoon rest, I babbled vaguely of pressing appointment and slithered out. I only wished I hadn't gone there, for a more depressing sight than that household you can't imagine. And oh, oh, I don't want to have pink and grey hair and sagging, discoloured skin and harsh voice and harsher mouth and a nervous tension that seems to make the air buzz like the sizzle of telegraph wires. But I know there's no getting out of it. There without the Grace of God I shall also go....

Reading what I wrote you about the job, I can see it reads rather confusingly and not very plainly, but I guess you will see what I am getting at, which is that after all my high hopes of getting a journalist's training on the Reuter desk, I'm not making any headway at all. It looks now to have been a false start and unless some change takes place (which may well happen in view of the war).... I haven't progressed very much from the International Metal Market. However, I suppose so long as I don't let the urge to do something about it expire, there's still hope for me.

Gosh, I'm tired tonight; can hardly type. Fresh as a daisy when I came on duty but it's worn off. I'm sending you more news of the mad hatters at number six when I'm not so tired; also about my P.A. boyfriend who is rather too keen, says he is suffering, isn't that beautiful? Rosalie says Goyim* are too easy and SHE wouldn't touch one with a bargepole, which is a bit funny because the one-legged one also is.

Cora wrote me, 'Vivienne simply hates food.' Extraordinary, isn't it? But she can say 'Beryl' and 'Olga'. And she puts her arms round her neck and says, 'Nice mummy.' Kiss my lovely Ricky for me and look after him.

Love, Og

*Non-Jews — a derogatory description.

March 1941
86, Canfield Gardens
West Hampstead, London NW6

Dear B,

Everyone in this boarding house says how well I am looking. They say it is a scandal I get more holiday than work.

I dropped a line last week to Dr. Margolin telling him I'd got this job on the Foreign News Desk at Reuter in Fleet St, and I received a typewritten reply from some doctor on his behalf, saying that Margolin is very ill with pneumonia and he will communicate with me as soon as he gets better.

Several women here who have graduated from this low job (the sub-editors mostly quite young men look down on us scum) up to being sub-editors translating the foreign cables from French and Spanish etc. into news stories ready to be teleprinted for the morning newspapers ... have certainly not qualified on account of their charm or good looks. They are mostly old and ugly and a bit poisonous. They do not even acknowledge our existence and the way they have of looking right through me, gives me quite a disembodied feeling. I get the impression they don't like me or anything on me and I feel they would be only too pleased to smack down on me if I tripped up on my work. But I've no intention of letting them catch me out, bleeding lung or no. I turned in my communiques right to the minute and they were taken down in shorthand at some speed. God knows I'm no beauty, but if you could only see the mug of the woman in green who sits at the Editor's desk at the top of the long room, you'd sure to find me bedazzling by contrast.

At 3 a.m. I go down for a sleep and apparently the men on this shift wangle some 3-hours sleep so they've advised me to go down at 3 and sleep say until 6 when I hope to get a bus or tube and then claim I've done an hour's overtime which will be refunded to me in due course.

Monday afternoon. I am quite better. Went to bed and slept this afternoon. No more cough. Why doesn't Betty write me? Rosalie threw a party last night in Harold's honour. Lots of smoke, noise, dirty jokes and Sally's chopped herring. Harold very subdued and refusing to be vamped by any of Rosalie's painted girl-friends ... painted specially by Rosalie for the occasion too! [...]

March 1941, 1.30 a.m. Wednesday
c/o Reuters
85, Fleet Street
London EC4

Dear B,

Thanks for yours. I sent our Betty a £1 note for her birthday and told her to buy something nice, not being sixteen every day. I think she is obscenely old. Glad she is going to have a holiday at Easter; expect she'll be a help to Corrie in minding Vivienne; hope she has a good time.

Don't forget to let me know about the skirt old girl. I am dogtired tonight, as you can imagine we've had a pretty rough time over the weekend with Jugoslavia [sic] and Greece and wotnot. I worked like a dog Saturday and Sunday nights and I am on duty tonight until 7am Wednesday. Went back to the bawdy-house and fell asleep one morning eating my breakfast; next thing I know I'm awake and its 6pm in the evening and my breakfast tray has disappeared. Anyway I was just in time for dinner!

The news just came through from Athens was not so good; the buggers have almost cut off Salonika from the other Greek forces.

The last couple of days I made two interesting contacts and feel better. The first was THE Press Association Editor himself, a real topnotcher who has been mooning at me for weeks through his gold spectacles. He comes from some place called Falkirk in Scotland. He came over to the Reuter side of the joint (we're all in one huge office together, Reuter and the Press Association, but divided by a wall of green Lockers where the staff keep their bits and pieces) and said would I do a flick with him one night when I wasn't on duty. He is a great big man, tall blond Scotsman name of Walton Adamson Cole* (they call him King Coal) Making discreet enquiries I learn he is a bit of a wolf, so tonight I amused myself eluding him while he tried tracking me round the huge office for about 4 hours. At 1 a.m. he gave up and went to bed. I'll give him a chase for his money; wolves I can always handle. But the 'conquest' cheered me up a bit; I kept it dark from the other girls – they're all Lonely Hearts on this desk.

The second date I had was when I got chatting on the telephone with one of the Radio Room News Translators who 'phone us the news inwards from the Radio Receiving Room just outside London. He pressed me to have lunch with him and made me promise to phone him the

135

following day to fix time and place. So I asked one of the chaps what is Mr. W. J. Peace like and he said oh not much, about 35, rather small, greying temples, slitty eyes, not very good looking. That put me off properly so of course I didn't bother to phone. Next night I was on duty, he was very hurt, so we fixed a lunch definitely for the next day. Not being able to get out of it very well I said yes. I then thought of leaving a message with one of the boys to phone and say I couldn't come. But Monday he was not in the office and couldn't be reached. I phoned Tuesday and arranged for one of the boys to give him a note saying I'd been called away. Then lying in bed that morning I thought how embarrassing it would be to have to take work from him every night over the phone after treating him so rudely.

So cursing my inanity and eternal inability to say no to anyone at the right time, I got dressed, got to the office just in time to cancel the note and kept the date. After what I'd heard from two chaps in the office I naturally expected something pretty awful (Funny one never expects that MEN will say anything disparaging about each other like girls will) so I was quite pleasantly surprised when he turned up. Certainly he was no beauty but he was not at all bad. Rather nice in fact and what he lacked in beauty he made up in brains. Also he does another more interesting job, as Assistant Editor on the fortnightly Review running since the war called 'Free Europe'. He translates the German Polish Russian for Reuters but of course he likes the other work better. He has a house in the country and two other bachelor members of the staff share it with him. He took me to lunch at Bertholi in Soho and is going to ring me at home some time when I am not in bed – it's hard to indicate any time I'm not likely to be in bed; I seem to be always there; the boarding house staff have to lie in wait in order to make my bed and dust the room.

Later editor-in-chief at Reuters.

5th April 1941
86, Canfield Gardens
West Hampstead, London NW6

Dearest Beryl,

Please tell Bettina I didn't forget her 16th birthday but had no time for shopping; I hope to get her the promised powder-compact sometime this week and send it on. I have a pair of brown lisle stockings of yours or Betty's taken by mistake. I hope Ricky is being a good boy; please kiss him for me and give him all my love.

I didn't get home until 4-45 am this morning so that I spent half my day off in sleeping. The Morleys are thrilled with your mayonnaise recipe so I gave them some to taste. Mrs. Morley asked whether you knew how to make lentil cutlets which she wants to give us as substitute for meat; do you know any way of cooking these? My stomach has settled down once again after its orgy of gluttony; next time I come to Malvern, shall try to refrain from overeating ... I think this is the cause of extreme tiredness.

A new regime has started on Reuters foreign news desk, with the assumption of command by Walton Adamson Cole; at first I could not but admire the calm poised competent way he took over, but now I'm thinking (though it is not really fair to judge yet – he only started this Monday) that he is going a bit far in his methods. I think he is a little punch-drunk, intoxicated with his own power. He takes charge in the evening and by sitting at the top of the editorial desks; examining every sub's and every editor's copy before it goes out; summoning them all, oldtimers and new ones to his desk like schoolchildren; altering their copy and often rewriting it himself; he has sent ripples of panic through every desk. No one feels they can relax so long as he is in the editorial room; he is exacting and many of the older sub-editors have been aghast at getting their copy back streaked through in blue pencil and scrawled over like a schoolboy's essay. I expect there will be a few nervous breakdowns or sackings before he is through.

As regards myself, he graciously stopped and chatted with me about the job, which I hardly expected now he is such a big-shot and, unasked, he repeated rather vague promises about trying to get me editorial status. Frankly, I think I know him so well I have not a great deal of confidence in his world.

I never pay any attention to what he says but always try to read between the lines as it were. He says I must be patient and wait a few weeks and he will do everything he can; nothing, he says, would give him 'greater pleasure' than to get me editorial status but the policy of Reuters administration has always been set against dilutees, particularly women; and moreover there are apparently any amount of male subs over forty-five or so who are willing to come for the minimum wage. Actually status will not benefit me very much for I would get no increase in wages apparently; the Union only stipulate you have to get the minimum rate after a specific training period of either one or two years. Cole is an absolute genius at making use of other people; I think this is how he got ahead; and although he says he has decided not to take me off the news-desk to work as his secretary, as this would be only routine stuff and I should lose contact with the Desk, he nevertheless gives me plenty of his private jobs to do, which is what kept me working until 3 a.m. this morning, and then I had to wait for a staff bus at 3-45. He dictates a few words, gives you some details to sub and with a few hopelessly vague instructions, leaves you to piece a story together yourself. Perhaps Cole is sincere; I really wouldn't know.

Anyhow I couldn't change my job now without permission of the Ministry of Labour because being under 30 I should be called up immediately for the Army though I doubt very much whether they'd pass me medically; this is no time to think about improving one's position; at Reuters everyone is more or less exploited now.

The awful hours do have their advantages; today I went out and got caught in the rush-hour coming home to dinner; oh how you would hate London nowadays; there are long queues everywhere for everything; you queue for a restaurant, a cup of tea, a lavatory-seat, a picture, a bus, a tube, to buy a ticket for the tube. It is exhausting in the West End and the City; I can't imagine why servicemen on leave come to London instead of going to some nice country spot, for I can see how anyone can enjoy themselves when they must queue for up for everything they do. And yet the West End is so crowded; you have to squirm your way through milling crowds, and the faces of the sailors and merchant-seamen are scornful and hating and disappointed.

Cease please to worry so much about me and about my life which you do not like. Neither do I, but I hate to think of you spending a single moment fretting over me. You do not think of yourself or your lot as important; therefore why treat me as though I were important either; I am used to my life now; and used to walking the long Hampstead roads in chilly dawns watched by a few inquisitive stars among the searchlights; eating baked beans at midnight; how my feet clatter on the pavements.

Tomorrow I am doing a day-duty for a change. We have been very busy with India. Tonight the Indian news seems a little hopeful. I could not help feeling pleased at the discomfiture of the hated Mr. Pigg who hates women; he is the Day News Editor this week and he came specially to the office last night to write a story on India for the American papers; and Cole tore it up under his nose! (and mine) and simply said, 'Sorry old boy but really it's just a web of words!'

I was asked out tonight but was too lazy to go. We have a new Scots sub, Colin MacFie; he is an M.A., and nice and intelligent, and he asked me to go along to see the hostel where he stays in Camden Town; once I thought of going there but the district is so dreary and it is one of those longhaired vegetarian places. Mac says they are all more or less freaks there including himself (who doesn't smoke or drink or eat meat).

I have finished the heavenly Malvern jam you made; should there be any more of that wunnerful [sic] Loganberry that Betty hates and Frank hates, remember I don't hate it at all! I did give a little of it to one of my favourites; a nice boy invalided out of the Navy with bomb-shock; he is rather like me in that he doesn't like people much (unlike the too sociable scotchman) and he lives all by himself in a cottage in Aylesbury, Buckinghamshire writing poetry and pottering about preparing his own meals; and he was so grateful for a couple of pieces of bread and jam. I expect if he knew the sort of people I mix with sometimes, he wouldn't eat my jam for he is proud of being Quote One of the yes-men of the boss-class; he despises socialists, thinks we ought to restore a feudal rural England; and he does almost no work at all, but either reads Tennyson or writes poems (furious when I called them Verses) he is a typical example of the sort of thing that can happen only at Reuters; he will be safe because he is a friend of the Chancellor family.

Mr. Chancellor, son of Sir John Chancellor, is the Business Manager of Reuters and the only one who is now 'over' Cole. By comparison Cole himself is an upstart, he told me himself he was just a young football reporter from Falkirk but he worked hard and earned so much money sending sports stories to the Press Association that they took him on the London staff as an economy measure! Cole likes to boast that he's never read a book in his life and his favourite reading is the Daily Mirror. The point is he gets things done; he's really a sort of genius.

Anyway that's the story of my nice friend; I call him 'Commodore' Peel the ex-navy man, the poet who gloatingly ate your jam right up; his name is really J. H. B. Peel and his book of poems will be published soon.*

I hope you don't find it too boring to get so much detail about the office and the office folk but I spend so much time there. One of the Soviet Russians, a Tass Agency correspondent working on the 4th floor (one above us), took me to the Tatler in the Charing Cross Road to see an amusing Soviet film called 'Musical Story' which was lovely with Tchaikovsky's opera Eugene Onegin and showing a witty delightful side of the USSR one had not expected; also showing scenes taken of four soviet scientists at the south pole.

Felt a bit guilty not doing more to help during the London bombing, so I signed on as a part-time nurse at an East End hospital.** Mostly the work seems to be comforting old people or getting them washed and dressed or undressed for their operations.

Love, Og

PS. I can do the nursing job, you see, when I have two or three days off in a row.

*John Peel (1913–1983) was a successful journalist and poet and had a column called 'Country Talk' in The Daily Telegraph.
**Nursing seems to run in the Davis family: Olga's mother and Betty were nurses.

1st May 1941
Thursday morning, 5.30 a.m.
c/o Reuters
85, Fleet Street
London EC4

Best-beluved B,

I was on duty last night and I am still on; it is going on for six; the dawn is grey and I am yellow; I am getting to look more and more like a cup of tea; made at least seven pots last night, after which I carry whole tubs of it around to staff on the Foreign Desk.

Now my colleague has gone off gaily on his bicycle and I am all alone; it was very quiet in the night and not really enough to keep one strong, though teacoloured, female busy.

I went down to sleep in the shelter but was driven up to the 5th floor again by fleas; I think they have invaded the one grey army blanket we all use for bedtime; most unsavoury. In future I shall park on two stools with a pencil in between to support sparsely-covered bony trunk. (Am down to 8 stone again and very bony; probably due to acidosis occasioned by too much tea occasioned by having to keep awake.)

I am getting very tired of the bawdy-house in Canfield Gardens; when I am in bed during the day I can hear above the noise of the vacuum cleaner, loud voices (female) soundfully and unnecessarily declaiming, 'Is she still asleep? She was asleep LAST night as well' (and similar witticisms). Wot do they expect me to do in bed; community singing? Such an invasion of my privacy is unwarranted; if I had a tommygun I would make them scatter. They are bitchiss; all wimmen are bitchiss [sic].

Those dam fleas are still biting; I am glad I am going to have my hair washed this morning. The news makes me very gloomy, but everyone is smiling so I shall smile too.

At the L.H. (Lonely Hearts) Club, Sally has disappeared altogether from the scene. Declares she has had enough of Luv and its effects to last her. Now she is tired. And the Spirit World she says is not so exhausting to be with as Freda and unsuppressed suppressions. So Sally comes no more which is Unsatisfactory as the 'Girls' have to prepare the food now as well as eat and wash up after it. (Rosalie can't abide doing Pans; I have to do all those.) I wouldn't mind only it is not often I get invited to share in the Repast.

Rosalie was in good mood and looked Replete. She spent Easter with her one-legged soldier married boyfriend. And told me she had a gorgeous time. Seeing four shows and three flicks and Drinking. Four shows and 3 flicks represent for Rosalie a very good time multiplied by 4 and then by 3. That disposes of Rosalie. And leaves Freda.

The seven-year-courted Jack is still procrastinating. He is holding out just like the heroic Greeks, but MUST like them capitulate eventually. Or so argues Freda. I am sympathetic but tired of Jack. He is very plain, with red face and butter-coloured hair and I cannot love him. He has also meaty buttocks and Freda is very much attached to them. She says dramatically, 'I cannot marry a Thin Man.' In the meantime she has found a man with a limp (this story has nothing to do with William Powell*) who feels very inferior like the one in Of-Human-Bondage** and claims he has never had-a-Girl, and Freda is set on winning him, just in case. Phyllis is still very keen on the Bond Street Marriage Bureau idea; so it may yet come to something.

Am now Hardbitten Newspaper Woman myself. And have to live up to the part. Have therefore also acquired married boyfriend like Rosalie. This all due to Ambition. Cannot face working always as inferior news-taker on this Desk ... and it seems the only way to Get On is to Have a Man Behind you. (Frank; you would make customary lewd remark). It is of course the Press Assoc.Editor I told you about, the giant Scotsman and he has fallen for me like a mass of debris or a torpedoed boat transporting high explosive (the wife does not understand him). It is so good for My own inferiority complex which beastly Natey gave me. I found out he was wed before I went out with him (or rather I was told about it by the Other Women on this desk who watched him prowling

141

around me) and I broke the first date with him and eluded him conscientiously only to be pursued relentlessly.

Having nothing better to do on Thursday last, I went round to see Natey (cannot understand how I ever thought him good looking) and got treated to a luscious steak and lashings of beer and things. The steak was more than just a novelty. I did not let the shock of this unwonted generosity put me off my meal, which was much appreciated.

I had a letter (only a few lines) from our Coralie. So I wrote her a reply telling her I was a survivor. 'Fraid London looks now very shabby. At one time you could walk around and not see damage unless you knew where to look for it (chiefly in the City and Holborn). Now it is difficult to find anywhere that is NOT damaged.

Love, Ogg

* *William Powell starred in* The Thin Man *(1934).*
** *Based on one of the characters in Somerset Maugham's novel* Of Human Bondage *(1915).*

18th May 1941
c/o Reuters
85, Fleet Street
London EC4

Dear B,

Went round to the L.H. club last night; embarrassed on arrival at finding battle in progress.

Freda dressed in pale blue, wearing pale determined air sat on the divan with Jack; he discomfited and toying with a tea-cup. Rosalie and Sally sat in the hall having their supper & craning their necks at the half-open door.

'When's it to be Jack?' I heard Freda say with never a quaver in her voice.

Jack replied, 'How can you ask me NOW when I've got Sinusitis. Sinusitis isn't a thing to be played about with, it's serious. NOW's not the time to ask a man…'

Said Freda with bitter knowingness, 'It's always the wrong time to ask you anything, if you haven't got dermatitis or pendicitis you've got sumthing.'

Jack sniffed. Sally was humming carelessly & tucking in to her salt fish.

'You offer me,' shouted Freda dramatically, 'the back-street of your life. Back streets, always back streets for me.' (After Jack had gone, Rosalie told me Freda had taken Jack that afternoon to the flicks to see the new Charles Boyer-Margaret Sullavan version of the old Fannie Hurst story;* the critics said it was full of woe so I guess it must have preyed on her.)

'Sinusitis or no Sinusitis,' said Freda, 'if you don't make up your mind soon, I'll leave you Jack, God I mean it.'

'Will you?' said Jack hopefully. 'Seven years,' Freda was moaning, ignoring this interruption, 'all of seven, in a Back Street, God!'

Sally was giggling. Jacob served twice times seven for Rachel; these modern girls are so impatient. Jack was retreating towards the door. I gave him my practised version of a sweet understanding smile & then looked carefully at Rosalie's salt fish; he looked all knocked about and his face was red against his butteryellow hair. Funny how a little thing like Sinusitis can get you down.

Jack gone, the storm broke; Sally bent lower over her fish; I rushed to minister with the tea-cups. 'Men are such SWINE!' Freda boomed at us. 'He's ruined my life and now he walks out with Sinusitis. Just like that.' Freda was tossing her eyeballs at the ceiling, her hands threw frantic gestures, her lipstick had been chewed off in agitation and the mascaraed eyes burned forbiddingly above the long white column of her nose. 'Sinusitis. The back streets,' said Freda, and wept. 'Have some salt fish,' said Rosalie.

We were in for a long session that night, and we knew there was no evading it. Freda rallied a little after the fish and as I cleared away the remains of her stewed rhubarb & custard, Freda told us about life, and love. Sally had gone. Freda expanded.

She told us how surprised she had been by the new boyfriend with the lame leg and the inferiority complex. The lame leg had proved indisputable but the I.C. had turned out to be a put-up job. Freda had offered herself, and had apparently been accepted, without much concern. 'Men are such Swine,' she said again. 'They kid you along they're almost virgins. Liars! Why he obviously had had as much experience as I had!'

'But Jack?' I said confusedly. Freda rent me. 'Seven years,' she intoned with fury, 'in a Back Street.' I stammered like a fool, 'But this other man?' I said. 'Jack doesn't know, you silly,' said Freda with scorn.

Rosalie threw Freda a warning glance; 'Don't tell her too much,' it said, 'she's a bit simple.' 'There's a bit of the salt fish left,' said Rosalie. 'Thanks awfully,' I said, 'I just had oxtail.'

'WHY can't we get married?' Freda was asking. 'What's wrong with us, with all our gang, we've none of us done any good. WHY? There's me, there's Rosalie, and Letty and Mitzi and Anne and Phyllis; we've all tried something different, where do we go wrong?'

'You think too much about it,' I said weakly. 'Marriage isn't everything. Why I've got one cousin who knows a girl who's ever so unhappy.'

'Marriage! Huh!' said Rosli with disdain, and dug the hot iron into the crease of her pants as she ironed them on the table. 'I must marry!' screamed Freda. 'What's wrong with me anyhow? Why can't I bring it off? I'm smart; I'm even brilliant.'

I looked at her and forbore to answer. I thought of a Vulturous bird I had seen in the Zoo at Regent's Park. 'It's only the bloody jews,' said Freda, 'any freak of a girl can get a Goy; they're too easy. Ah, how I hate jews,' she said. 'Jewish men are so tough,' I said apologetically.

'Yes,' said Rosalie, 'it's the men, of our generation. They're rotten.'

* Back Street *(1941), based on the 1931 novel.*

May 1941
86, Canfield Gardens
West Hampstead, London NW6

Dear B,

First of all thank you for the perfectly lovely photograph of my Ricky-ticky which has already undergone a good deal of inspection and will soon look a bit ragged at the edges so will have to keep it in envelope. It is the best yet. Aunt Sally says yes, just a shade like your Father Izzy but much more like You. I miss Ricky and his passionate kisses; hope he realises this. Can he now walk manfully? Sorry I missed seeing Vivienne; looks as though she'll be a grown woman before I have the opportunity of meeting her.

Smiled at your reference to Pauline [Cora's sister-in-law] completely dressed in rings. However, this is I guess an investment these days, nicht? Also amused to hear our sister Cora is grown so rich; do you think I could tap her for a fiver? What shall I give Betty for her birthday, money or goods, it is next Saturday, isn't it? As usual I have a big income tax bill and a large bill for storage of my belongings not yet paid. (Do you think there is a chance of Frank getting me a piece of black velour sufficient to make a skirt?) Congratulations on our having another member of the family engaged. Have you sent any felicitations to Aunt Ethel and Uncle Mo and does Betty know her favourite Cousin Valerie is to be married?* It may even put Betty on her mettle.

I am very well in health though a little depressed in mood, but this will pass. Everyone says how well I look and apparently the numerous days I spend in bed are the very thing for me. After one night-shift I came home and went to bed in the morning, sleeping eleven hours without waking; until finally someone banged several times on my door to tell me dinner was nearly over. Working at night I do not get tired, even on a 14-hour shift, because I sleep so much in the day.

The red-headed Night Editor Geoffrey Imeson deigned to speak to me the other night and I nearly swooned with excitement. Unfortunately I do not get on too well with one or two of the girls; we are all spiteful, catty and ragingly competitive, and with the exception of one or two cronies I get on much better with the men. This seems to throw a most unpleasant light on my character, nicht? The fact was only that a certain tactless remark I made regarding one woman's incompetence was referred back (with frothing joy) by an ardent troublemaker to the party concerned; with embarrassing results. Moral: I keep my mouth grimly shut now and my confidences are for Males only. Also the other women have apparently been discussing me deprecatingly behind my back with reference to my unseemly appetite for work. Unseemly it would seem in a Beginner, and the Lastcomer at that.

However, I have no apologies to make, and without undue boasting it is simply that I can work twice as fast as any of them, new or old hands, and rather than sit idle while they dither about with the work I always make a dash for the telephones and take all the work before they have time to turn round. Quite naturally they resent this and one or two have said so. Tactless of me I suppose and shall have to go a bit slower in future.

Also .... I did not get on with Natey at all ... we simply fought and have parted again. He bores me. He also does not like me reading the New Statesman; we do not agree on anything. He is good looking but not at all exciting if you understand what I mean.

So my only light relief comes from Grove End Gardens and the Girls who gather there in Rita and Rosalie's flat... so read all about it in my next letter.

Love Ogg

* Valerie Davis had a daughter, Lydia (now Eisenberg), who settled in Israel and now lives on Kibbutz Mishmar-Emek where Olga's Aunt and Uncle Becky and Ernest settled in the 1930s.

June 1941
c/o Reuters
85, Fleet Street
London EC4

Dearest Beryl,

Your handsome hamper just arrived and joyously received. The butter is a delicious luxury but I wish you wouldn't send me Ricky's chocolate! I hope to bring both choc and jellies when I come over. I don't know yet when that will be but will let you know.

The Russian war* makes a frightful lot of work and Mr. Neale, Editor on Night Desk, says that I (being the star worker, said she modestly) cannot be spared.

I have found a shop with pure silk stockings for 9/11d per pair or 10/11d [that would be over £20 now]. Fully Fashioned. Will you send necessary coupons if you want any? I think it's a grand and marvellous idea if you can afford to keep Betty at school for another year or even another term. I had a pathetic letter from her saying she would weep buckets at having to leave school but that I was not to tell you she said so.

I would be glad to contribute if at all possible – though I guess that sounds funny in view of my creaking, groaning exchequer which refuses to give birth to my honourable debts. Enclosed find a further £1 which I owe to Frank and which leaves me limp from the effort of putting it in the envelope. I am well and thriving in the cold and rainy weather.

Sunday morning 7-30 am. Just going off duty. I have got some extra days off next week, so shall see you then.

Best love for baby Ricky and you and Frank, Og.

P.S. Naturally with the war situation so critical, anything is liable to happen but I hope to snatch these few days off come what may.

* This was Operation Barbarossa, the Nazi invasion of Russia.

June 1941
86, Canfield Gardens
West Hampstead, London NW6

Dear B,

I am going to tell you about the latest events at Grove End Gardens. But first ....I attended a lecture in Hampstead Garden Suburb (which is quite beautiful and on top of the Heath but it was awfully cold; I wore two coats). Professor Harold Laski spoke on the war and the Afterwards. He is well worth hearing, if only to admire oratory at its best, though he has nothing new to add to the situation.

Mr. Friedmann said when I called in at Metal Supplies this week that he had never seen me look so well; and although still a trifle skinny I do look rather blooming fit (the evil eye avoid me)!

However, to my sweet Coz and her satellites. The House (or rather the Flat No.6 Grove End Gardens) has been in session now for the past fortnight, and this to such an extent that Aunt Sally has, so to speak, left home and retreated to the peace of her own small apartment round the corner (just facing Lord's Cricket Ground). Sally now attends only upon the minimum of occasions, which is about 3 times a week and cooks and prepares the meals for the nights she no longer comes. This is of course regretted by all, as all have to turn to, in their utterly incapable fashion. Imagine a houseful of females, all mature, and not one of them able to cook and all pining to get married!

But Sally says she has had enough, come Blitz, come Bomb, come All High Explosive, she refuses even to seek sanctuary in the Grove End walls when the price exacted is each evening's interminable session on the unchanging subject. How to Get Married at All Costs and Soon. The position is that Rosalie, Freda (her girl friend age 36) and Phyllis, the Paying Guest (a vague thirtyish), have recently parted from Him. Freda has told her Jack with whom she has been sleeping for 7 years that either he marries her now, or else. To which he replied he will let her know in a fortnight.

This was a month ago and she is still waiting. But not patiently. There is also Mitzi who has no boy at all at present and who takes part in the debates. There is also me, now a privileged member of the magic circle on the grounds that I also have been lately spurned by the all-conquering male and although I am not permitted (nor willing) to exhibit my Operation (there is naturally hardly time when there is so much more pressing agenda to be dealt with) ... the fact of my 'wound' entitles me to be present and to enjoy confidences which might otherwise be withheld.

Phyllis, who has been courting a boy for 8 years (Phyllis enjoys the inestimable novelty of being a virgo intacto and I think secretly rather shocked at it all ... and this is fortunate, preventing as it does that Sally on her evenings-on should start throwing the frying-pans about on account of discussion which is not often nice and very often obscene) ... Phyllis has just received an invitation from her ex-boyfriend to his wedding with a Very Rich Girl.

And finally there is Rosalie herself. You might call us the Lonely Hearts Club; but this state of affairs, says Freda stoutly, is not to be allowed to continue. Marriage is her goal and she is going 'all out'. So, during the night hours between the first Air-Raid warning and the last All-Clear, in between the deep, deep thud of bombs dropping somewhere in the West End as they have done so often lately ... a Strategy for Marriage is discussed.

Last night matters reached a climax. Rosalie confessed (by the way, she told Mark, the one you saw here, very fat, to marry her or Go; and he went) ... that she had a while back attended the Marriage Bureau in Bond Street and had considered having her name registered.

Now she and Freda have decided to Do it. You pay £5 down before you can register and £20 down on acquiring a Husband. Or else the man pays, always provided he can afford it. You specify what kind of man you want to meet and an appointment is arranged. Freda is going tomorrow night and Rosalie the night after. They then turned on Phyllis and vowed they would force her to go; this resulted in blushes and giggles. My turn came next (I stood quite a good chance I was told kindly, as many men prefer a nice juicy widow!) and I said yes yes, and I swore (in face of their watchful interrogation) that the obstacle of the five pounds only prevented me from going that very minute to register.

Terrified that they might doubt my sincerity and thus exclude me from the fun which is to come, I urged them on to show my enthusiasm and to encourage further revelations. (Surely Natey is right and I am the most spiteful of females) ... but I was enjoying myself, who wouldn't? Rosalie remarked in all seriousness that she must contact Rita immediately, as she being luckily possessed of many fivers (that's showbiz you see) and to spare, would not jib at laying out for herself also in such a good cause.

Whereupon Freda phoned her widowed mother somewhere in Belsize Park, to tap her for the necessary amount which she said her mother would scarcely withhold in view of the importance of the matter and indeed to achieve a Match or Shidduch* at long last, her mother could be prevailed upon to part with a much larger sum, so said Freda.

Later the talk took a more detailed turn and essential items were dealt with, such as, should they specify Jew or Gentile (the Gentiles being much more in favour as being a so far untested quantity) .... the height, weight, income and habits to be demanded of the Intended. Rosalie admitted a preference for a widower of forty, Freda for a large fat man with pocket-book to match, and Phyllis, giggling, specified also a widower, possibly with children, and was magnanimously willing to waive the 'love' question in her case.

For poor Aunt Sally all this acts as a kind of emetic; for my part I find it delicious, when not pathetic. And with all due admiration I think such perseverance deserves its true reward.

Rita perhaps will be less interested at the moment, being a busy business woman. She is starting her own Theatrical Agency and already has many famous clients like Bonar Colleano,** Alfie Bass and is visited by the most beautiful girls like Moira Fraser and many more. She also has a devoted boyfriend in tow as well. He is a Viennese composer named Hans May who is working on some Operetta ...I think it is called Carissima but I can't be sure. He has a wife to whom he is devoted but her health is failing so they all go around a trois.

Rita's health is delicate too. Since her operation she has apparently developed Liver. She now travels about accompanied with the requisite Vichy water, haemorrhoid suppositories, opening medicine, piles-preventer, acid-manufacturer and sedatives. She is sworn off all liquor for some time to come. She has got rather plump although eating very little and I thought she looked well enough except for heavy bags under the eyes like Harold also has.

Now ...dear sister .. if ever after a hard day's washing of nappies and preparing for the unworthy spouse's dinner you are inclined to feel dissatisfied with your lot ... think on these things and bless the husband who conferred upon you the inestimable gift of himself.

For these women, one and all, except of course Sally, in their obsessed, sub-mental condition, look upon marriage (they confess to almost anyone – short of a very black negro) as the Solution to ALL their problems and the One and Only Good. They confess, except Phyllis, to be now prepared to go to all and any lengths to achieve their object.

Sally is very nervous of bombs so you can visualise just how bad the situation must be if she will brave any blitz rather than Freda's prostrated and frustrated sexuality.

Freda (and also I forgot her special pal Letty Dejong who also has a boyfriend who won't marry her and who also attends the discussions) has been out of a job for weeks. (Did I tell you Freda is perhaps the most talented of all of us; she does cartoons and illustrations etc., which are really good.) In the meantime they sponge on their Mamas and buy expensive new hats off Rosalie in George Street.

Needless to say, I showed the new photograph of Ricky only to Sally and Phyllis (Who are both like oases of sanity in a desert of boggy inanity) because the subject of babies, like that of Cooking, is anathema to the others! I hope to give you new full instalment with my next letter.

Write soon. Ogg

Shidduch – Yiddish for arranged marriage
**Bonar Colleano was a successful radio and TV performer; Alfie Bass was a* *character actor who made his name as Bootsie in the TV sitcom* Bootsie and Snudge.

6.45 a.m., 8th July 1941
c/o Reuters
85, Fleet Street
London EC4

Dear Beryl,

You must think me a perfect sod for not writing; these beastly night duties make me so languid especially in the indescribable heat of the office when windows are shut and blinds drawn, during the black-out and bombing, and I'm shut for hours in the little telephone box which is like a Turkish bath, taking the Soviet communique which is always ghastly long. I can't understand how people can actually like this weather.

I haven't much news; have to work three times as hard since the Russo war as there are many more news sources to tap; the radio room work all night instead of dozing off after midnight, and often the busiest time is now between 2 a.m. and 7 a.m.

I didn't have any money to buy you some chocs for your birthday so shall leave this until I come to Malvern. I hope soon ... but I've no idea.

I'm so hard up this week that I can't send an instalment on my debt until Friday; had to have two pairs of shoes mended, broke my watch-handle, that's 5/6d, owed 2/6d to start with; had to have my hair washed, and had to pay 3/6d; wot a price for some dark glasses, because I have had such bad headaches the last couple of weeks from bad eyes. I hope you will forgive me for the delay. I'll send off money for sure on Friday.

I saw a couple of pairs of silk stockings marked U.S.A. in that shop I told you about which had them for 10 bob. They are marked 15/11 now and there are only two or three pairs left; also they are very sheer and couldn't last very long. They are the only ones to be had in London, at least that I have seen. Do you want to pay this price? I haven't used a single one of my Clothing Coupons yet on account of not having any money to spend.

When I come home I'll tell you the whole megillah* about the job at Barnet where they've moved Reuter radio station and how I came to flop on the German monitoring ... but no energy now. How does Ricky fare in this hot weather, does it suit him? And how is Frank? No word from sisters Betty or Cora for months now. How are they?

My old pal Henry Rose is writing a book called 'Before I Forget' on his trip to the Continent and the U.S.A. There's energy & enthusiasm for you.

I saw the picture Love on the Dole, very good, wept bitterly.

I'd rather work in Fleet Street offices than in Barnet actually because in Barnet they're nearly all wimmen and bitchiss [sic] & here they're mostly men. I'm sorry this is such a dull letter; all I can think of is brekfast & sleep. I'd rather be talking to you but can't afford the fare to Malvern until I've paid off my debt of honour. A hug for Ricky-Ticky-Tavi; how does he look now? PS. Have you got a LITTLE tea to spare? If you haven't, it doesn't matter.

Love, Og

*Megillah – Yiddish slang for a dramatic or unusual story.

July 1941
86, Canfield Gardens
West Hampstead, London NW6

Dear B,

As regards the L.H. club at No.6, matters proceed apace. They didn't (as far as I can gather) so far register at the Marriage Bureau. Apparently something turned up in the meantime. So it is postponed a week or so.

This is because Rosalie's one-legged boyfriend returned to 'Somewhere in England' as the boat in which he was going to the Near East mysteriously put back to home waters. I gather he is everything she could wish for only he's married and this for Rosalie is a serious drawback as you can imagine. Anyway she may be seeing him which has cheered HER up; (thank God one L.H. is disposed of for a little while at any rate) and she has a smashing new outfit in brightest green tweed, green costume beautifully tailored, green straw hat to match with black ribbon and tailored green blouse; looks like one of those bright birds in the aviary in Malvern Link, but rather smashing; her attention to detail of her outfit, incomparable.

With Freda, however, things are not so good. Things were looking up with the 7-year-slept-with boyfriend; who had gotten to the point via sheer exhaustion of saying, 'Well, he might marry her, he'd have to see,' etc.

She was thrilled to bits & actually asking for cooking-hints and had decided to join a cookery class. However, this week-end apparently he changed his mind again and doesn't feel so sure. I felt quite sickened when I heard her 'phoning her poor mother to tell her the latest; apparently Freda has promised to find him £500 from somewhere if he'll only make her a Joyful Married Wuman [sic] and she has prevailed upon her mother to promise to raise it somehow somewhere. But now he ACTUALLY says to Freda (over the phone) quote – you keep talking in generalities instead of saying something DEFINITE about the money – unquote. Which means he isn't taking any chances. Freda says she is sick of the whole yiddisher business but she refuses to give up hope. And you ought to see the fellow, he is not worth (everyone agrees) five pence let alone 500 smackers; but Freda has gotten this almost crazed obsession; she MUST get married. Admitted she's very plain, but the fellow himself is even plainer.

Phyllis still maintains her ladylike calm except when over-tried by Letty, still without job but plus boyfriend and minus wedding ring. Freda now has a job but unsatisfactory, 55/- a week [£2.75] clerking Government job; and Sally puts in an infrequent appearance.

I go there to get a hot bath which unobtainable at No.86, Canfield Gardens, where competition to get in the bathroom even when the water is hot enough is pretty fierce between all the boarders, gents and ladies....

It's now 2.30a.m. here in Fleet Street and quiet. At 4, thank God, I can call my colleague, one of the younger men and not quite so bad, and then I go to bed myself on a camp-bed in the basement until six. The P.A. editor I told you about has a bedroom in the building and apparently lives here; being on duty every night but they don't work all night like we do. Cole himself is the hero of the whole Street because when the pre-Christmas bombs wiped out most of Blackfriars and nearly all the printing machinery, he quietly and calmly organised everyone. It was found that the News Chronicle building and printing equipment was intact, so Cole had the whole P.A. and Reuter 'show' moved in there and we were saved! So the news went ticking on all night. Everyone is very pleased with him and he still gets slapped on the back so forcefully, he gets to wince a bit from the bruising. Not that he bruises easily, being huge and fat. The Press Association are of course more or less OVER Reuters, apparently they own us and can buy us out tomorrow if they want to. So things are a bit dicey here even for the tried and trusted old staff ever since the Reuters boss Sir Roderick Jones retired. His wife is the rather beautiful Enid Bagnold.* I'll keep you informed how my silly dates go on; I intend to keep both running at the same time if possible; it's such a long time since I had anyone interesting to talk to.

Sorry now I mentioned it; the anti-aircraft guns have started up again and are going like mad tonight. Best love and kisses for Ricky-Ticky; hope you and Frank both well.

Og

* *Enid Bagnold: author of* National Velvet.

29th July 1941
86, Canfield Gardens
West Hampstead, London NW6

Dear Beryl,

Last night I thought I would pay my first visit to the Caves in weeks. However, all were out, except for Rita. I found her just going indoors with a withered-looking girl-friend from the celluloid-picture-world. Rita was ravishing in navy & white, a heavy navy linen with white reveres and a navy straw hat with a white heart-shaped halo. She looked only a very little faded.

Now that O.D. is gone (no, not olga davis) but her appellation for her late boss & friend Oscar Deutsch* who built all the Odeon cinemas in Britain, Rita has come back, accompanied by a vast quantity of clothes, from Cookham to start life afresh in St John's Wood.

This necessitated the summary dismissal of poor Jane Davis from Flat No.6. I was told that Jane's presence alone could have been endured, even be welcomed as a buffer (luscious buffer is fat, blonde Jane) between Rita and Rosalie ... but Jane and Jane's clothes and Personal Effects took up far more room than was available. So Jane had to go ... but has found refuge in a little flat with Mitzi Metz only a few doors away. This arrangement should work well; and Jane and Mitzi will be able to exchange cris-de-coeurs about brutal lovers who do not marry them, almost without interruption. And as neither will listen to what the other has to say, everyone will be comfortable.

Not so with No.6. There ... it is war to the knife. Here I confess I must support the side of Rita who is already so well able to take care of herself. Because living with Rosalie I am told is like living with the gentleman of Berchtesgaden. With the sole difference that Rosalie would always carefully shed blood where it would leave no mark. And though she is capable of biting Rita's ear off, I'll wager the carpets will be left intact.

Joking apart ... it is more than unkind of fate to condemn these Two, in their final forties, to live together. It only confirms my belief that the fates have indeed a perverted sense of humour. Be prepared therefore, any day now, to see the Family figure in a murder case. Rita spoke to me very strongly of Rosalie's habits and pernicketiness. And her voice was quite firm when she said that 'Rosalie will have to learn.' Rita is now working in London; she is Talent-Spotter for Ambrose.** She did not specify the talents. I looked very impressed. She told me she was very hard-up. She insisted on showing the withered one, whose name I cannot recall, but it sounded rather like 'Carp', the view from the roof of Grove End Gardens and the basement-bar. I paid for the beer.

Today being my birthday I recklessly laid out a few shillings I can so ill afford and bought a handsome green silk tie to wear on my red-and-white striped blouse. I have combed my hair and put a bow on it and am ready to sally forth to work. Madame Kissack (the newest boarders are an interesting French couple; she is older than him) says I look quite well. She also says your Raspberry jam is 'magnifique' and has apparently filled her with 'extase'.

Rita Cave says she now finds herself lonely in London, having lost touch with all her old friends; and everyone else, she alleges, is so inferior. She tells me that all '... We Davis's are colossal Snobs' and that apparently Grandma Davis is to blame for having passed on this 'disease' to all of us. So now you know.

Havin' told my landlady Mrs. Morley that it was my birthday, I got Chocolate Blancmange (my favourite) for lunch!

I was just told that George Bonner, one of the pilots from the Argentine who stayed here now and then (Mrs. Morley and her daughter Miss Morley lived in Buenos Aires till the war) has just been killed out in the Middle East. He was about 27. I feel very conscience-stricken about him because he was one I 'led on' and then rejected for no especial reason.

Love, Og

*Oscar Deutsch was another Brummie and founder of the Odeon cinema chain. His son Ronnie married one of Olga's cousins Jill Davis. He died relatively young in 1941. **Ambrose was a bandleader famous for, among other things, discovering forces sweetheart Vera Lynn.*

July 1941
c/o Reuters
85, Fleet Street
London EC4

Dear B,

Thanks for your letter and the tomatoes were very good tomatoes. Just going home after night duty; if you can spare a moment, please write me some news about Betty as your letter worried me very much. I remember how nervous I was starting the first job and I was properly trained; I'm afraid the child will make herself ill. Are the spots better and are they as bad as she's had them before? Why does Aunt Ray talk such bloody rot? I'm properly upset about Betty, particularly about my inability to contribute to her continuing with school. I have been doing a night shift midnight to morning for 7 nights running; done 5 and still have 2 to get through; they're a bit wearing.

My landlady has raised my rent 7/6d a week now because with the changed duty roster I am in to more meals. I now pay 37/6d a week.

I hope you get some rest now your visitors have gone. There is not a tomato to be seen anywhere in London since a month. I gave one of yours to my favourite Editor. No one anywhere can grow tomatoes like they do at my beloved Evesham.

Love, Ogg

28th November 1941
c/o Reuters
85, Fleet Street
London EC4

Dear B,

I haven't had a chance to write before. The parcel was lovely. It came last Tuesday afternoon just when I was wondering what on earth to take with me for all-night duty. The parcel contents lasted me all week for which I was no end grateful as I had no money and I don't wake up till about 7pm when it is too late to buy anything for the night and in the canteen you can't get anything except bread and marge.

We have an awful job getting milk. I missed being able to get milk this week … having contracted slight bronchitis, but shall be all right in a few days. Am on day duty this week but there has been thick fog every morning when I leave the office at seven am.

Am longing to see Ricky and all. I don't know yet though whether possible or not. We don't get anything like as much time off as we used to. I don't know whether I shall be conscripted for the Army or not. No one is talking about anything else. I expect there will be a hot debate in the House of Commons tomorrow. We are frantically busy all the time now …. with Parliament and all the war communiqués. I have worked late every day but am allowed to claim for overtime. Stockings just arrived – they are gorgeous! Who are they from? From the G.I.'s in Worcestershire?

Shall I join the Wrens? I am keen on the idea of Nursing for Betty now, because I should not like her to be conscripted into the ATS. […]

4

The War in Fleet Street

1942

As the year started the Red Army began its counter offensive. The Japanese captured Kuala Lumpur and the Nazis started deporting Jews from the Lodz ghetto.

January 1942
c/o Reuters
85, Fleet Street
London EC4

Dearest B,

We've all been told to take our summer holidays as early as possible this year… very early, starting April as it is believed the Invasion will come sometime in the summer. Had a bad cold all week and bronchial catarrh; better now but here's so bitterly cold it is difficult to keep warm.

When is Frank having the operation and how does he feel about it? I hope Ricky is quite better. I am saving this month's sweet ration for him so I hope to be able to bring him two or three months' rations when I come. Shops all refuse to send parcels so I'll bring all with me.

We have two glamorous new women at the office; one comes to us from Everywoman's Magazine and looks like she came off the cover itself. We all felt positively scruffy beside her. It has done our woman status heaps of good on the News Desk. Even Mr. Pigg looks impressed. There are now 3 of us trainee subeditor women on the Desk apart from Connie Smith who is a bit older than us so it is a sort of breakthrough for women!

One fair haired girl who is my special friend is named Madge Whittaker and turns out to be Whittaker's granddaughter (I refer of course to the

Dictionary in case you didn't recognise it).* In between jobs we sit whispering together about those Editors we love and those whom we hate, until Miss Muriel Penn, who is rather a stern Gorgon and sits at the top of the table on Night Shift (She is brilliant of course but fearfully strict and the men have to put up their hands and ask her permission before going to the lavatory for a few minutes …that's in case a red-hot cable came in suddenly about the fighting round Smolensk** and as that's the Big News she couldn't trust that to Little Midge and me) glares at us …..Everywoman's Mag girl is intellectual and reads War & Peace when things go quiet after midnight….

As regards my own work, I seem to be doing better now. My Pacific and particularly Burma Round-Ups have been hitting the headlines (in case you noticed … I am now called The Burma Queen). Luckily for me the 14th Army does not move very fast, but every few nights they cross some dreadful Burmese river and I have one helluva job trying to find it on the map because these rivers have got at least four different names depending on which map and which year it was printed and which military regime was in charge at the time.

Love, Og

PS. I have discovered that Journalists are the most generous of men. What is more they do not think that women are too dim to work alongside men and do men's jobs … or what are usually thought of as men's jobs. What I enjoy is being with men I can honestly ADMIRE. Harold King helps me with my bad French; he is witty and clever. Michael Fry who is brilliant (he lies on the floor doing Yoga during the night to relax his brain end muscles) is training me how to write a good headline and how to get the red-hot news into one Short, sharp paragraph.***

Sometimes chaps come on here from the House of Commons (MP's or Ministers or so) and walk around our desk, looking over our shoulders. Or they come to talk to an Editor with the funny name of Rickatson Hatt. One night a dark, dour fellow named W.J. Haley**** came and walked round & round, making me nervous. It's said he may be our new boss.

The Moscow news gets worse. We go up to the 4th floor to try & comfort the Russians in the Tass Office. Misha Baharin walks up and down with the news-tape in his arms as though it were a child; he looks white and drawn and so thin with his white face and steel teeth. Or we sit in the canteen with the yellow tea and yellow cheese. Two English subs, Harry Cousins and a blond named Phillips, speak a bit of Russian; Cole's pals, Doon Campbell***** and Jimmy Nicholson.

Olga may have meant Whitaker's Almanac, *first published in 1869.*
**This would probably be the Russian counter-offensive pushing the Germans back towards Smolensk.*
***Harold King was head of Reuters Paris bureau after the war; Michael Fry became a UN correspondent.*
****W.J. Haley later became Director General of the BBC and also editor of* The Times.
*****Campbell was the first reporter ashore on D-Day.*

29th July 1942
c/o Reuters
85, Fleet Street
London EC4

Dear Beryl & Cora,

With the aid of a little carbon-paper I can write two letters at once; to both of you if you've no objection. This helps me; being always hard pressed for time & disliking the typewriter if I can avoid it ... (which reminds me, Cora, your typing – vide today's letter – is so exquisite you will always be able to make a good living as a typist if all else fails.

Many thanks for the birthday-gift of the stockings; I will return the lisle pair as requested and you may have the coupons – how many is it per pair? Is it all right to snip the coupons off the card & send?

I do wish you and Viv would move out of Birmingham which appears to be the target for the Luftwaffe's especial spite. How did you fare the other night? People could see Coventry burning for more than 25 miles away....

I wish, Cora, you could induce Beryl to accompany you to Devon. Apart from everything else it is so good for Richard and Vivienne to be together. And Richard has never seen the sea. And seems badly in need of a change & entertainment.

Thinking things over, Beryl, I am sure Richard would be a different child with a little entertainment. Recall how good he is in the pram when he has something to look at.

An Argentinian lady staying in this boarding house (No.86 Canfield Gardens, NW6) says Richard sounds to her like an unhappy child. Happy children, she says, are almost never naughty. She says he ought to be swamped in toys and entertainments. She was so full of advice I was left quite breathless. She has a good little boy with her, aged 8, who sits very straight at table, and even Mrs. Morley can find nothing to complain of.

Returning to your letter, Cora, your facility of expression and faultless English is such I am inclined to think you more deservingly called the 'litry one of the family' than I.

Your references to Felix and George* always make me sick with misery. Naturally the poor fellows are convinced they have some mysterious nerve complaint when the Army authorities specifically rejected them both on this ground. How about advising them both to try again for Army or Navy? I am inclined to think the Authorities might give way to enthusiastic pressure.

As far as Betty's future is concerned, my advice is to wait awhile. Seventeen is very young. Time enough when she is 19 or 20 if she still wants to embark on a new career. I hope to be in a better position to advise her now, as I am doing voluntary nursing at a hospital in Stepney. Matron was very sweet and showed me round the nurses' Home equipped with everything including electric hair-dryers! I told her that our Mother had been a hospital nurse in Manchester and made a lot of bold comments about the nursing career but she had an answer for everything and I was utterly routed. I saw the Lecture room and was horrified to see a stout dead body in one of the beds there which turned out to be a large female dummy with blond curls.

I start work in the out-patients' department at 10-30 before going on duty in Fleet Street at 4-15pm. Matron promised to read Monica Dickens 'One Pair of Feet'. If all Matrons were like her, I'd advise Betty to go right ahead.

Did you know the East End of London used once to be the West End. It looks a bit like Bury Old Road in Manchester. The hospital is flanked with trees on both sides and has a little park full of hollyhocks and dahlias.

Love, Og

Betty studied nursing, winning a gold medal in the process, and became a successful midwife

* *Olga's twin brothers both had problems with depression, with Felix eventually committing suicide.*

19th November 1942
c/o Reuters
85, Fleet Street
London EC4

Dearest B,

I hope you are all well. How is my Ricky? I miss him terribly … and you and Betty.

I am trying hard to get myself a new job. I registered today with the 1912 class but was dismissed without any questioning.

The atmosphere at Reuters is awful. I have the impression the bosses are fearful of the NPA (Newspaper Proprietor's Assoc.) taking over, as they are the ones who will have to go I expect if the NPA are not satisfied. Also Reuters have lost a lot of money from the fact of Europe being, so to say, closed down the past year.

I duly made my complaint about the anti-feminist movement on our Foreign News Desk instituted by Mr. John Pigg, and Mr. Neale said he could do nothing as Pigg had been put in charge by the Administration and Mr. P was responsible. He suggested I could always transfer to the Barnet radio station, translating the German hell tape and taking English radio in shorthand, which is quite a good job but I don't want to go. I don't like the three quarters of an hour's walk through the countryside in winter, miles from any station or bus. I don't like the company; elderly bitchy women, eccentric White Russians and a few sinister foreigners.

I now have sixteen shillings and five pence deducted each week for income tax, so shall have to try and find somewhere cheaper to live.

Cole is going to ask at Assoc.Press if they need a subeditor there. I think after all I'd prefer war work in a factory or joining the Wrens if they'd have me; the Wrens are the only service with a waiting-list so it must be better than the others. I am not the only one unhappy here; everyone at Reuters seems to be leaving or going after jobs or looking elsewhere. I am sorry to keep writing you all this boring stuff about jobs and Reuters and so on. It's a sort of closed-in world here; the Editor-in-charge sits at the top of the long green table with his green eye shield. We all have yellow faces under the electric light. Not a peep of daylight, all boarded up behind the blackout shutters when we start work at 4pm and it's still dark when we finish at 8am next day. Yellow-eyed, orange-yellow tea and hard, stale-smelling very yellow cheddar cheese.

Love, Og

November 1942
86, Canfield Gardens
West Hampstead, London NW6

Dear B,

I can just manage to stay on here for a bit by taking some temporary work on my days off or hours-off during daylight. I am glad the fierce cold has broken; today for the first time it is warm but with pouring rain all day. I have several days off and thought of coming over only I had no money for the fare; no money at all, so I thought I'd better go out to work first and earn some and come next time I'm free.

I saw a wonderful flick, Bette Davis in The Little Foxes; a picture which impressed me very much (as did Citizen Kane), I hope you will one day eventually see both these; in the Little Foxes there were so many characters to match those of our own peculiar family, but most amazing of all was the heroine whose name I forget who takes the part of the young girl Alexandra*; she is the living spit and image of our Betty; such a likeness! in features, colouring, manner, the same sulky funny ways, the same sudden docility, the same everything. [...]

*It was Teresa Wright.

November 1942
Brook Street, London W1

Dear B,

I am writing this at the office where am at present working on one of my off-days from Reuters. It is a luxurious office just off Bond Street of a little fat Estate Agent named Marcus Leaver. All the offices are carpeted with thick beige pile carpets. Leaver's office is awe-inspiring and it takes an awfully long time to walk over from the door to his desk; am quite breathless by the time I get there and sit down in the dim light of the artificial fireplace which is the size of a front door. He watches you triumphantly, stumbling across the waving carpets and observes I'll be damned that I have a hole in the seam of my Skirt, a hole in my left shoe and several ladders. The business deals with War Damage due to Enemy Action, but this is the only warlike thing about it. I get quite a kick out of this temporary work because in all the offices so far they never had anyone as quick as me yet in their lives and they are so astounded, it makes me giggle.

I get sent on these jobs by an Employment Bureau; on Monday the bureau nearly messed my day up and I was wild, but it came out all right in the end. I have to go to the bureau in Coleman Street, Moorgate at 9am and wait until something turns up. Sometimes you can wait all morning and nothing turns up but that hasn't happened to me so far. Anyway they sent me out to Tottenham to a factory and although it was such a long way I thought it's better than losing a day's work so I went. I took the tube to Finsbury Park, changed to Manor House, took 3d trolleybus ride to Northumberland Park, Tottenham then ten minutes' walk, only to find the factory didn't exist; they'd given me the wrong address. So back I walk, search for post office telephone; post office have no coppers so I go another walk, find some shops, get change; return to post office, ring the bureau and ask them what the hell; they say sorry they've given me the wrong address, but meanwhile there's another booking at Fenchurch street; please will I go back to the City; So back I trek, bus to Manor House, wait in queue for train to Mark Lane which is Inner Circle and goes all round the City first; lose my way owing bombed streets are quite unrecognisable to me and finally arrive 12-15 for work at Wm Cory & Sons, marble emporium, big coal people in the City. Next day they sent me here ...to toast my toes in front of the gas fire. Some people seem to me to have too much money to waste, employing labour where it's not needed or because their own staff are slow and incompetent often as not .... and anyhow it all doesn't seem to tally with Stafford Cripps' scheme for more and MORE work and sacrifice.

Anyway I shall make about £2/10s clear this week; unfortunately I owe Rene £1 dam it. How is Ricky? I'm going to send him sweets and jellies for his birthday.

I had extra time off this week because a woman loaned me two days as she wants me to pay her back two days later on when she's going away. Nearly succumbed to the temptation to come to Malvern ... but it's no use borrowing and going on borrowing from this one then that one; best to earn the money first and then come; have made Vow not to borrow again.

At the bawdy-house, Mrs. Morley now has no coal and no soap; or very little soap,.... having neglected to get stocks of either. So she is claiming half our soap-ration each month for household use!

And for bath I have to boil a kettle each night.

I heard from Parliament end that the Govt are considering or rather had decided to cut meat ration to 10 penny worth per week per person.

Love, Og

December 1942
86, Canfield Gardens
West Hampstead, London NW6

Dear B,

I had a very nice letter from Corrie; don't know how she finds time to write letters and everything else as well. Is it true she may have twins? My first thought was oh God, no. How can one not fear they may be twin boys and turn out like our own unhappy brothers Felix and George? I rather wish she was with you in the country. I do wish you could get up to town a bit oftener; perhaps you will when the weather gets a bit warmer; please God (it's snowing today); it must be hellish dull for you in Malvern living next door to the Rainbows* etc. Still you have the compensation of that view of the Malvern Hills from Malvern Link. My next free time I shall come over, if I may, but I know you'll understand I couldn't come over when I didn't even have the fare. I just eke out a living, from week to week from hand to mouth. It's no use saying be more careful; the money goes nowhere; I spend on barest essentials and am still in debt.

The little fat man in Brook Street offered me a permanent job and seemed quite taken aback when I turned it down; these fellows don't seem awake yet to the idea they will have to be glad of part-time labour eventually when there is nothing else to be had. Tomorrow is, however, my last free day and I have to go to Fleet Street at midnight. I like work; work is the best thing; it is the solution to so many of my problems. Rene keeps phoning and badgering me to go round and keep her company, no matter how cold it is or how tired I am; she is selfish in that way.

But I mustn't get like the landlady's daughter Miss Morley: rather pretty, rather nice but so conventional. She works till she drops. They've been unable to get any household help for weeks since the last charwoman walked out on them and Miss Morley has been running the place and got herself properly knocked up. So she got two whitlows on each hand

and has had to have two fingernails removed by the doctor, and she's all bandaged up and can't do much; but she still potters around carrying trays and whatnot.

So you'll forgive me old girl if I dissolve into bed; I'm sitting on the edge of it. I know I'm a rotten correspondent, as Cora says, Betty says, you said; ... but there's times when I'm too tired and times when there's nothing to write. But there is never ever at all a time when you and Ricky are not in my mind. When will Betty write me? Is she going to start her nursing training right away, or is she still too young? I hope she does because I don't want her being called up for the ATS. Is she still practising piano? And has she any friends? this letter is all staccato .... but old brain too worn out to think except in spurts. Please don't think I am going to be like Aunt Phoebe though this letter reads like it. Perhaps I am getting a whitlow on the Brain!

Love, Og

The Jaffas were living in Malvern Link next to Beryl's cousin Bob Rainbow and his family.

1943

January 1943
86, Canfield Gardens
West Hampstead, London NW6

Dear B,

Miss Morley brought your letter to my room. I sat on the bed, rocking back and forth with misery. We have had so much ... death, loss, anguish.

The thought of Cora opening the door to a postal messenger with a telegram saying Ivan had been killed serving with the RAF in North Africa, and the War Office official condolences. I can understand Cora saying that the 2-year-old Vivienne is no real comfort to her, in spite of what sister-in-law Pauline says.

I have since learned that the whole of that RAF unit which landed, secretly it was hoped, on the North African coast near Algiers was wiped out THE VERY FIRST DAY by the Luftwaffe.

Miss Morley was marvellous to me; helped me get my things together. I went straight to Cole and he said, 'Of course, you must go to Birmingham

165

right away.' I shall come to see you as soon as I can and shall try to bring Cora and Vivienne with me.

Ogg

July 1943
c/o Reuters
85, Fleet Street
London EC4

Dearest B,

Many thanks for lovely parcel. Why have I not heard from you all this long time? Is everything all right? I hope you will forgive if this letter is not so long as I intended, very tired. Am on 7-30 am duty this week and am up at 5.30am.

Also am very depressed today; having made silly blunder and Cole was so annoyed and I cannot blame him. It was too awful! It got on to the front page of the first edition of The Times, and if there's one thing our super-efficient Reuter boss hates more than anything else, it is having to publish CORRECTION on the ticker-tape to All Morning Editions.

The Editor of the Times 'phoned him up ...only just minutes before the first edition 'went to bed' so they had to rush like mad to correct the front page before it got on to the vans and into the streets. Oh dear! I am so crushed ... feel like a worm not even worth treading upon.

Of course the whole office heard about it ... and afterwards I found out I'd become famous overnight. Everyone loves a really good Bloomer, but not my boss. And he's quite right. After all, supposing I'd been handling the Stalingrad front ... and fell right flat on my face like this!

It was a Vichy dispatch ... and a Sports item at that ... but that is the kind of thing the papers always look out for. You'd think there wasn't a war on at all.

It was a French cable which I translated and interpreted all wrong; I said that Vittorio Mussolini, Il Duce's only surviving son, was going to Budapest TO BOX IN A BOXING MATCH. Actually he was only going there to rejoin the Delegation attending the boxing-match ... 'to participate in the judging' ... and what's worse I give it a headline: 'Mussolini's son to box in Budapest.' When I told Cole afterwards how sorry I was ... but I knew nothing at all about Boxing, it didn't help. 'It's your job to know all about Boxing. Football ... every Sport there is. I warned you about that when I put you to train on the Desk.' Which is quite true, he gave me a sort of test back in the winter of 1941 ... asking me to name the Captain and Inside Right of the Tottenham Hotspur team and was horrified when I said I didn't know.

If you could see me now I sit here brooding and looking exactly like our Betty when she's been ticked off about something. It's my first bad mistake, but it must be a Whopper because the whole Street, according to Cole, is talking about it. My vanity is hurt the most, of course. You know how I pride myself on being Supersub! Me, my God! Cole seemed to get over it a bit later; he came up behind me, sitting broody on the Desk... 'Cheer up,' he said. 'It was a lovely story. Wish it had been true.'

Everyone was watching us and I felt like the lowest thing that crawled. Of course I knew they were telling each other that he is lenient with me as one of his ex-mistresses. The worst thing about that is that it is true! Don't be sorry for me. I don't deserve it. I always did take things too seriously, though it was Cole being so angry with me that upset me the most. I can be as Touchy as Betty, you see...

I felt quite ashamed too when I was called upstairs later this afternoon to pick up the overtime money Cole had wangled for me because I had told him I was hard up. He had put in for a month's overtime; so I got £4.4.0 all for nothing. Also I am now getting £5.0.0. (minus income tax of £4) soon rising to £300 a year, that is £6 a week! So Cole has really treated me decently ... and I was so un-nerved at making a mistake, I made a lot more in quick succession. Oh oh. Humiliation and Ignominy, as our Frank would say. Only this is for real. On days like this the job is hair-raising, though I guess for everyone, even oldtimers, it is always pretty nerve-wracking[...]

Well you must be good and bored with me and my job. Am going to send you my month's ration of sweets this week in the form of choc peppermints. Couldn't get them today as you have to go in the morning early. They get sold out, being the most popular item! Oh that raspberry jam of yours is heavenly.

I am still looking out for somewhere to live. Rita Cave is very fed up with her talent-spotting job for Ambrose and is looking out desperately. She and Cousin Jane Davis are a couple of twirps; they haven't registered in case they get called up for war work!* They'll get to gaol yet. Jane hasn't worked for months. I don't think she did for more than about four weeks. I think that's her limit; then she gets funny 'health' turns and takes to her bed. Ha ha.

Rita has new boyfriend, an American Officer, a solicitor, about 36, married. Like you'd expect a solicitor to be, blond, big and comfortable, not bad-looking. She picked him up at one of her smart clubs in Park Lane, the Deanery. She took me there; it was very dull and the food was awful. The solicitor friend insisted on going home with her that same night although she begged him not to; but she is spending his pay so fast you really can't blame him for wanting his money's worth quickly. You have to hand it to Rita; she looked all right; she can still hold her own. She had on a nice costume though marred, like Rosalie's outfits of course, by bits and pieces; a jewelled clip on her hat, a heavily jewelled wrist watch, a bangle, two diamante clips on either lapel and rings and coloured flowers and anything else there was room for. However, Captain Lutwack from Texas liked her all right.

They are terribly dull these officers you can't imagine, they are So giggly and inane. I suspect they are quite nice normal people really but they insist on 'going to town' whenever they go out, which means being completely nitwittish and boring.

Guess they've got the 'before the deluge' complex. But it's a great pity. I see them in their loud-mouthed hordes coming home on the last tube-train which I have to take home from work, completely sozzled so they can hardly walk. Their idea of fun is to climb down on to the rails and lie down until the tube train comes. It's making our 'British' girls so affected too; you hear them call to each other now in the streets, the girls always using such expressions as 'get a load of this, honey'. Yah!

Rosalie, whom I had a grim tea with one afternoon on her invitation, told me about her boy-friends, A Greek and a Pole, 'It galls me to death the Greek won't marry me.' Excuse – he has told her that he has instructions from the Greek Legation he must not marry out of his own nationality if he wants to get a decent job in the Ministry! Anyway, as you see, my cousins are doing their bit for the War Effort. (I believe even Paying-Guest Phyllis has a so nice sedate American officer.)

Rosalie & Rita still share the flat (No.6, Grove End Gdns), which must be a bit awkward if the Yank comes home the same time as the Greek or the Pole, but the sisters haven't spoken to each other for weeks.

I should like to tell you also about Freda, and how I met her one day in the road when she was rushing out to make a call, and she was expecting a visitor and had been waxing the whiskers off one side of her mouth, but had only had time to do one side. But my back is breaking sitting on the edge of this bed....

I hope Stalingrad goes on holding, and if it does, anything might happen. I saw Leslie Howard in 'First of the Few' which I liked very much indeed. I reported a Zionist meeting at the Dorchester for Reuters, which is where I met the Cave girls; I wore my black straw probably for the last time this season. It has turned very cold today. P'raps I'll invest in new one with my overtime money. Must fall into bed now, dear & probably have nightmares about that bloody Mussolini.

Love Og

Registration and possession of an identity card had become compulsory.

July 1943
c/o Reuters
85, Fleet Street
London EC4

Dearest B,

I was upset you can imagine after you're going to all that trouble for me. But the parcel arrived completely shattered. I hate having to tell you but for the fear you might do it again. Apparently tins are the only kind of thing one can safely send through the post nowadays. I wept at having to dispose of the remains of that gorgeous gooseberry jam, just what I could do with now, but it was quite hopeless. The jam and orange (the Horlicks was intact) were not just broken; they were simply shattered into a thousand little pieces of broken glass. You'd have thought they'd been playing tennis with the parcel.

Don't be upset ole girl. I do appreciate it terribly your having gone to all that trouble for me but I shall simply have to wait until I come over to see you. Was this your new lot of jam just made? It certainly is heartbreaking!

Actually I think my loss of weight is less due to lack of food than sleep. I expect it is due to the constant late nights and then often when I get to bed I can't sleep because my mind is always in such a turmoil – especially lately – over the dam job.

I have to go to Barnet radio station, and the alternating hope & despair over the prospect of a new one. Did I tell you that some months ago Cole suddenly took to religion! Surprise. He joined the Buchmanite Oxford Group who have quite a big following here because the Press Association Editor is a leading member as well as the 'Express' columnist who first joined and has been, so to speak, 'recruiting' all along Fleet Street. Cole told me about some of their meetings.

They all sit in an audience and listen to each other confessing their 'sins'. Except for Cole who says he 'confessed' about me and a lot of other girls ... the sins are a bit nauseating like 'self-abuse', 'nose-picking', pinching someone's sweet ration or 'having adulterous thoughts'. However, his membership hasn't fortunately affected his consuming passion for work – he takes the Page One Lead on the Stalingrad Front to bed with him just to check whether it can be hotted up or not – nor does it stop him from chasing after a new blonde in the office, just like he once did after me. She is Peggy Butler and sensationally pretty in her white silk blouse and even more romantic she has been widowed recently after her pilot husband was shot down. I keep my head down over my unending accounts of the 14th Army in Burma and feel poisoned right through with evil jealousy and humiliation. Serves me right, eh! Still it does help me to cross those dam rivers which change their names so often, without so much as getting my feet wet.

You'll be pleased to hear my old paltie Henry Rose, now a top columnist on the Daily Express in Fleet Street, after his promotion from Manchester office, has got me an interview with the Great .... with Arthur Christiansen himself, no less, the famed Editor of the Daily Express. Really Henry is a nice, kindly fellow and has behaved very decently ... (especially as he is one of those many to whom I refused my 'favours' for no particular or even sensible reason!) ....I can quite understand why Henry's reputation for good nature and great kindness to people is even bigger than his sports-reporting one. I am to have my interview with Christiansen at 3-30pm on Tuesday, so keep your fingers crossed for me. I do hope you approve.

Well that's all for now honey. I hardly have time to get home & have a bath and write a few lines before it's time for me to get ready & go back to work again.

What shall I wear for the interview? Am already sweating at thought of it. Shall I wear YOUR costume without hat which suits me very well or my best black with black hat. Suppose it rains?

Love, Og

July 1943
c/o Reuters
85, Fleet Street
London EC4

Dear B,

Last week I had to do my stint out at Barnet. The woman where I am
billeted for sleeping out is especially charming. She keeps chickens &
rabbits and has a smashing garden.

I have an egg for breakfast almost every day! She often puts a little cluster
of fresh strawberries from her garden on to the breakfast tray; she puts
them to nestle in a few tender baby lettuce leaves. She often puts a rose or
a bit of blossom on the tray and I can never eat a half of what she gives
me, which seems to worry her quite a lot. I think she must like me.

Last night she left a glass of cold milk for me at the bedside. Human
nature is really not as bad as one might think what with wars and all.
What with the kind Henry and my temporary landlady and you.

Love, Og

Dear B,

I found Christiansen tucked away between the fastnesses of a lot of
royal blue carpet. He told me about His Ministry of Labour quota and
the resultant restrictions almost before I had finished my journey across
the royal blue to reach a seat. He told me if he took me on it would
mean sacking someone like Morley Richards!*... Intended to dampen my
girlish enthusiasm, this particular shaft went further; I dissolved like a
fleck of foam on that very blue sea. After that (isn't it called the softening-
up process?) he was able to make rissoles out of me, and did.

He suggested I come to the Express office on some of my evenings-
off from Reuters and try my hand at Express subbing. I thanked him
for his kindness in seeing me and withdrew, realising that he obviously
didn't want me and was in fact just trying to do Henry Rose a favour.

He did say one thing which I feel was helpful. He said if I could go
North and get experience as newspaper reporter in the police courts etc.,
of say Manchester, Newcastle, Glasgow ... for a year, then I could come
back and see him again, when 'you would certainly be much more use
to me'.

I've gotten over my disappointment now ... helped possibly by colleagues who tell me that in the past couple of years, several well-tried, experienced and hard bitten women subs have been either sacked or are on their way out ... from the Express editorial. Three months there is considered a really long session for a woman sub on the Express. Reason? The paper has a fancy slant on most news stories that you either get or you don't, and mostly you don't.

I've written Henry to thank him for giving me the chance and telling what happened.

Meanwhile I've been writing around for jobs in the provinces and had several offers, mostly from Wales. Neath and Merthyr Tydfil are willing to try me out ... I'm all for taking chances ... even big ones.

News! Rene is expecting a baby. She asks me if you have time would you please write her some advice. She knows nothing about babies or baby clothes or anything. She is fearfully interested in her condition. And though still slender as ever, she walks about with her skirt undone and half hanging down, just to show the world she means business.

Love, Og

Morley Richards was a leading member of the Daily Express *editorial staff.*

August 1943
c/o Reuters
85, Fleet Street
London EC4

Dear B,

I asked Cole if he would give me a letter releasing me. Without such a letter to show the Ministry of Labour, I would not be able to change my job anyway. He was reluctant ... possibly because so many subs have left lately, but I insisted. On the whole I think he has been a good friend to me because it is all due to him that I am now a member of the NUJ (National Union of Journalists) and you know that without a Union Card I could never get work with any newspaper.

I showed him the offer I have had from the Editor of the Oxford Mail to join their Reporting staff in Oxford; he says he approves and it will be 'good for you'. He thinks, he says, that Subbing is not for me. Reminded me, of COURSE, about the Mussolini bloomer. 'You'll do better out on the road,' he says to me, and I know he's right about that.

Bumped into Aunt Sally yesterday with a Medium friend .... on their way to a Séance. She gave me a piece of eye-opening news. That Uncle Abe's illegitimate daughter is in Fleet Street too! Calls herself Sally Davis. I asked whether Cousin Jane knows her. 'Of course,' says Aunt Sally, 'everyone knows except you.' Well I know now. Our family!!

Will write you as soon as I get settled down in Oxford. Miss Morley has given me the address of a nice landlady she knows in Woodstock Road.

Love, Og

5

Oxford and the G.I.s

September 1943
c/o Oxford Mail, Oxford

Dearest B,

Am getting really worried now at not hearing from you.

Please ask Betty to drop me a line & say what is happening your end. Have not heard from Cora either ... in fact from no one except a girl friend at Reuters who tells of more sackings & intrigue and says she is thinking of following my example as she is not happy.

I was too busy to write you a decent letter. Apart from the routine round of police court and meetings and so on, I go out and look for my own stories and the Chief Reporter seems pleased about it.

I interviewed two College Dons (at their request), one incredibly dirty and the other rather nice who gave me sherry. And written up my landlady Miss Groves (friend of Miss Morley) about giving us hot milk and hot bottles and she was tickled pink to be in the paper.

Then I persuaded a wounded U.S. pilot to offer to take me to the Churchill Hospital where all the wounded American flyers shot up in action over Germany are stationed. This hasn't come off yet and the Editor thinks they won't let me in but I intend to have a jolly good try as it would be a scoop to get past the censorship. The wounded pilot is taking me out to lunch this week to discuss tactics.

Have also been doing the rounds of Oxford's wartime nurseries with permission from the Medical Officer of Health; it seems there is a lot of opposition to them in the County and I want to find out why.

My last days at Reuters and especially out at Barnet were a bit tense, and tempers got a bit frayed. At the height of the North Africa excitement recently when Richard Loewenthal of Heidelberg University was trying to 'phone a communique from the Fuehrer's HQ to head office at the same time as Vladimir Apraxin of Voronezh was trying to listen in to the communique from Allied Force HQ in North Africa in French – both men were screaming and nearly in tears – neither could hear or be heard and they knew the inquest that would follow if they were as much as 30 seconds late with the news; when the German chap's morale cracked as he sprang from his desk and threw the telephone from one end of the noisy, dirty little room smack against the opposite wall. Then Cole had a tip-off that Sicily was going to be invaded – and we all had to come on duty even if we were 'off'. Nothing happened.

Next week after that he had another tip that Spain was going to be invaded and he sent an army of Spanish translators to cover Madrid radio, though we already had several Spanish linguists. The Spanish gentlemen returned to Head Office in a fearful huff that night after that terrible journey, most of it uphill on foot, to Barnet, simply to hear Franco mouthing the usual platitudes. Cole says the news is 'climacteric'.

I am looking forward to seeing Vivienne dance like a ballerina in her little red shoes. When are you going to sell me your green costume? How much?

Best love to all, Og

October 1943
c/o Oxford Mail, Oxford

Dearest B,

Thanks for yours at long last. I couldn't think what I'd done to be so neglected. I am grieved to hear you are having to work so hard in Malvern; perhaps it will be a good thing to go back to B'ham after all, but will you be able to get any help there? Oh, how I love being in Oxford. I love every bit of it.

Christchurch meadows are full of pink rose bushes as though it were high Summer. I love the greystone Colleges and the slate grey of the river. The climate is adorable, being mild and damp and hardly any wind. Everything looks mellow and green and gold.

The office itself is mellow with seasoned wood stairs and doors; it has a pre-war look about it, an atmosphere like a J.B. Priestley play. Chief Reporter is an ogre of a fat man named Mr. Gibbs who is also News Editor. All the reporters are lovely, including the Crime Man who has just come out of the Navy and a golden-haired slender girl with a present as racy as her Past and she loves going on about it.

The work shifts are long – from breakfast to midnight usually but I am never tired because I love every minute. Mornings I spend in the police-court usually, afternoons are for cycling out to do interviews or to report on church or Cathedral ceremonies ... for a new Cardinal, or a stone-laying. Then I have to go to a cinema or theatre or some University function and write a Review for morning paper, with another version to do for the weekly paper the Oxford Times. Then at night back on the old bike to write about some political meeting at one of the Colleges ...or for a lecture or madrigals or something...

I have good digs in Banbury Road with Miss Morley's former housekeeper who cooks lovely hot dinners at lunchtime like I've not had in years.... My only worry is not getting enough news from you. I have just wired Betty to let me know about the new baby* because I get pretty worried.

I enjoy every day here. I seem to talk so much to so many in so little time that I make myself dizzy sometimes. All the most interesting people are here; you bump into them every day. This week I had to interview a nice rather balding chappie named Frank Pakenham** who is Prospective Parliamentary Labour Candidate for Oxford who talked nearly as much as me, so I didn't get a chance to put all the questions the News Editor wanted answering. Sir William Beveridge is here and who d'you think too? Neville Laski has been living here for about 3 years. And of course there are the Yanks. But you've got THOSE too...

College starts tomorrow again and we expect to be very busy. There is a Conference or Concert at one College or another every single night. The town has filled up with very young lads who have got to squeeze their education into a tiny portion of time before joining up. They all look clean and earnest and not a bit sophisticated like the usual undergraduates of 21 or so[...]

I am going to try and do my evening stories and reviews in my room on my old typewriter and get up early and bring them in at 8 a.m. because I am scared of the Rats. Oxford centre is alive with them, great monsters like in that Hamelin town in Brunswick, that famous Hanover city ... If ever a town needed a Pied Piper. It's scary in the blackout; I find myself almost running them over, cycling down the Woodstock Road! Every day I cycle past the huge laboratory where Professor Florey is working; they say he's the man who discovered Penicillin or something.

Had to interrupt this letter to cover the County Juvenile Court but luckily it was short. Was able to snatch an afternoon off on Monday because had been sent to review a film I'd seen in London. We always have to do the films on Mondays. The one I wanted to see 'Carnet du bal' I didn't get.

Everyone said I'd never manage to get into the Churchill Hospital to interview the Yanks, wounded or otherwise. So of course I was keen to go as I hate to be defeated. My first approach failed as the American Colonel had given me the wrong man to try, but the second produced something. The Public Relations Officer, a chap named Talbot from the U.S. Army GHQ at Cheltenham is coming up to Oxford on Tuesday morning by car specially to take me out to the hospital. He phoned three times before we could contact as I am almost never in the office. He says he will give me lunch at the hospital, so you can guess I am looking forward to it. No one from the Mail or the Times has been allowed in before.

Oh dear Berylline, I do hope you're all right. Hope to hear something today. Have you been 'turned' again by Dr. Jefferson? Do let me know or ask Betty to write me. Love to Ricky & Frank.

My phone number is Oxford 4141, but telegrams just Franklin Mail Oxford is sufficient.

All my love, Og.

*Lucille (Lucy) Jaffa, Beryl's daughter, was born in Malvern in October 1943.
**Frank Pakenham became better known as Lord Longford.

October 1943
c/o Oxford Mail, Oxford

Dear B,

It was lovely seeing you all. I'd come oftener but it costs 13/2d each time so perhaps it's just as well I can't come every week! That porter at Malvern Link had given me all the wrong dope. The 6-12 am didn't get in until 6-45 at Foregate Street. Meanwhile the Oxford train I wanted left Shrub Hill at 6-30. Oh oh. I had to wait till 8-20 for the next one, after getting up at 5 am.

The weather here is still lovely, all golden & October. The mist and damp seem to suit me better than any climate I've yet been in. Am still enjoying Oxford like mad, made many friends and just adore meeting all the Professors and writing about their lectures and things. Had my first byline here with my story on St Ebbe's school.

Above left: Olga *(l)* and Beryl with their Mother, 1912.

Above right: *(l–r)* Beryl, Olga, Cora. Circa 1915.

Left: Olga, 1932.

Above: Olga and Norbert's wedding at Singers Hill Synagogue, Birmingham in 1934.

Below: Beryl's wedding to Frank Jaffa. *(l–r)* Rita Rainbow, Frank and Beryl, Cora (seated) Jerry Simons, Betty and Olga.

Above left: Betty as a trainee nurse circa 1946.

Above right: Aunt Phoebe Cave (centre) with her daughters Rita and Rosalie.

Left: Olga on the balcony of Hitler's Chancellory in Berlin, September 1946, with the children of the British Control Commissioner, Col. Guy Hughes.

IMT VISITOR'S PASS № 80677

The Bearer MISS O. FRANKLIN

is authorized admittance to the Area of the Palace of Justice

to visit COURTHOUSE Room

From 0800 To 1800

Security Officer *John D Ellis Lt. Inf*

Countersigned

Person Visited

Date issued 6 SEP 46

FIVE DAYS EXPIRES 10 SEP 46

Olga's press pass for Nuremberg, 1946.

Stunts for the *Daily Mail*:

Left: learning to fish;
Below: building the M1.

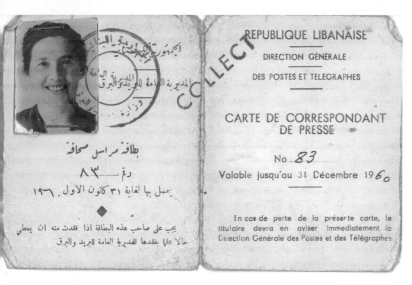

Top: Lebanese press pass 1960.

Above left: Telegram to Olga in Moscow with instructions from her editor.

Above right: Olga as seen on one of her TV appearances.

Below: Olga depicted by cartoonist Leslie Illingworth, celebrating her green fingers in her new home in Caterham.

Above: Olga in 1963 at Ladies Night *(l–r)* Frank, Beryl, Olga, Louis Mintz and Betty.

Below: Olga at Richard's wedding to Jane Guest in October 1968 *(l–r)* Alfred Wieser, the Mintz twins Bernard and Simon, Olga, Betty and Henry Mintz.

"HEWWO . . . Olga Fwanklin speaking . . ."

Above left: Olga for ever in a rush as drawn by Leslie Illingworth.

Above right: Emmwood's cartoon of Olga with her series on the rejuvenation drug H3. © *Associated Newspapers/Solo Syndication.*

Below: The four sisters together on Beryl's 70th birthday in 1979 *(l–r)* Olga, Beryl, Cora and Betty.

Another stunt – in the recording studio with Skiffle king Lonnie Donnegan.

The only problem is the lack of Crime here! Day after day I go off to the Magistrate's Court hoping for at least a decent smash-and-grab if not a decent murder. Instead the Charge Sheet looks quite indecently bare; same old stuff, Riding a bicycle without rear red lamp (the lamps get pinched every night) or urinating in sight of the Mitre or the Randolph hotels ... and who can blame them when there aren't any toilets for miles and the Council isn't keen to build any.

Try getting a headline for the Evening front page out of any of that. It means I'm getting no experience where it really counts. Our Crime Man was very apologetic to me about it. He said Oxford has always been a bad place for Crime. He said things would get better when the Assizes were on, but for the time being ... All I've had this month was one American Court martial which, hooray, earned me an extra ten bob through linage, as I was able to 'phone a different shorter version to one of the London morning papers.

Went to highly enjoyable Thanksgiving party with some really nice Yank officers from the Churchill which I had to write up for the paper. When I had to cover an inquest, or rather two, at the lunatic asylum at Littlemore, went with the Coroner in his car, a certain Mr. Harold Franklin. One inquest was on a man who hanged himself in the asylum lavatory with his pyjama cord. En route Mr. Franklin, very prim and spectacled and kindly, said to me, 'I expect this is the first time you've ever been to a place like this.'

'Yes indeed,' I replied demurely.

Suppose ... he could have asked that question of 99 females out of 100 and got a truthful reply at least.

Love, Og

October 1943
326 Banbury Road, Oxford

Dearest Beryl,

How are you and the baby? Do let me know. Oh, I am looking forward so much to seeing Lucille. I am glad her cold is better and even more glad she is so good. Hope you have strength to give Ricky a good beating when he is naughty.

Cora and Vivienne came over on Sunday. Cora did not look too well. She is calmer though and tells me she works hard at her Army canteen

work. I don't think she feels she has any talent for business and prefers
to leave a woman in charge of it and spend most of her time looking after
her Canadian and British officers. I think she is quite right. I understand
her need to keep working until she's so tired she can sleep at nights. Vivie
looked very pretty in a Fairisle beret and gloves, dark green jumper and
plaid skirt and plaid ribbons on her little plaits. She was as good as gold
all day and did not complain when we hiked her round the Colleges. We
did not go very far, however, as it was so bitterly cold. Cora tells me that
Betty is going to apply to the Accident Hospital; please tell what happens.

Had big row with the horrible Mr. Gibbs who has threatened to sack
me. He doesn't like my doing the 'lineage', that is phoning stories to
Agencies and newspapers when they are of 'national' interest. The reason
is that he likes to do these lineage jobs himself. The other reporters who
had all this same trouble with him long ago, gave up the ghost and do
not handle any lineage for anyone so as to avoid any friction. I hate
having to give in unless I absolutely must! Gibbs is doing his best to
catch me in any slackness, so I'm always 20 minutes early mornings and
don't go out at all to lunch. I complained it was against Union rules to
be on duty from 9-30am till 9-30pm ... and then an evening job as well,
writing it up & walking home about 10-30 p.m.; he said, 'It's not my
fault the buses don't run, I don't give a dam about the Union, and you'd
have to walk a good deal further if you were in the ATS!' There baint
no answer to that one, as they say in Cinderford, eh.

He also said, 'I know you come from London, but – I'm your boss
here, remember that.' Pocket-Hitler. The other reporters say why worry;
we had to give in to him long ago for the sake of peace; he treats us
all like schoolchildren but what can we do? We can't afford to get the
sack. Just ignore him.

Sorry I haven't any cheery news for you apart from my moans. Cora
says, and she's probably right, that my letters have got horrible, all
egotistical and whining.

What's all the Malvern news? If you haven't time to write, ask Betty
to do so and you dictate to her one evening; I know she won't mind.
Are you slimmer now? .....me, I'm getting fat as a pig.

I think the Easiest life is in the Army, particularly the American Army!
My Irish American Sergeant who has now got another stripe making him
Sergeant Firstclass told me that since being in Oxford (about 3 months)
he has saved £150! This ...apart from the fact that he has to pay 35/-
weekly for bed and breakfast and buy his own lunch and dinner. He says
all the boys are saving & putting their money in BANK DEPOSITS and

some of them hope to have enough money to start their own business after the war. What a war!...

Love, Og

October 1943
c/o Oxford Mail, Oxford

Dear B,

I was in London yesterday and saw Roslie and Rita. I found them splitting the home up in a great Divide. Rita has taken a tiny flat in Jermyn Street and is starting in business on her own as a Theatrical Agent.

Flat 6, Grove End Gardens was the Theatre yesterday, however, as per usual ... where the sisters were busy apportioning out the furniture & effects, who gets what and so on. Rita was bitter at being turfed out. But there are compensations. Both are still busy plodding steadily through the U. S. Army.

Please tell Betty I will send that 5 bob I owe her by next post; do you think she would like to sell me a couple of coupons?

Love to you and Frank and Ricky and Betty and Lucy-Lockett,
Og

October 1943
326 Banbury Road, Oxford

Dear B,

I presume you are too busy to write, but I wish you could manage a line. I am fine; it is a very good bike Betty sent me. Tell her I will refund the 5 bob carriage. It is a great help in getting about as the bus service is so impossible. Everyone cycles here, even the Yanks when they can't get a jeep. This is the loveliest town I ever was in and the work is so interesting. Had to cycle to Blenheim Palace on a story this week; the countryside all lush and golden. I thought I was in heaven. I never want to leave here, but I know I must. You see, owing to my pique over the row with Mr. Gibbs who objected to my earning a few bob doing lineage, I dashed off a few letters after jobs. So I've had a few offers and went up to London to see a few people, get advice, etc.

I went to Reuters of course and there saw Bob Petty of the Manchester Guardian ... he's the Editor who first advised me to take a reporting job. I told him that the Newcastle Evening Chronicle have offered me a senior reporting job at the minimum rate for Newcastle which is £7.2.6 or slightly more than that. Bob Petty's advice was .. Go to Newcastle! He says if I am comfortable at Oxford, all the more reason to go despite distance, loneliness, cold, etc. He says it is a much bigger paper and a live town and will mean much more Experience. He said: suppose the war is over soon, and all you have to show is the Oxford Mail, you won't stand a chance.

So I went along to see a man named MacLean who is London representative of the Newcastle paper and he offered me the job and gave me £1 for my expenses which just paid them nicely. He talked to me for nearly two hours ... all about Tyneside etc., and seemed pleasant enough except he was the kind who comes too close with his smelly pipe and presses your knee ... which I didn't much like.

So, chum? I'm all for taking risks as you know and would certainly like to be on a better paper instead of a local rag. Please advise. Guess a year in Tyneside won't kill me, but ...oh dear I do love it here; I've made so many friends. Up there in the frozen North; I never even knew anyone who went so far North; it's sort of off the map, a new, entirely new world. Still I've been lonely before and can handle it; it is the job that counts; so give me a push old girl, yes? Must stop now to rush out; am getting almost too fat to ride a bike...

Best love to you and all the family, Og.

November 1943
c/o Oxford Mail, Oxford

Dearest B,

Bumped into Neville Laski in the road; he asked me round to the house yesterday but of course I couldn't go. His wife said come today but I don't think I shall be able to make it.

Yesterday morning (Saturday) I had the County Police court until 12 noon, then the Mayor opened a Merchant Navy Exhibition, office duty all afternoon and a concert to write about at Exeter College in the evening at 8. The concert turned out to be the nicest University function yet. And thank God it was warm. Most evening jobs one sits in some icy hall & freezes. In the great raftered hall of Exeter college, I sat in front of one of those huge Elizabethan hearths where a fire blazed so huge it took two men to carry the one lump of coal on top of it and logs round that! There were a few table-lamps so that the dim light just revealed the colours of the Elizabethan portraits on the panelled walls.

The students sang madrigals (Elizabethan ones) round a big oak table while the others listened. A brilliant student played Beethoven's Sonata in E Major and a world-famous Dutch cellist gave Boellman's symphonic Variations. Tell Betty I hope she will be able to play like that one day! One old post-graduate in officer's uniform brought a beautiful blond wife; she had my shoes on.

This afternoon I have to go out to Headington to a Labour Party conference. Labour M.P. for Middlesbrough is speaking ...and who do you think the other speaker is? Prospective Labour candidate for Reading and it is Ian Mikardo (there can't be two of that name) who used to lecture to our student debating society in Brum.

On Friday I covered a Sir William Beveridge lecture to American and Canadian officers attending the course at Balliol and speaking on his 'American impressions'. The Americans all called him 'Sir Bill' and seemed to love him a lot. Afterwards I had supper with one of the American officers, Lieut. Leonard Paul of New York and then I had to go on to a Trade Union meeting in Morrell Hall which was ice cold and then back to the office on the old bike to do the two stories. Then I met the Lieutenant for a drink, but he got fresh like they all do.

The officers are worst. My landlady ticked me off for having a Sergeant (U.S. 1st-class) in my room so am in her bad books and get no second helping of bread pudding or bubble-and-squeak at lunchtime. It was most undignified I know, but I would never have asked anyone only she said I could do as I liked when I first came. There are no locks or keys to doors so we put a chair against it. It was the blasted British Army sergeant's wife in the room next door who spied on us and reported to the landlady ... so up she comes and marches straight in – oh golly!

When Cora came to see me at the weekend I told her about it and she threw up her hands in horror. So I told my Sergeant to get on his bike and come no more. He is a tall, dark very serious Roman Catholic, one of those spectacled introvert intellectuals. He has taken a hate against English landladies now; he said, 'They think it's enough for us to exist but not to live!' After that we do our 'courting' in a cemetery off the Woodstock Road, on a wet gravestone; it rains a lot here in late autumn. The Sergeant is divorced and thinks he ought to be analysed. I know you'll be horrified too, and amused with it, and will see I'm no better than Ros or Rit which is true, only they'd draw the line at gravestones I can tell you[…]

The Yanks are everywhere now, just like it is with you in Malvern and Evesham. They certainly outnumber the English in Oxford. What I like is they're good-tempered, happy but the people here all say 'so they should be on THEIR pay', which sounds a bit jealous but understandable I suppose.

I like learning about new kinds of people. It's easy to see why the Yanks, whether officers or rankers, are jolly and easy to get on with. Their conditions of life are not just tolerable but awfully good and comfortable. I go to a British Army camp HQ for an interview and it's stiff as hell and they can't get rid of you quick enough. Call on the Americans and whatever your queries or demands … it's 'come in, take a seat, and bring the lady a hot coffee or whatever'. You sort of warm towards that kind of easy goodwill and trustingness. Okay, so they haven't been tested yet, or tried in the Fire, so we'll have to wait and see.

One lesson I learned about visiting American army camps. Whatever you do, avoid the 'clergy'. The real topnotcher Officers are their Preachers-in-charge of the regiment. Boy … are they the sexy ones! On the whole most Yank servicemen don't get rough …unless you start acting a bit coy and come-on. In fact, I find they tend to be even a bit MORE respectful than the British …The grand exceptions are the U.S. army chaplains. Each has a separate office, with all the Comforts of home. Protestant, Catholic and Jewish, and the three usually go about together in proper mateystyle. It's nice to see the Denominations so cosy, but absolutely FATAL to go and visit anyone of these Passionate Three alone, on your owny-own. Never again.

At least the Protestant Chaplain finally, after long struggle, agreed to take 'no' for an answer. But the other two, especially the Rabbi who was a sturdy, thick-set chap looking more like a Kosher Butcher than a man of God. He wanted a weekend in Bournemouth if-you-please and, clearly, had never been refused before. Just couldn't believe it! They've all got this idea that Englishwomen are really sex-starved and hungry. He wasn't so much the butcher as the boxer too and when I finally made my getaway, slightly scared, I'd got good bruises all up each arm from his hand-grip stuff.

Anyway it's not the sort of stuff they want written up for the Oxford Mail. I got back to the office in good order in an army jeep, only slightly shaken. It was quite a scoop to get a whole set of interviews though inside their Churchill hospital. I sent a copy of the paper with my American story in it to Cole at Reuters and he wrote back full of congratulations. He has appointed me Reuters man for Oxford and I send anything I can ... as long as I can keep it dark from Mr. Gibbs.

I have still no fire in my room and the conversation of my fellow lodgers gets me down. I mean of course the Lancashire army sergeant and his wife. Cora laughed when I told her about them. She said, 'Don't tell me, I know! They KNOW everything.' The Sergeant has two stock phrases: 'Pretty!' and .... 'D'you want to make sum ink of it.' This passes for wit. They certainly made 'sumink' of my friendship with the American Sergeant and they're even greedier than I am when it comes to mealtimes; that is they're still eating a good halfhour after I've finished. Even So I've put on weight from all the bread pudding and stand 8½ stone in my bod .... so heaven only knows what I weigh with my clothes on. It won't do[...]

Had to push me bike to Headington as back tyre flat; must buy pump also lamps. Glad the cold is over despite the rain. Am still stockingless and corset-less. Mrs. Rogers (that's the British Army Sgt's wife in the room next door to mine) makes her own pithy comments at sight of my bare legs. 'Needs her ruddy head looking at.'

I don't feel cold here. They threaten me with frostbite and every kind of fearful skin disease. They annoy me ... always being so bloody 'right'. It just goes to show. Cora says all Lancashire people are like that, witness Aunt Ray and Uncle Joe Kennedy. Mother wasn't like that, was she? ... or p'raps it got rubbed off in Warwickshire.

I had supper with Ian Mikardo* at the Mitre Hotel, famous sort of place, and had a lot of drinks. He has had catarrh for which he is taking a course of 70 injections but he is very nice. He remembered you but couldn't place me at all. (Until I reminded him how I'd insisted on going on the platform at the Arts Society meeting and singing in German one night ... 'Hor die Nachtigalen Schlaagen' .... ('komm beglucke mich' and he'd called out a derisory 'ganz gut' which made everyone in the audience howl with laughter but it shut me up all right...) The political meeting was very successful; he is a very good Speaker.

There was a lot of excitement about Oswald Mosley** being released from prison under the 18B rule ..... Everyone made protests and shouted a lot. The hall was very cold but that hotted things up a bit. I did not get home until 1 a.m. But I was up at 7 a.m. and had my monthly egg. 'Pretty!' shouted the British Sgt. Rogers when he saw his.

That's all for now. Love to all, and do please write.
How are the kids? Og.

PS I've got an interview with Oswald Mosley and Cole wants me to wire 500 words to Reuters.

Ian Mikardo (1908–1993) was the son of Jewish refugees and a leading Labour politician.
**Oswald Mosley (1896–1980) was the founder of the British Union of Fascists and was interned for a period during the Second World War.*

6

The Frozen North

December 1943
c/o Oxford Mail, Oxford

Dearest Beryl,

Am spending this weekend in London. I plan to spend Christmas with you, but should like to know what you think about that? Is there anywhere I can sleep or can you have me put up at the pub?

I aim to agitate to let the Oxford Mail let me go at Christmas and not go back, which will give me a few days before going to Newcastle on the 1st January which is a Saturday, to start work on the 3rd the Monday. Will you let me know if you can have me?

I am having a board and easel made for Richard for Xmas and it will be a nice one so I hope you haven't already bought him one... and lots of coloured chalks so he can be kept busy and quiet, let's hope...

Had a very nice note from Henry Rose giving me several introductions to people he knows in Newcastle. He says he likes the place and knows a lot of people there and hopes to come over.

Am looking forward very much to seeing Lucille. I feel pretty badly about not having yet sent Bettina the 5 bob I owe her, but have decided to look in at Harrods and see if I can pick her a nice collar or something instead. I want to see a few people in London as it may be a very very long time before I can go south again. Do you know what Cora's plans are for Christmas?

I hope you are all well and keeping free of flu. I have a little cough, nothing much though and as fat as ever. You won't recognise my shape-less rotundity. My landlady Miss Groves had a chicken the other day but the Rogers lodgers ate it all up. Not even a wishbone left; twas to show I am not yet forgiven for outrageousness and now there's only about a fortnight left so it is too late to try and prove anything ... I only hope that Miss Morley at Canfield Gardens never gets to hear about it . . . . .

I'm sure looking forward to being with you again so hope you can have me. I also hope you've not been feeding chicken soup to half the American army at Malvern camp. If you are likely to be decamping back to Birmingham by Christmas, let me know, in which case I hope to see you there.

Best love to you and Frank and Betty and Rick and Luce, Og.

PS. Don't worry about those London air-raids; they were very noisy but that's about all.

1944

January 1944,
Regent Hotel,
Osborne Road, Jesmond Dene
Newcastle-upon-Tyne

Dear B,

Tyneside: Sunday,

Typing in bed, fully dressed with overcoat buttoned to the chin & feet on hot-water bottle because smoking-room entirely full and coal-fire there, which is the only one lit in this Hotel, is ringed in by tight circle of tight-lipped people who are not going to let anyone inside ... let alone pushful typists with noisy machine.

It is said that if women do not have children, they take to dogs. By the same reasoning therefore if they cannot have live dogs they will have stuffed ones.

Clearly, hotel life does not cater for these little eccentricities, though I believe there is a lonely two-year old child incarcerated in one of the rooms of one of the houses of this vast hotel (four large old houses are turned into one building by virtue of a long tunnel or corridor which connects them). This child is rarely seen, never heard and has within living knowledge only on rarest occasions been out of doors. It is said to be a Scandal.... and the child is without any animation whatsoever. There is even a scruffy little pekinese dog belonging to the four elderly sisters who own the hotel who cannot hear. There is also one brother

Cecil who cannot and one tall, thin sister who can. But there... the facilities for normal expression of human affection end.

I suppose therefore I ought not to have been so surprised when I came upon the Stuffed Dogs and other Animals in one woman's room. She invited me to visit her after our meagre dinner one night; she was friendly, rather attractive. I went in and there... the stuffed dogs lay or crouched on her bed so lifelike and so enormous and shaggy that it gave me quite a turn when I first saw them. It was quite a small bedroom like most others in this hotel ... but this big-hearted woman had room on her bed for more than just stuffed dogs and a little husband. Seated on the pillow as though conducting a doggy class, the head boy as it were was an enormous hairy ape with jointed shaggy arms which could be made to clutch the lady round the neck when she raised him to sit on her shoulder, like the raven of Barnaby Rudge. Friends of mine who are very fond of Psychology, maintain that the combination of the shaggy ape and the little grey-haired husband form a very proper picture of subconscious frustration.

It was an interesting evening and easily made up for the intense cold, very small meals indeed and having to go up in the darkness to my own room on the third floor which is so tiny that I have to enter sideways in order to insinuate myself through the doorway between the bed and the wardrobe.

This is an exciting town, full of sailors and merchant seamen from all over the world. It is a very masculine society. Hardly any women to be seen, except a few in ATS uniform. The talk is like something out of a W.W. Jacobs story but so many Scandinavians that sometimes it is pure Joseph Conrad. All this against the background of the weird sisters and their deaf brother who are of course straight out of Hitchcock!

When I started work at the Newcastle Journal (the daily paper) and the Newcastle Evening Chronicle (the evening one .. we work for both), I found the office in Westgate Street even more old-fashioned and charming than the Oxford Mail. You go upstairs to a little wicket-gate where an old, old man surveys you with some excitement. New faces are not often seen ...even in wartime. He hobbles away to fetch Authority. I am shown into small office by small, whitehaired Geordie with charming smile ... to meet my new boss, Mr. Arthur Wilson.

More tomorrow, goodnight luv, Og

January 1944
St Margaret's Hotel
Osborne Road
Jesmond Dene, Newcastle-upon-Tyne

Dear B,

Thank you for your letter and thanks to Cora too for hers; both much appreciated. I do miss the children and was awfully glad you gave me news of them. Please do not fail to include all latest sayings in all letters which I hope will be long & newsy.

I feel that in a world where a woman can send your grim and gloomy brother-in-law Mr. Murray a book called 'Great Lovers thru' the Ages', anything can happen.* I am prepared.

Cork, you say in your letter that you bar Married Men ... but I believe Mr. Taylor whose wife so-utterly-fails-to-understand him, is still included in your life. There is some discrepancy here?

I liked very much your story of the greeting exchanged between Ricky and Viv; also Richard's hope that his sister will one day be cured of widdling. I do not think Richard a problem child at all; he is a charming little boy – away from his overfond Papa.

I am writing this in the sewing-room which has been put at my disposal as it has a gasfire and the snores of the guests in the lounge must not be interfered with. My hands are icy. However, I had an egg for breakfast which was a great thrill.

It is very cold today. I do not think it is any colder than in the South; but it is a very dry cold. I find I have to wear two woolly jumpers, with costume jacket and coat and scarf, to be comfortable, but am still barelegged, having no stockings and no hope of acquiring any.

The town is full to bursting with naval officers and ratings, and I cannot keep my room for more than a few days. When I arrived at the Newcastle Evening Chronicle, my boss Mr. Wilson asked if I had anywhere to live and when I said no, as this Hotel would be throwing me out this week for some resident Ministry civil servant, he sent me straight out to try and locate a permanent room. All I got was the promise of temporary accommodation at another hotel across the same road while some Naval Captain was away on the high seas.

Had nasty little interview with the Ministry of Labour where highly efficient and officious women told me I had infringed something or other by not letting them know I was coming to Newcastle. One said something darkly about not letting me keep the job. I kept very calm and referred them to Moorgate Labour Exchange where I registered and where my records will be. They said I was all highly irregular. I could have shown them my doctor's certificate granting me exemption from Army call-up but I did not feel so inclined and I left it to them to settle how they like. Actually the firm are to blame for not informing the Labour Exchange about me, i.e. that I had transferred from the Western Press (Oxford Mail) to the employ of Lord Kemsley who owns the former Allied Newspaper group which includes Newcastle.

If there was an absence of crime in Oxford, here it is plentiful. Am getting slowly into the police court work; it is ten times more difficult than in Oxford. There is no charge sheet to get names & addresses and the Tyneside accent is still beyond me. Here, we have Court every day, morning AND afternoon, sometimes 3 Courts a day: matrimonial, juvenile, county court, civil actions and the Assizes start soon. There are at least four top feature reporters and four or five first class Court reporters as well as me, but I think the competition is good for me. There are also masses of Juniors. Court cases are endless; it is a wicked town[…]

Some of the people are quite barbaric. One poor old man was brought into Court on Friday with his eye and head all bandaged. His 24-year-old married daughter, an extremely pretty little woman, had lost her temper in an argument over an old overcoat and hit him on the head with a torch six times. He had to be taken to hospital. The husband, a Cook in the Royal Navy, assisted her by kicking the old man in the eye.

There are endless girls, some of them beautiful, who have deteriorated since their husbands left them to go to sea. They get brought in for stealing and are found to have dissolved into varying stages of prostitution. Many have married Danes or Norwegians. There is no formality about the Court and victims and magistrates bellow at each other. There is no mincing of words and one very pretty blonde charged with stealing was loudly told by the magistrate to change her ways before she picked up some disease she wouldn't get rid of in a hurry. They are mostly pathetic because though they are often earning good wages, they cannot get along without a man or friends to look after them and they simply deteriorate. The Courts act, to some degree, as a deterrent on my own wildness. These girls obviously never had any sisters.

Norwegians and Danes are held here in the same disfavour as the Yanks are in the south. This is a hard town for girls, much more dangerous I should think than London. Half the people are semi-barbaric and the other half dangerously narrow and presbyterian. Friday I had a whole spate of child-neglect cases which were quite horrific. One case of a 21-year-old mother of three children alleged that the girl had gone crazy about coloured men, Indian pedlars and had left her children to be with them. The magistrate banged his fist on the Bench and forcibly shouted, 'We want all the evidence in this case.' Typical of crude Northumbrian humour is the story about the girl-shipyard-worker who was doing her job with her left breast hanging out. 'You can't go about like that woman,' shouted the foreman. 'It's those bloody riveters,' said the woman, 'they never put anything back when they've finished with it.'

Tuesday is my day off and I might go to Whitley Bay and inspect the hotels there. Though this place is wickedly expensive, I haven't spent much outside of it. A Norwegian sailor took me twice to the pictures (he had quantities of real milk chocolate he had got from America!) and other men from this hotel have taken me out for drinks. I don't like to miss my dinner if I can help it because of the expense....

Colleague Dorothy Whitfield is a great sport but she is always nagging me to come out on a binge with her and Mary Selborne who lives at the Embassy and works up here for the News Chronicle. So far I have gotten out of it because I am not such a very keen drinker and I am too mean to want to pay for my own drinks. Naturally if you are all boys & girls together, you each pay for a round. I am now going out with a policeman, which is quite a novelty, and seems a bit safer than the Norwegian. He is a C.I.D. man I met through the theft of my typewriter ... but he is so wild and reckless in his habits I don't know how he comes to be 'on the strength' at all. He is taking me down to the docks to see the night-life in the waterfront cafes and the Danish Seamen's hotel. He does not carry a gun but fortunately he is a very large policeman.

Love, Og

* *Beryl's brother-in-law Louis Jaffa was known as Mr. Murray; family history has it that he was married for two weeks but then returned to live with his mother for the rest of his life.*

February 1944
c/o Newcastle Evening Chronicle
Westgate Street, Newcastle-upon-Tyne

Dear Beryl,

When our News Editor Arthur Wilson gets his teeth into a thing, he never lets go. He comes from Sheffield. When I ask our Industrial Correspondent George Thompson what that's got to do with it, he says all Sheffield people are like that. George says Mr. Wilson doesn't really trust anyone who doesn't come from Sheffield.

This morning he comes in and says there's a Greek prince in town and I've got to go and find him. 'Well, don't just sit there, Girl,' he says, 'I want that Prince and I want him in here 4pm sharp, not a minute later.'

So of course I shuffle off to look for Gotha ... that's the book they taught me at Reuters you use like it was the Bible. If people aren't in Gotha, then you really needn't bother; it's like Debrett's, only for Royals, real ones. And there's no guarantee (they taught me that much on the subs desk in Fleet Street) that it's a real one just because he calls himself Prince Philip of Greece.

Would you believe it? They've got no Gotha here in Newcastle. And while I'm still going on about it ... and all my pals Dorothy and Steve and George and a marvellous girl named Eve who used to be a reporter at Whitley Bay are fascinated to hear ... the door opens and back comes Mr. Wilson, as usual with his little white haired Assistant (he's the Copy Taster) at his heels.

'Well lass,' he says, 'are you still here? I thought I put you on to a Greek prince.' When I say I'm on to it but first I've got to find out how to find him. I get the same old speech I get from him day after day. 'I've told you lass. Ring the fire-station first, then the police hospitals next to see if anything came in during the night. After that get the 'phone book and ring every hotel and lodging-house in Newcastle...'

It took until nearly teatime, and I didn't even get out to lunch – for the usual dish of mashed Swedes in gravy in Westgate Street – and I got fed up with hearing, 'No Hinny, we got no Prince here.' Then, right at the end nearly, I found the right one. Which was a bit odd; it was the Jesmond Hotel, Osborne Road about three doors away from our own Regent Hotel with all those beetles.

I dash in to tell Mr. Wilson and the Copy Taster, sitting there having

their tea and biscuits and me not even any lunch. 'Right ... off you go!'
he says with a wink to the Copy Taster. I have this feeling he's really
having me on. After all, you don't just burst in on some chap just because
he's a Prince and demand an interview. Prince Philip – that's his name
– Prince Philip of Greece might just possibly be having his tea too; that
is if they serve it in the Jesmond lounge because the Four Sisters certainly
refuse to serve it in the Regent Hotel one until 10 pm at night.

He wouldn't even give me time to powder my nose; so I just clapped
on my old brown leather coat – only garment I have left as reminder
of my old married life ... how many years ago, seven it seems more
like seventeen ... and run for one of those big yellow trolley-buses, one
of the few comforts of this roughneck town, for the five-minute journey
to Osborne Road, Jesmond Dene. I can see the Regent Hotel as I leap
from the trolley, but I look like being too late for dinner tonight. If
you're not on the dot of 7, someone else gets it. Hope it'll be one of
the maids gets it tonight.

It's quite a nice place, the Jesmond, nothing fancy, but nicer than the
Regent with a proper Reception Desk and a respectable lady to answer
questions. What's more, she speaks straightforward English and seems
uncommonly calm about having a live Prince as resident. The relief! She
didn't even flinch when I said my usual speech, i.e. 'I'm from the Evening
Chronicle and I've come for an interview.'

'Oh yes,' she says, almost without interest, though she could be
pretending. She's clearly one of those English types you hardly ever find
in Newcastle who give nothing away and keep their own council. The
Geordies have a way of buttonholing you and telling their life histories.
I knew at least I could get some sense out of her so I took the plunge.

'Is he a real Prince or what? ....'

'Certainly, I can show you his name where His Royal Highness signed
the Visitor's book.' And she shows me and there it is, and Mr. Wilson
is not having me on, and I've got to see this darn thing through ... but
oh for some lovely dinner. I notice she refers to him as 'Royal Highness'
which sounds a bit odd.

She showed me into the Residents Lounge and it looks all right, a lot
better than the Regent which has hardly any armchairs. It even has a
divan, a lamp or two and the odd cushion. Yes, it's better than the Regent;
it's the sort of place where you can get morning tea if you order in
advance, which they'd die rather than give you at the Regent, even if
you let them have your whole tea ration to do it with.

The point is When is the Prince coming in for his dinner? It is now

194

about 5-15 pm. The lady receptionist cannot help me there. He comes in 'at all hours'. He might come in this very moment while we're speaking and he might not come in till very late. My heart sinks. The only place where I'll get a single crumb to eat tonight is the only place that's open which is an Army canteen, only a sort of tin shed really serving mugs of tea and a few packets of what are called 'cheese biscuits.' Impossible to ring here in the Jesmond Hotel for something. It might cost the earth. Besides hotels nowadays even those fit for Princes to live in, and especially those on Tyneside, didn't serve snacks to down-at-heel reporters. Hotels just didn't have the rations to feed any casuals.

One hour goes slowly by; then another. I sort of doze. I keep my leather coat on because at least it's respectable-looking but I'm a bit shabby underneath. It's warm enough to sleep here, although there's no fire to be seen. I sleep.

Hours, it seems, later the door opens very suddenly and there he is; I struggle to my feet. I get dizzy looking at him. His beauty is so dazzling. People don't look like this, surely, in real life? For once I'm at a loss for words, just when I need them most. He looks almost exactly like the late Duke of Kent, only far more handsome. I remember seeing the late Duke quite close, on his honeymoon, when he and Princess Marina drove in a big Daimler car up the Hagley Road towards Staffordshire right after their marriage. This Prince Philip is stunning, with hair like gold coin only paler, a sort of ash-gold, eyes of deep blue almost violet in the electric light of the Jesmond Hotel lounge, tall, fine-featured, really a shockingly beautiful figure in naval uniform. It takes what feels like minutes getting my breath back. I think it's the surprise. Mr. Wilson said a Greek Prince and I thought, well a darkie perhaps, with a nose arched like his own and perhaps a Cypriot curl to the hair. I manage to stutter out my set speech:

'I'm from the Evening Chronicle.'

Could have bitten my tongue – Why hadn't I the dam sense to mention it was The Viscount Kemsley's own newspaper organ I was referring to. After all I'm nothing, hatless, bare-legged, crumpled. But surely the Prince would think twice before turning down the Viscount?

'Oh dear!' he said, which wasn't much but I was going to need every single word in clear Gregg shorthand outline to satisfy Mr. Wilson.

If only I'd thought of some good questions to pop instead of dithering in a daze. Where you from, Mate, was my usual style. Caught off guard, I was scared. What saved me was ... I was even more scared of going back to Mr. Wilson empty-handed.

'My News Editor heard' … I stuttered at last … 'and sent me … hoping for an interview.' I thought a flicker of relief showed on the aristocratic features. 'Ah,' he said. Not a Big Talker this one. But I felt it was coming, so I waited.

It was quite a speech. 'The thing is,' he said (with a restrained sort of smile) 'I should love to give you an interview but I'm not allowed. I'm a Serving-officer in the Royal Navy … well the Admiralty would never give permission, I'm so sorry.' He looked smiling and happier now he'd got that settled. I felt better too. That settled things nicely. Not even the great Arthur Wilson, Sheffield-born and Sheffield-trained could complain now. Then a terrible thought struck. Suppose … God forbid … but just suppose the Competition came. Suppose the unknown chap down at the Wallsend dockyard who'd given Mr. Wilson's informant the tip-off about a Prince messing about at the Docks … went and sold the same tip-off to the competition, the local rep of the Daily Express for instance. The mere thought put guts into me.

'Then you wouldn't?' I said, 'you wouldn't, would you? … to my .. any of my colleagues, … anyone … the Express, say?'

I felt some wetness around the eyes. It'd been a tiring day. Any minute I'd be turning on the tap.

It seemed to work wonders though. The Prince was smiling, a real grin this time. 'Absolutely not,' he said, 'you may take my word for it.'

I felt things were going swimmingly now. 'So,' I rattled on, 'I can tell my paper that if the Admiralty gave permission, you'd have been only too happy to grant us an interview and answer questions?'

'Yes,' said the Prince, 'that's the position.' He gave me his broadest smile yet. 'I'm absolutely confident the Admiralty would never permit.' He added: 'We're not even allowed to tell anyone where we are.'

He looked cheerful now and quite friendly. I felt more cheerful too. 'I am grateful,' I said fervently. He thanked me for coming … ha ha .. turned smartly and withdrew. I flopped on to the divan for a moment or two … seeing myself in the office tomorrow telling Eve and Pauline and George and Mack … this gorgeous creature, the ash-gold hair, the eyes, nose, oh boy!

It was only on the way back by trolley to the office to report to the Night News Editor and the powerful but alarming Chief Subeditor Mr. Percy Edwards, sitting there waiting for my red-hot news story … it suddenly struck me I still didn't know what a Prince of Greece was doing in the Osborne road that night, and hadn't thought even to try to ask.

I left a message for Mr. Wilson who'd long gone home for his tea. 'Only if the Admiralty give permission,' I wrote. They wouldn't, would they? Well, that was only the beginning. I'll give you the next instalment, dear Bella, in my next epistle.

Love, Og

February 1944
c/o Newcastle Evening Chronicle
Westgate Street, Newcastle-upon-Tyne

Dear B,

No letters from any of you. I hope all is well. Perhaps I shall be dashing into the office at 9 tomorrow only to have a letter from young Bettina thrust into my hand. Who knows?

I have still not found a hotel or other accommodation and continue to hang on in the Regent until I am turned out.

The other two young maids aged 16 and 14 are leaving next week, which leaves only the four fat sisters and the tall thin one.

The little maid told me that they would have stayed if they had been given proper sleeping accommodation. The sisters have old-fashioned ideas. The girls sleep in the basement where the beetles are so thick that an anti-beetle powder has to be sprayed over the ground; they do not get proper food, chiefly only vegetables (which in Newcastle this time of year means nearly always just SWEDES because there are practically no potatoes) .... unless a guest fails to turn up for dinner and then it goes to one of the maids.

The three young girls work from 6-30 a.m. until 10 p.m. and almost never go out. One dropped a boiled egg on the floor while carrying it to a table at breakfast this morning. The tall thin sister was so cross.

The Embassy Hotel – the only comfortable one apart from the Station one – still has no vacancies though I am supposed to be No.1 on their waiting-list, according to Henry's friend Mr. Schaffer. All the other hotels in town are full and have waiting-lists. A sudden invasion of American troops into Newcastle does not help matters.

Henry Rose's friend Mr. Schaffer took me to a show at the Theatre Royal. It was an all-American show. I thought it very poor. Sitting in the front row, even when the music is Cole Porter's, is rather deafening and you can see all too plainly that the Americans are plain and old and the girls have fixed artificial smiles and bookings in the States must have been small-town and few.

This hotel has just informed me that if I am not gone by Saturday I have to go on daily terms of 10/6d per day! Two more people have notice to go. I have not been able to find a vacancy anywhere and even if I could get a room, no one is willing even to do breakfasts.

I have a whole circle of admirers here now, including two elderly gentlemen in their seventies. When I had a cold last week, one gave me aspirins, another gave whiskey and another fetched a hot bottle. We are to have a gin party on Sunday as the RAF officer whom we all like is going.

The two old chaps – my Old Faithfuls who dote on me – are going to take me to Jane Eyre tonight if we can get in.

Love, Og

PS. oh dear – Mr. Wilson just came in, triumphant, so I knew it was trouble, touting a great, long piece of news-tape. He starts tearing off an enormous sheet of it and shoves it in front of me. It's a lengthy message from the Admiralty running to about eleven paragraphs. 'Here,' he says, 'you can take this with you to show Prince Philip. I told you the Admiralty'd not say 'no' to me.'

7

The People You Meet on the River Tyne

1944
Regent Hotel,
Osborne Road, Jesmond Dene
Newcastle-upon-Tyne

Dears Beryl and Cora,

Richard and Vivienne clasping hands so sweetly lighten my darkness in 'my lonely little room' which is ugly and squalid beyond words. The hard bed, the washstand with its pink china, wardrobe and dressing-table entirely fill the room. I can just pass from door to window if I edge sideways carefully, with a fearful eye to the pink china.

Rick and Viv in their loveliness are an incongruous sight in such a setting. I am ordered to make my own bed and see to my room myself. Thank you sincerely for the lovely photograph and attractive frame which I shall treasure.

The comfort of St Margaret's Hotel, where I stayed about a fortnight, has demoralised me and I feel the change of moving over the road sharply. I learn the 'owners' of this hotel are trying to sell the place which means some 45 people will be on the streets and send hotel prices soaring a bit further still.

Also I do not so far get asked out any more at this hotel; the people are one grade of society lower and probably cannot afford it. There are several young men of the insurance agent type who ignore me completely so far to my chagrin. There are several Jews; one night-black is in films.

There is a pretty blonde at my table, wife of a naval officer who picks up other officers and is out most nights. She wears a different costume each day and admits to having extra coupons. She showed me her room, which is like mine and also without any fire but we had to push our way inside as the doorway and room itself is entirely blocked with clothes.

Two fur coats hung on the door. She said this is only half 'her stuff' as most of it is at the Cleaners.

Also at the table is a charming woman teacher Froebel-trained, and student of child psychology who tells me that Richard only needs occupation and encouraging to do some work with his hands. But she says that such children, who are always highly intelligent, will always behave badly at home once they have been spoilt even when they start to improve at school. She says, however, that 'good' children are rarely intelligent.

Then there is Dr. Gladden, middle-aged man, who, all alone, studied for a Science degree at the age of 20 when he could barely read or write. He has, however, had no time for social graces and reads a book on electoral reform throughout meals. The food is tolerable. Compensations are I can get a cup of tea for 3d at 9pm and bath water is always extremely hot at any time of night or day.

This must necessarily be a short dull letter as my typewriter is at the shop being repaired and will cost me £2/2/0. Next week we expect to be busy with the Newcastle Public Enquiry. Dear Be, the jam arrived with thick mould on top. I will see if it can be scraped off.

Had to cover meeting of Licensed Victuallers at County Hotel today. They started drinking before they began the meeting. Also went to interview the Canadian press delegation but they wouldn't talk; they're doing a 3-weeks tour of Britain but now they are bored and don't want to see any more. At Berwick the lord mayor turned out to greet them complete with civic party and they just didn't turn up.

Love Og

February 1944
Regent Hotel,
Osborne Road, Jesmond Dene
Newcastle-upon-Tyne

Dear B

Snow fell thickly in the night. My room is so cold I have been driven to typing this in the smoking-room but I don't know how long it will be before people will come in and object. Those present, an army captain, a man who mends radios and has nightmares in the room next to mine and a Mrs. Alec Wolf darning the socks of her National-Fire-Service

husband who is still in bed and a good-tempered old man named Dobson
... have not objected.

Friday night I was invited to Jacobsons again and am also asked to
tea to the Rothfields over the road but I expect I shall stay in and go
to bed for a nap. Bertha Rothfield is headmistress of a Jewish approved
school at St Albans near London and is about my own age. She phoned
me some weeks ago when I was at St Margaret's and introduced herself
as a friend of Natey Zamet. She is very musical whereby I believe they
met. The mother and father were an extremely pleasant old couple. He,
wearing Skull-cap, toasting the shabbos out in good Tyneside language,
tickled me.

He is a watchmaker, they have a cosy little house and there was
excellent tea of savoury sandwiches, jam tarts and chocolate biscuits
followed by supper of gefillte fish and coffee. Bertha was a teacher in
a village school until recently and the parents are somewhat aggrieved
that their Bertha, nice but plain, should give up a good home for what
they call a 'wardress' job.

We gossiped until midnight, had cocoa, then I dug my way through
the snow to the hotel.

The food here is not half bad; it is only the place itself which is not
very comfortable. Breakfasts particularly are excellent with kipper (done
I regret in water), grilled herring and so on. The portions business is
annoying; ladies' portions and gents' portions are two very different things;
then there are the 2½-guinea-payers and the 3½-guinea payers. If, like me,
you are a 2½-guinea 'lady', you don't get a chance to fill up very often.
Still ... they got me 3 oranges this week and I had a boiled egg this
morning; I can't grumble.

If you'll forgive me keeping on about food, we had some good wallop
at Ruth's on Friday, starting with gin which bowled me right over as I'd
had nothing to eat all day, then roast chicken with tiny roast grouse, veg
& gravy, followed by apple charlotte topped with meringue and marron
glaces and touched with marron glace juice. Oh boy!

Ruth is going away again for another wedding. Her husband and the
Schaffer man are taking me to the theatre on Saturday and Ruth says
behave yourself as all the elite of Newcastle will be looking on. They
are very kind but damnably possessive which frightens me. The idea to
get me to come today was to spend the rest of the day with Nanny
who is lonely while they go to Bridge. They tire me too rather as the
conversation must necessarily be kept as near as possible down to Ruth's
level. The Rothfields were very intelligent.

201

Everyone in Newcastle knows everyone else[...]

The infants teacher woman Jo Parker who sits at my table for meals, claims to be Dr. Sammy Caller's 'shiksah'.

She invited me into her very attractive room (she has been here 5 years and pays £2.12) and confided in me. Not because she is the confiding sort, on the contrary; but I think as a kind of Warning in case I should meet him, to layoff. Sammy Caller is the bachelor doctor brother 'helluva good sport' recommended in Henry Rose's letter to me if you remember. Maliciously I thought, she described how she is hated by all the girls in Tyneside because he is the 'only eligible bachelor'. Several Jewish doctors who stay at the Embassy all 'go with shiksahs' she said. But petulantly she told me she suffered from the converse of anti-semitism. She is the victim, she said, of the Jews' own anti-racial feeling.

Sammy refuses definitely 'to marry her because she is not Jewish'; though she is prepared, she alleges, to become a good Jewish housewife and even to try & learn how to cook if he will marry her. Big of her I thought. The affair is now nearly eight years old. She is a catholic, turned out of her home because she has given up Catholicism. Her mother, who will have nothing to do with her, is also a teacher and ardently Catholic. She says she does not come into the smokeroom here or fraternise with the people because they often whisper to her 'when will you give up your jew?' They think he is spoiling her chances. Equally she knows she is spoiling his; he is 40 now, but she told me grimly she will not leave Newcastle & give all the girls the satisfaction of thinking her defeated. Shades of Fannie Hurst, or worse.

Then there is Dr. Sidney Wolf, brother-in-law of the woman here, sitting with her darning. I also met him in Court. He handles all the N.S.P.C.C. cases. He says he will be my panel doctor if I like, but it is rather far to go. Both Wolves are nice little chaps who married awful women for money.

Old man Rothfield told me there is a comic little jewish community in Gateshead where he comes from ... just across the river by the little yellow tram ... Some have beards down to their waists; the women quite young wear wigs.

I saw something of the dreary rotting shipyard towns this week. I was sent out to Hebburn and Jarrow because a 13-year-old schoolboy had been so severely caned by his Headmaster at Jarrow secondary school that his hand swelled up and the mother was exceeding wroth. I got the mother's story and saw the boy but though I traipsed from Hebburn to

Jarrow, could get no corroboration from any official person that the matter was being taken up.

The suburban part of Hebburn, which is one vast shipyard, has all streets named after poets. I don't know why. Perhaps the streets are named Shakespeare Avenue, Wordsworth Avenue and so on out of the canny Geordies' sense of humour. Endless streets of an uncommon ugliness lie between the docks, places where Wordsworth would have hated to wander lonely-as-a-cloud.

I stood on the rain-swept icy corner outside a Jarrow public house waiting for a bus and wondered how people got the courage to live in such towns forever. I felt they ought to be paid a special bonus just for living there.

Yet the people as they poured out of the shipyards looked lively and spirited enough; wild shouting children and cheerful workmen.

I got back to the hotel late, sat watching gent eating gents' portion of swish Fried Cod. I got cold Pork. For my part little Jimmy Ewing could have had 20 strokes instead of 12. He played truant for a fortnight anyway[...]

Monday was an even colder day and I got sent to Consett in County Durham. This is the coldest mining village in the country.

I had to wait until 7pm to get my man, Christopher Bell the besom-maker, and I was frozen nearly stiff.

Christopher Bell kneels out on the moors in all weathers picking heather; sometimes he has to shovel the snow from the heather before he can kneel down with his sickle to cut it. Mostly he kneels on bog-wet heaths or in the knife-sharp frosts so that his wife has to cut the stiff frozen trousers from his legs when he gets home.

Again I got back to Newcastle too late for dinner. However, my expenses came to 14/- this week.

A colleague and I tried petitioning the canteen for better meals but we got almost threatened with the sack for causing alarm & despondency among the canteen-helps. Mr. Berry was furious. We only offered to spend our free afternoon showing them how to cook and suggested the introduction of some fresh vegetables occasionally.

Mr. Ewart Berry is said to be married to one of the sisters of the famous Berry brothers, Lord Kemsley, Lord Camrose, etc., but he is actually not a real one. He simply took the wife's surname. He is the Big Boss up here, proprietor of our newspaper group as representative of the Viscount and Lady Kemsley. However, he does not eat in the canteen, at least as far as I can tell.

My colleague Dorothy Whitfield, the drinking-smoking-swearing woman, played a dirty trick on me this week. I fear she may have become rather jealous because I am given Specials to do as well as Courts. She walked in and told the Editor that I had promised a man at the police court to keep a story out of the paper. It was a downright lie. I had told her in course of conversation that I had been approached by the Probation Officer about a young kid of 17 who was charged with wearing an Officer's uniform and he asked whether it would be possible to suppress it. Naturally I promised nothing; it's more than a reporter's job is worth. Nearly every week someone comes sidling up to the press bench: 'can I pay a Shilling to keep it out of the paper?' The Editor yelled at me. He said ... next thing they'll be offering you money! No one in the office can understand what made her do such a thing to a colleague. I tackled the editor later in the day (he was so enraged he wouldn't let me speak on the first occasion) and protested that there was not a word of truth in her story.

In the office each one is surrounded with enemies like that. We watch each other treacherously. But I cannot imagine myself doing a thing like Dorothy did. In the Regent Hotel here my talkativeness is already a byeword I'm afraid. Also the intimate friendships I so soon establish with elders of the Male Sex. The whiter the hair, the more doddering the tread, the longer the whisker, the more pliable they are in my dominating hand. They are inclined to get overstimulated by my racy talk from time to time and have to be soothed. Sometimes there is gossip of the unkinder sort whereto I turn blind eye and deaf ear. Jo Parker and her girl friend Mrs. Basham tremble at every covert whisper ... but then Jo Parker has 60 children in her care, Mrs. Basham represents Barnardos ... but nothing better, fortunately is expected from me representing the vulgar penny press ... and when my common laugh rings out ... the Misses Lane and the Misses Armstrong and one brother Cecil who run the hotel from the top 'family' table are all stone deaf bar one Lane sister ... so the tall thin one who hears, nudges the four short fat ones who do not and is heard to say: 'Don't look dear.'

Love, Ogg

March 1944
c/o Newcastle Evening Chronicle
Westgate Street, Newcastle-upon-Tyne

Dear B,

I'm getting a persecution complex. Each morning Mr. Wilson is waiting for me, clutching that long piece of tape like a giant toilet roll; I think he's scared to part with it ... being so proud of his victory over Admiralty censorship, you see ... 'Has tha' been to the Prince today, lass?'

And God help theee, if tha' hasn't. The other reporters & feature writers are tickled pink that I'm stuck with Prince Philip of Greece and they're NOT. If I only go to the canteen (you'll not believe this, Bella, you never will ... only I saw it with these poor old eyes; in this canteen they serve Fried Fish WITH GRAVY. Yes, you heard. Gravy!) someone comes, 'Mr. Wilson wants you.' He's just checking, he says, to see if there's any news from me on THAT Prince. Prince Philip has been away, probably on his Destroyer that's getting a re-fit.

So every day I go in to his hotel to check, 'Is he back yet?' and thank my lucky stars he's not as I don't relish showing him that long poem from the Admiralty. It's got 8 verses to it, half of them in naval lingo ... naming at least 8 Questions I'm not allowed to put. I dread having to show him. It doesn't seem to occur to Arthur Wilson that if I hang around the Jesmond Hotel much longer in pretty sordid Osborne Road, I may get asked to Move Along There....

I was to have covered a Conscientious Objector's Tribunal today but the Judge is ill and it is postponed. I have to open an Art Exhibition instead.

Talking about the Osborne Road again ... it's a proper haunt for crooks as well as princes. It has just now the only vacant room in Newcastle, No.24 .. or did have ... I expect it's taken already. The man who occupied it was in Court on Monday and went back to prison; that's how I know his room's vacant. He escaped from gaol and in his room they found a large quantity of jewellery, an officer's uniform and ration books from all over the country.

No lack of crime in Newcastle! Even the Chief Constable is up on a charge. For stealing a Fire Engine. The scandal has turned into a big national story, with other revelations of banquets and blankets and burned cheese with other goings-on ... a lot of it sited in our now famous Osborne Road, Jesmond Dene. Half the staff are busy each day reporting the Charges, etc., at the Newcastle Enquiry...

At last I found the Prince at home in the Jesmond Hotel. He studied the Admiralty tape thoughtfully. What a real, true gentleman; if it were me I'd have raised my voice and cursed the Admiralty to high heaven. All he said was that he was surprised! I was sweating a bit; if he turned me down now, I'd never dare go back to the office. I was muttering about having a dedicated News Editor, very hot for the News, a Yorkshireman, frightfully keen. The Prince looked at me … probably thought I was going to turn on the waterworks again. I turned the screw … sudden brainwave. I get them sometimes. 'I think he might give me the sack if I let you get away…' I gave a nervous giggle.

No response. God, he must have a heart of stone. Suddenly the Prince's face brightened. 'I've just noticed,' he said, 'it says here …that my Commanding Officer must also give permission and be present at the interview.' He looked almost gleeful.

'My C.O. is away on leave … for another three weeks.'

I could read his thoughts like a clairvoyant. There's a war on mate. I went right back to the office. 'Not for 3 weeks,' I said and watched Arthur Wilson go up to the big calendar on the wall and draw a big red circle round the date. There's no escape. […]

Olga's encounter with the youthful Prince (later to be the Duke of Edinburgh) is described in some detail in Basil Boothroyd's biography of the Duke, published in 1971.

8

Back in Fleet Street

1945

While working in Newcastle, Olga kept in touch with the contacts she had made in London to try and find an opening in Fleet Street but wartime restrictions made it difficult to find openings. But the Kemsley Group who owned the Newcastle paper agreed to transfer her to their London paper, the Daily Sketch.

January 1945
c/o Daily Sketch
Room 311, Kemsley House
Gray's Inn Road WC1

Dears B & C,

The journey from Newcastle to London … it actually took 24 hours!

The Union minimum for London reporting is 9 guineas but the Sketch have offered me £10 plus war bonus (don't know how much that will be at present) and expenses of course...

March 1945
Monday morning
Hampstead Towers Hotel
Ellerdale Road, London NW3

Dear Beryl,

Can see you rolling your big eyes already. In my customary extreme manner, have transferred self from Kings Cross station to Hampstead

207

Heath. The cost is prohibitive so I had better enjoy it as long as the money lasts. It is rather a change from my room in a public-house-digs right opposite Kings Cross station where pimps and prostitutes stroll in the smoky darkness; where the bare bedrooms smell of cheap soap powder and the commercial travellers partially undress in front of the smoking-room fire. They unlace their suspenders, undo most of their buttons and then glare at me in the hope that I will go to bed and they can undo the other button. The only other permanent guests are one small, coloured man and a retired policeman.

Rosalie gave me an egg one day and it caused quite a stir. Everyone glued their eyes to me while I ate it. Eggs have totally disappeared from the shops and even powdered egg is getting difficult to obtain but I notice that the van-drivers in our Kemsley House garage at the back of Grays Inn Road are doing a steady Black Market in fresh eggs, oranges, even bananas, and petrol. (Lack of petrol means we can only use the Office Cars (3) at present on really urgent stories, like the murder hunt for the monster-rapist-sadist with the posh RAF accent Neville Heath who killed a girl horribly in a ghastly old house in Porchester Terrace, Notting Hill Gate and then killed another in Bournemouth). I had digs in the same road...

I spend all my spare time hunting for new digs. Each room is more horrid than the last. And freezing cold without fires; one in Barons Court had a gas-fire but hardly any gas. Partly of course it's the bomb damage; no one seems able to begin cleaning up; most ground-floor windows are still boarded up but even the boards are disintegrating now; front gardens are piled with rubble or rubbish and the only consolation is the grass and weeds which have taken over. In the City and round our office in Holborn, grass sprouts along the pavements and the rubble of smashed buildings is almost hidden among tall weeds with lovely purple and yellow flowers.

When I have time I plan to visit Rosalie in Grove End Gardens; for one thing she may know of a vacant room somewhere and for another she is now MARRIED and absolutely respectable. Did you hear about it? I will get all details and let you have full report; all I got so far was a bit garbled, over the 'phone from Sally. She was too excited about it; apparently he is 'a very cultured man and frequent visitor to Buckingham Palace'. Now calm down, girl. I mean by the Back Door. Sally called him an 'artist-confectioner' ...I suppose she means a Cook! Well, we shall see.

Well ... back to Kings Cross and my Powdered-Egg breakfasts in the

Residents' dining-room smelling to high heaven of detergent, presumably to overpower the aroma of last night's beer....

That was all for £3.10s per week.

Now I pay 6 guineas all-in. When I phoned a week ago & fixed it, the Receptionist said 'from 5 guineas'. When I got there, no 5gn rooms only 6. The 5-gn room she showed me that might be free later was like a little cell. My room is glamorous! Fitted crimson carpet, pale walnut suite with large wardrobe, telephone at bedside, h & c, radiator central heating, big gas-fire, comfortable bed. The 6gns includes everything, bkfast, lunch and dinner, but morning tea is extra. The hotel is de-luxe; all luscious carpets and pale wood panelling.

The company is amusing to watch. There is a very Poona family complete with Indian Rajah, handsome black-bearded and very effeminate in natty grey suiting and beige turban. An elderly elegant believedly Polish couple read the Daily Worker at breakfast! The woman wears a pale blue woollen tea-cosy on her head, Scrooge-fashion. There is a man who looks like Lord Halifax, very tall, he likes ITMA; radio is in the enormous chintzy lounge which has queer little alcoves like small chapels cordoned off by gateways; oil paintings, iron coke fire in great stone hearth underneath multi-coloured panel piece which looks like it was pinched from Durham cathedral.

The dining-room (small tables) has silvery panelling topped by tapestries like an old dressmaker used to have in the Bristol Road. She had screens of it where you undressed behind. The maids are the quiet unobtrusive, elderly, efficient kind that belongs to a gone forgotten age. Their voices make me think they were sent along by the Association of Decayed Gentlewomen. When I say to her I'll take porridge, Theresa, that's one of them, says, 'Thenk you Moddom.' They had chicken for dinner Sunday but I wasn't there! Could you please send my ration book on here as I have to surrender it to qualify for three meals a day which I intend to devour every chance I get ... Thanks for the butter you sent me ... but oh so much! It must be nearly your whole month's ration. The only thing I need is orange juice but I know that's impossible. Feel much fitter already[...]

The hotel is bang on Hampstead Heath, in the exclusive residential part which is the poshest part of North London. It's just off the famous Hampstead High Street with its quaint arty crafty antique and bookshops. At the top of the street, you reach the Heath itself where you get a view of rolling green moorland and woods way over the Heath for miles.

209

Hope to be able to stay here for a week or two anyhow. A pal at the office says he will give me some names in magazines who will buy feature articles. Says it's the only way he can endure the Sketch and his frustration at working for it.

Saw Aunt Sally to get details of the Romance ... which I hear has galvanised the still unwed members of the Grove End Gardens lonely-hearts towards 'new efforts' to achieve the oh so desirable target of a Good Husband for each. More on this next time.

Love to all, Oggi

May 1945
Room 311, Kemsley House
Grays Inn Rd WC1

Dear B,

I haven't spent my coupons yet ..... though I received 5 guinea cheque from Newcastle for that Japanese prisoner-of-war story you saw in the paper. Also this weekend we are getting approximately one week's salary minus income tax as a 'Victory Bonus' on top of our wages....

I'm still at the same digs in Swiss Cottage, No.11, Adamson Road, NW4. Two men are leaving the boarding house on Friday! One, the nicest has been ordered out! Because he asked if his butter was really butter or was it marge? Housekeeper Frau Loewensberg was Furious at not being Trusted. So he's getting his own back. They have been charging him electricity for an extra lamp in his room where he does a lot of writing. He has taken this up with the 'poaleece' he told me, because Landlords are not allowed to make money out of Public Services like light and water. There is going: to be a Lawsuit. Ha ha. It is that kind of bawdy-house. German. Full of fun.

I was out at Chalfont St Giles in Bucks. yesterday to see British prisoners-of-war back from Russia. The War Office gave us a slap-up tea.

Love to all, Ogg

June 1945,
Hampstead Towers Hotel
Ellerdale Road, London NW3

Dear Beryl,

Am down with streptococcal tonsillitis ..... and only hope the hotel will
let me stay on a few days longer as the doctor says I can't get up till
Tuesday. Had a high temperature when I reached London on Monday
and struggled on until Wednesday morning; went to see the doctor today
who said I should have stayed in bed. I am on the old M & B which
Dr. Margolin gave me back in 1937, every 4 hours including the night;
you can imagine how the hotel like me! They've already let my room to
a couple and anyway the plan is to reduce the hotel facilities now through
lack of staff or something. Would you be a sport and tell old Cork I
am bad as I have no strength to write her. Lost me bit of carbon paper.
Don't worry about me.

   I feel hungry despite painful throat and high temp so I must be all
right. My Russian teacher Ms. Grun* ticked me off for being too
'melancholy' and she oughta know, she's a Russian. As I've got a phone
thank God by my bed I might ring up the Happy Bride old Rosalie but
I Expect she'd be scared of infection. Being ill is a horrid bore.

   Love, Og

*Mrs. Grun taught Olga for many years and became a close friend. It was her teaching
that enabled Olga to become Fleet Street's first Russian speaking journalist.

July 1945,
30, Kensington Place
London W8

Dear B,

Am renting a basement flat here from a charming American couple with
child on the floor above. Very friendly and helpful; showed me how to
stoke the coke boiler which heats the place which needs it badly, being
rather damp. It is one of those old Regency houses circa about 1799 which
means it's delightfully pretty, but I sit up most nights in terror in case one
of the large family of mice who also live here dare to cross my floor.

Was round at No.6 Grove End Gardens for delightful dinner cooked of course by Paul. He is totally devoted to Cousin Ros who I must admit is a lot sweeter since her marriage than she ever was before. While Paul and Aunt Sally were washing up (first time I've ever been at No.6 without having to do the washing-up so you see what I mean) Rosalie told me that her Romance has galvanised all Les Girls who have all declared it their immediate Post-war Aim to find a Good Husband like hers.

He is an Austrian, Catholic, came to London early in the Thirties and stayed ... was jilted by an British girlfriend; (Les Girls never tire of hearing this bit; they can barely conceive of the Good Fortune of a Girl in a position to Jilt a Man) ... and one day in the autumn of 1944 – while I was still in Newcastle which is how I came to miss the full drama – Rosalie happened to pick him up in Baker St Classic cinema. It was when the lights went up during the interval of one of Bette Davis's weepies. Austrians, happily, are romantic. Sally wouldn't fill in the EXACT details but as they don't smoke I reckon he must have offered a Choc-ice while the organ played. They were both on the Rebound; he from the English girl and she from Her Last American ... which by the way are getting a bit thin on the Ground at last, that is as far as Officers are concerned. The poor bloody GI's seem to be trapped in Grosvenor Square judging by their constant demonstrations.... Sally tells me Paul is a True Gentleman 'and an angel with it'. It has worked wonders for Rosalie's character; she is positively Sunny. They also have a little dog, a black Poodle called Peppi, horribly spoilt who eats and as far as I can see, sleeps with them too.

Paul Gottl has changed his name to Gough; I thought him terribly nice and charming and I couldn't help thinking, far too good for our Sweet Coz though I do admit that at 45, she is terrifically Improved; he is about 3 years younger. One of his specialities is making speciality chocolates for the Queen.

Love, Ogg

By now Olga is taking her Russian lessons very seriously, which turn out to be a good investment for the future. And then there is the first post-war election and Olga is on the trail of Winston Churchill, although she ends up with the Atlees. At some stage this year, she spent time both in Nuremberg and Berlin but doesn't mention it in her letters.

August 1945,
c/o Daily Sketch
Room 311, Kemsley House
Gray's Inn Road WC1

Dear B,

Having a day's rest at home today before the deluge tomorrow. How are you voting? Mrs. Grun, my Russian teacher, will hate me if I vote Labour because she thinks they are both weak and treacherous and she hates Ernie Bevin. She says I should either vote Liberal or abstain.

I find it quite upsetting attending all the meetings of all the parties all over the South-East because the Tories and the Labour people all say such spiteful, malicious things about the other lot. Sometimes they decorate the various meeting-halls with little papier-mache models of whoever it is, Bessie Braddock, Nye Bevan, Herbie Morrlson or Cripps or Eden or Macmillan, and then they string them across the platform swinging from the gallows or something just as horrid. After a few weeks of it ... you don't know where you are or WHAT you believe. I mean .. it all gets rather childish!

For me the worst part has been trailing after Winston Churchill on his long, long car drives from his Woodford, Essex constituency. If I had only a tiny particle of his energy, it might be fun. But not one of us can cope! Each day he sets out in his car, usually standing with his head through the open roof most of the way. Every village and town we come to, he stops and makes a speech and we have to fight to get near so we can take a shorthand note of what he says and the questions they ask him. He gets an ovation in most places, and there's an awful struggle to get his car and the Party officials in THEIR cars following behind through the crowds ... then the people run into the road after him ... and at the back of it all, THERE we are with our sad, sad photographers and wire men (who have the job of telephoning the pictures and messages back to the Fleet Street or to Gray's Inn Road) in time for the Early Evening Editions. Our lot has to try to be quicker than anyone else because we've also got to send stories and pictures up to our sister papers belonging to Kemsley in Newcastle, Manchester, Glasgow, Aberdeen and so on.

Our group of newspapers has started an even more ghastly method of Getting the News Before the Others. All our cars, even the most decrepit of them (the back wheel suddenly came off one Vauxhall model when I was sitting in the back with all the heavy photographic and wire equipment so it was lucky we'd slowed down a bit or we'd all been killed) have now got radio installed so that our News Editors can call us in the car any time they like. That is pure hell. You can't stop for a beer or a cup of tea for five minutes ... if you do, there's Mack's or Jock's bloody voice calling, 'Come in Daily Sketch ... where are you? Come in there.... where's that bloody girl got to?' You know me, dear Sisters ... all I want is the odd cup of tea from time to time to cheer me and sustain. On the Churchill tour which has lasted all of 3 weeks now, no cups of tea, no nice sit-down. Every time we get to a new village and we all stop and crowd round while the Grand Old Man gives the V-sign and starts talking ... We all start to get hopeful for a minute; you'd think, wouldn't you? that a man of his Years would want a sit-down, a nip of his favourite brandy or a cup of tea. No luck. Off he goes again, bloody mile after bloody mile. Can you wonder that by now we're all so exhausted we don't much care what kind of a Government we're going to get. Eine kleine Pause is all we want. When the actual voting starts, we're all on duty- non-stop until it's over.

Election votes results are coming in now ... over the ticker tape. We all sit around exhausted[...]

I'll carry on with this letter while we're still waiting to know who's won......

One Labour candidate in Streatham is threatening to sue me for a story I did which mentioned him on Sunday. You would not believe that a barrister age 28 could be so childish. But everyone's nerves are on edge with all the shouting and yelling...

I went slumming with Lord Derby down in Poplar E., and Stepney on Friday night; the amount of beer that man can drink, well you can see it from my expense sheet if it ever gets past the accountants.

Ha, here it comes. I'm not sure what.... with all the bawling and shouting. A sudden dead silence, except for the ticker tapes all going at once like a lot of lunatics...

The door opens and our elegant Cricket Correspondent enters. Making us all look even more unwashed and smelly than we are ... He goes over and checks the results on the tapes; then he puts his hands to his sleek dark head as though he's going to cry.

Then he stares at all of us round the big dirty room with all the war maps still hanging greasily with usually one drawing-pin missing, all askew on the stained yellow walls, and he says with a sort of low moan:

'It's the end of my world.'

We watch his back as he sort of sways himself out of the room. Then we all rush to the tapes. 'It's a landslide,' everyone Shrieks.

'That'll show 'em,' another cry goes up.

'That'll teach 'em to stop cutting my expenses.'

'My God, what does it MEAN?'

'Poor old Winnie.'

'Yes ... but what?' says someone. 'What did Victor Lewis mean about it being the end of HIS world?'

'You know damn well what it means.'

But louder and above all that comes the sound of Mack the news editor calling: 'All of you get on your bikes ... OUT. I want atmosphere, colour, joy, tears, triumph, despair, the LOT.'

'Olga, get the hell out quick, with cameraman, get the Clem Attlee family celebrating, do the whole champagne how-I-won, the Great Labour Landslide, the Victory. Did you hear me, Girl? I said OUT....'

Better end this letter here. I'm off to the Great Western Hotel, Paddington for what looks like the rest of this hot, sticky night. There the whole Attlee family, kids and all are installed ... to celebrate.

More in my next, Love, Ogg

August 1945
c/o Daily Sketch
Room 311, Kemsley House
Gray's Inn Road WC1

Dear B,

It was a long night waiting for the Attlees, with standing-room only in the corridor. I was the only girl except for the Daily Express brilliant Eve Perrick; both of us pretending we were not watching each other's every move. When she disappeared once or twice along the carpeted corridor to visit the Ladies, I followed; when I went she came after me.

Every hour or so, the new PM, Clement Attlee or his pretty wife or the grown-up son or daughter opened the door a crack and said; 'Not yet, not yet. We need more time.' I just caught a glimpse of a table with white cloth but no sign of any champagne or anything like it. It was going on for 11pm when the door was at last opened wide. Mr. A is so insignificant to look at that it almost makes him look important ...

if you get my meaning. I mean you think there's sure to be genius there tucked away, otherwise how? But the wife is so good looking in a girlish, English way; how clever of her to marry a PM. We all push and squeeze in, a bit sheepish. It's a GWR hotel room like any other, and just the family all on their own so God knows what they've been talking about all this time. We all look around for the champagne; my News Editor said don't forget to say which brand and the cameras get ready to do him holding a glass high. To our astonishment we don't get offered anything .... but on the table there's just the remains of a modest tea-party. Even the PM's first speech is only about ten words long; yes he's pleased with the Labour victory. I notice the remains of a large Seed Cake on the table as we get pushed out fairly quickly.

'Socialists!' says Eve as we rush for the lift. 'Now we know what to expect.'

Back at the office I get ticked off for a dull story. What does he expect for a slice of Seed Cake which I didn't even get!

What with having Laryngitis and a gas strike this week ... I had to go to the House of Commons to see ex-army cooks doing all the cooking there on improvised field kitchens owing to the gas strike. 'Food marvellous; all the chickens and geese in London must have been there on the slab. I don't know why ... Sir Stafford Cripps is strict vegetarian; I see him often at the superb Vega restaurant run by a very efficient Swiss couple in Panton Street just off Leicester Square. They also make terrific real 'Bulgarian' yoghourt which is the real thing and George Bernard Shaw sends his chauffeur and car all the way from Chalfont St Giles once a week to collect a supply.

Am lunching at the Churchill Club on Saturday before it closes down altogether, with the USA Captain who appeared in a Sketch interview with me. He wrote and told me the picture of us lunching there was splashed around the world ... fame at last.

Then out in the cold to stand listening to the gas strikers' meeting on some waste land at Barking, so what with the football games in a few days I don't look like getting my voice back just yet.

Love, Og

November 1945
c/o Daily Sketch
Room 311, Kemsley House
Gray's Inn Road WC1

Dear B,

In case you saw the front page pictures of the 100,000 people trying to get into the Chelsea football match against the Dynamos yesterday, perhaps you saw me among them trying to get in. Guess I made football history by getting in 15 minutes late, getting good seat and having no ticket, while thousands were turned away or hung from the roof-tops, trees and lamp-posts. I had no intention of being turned away.

Actually I wasn't keen to be sent to Croydon airport to meet the Dynamos – London's first-ever Soviet Russian footballers – but the News Editor insisted as I was the only one able to speak enough Russian to interview them. Two days earlier the Royal Free hospital pulled out my two wisdoms just like that – bang .. and it was really free except for the x-rays so I'm not grumbling about them being a bit rough. But when the pain got a lot worse and it felt like another tooth had come up overnight I went back to hospital. Dentist found long piece of jagged bone, and whizz just pulled it out. Did I yell ... Then I got bad earache from the cold weather. Mind you, I'd do it all over again because I think they're good, cheap and efficient at the Royal Free. Not like my dentist Mr. Bodenharn in Newcastle who struggled an hour trying to get my tooth out and then it was him who collapsed and was taken to hospital....

But the day after this 'operation' (I was on duty same day at night 6pm to 2am) I got sent to Croydon to meet the Russians, so my face was so swollen that someone said I looked all pregnant on one side. The news editor said I had to make the 'lead' for my morning-paper story .... about the Eggs. The Football Association made a terrific whip-round and collected two dozen fresh eggs so we could give the Russians a real welcoming party.

At Croydon, they were hardboiled and made up into the most tempting sandwiches you ever saw. So of course this made Page One News because no one in the whole U.K. gets two dozen egg sandwiches, not even the King and Queen, them least of all as they'd never do a black-market thing like that. So there we all were in the freezing cold and foggy with it, all the top brass from the F.A., and big, dark, handsome Henry Rose egging me on..... if you'll forgive the pun, yelling out that I was 'Olga the pride of the Dynamos' and then down comes their piston plane direct from Moscow and it is rather thrilling as they all troop out looking god-awful in the most ghastly trilby hats – the kind people wore in Germany in the early twenties – and they're all pale as pale and rather fragile-looking so I just don't know how they'll manage against Arsenal, let alone Tottenham Hotspur, Wales and Glasgow Rangers. Several are very good looking in a pale, dreamy, blond Onegin sort of way but looking all of them so terribly ILL. I get pushed forward with my big tray of egg sandwiches and I start my welcoming speech:-

'S priezdom!' I yell out from the side of my mouth and start to go through the team offering my beautiful sandwiches first to the Captain Semichastny, then to Angelski, Yakushen, Boskov and all... Would you believe this? They took one look at the egg sandwiches and shrank back as though they were poisoned!

Even the pot of piping hot tea they weren't all that keen on. It appears they've brought not only their own grub but their own Cook, Trainer, Physiotherapist, Doctor, even Dietician. Captain Semichastny ... I went back with my dish and tried again because I just couldn't believe anyone would turn down the eggs; they all looked half starved, pale as death and from all reports they've got even less food in Russia than we've got which is nearly nowt ... and he just waved me away, sort of joking about how did they know we'd not put something in the sandwiches which might spoil their football style...?!

Love Ogg

November 1945
Belsize Park
London NW

Dear B,

A worry at the office is that we most of us have been handed contracts for three years to sign and none of us want to. Also the Union say we should not. There is a Union meeting tomorrow. Don't know what to do.

Also have quarrelled ferociously with my mad landlady, and am hopelessly looking for rooms again. She is a Russian-Pole, a great white monster in tall black turban and used to be an Opera-singer, and famous for it she says, in the Old Country.

She sits in her room surrounded by objets d'art and rarely moves from her armchair which seems sensible enough for she could hardly be moved without someone to lift and propel her to the divan where she sleeps. At least I presume she sleeps there though I've not seen this.

The flat is nice and comfortable and I was overjoyed to get a room which was warm, centrally-heated etc. and not too far from the office, as Swiss Cottage and the No.13 bus is only just down the road.

There is always something. It is her parrot, the most bitter, evil, sophisticated, spiteful and talkative parrot I ever saw. Even though covered up at night in his tall cage beside her bed, he wakes at every sound. She did, I admit, warn me that I must be careful not to wake them both when I come into the flat after late-night duty, which is every other week and could be 11pm or midnight or quite often much later. I take off my shoes; I creep about like a mouse but that damn parrot sounds off the moment I enter the door. I presume its fearful oaths are in Polish but they certainly terrify me. Landlady summoned me to her armchair this morning, said that neither she nor her parrot really liked me; that I could not be a real respectable lady or I would not come creeping home on all fours in the small hours and said I must be gone by the end of the week. I was positively cringing in reply, knowing that I haven't the smallest chance of finding a room in the time. She is adamant.

Luckily it was a nice week, with three whole days sitting in the warm for a Breach of Promise Case in the Kings Bench Division at the Law Courts. The case was dramatic, beautiful Greek girl sued British naval officer for not marrying her after their romance failed. She followed him to Britain in the belief, she told the Court, that a British officer and a gentleman will always keep his word. He just said he fell out of love and you could sympathise a bit and see what he meant; she was lovely to look at but talked to excess and in very long sentences.

Thursday I interviewed the novelist Margery Sharp at her charming flat; she lives in the flat above J.B. Priestley in Albany which is a famous mews near Piccadilly. Friday went to a Christina Foyle luncheon at the Dorchester.

I hope to come to Brum for the weekend. Warning: let there be no coarse laughter when I arrive in my new hat. It is very stylish but rather large. It was fine for the Foyles' luncheon but causes alarm, even consternation, on a bus. People run after the bus to get a closer view. At the office I fear it came to almost a strike; the cameramen formed a deputation to the Art Editor (in charge of our photographic desk) claiming that my hat blocked every camera-shot for miles around and they charged me with causing an Obstruction. It is a big black picture hat of ruched felt which all Paris will be wearing by spring. Please brief Richard and Frank in advance about it as I have suffered enough rude comments and feel I have a right to walk unmolested in my own home town.

Love, Og

December 1945
c/o Daily Sketch
Room 311, Kemsley House
Gray's Inn Road WC1

Dear B,

I met Mrs. Roosevelt on Friday. A huge shouting army of G.I.s demonstrated all morning in Grosvenor Square. They want ships, ships and more ships to take themselves and their G.I. brides and babies home to America. Everyone else wants that too because the U.S. army now has nothing much to do except hang about Oxford Circus and Piccadilly chatting up the girls and moaning, 'You are my sunshine, my only sunshine; you make me happy when skies are grey...'

The 'demonstration' has gone on for weeks. Today we made an early start and trailed the noisiest lot to the General's h.q. in Grosvenor Square. When they got no change out of him, in spite of all their screaming abuse; six of them marched straight off to Claridges, trailed by me and half-a-dozen hungry newspapermen and cameras. It was 2pm and none of us had had any lunch. Mrs. Roosevelt was charming; she opened the door to me as head of the press delegation and invited them all in, but kept us out. No publicity, she said. She looked like she was going to kiss all the boys. I thought her beautiful. She is tall, slim in black and several rows of pearls. High-piled hair and lashings of charm. I was surprised. I had always thought of her as plain. Like she comes out on the photographs. Finally the boys came out and she let us in. It seems she has 'promised' them ships and they cheered her like mad. So we got our lunch, round about tea-time.

Married life is not all honey; Went to Cousin Rosalie's un-invited and un-announced, carrying an attache case she had lent me ...only to find her in dressing-gown, bad complexion and worse temper. After remarking bitterly that she had not really expected ever to see the attache case again

(I have had it 3 weeks) she added. She'd just been stricken down with the 'curse', bad tum, bad cold and could not care less about receiving guests, even a Kemsley Young Lady. Paul, frying himself some eggs & bacon with french beans in the kitchen, came into the hall bearing this steaming plateful and we all drifted into the lounge. Rosalie ate a bowl of gruel lying on the couch and glowering at Paul's dinner and the box of chocolates which I was picking at from a low stool before me. To make matters worse I was wearing the revealing black jumper I bought in Paris which made Rosalie remark that it was bad enough that I had come uninvited without ringing first and at dinner-time (!) although having had my dinner, without coming in 'evening dress' as well. I drew a cardigan over the offending shoulders and waited for the Bengers food to have its soothing effect which it did in the end and I was sent home with an egg for my breakfast and a chocolate dog which Paul said was my Christmas present. Rosalie and Paul now have their own car and plan a holiday in Spain and Portugal.

After leaving I bumped into Cousin Jane in the corridor who was also coming un-announced for our usual Friday night get-together. I soon put Jane au fait with the night's work and it was agreed it would be too bold a move for Jane to venture where I had already failed. Walking back into St. John's Wood Road we bumped into Freda who had also come on the same mission; to pay respects to the Goughs ... also under the same impression that the Newly-Married Rosalie Gough and now a totally-fulfilled married Woman would be only too glad to welcome her less fortunate and deeply-unmarried friends and relations. So we Three, remnants only of the gay company of Les Girls who in the bombing of London made the corridors of Grove End Gardens ring with our laughter, decided it would be safer to go to Jane's little pad instead. Jane who is as always the Perfect Lady had her work cut out keeping Freda's voice down to a minimum.[...]

Because Freda who has a Carrying Voice insisted on telling not only us but also the tube train occupants, the ticket-collector and the liftman, details of her recent visit to Paris which unfortunately are the kind you would not learn about outside a Kinsey Report. We left the ticket-collector at St John' s Wood underground station staring after us as though turned to stone.

Jane tried to remonstrate with the wildly gesticulating Freda who was bursting with rare information, but it was no use. Because, among other incidents, Freda who had 'met' a man at a tea-dance in the Champs

Elysees and had been taken by him in a glittering automobile to a palatial apartment, had found to her sorrow that the man who was a Very Kind man even for a Frenchman, wanted Freda only for his girl-friend who was a Lesbian.

Freda's French is pretty fluent but she had unhappily failed to catch this particular word in its French context. So the whole evening, as Freda roundly informed a petrified railway carriage, had been a failure. However, happily there had been other adventures but by this time a breathless, blushing, sweating Jane was grappling with the doors of the train trying dangerously it seemed to open them as we approached Regent's Park station. Freda, we gathered, does not agree with the Sunday newspapers that Paris had now been cleared of vice. We bore her swiftly past the station-porters and into the flat and turned on the Third Programme very boomingly.

Love to all, Oggi

1946

9th January 1946
c/o Daily Sketch
Room 311, Kemsley House
Gray's Inn Road WC1

Dears Beryl, Cora and Bettina,

Thank you for your several letters which I was enormously pleased to get. Am feeling very well after a whole week doing nothing at the Kemsley Training Conference. It suited me uncommonly well to sit round a green baize table, only woman among 20 men, graciously accepting twice a day at his Lordship's expense, four free cups of tea and the same number of ginger biscuits pressed upon me by a gold-liveried official and a whitecoated waitress.

We broke up for luncheon at one o'clock which was also free of charge and preceded each day by a free bottle of beer apiece. Then back to the baize table (after a sharp walk round Grays Inn Fields with a selected corps of the best-looking men among the 20 provincial and other correspondents) and another cup of tea into which we unceremoniously dunked our ginger biscuits while listening to more lectures about newspapers. During Question time, it was found that I differed in opinion from nearly everybody else and one colleague suggested that 'Miss Franklin should put in a minority report', but my witticisms were mostly taken in good part by visiting Editors from Manchester, Sheffield, Glasgow, etc. The tea was uniformly excellent throughout. We are allowed to draw two guineas expenses to cover this social round of teas and beers, etc!

My advice to Bettina if she wants to come to London is this. (I don't like giving advice and only do so by reason of long experience, etc.) That she should come to London ONLY if she comes to the finest most comfortable hospital. I will be glad to make enquiries or to visit Matrons or to enquire from my contact at the Royal College of Nursing. Two of my colleagues here have daughters (Probationers) at St George's hospital, Hyde Park Corner and if there is a vacancy and Betty wishes, I will go and have a look. I am told the nurses are well looked after; they wear an attractive green uniform outdoors. They have a good nurses hostel nearby at Knightsbridge with good food, electric fires and a Yale lock for their own rooms. Patients are of the cleaner kind, being drawn from the theatre and society. The hospital itself, though old fashioned and old, has a status for the 'George's girls'. Matron is only 32; it is next to the Park and it is important to be in the centre of London like that, and is on a direct 2½d bus to my flat. The girls get free tickets to many shows. Barts, Guys and the Westminster are the famous ones, but probably too big to be really happy for a young nurse.

I am not really in favour of her coming to London for the same reasons chiefly as you have ... I doubt if there will be enough of the right kind of social life for her, because although she can join clubs, etc, it is all vastly expensive and London nowadays is rather drab. What life there is belongs to millionaires. And of course the social-life aspect is more important than ever in a big lonely city. I want our Tina to be happy as you do, and I think it is more difficult to be happy in London than anywhere else. However, I do like the sound of St George's so please ask Bettina to let me know whether she wants me to approach Matron or anyone else. I do see how you and Frank feel about it, but of course she will do what she wants. In any case, if she comes, I will do my best to keep several eyes on her and my present little temporary flat (I hope it won't be too temporary) is at her disposal for her leave time when she doesn't go to Birmingham.

I was at Rosalie's on Friday night and everyone there thought we should certainly let her come..... but Jane and Rita are not good advertisements for the life. Jane has serious stomach trouble and is under the doctor.

Love Og

19th January 1946
Hampstead Towers Hotel
Ellerdale Road, London NW3

Dears B & C,

You will note I'm back at the above address, i.e. still living with the upper classes. It is making me very refined. My good morning bow would do credit to a debutante; my luncheon bow is more casual, just a slight incline of the head and I allow a faint smile to twist the scarcely parted lips through which a short hiss ensues. This is not due to former bronchitis. It is understood that after the prolonged exchange of good-mornings between some 35 guests at breakfast, the formalities are allowed to lapse at luncheon except for the ceremonies which I have described.

But of course, dear sisters, you are chafing with impatience to know how I make an appearance among the gentility at lunchtime. Subterfuge. Briefly, I slip on to the Northern Line underground at Kings Cross and am on Hampstead Heath in a jiffy, or at least 15 to 20 minutes. I then appear, breathing heavily it is true, but with an air of one who only works because of some eccentricity of mind, and after the aforesaid gymnastics are gone through with perfect poise I sit down at my lone table among the two Generals, one Admiral (Polish), one Air-Marshal, one barrister, one professional actor and three doctors, oh and the Indian Rajah too, lately in palest mauve or parma violet turban, among my vitamin tablets, the remains of my (I mean your) raspberry jam, with perfect Aplomb...

For the sake of dear Cora who is unaware that all this costs 6 gns per, I will dwell a moment on the more sordid side of Hampstead Towers. I find that by making an effort to attend ALL meals three times a day, one can almost save money. Lunch is a mere trifle, of cheese souffle or fish pie, but it suffices. It is insufficient, however, for the rather dim spinster in green velvet corduroy jacket who sits at the next table, and though a worker, also attends for lunch. Theresa, she gushed to the maid today, you have brought me enough pudding for a mouse, and she looked at Theresa with big, hungry eyes. Hev aye, moddom, says Theresa and haughtily procures another slice of delicious treacle sponge.

Do not assume the green-velvet one is unrefined. I believe the sharp weather prompts her into a course of action she would otherwise scorn. I know too that she likes to feel herself a woman of wide interests and sympathies. At every meal a copy of the Soviet News Weekly is propped against her water jug. I have never seen her either turn a page or read a line (and who can blame her for that!) but it is always there and together with the Polish Admiral's wife's Daily Worker proudly defies the surrounding tables decorated with The Times and the Daily Sketch. I think the Sketch has very little competition to face at the Towers.

Now and again, a proud upright figure, the Air Marshal breast sagging under the weight of his medals, bends over the hungry one in green velvet simpering behind her Soviet defence and says to her, How interesting, dear me, how interesting. Is it in the Russian language? This, in face of the words Soviet Weekly in bold black type. This does not mean the Air Marshal's sight is bad, but is a feature of the ancient culture of English gentlefolk to pretend to be blind as well as deaf.[...]

So-o interesting, coos the green velvet one. My deah, she addresses the Air Marshal's wife, you simply must see it when I have finished it. I think the AM's wife will have to wait a long time, seeing that Green Velvet is still on Page one with its bold title challenging the pale silvery panelling of the dining-room.

The Generals, tall, silver-haired with the ramrod-straight backs you would expect, never focus their eyes on any living person. Their line of vision is narrowed to their plates and the persons destined to share their tables. These destined persons presumably have some blood tie or are authorised to companion their Excellencies in some way. The Generals rarely speak. The one who sits with the Rajah and two ladies who appear to have some control in the activities of Hampstead Towers, spoke yesterday. His announcement was framed as though it were an Order-of-the-Day.

'The fish,' he says, 'was not quite done at luncheon yesterday.'

This statement appears to me to produce no immediate result except that the ladies at his table go into a prolonged huddle.

Later Theresa is summoned and dispatched to the kitchen on reconnaissance. I avert my eyes from this painful scene.

I am shocked to note we have a pregnant woman among us. In this enshrined atmosphere on the by no means wuthering heights of Hampstead Heath, I did not think such things could happen. But my dears, the expectant one is a lady doctor and her husband also a doctor watches over her at breakfast, so I am relieved to reflect that obviously the thing has been undertaken in the noble cause of Science. They have taken a suite on the floor above where they will await the result of their experiment.

We have another lady doctor who, however, is far removed from such coarse experiments. She is a spinster lady of advanced neurotic temperament. She sits in the lounge of an evening sewing a fur hat. It is not a stylish hat. Her face is pale, sharp-pointed, wild-eyed behind her spectacles. Everyone is afraid of her stormy moods. I fear she is scarcely robust enough to be a patient let alone a doctor.

Outside my door hangs a large metal breast-plate like soldiers used to wear for battle in the time of King Harold. Possibly a relic of the General's family.

Do not think Youth is not represented at the Towers. We have sundry youngish or middle-ish men. One, just back from the Gold Coast, has two young schoolboys with him. I am charmed to see how they mother each other. The man, who looks scarcely old enough to be the boys' father, has a buccaneering look as though he went to Africa to strike gold and struck it. He has a winning way with Theresa.

I am torn in pieces with my personal problem, which is, how many pieces of silver should I hand over each week in order to keep well in with Theresa. One man tells me she has one night off each week and goes on a drunk. But she is such a skilled tippler that she can manipulate soup plates safely while completely tight.

There is a tall man with a limp and even more bottles of vitamin tablets than I have, who is passionately devoted to the Daily Sketch which he calls 'Gallant'. He believes that Candidus (who is a nice friend of mine named Henry Newnham*, rather Fascist so he says, but otherwise charming) is the new Messiah. His wife is a vivacious woman with dyed hair who loves to talk of The Theatre. Once she wanted to be an actress. She thinks my life must be So-o interesting. I escape from her to my near-glamorous and cosy room. Outside, Ellerdale Road rolls down in one vast white precipice to Swiss Cottage and West Hampstead (where I was regularly bombed you'll remember in Canfield Gdns in 1941/2). For safety's sake its gleaming whiteness has been diminished with sand. But there is more snow in the air. Here, high up above all London, you can hear the birds in the mornings. Below are some eccentric novel houses of the rich, including the green-roofed one which Gracie Fields had built.

Love Oggi

*Henry Newnham – acerbic columnist who accused the left wing of the Labour Party of being cowards while their right wing opponents sacrificed themselves for king and country.

Dear B,

I tried everywhere to get size 6½ shoes for Lucy. Nothing.

Some shops display a notice, 'No children's shoes under size 8 or size 10.'

New Year's Eve I was a rather surprised guest at a noisy party in Muswell Hill, N., and for most of the evening not quite sure I have come to the right party. Loads of food and drink and an exhausted-looking hostess whom I vaguely recognise who is wildly unflaggingly gay, hundreds of people dancing in huge flat and after the dancing there are energetic games including Musical Hats, Embracing Games and throwing the bodies of male guests through the air like a jet meteor. I take part in many gay screaming games and drink a great deal of brandy to soothe my throat but in the end the 'hostess', whose name appears to be Hazel, wants us all to stay all night and fights with guests to prevent them donning coats and hats. I escape in the general melee......

My colleague Yvonne Tabbush, who was sacked by the Editor on the night before New Year's Eve, is reputed to have upset him, among other things, by trying to kiss him in a pub after a drinking party. So ... do not believe all you read in the papers about scandals in Fleet Street. Newspaper editors do not have a casting couch like Theatricals; they like their girlfriends to have a not too insignificant income of her own before consenting....

Love, Ogg

January 1946
c/o Daily Sketch
Room 311, Kemsley House
Gray's Inn Road WC1

Dear Beryl,

I had a most trying day on Thursday. I was scheduled to go to Tidworth in Wiltshire to spend a night with 700 GI brides who will be accommodated there en route for Southampton. Every other newspaper picked up the news that the ship was cancelled and postponed until next Tuesday. The Sketch failed to pick it up.

I rang up on the Wednesday which was my day off to confirm if the job was still on. I was told to take the 10.40 am train from Waterloo and to get off at Tidworth. There would be 700 brides. Nothing more. Except they would hold the double-page spread for me with photos, after all it was very newsy after the GIs have been demonstrating all over London and pounding away at their Government and ours to get them some ships to take their brides, babes, etc. home after all these months of waiting.

Arriving at Waterloo I find there is no 10.40 train. I ring the photographers' department to tell them so & I ask where is Davis, our photographer who is to accompanying me. I am told Davis has already left the office on his way to meet me. I wait thinking I have missed him in the crowd, I board the train. I note thankfully that it appears to be only a short journey as there is neither corridor nor toilet. The 10.54 for Andover, change twice for Tidworth, finally leaves at 10.54. Very cold and uncomfortable, no heating in freezing train, I arrive at Andover at nearly 2pm. The little junction platform is swept with Arctic winds. I am able to get a cup of cocoa in the buffet. No sign of Davis. There is an hour's wait for the connection so I try the bus instead. I wait for the bus. At nearly 3pm I reach Tidworth, a huge army camp the size of a town.

I stand forlorn in that freezing wilderness clutching my little overnight bag with its torn strap through which brown paper stuffing is protruding. Across the icy wastes of the huts and camps I see some GIs approaching. They are friendly. They take me to the Provost Sergeant's office some way distant. I ask where are the GI brides? He replies, What brides? I find I am nearly a week early on the job, which is quite a record for the Sketch which is usually 48 hours late. The GIs in the office laugh and say, Your paper sounds like the army. I ring the News Editor. He is quite unruffled. I shout and bang the table while the GIs look on, smirking. He says get anything you can on the Preparations for the Brides. I am speechless, nearly, and hang up.

Later things start to improve. I find the Press Office. Two charming and intelligent soldiers take me to a big kitchen where German prisoners of war are working. I am provided with two real live fried eggs on toast which is put in front of me by Nordic blond German, very tame. Later I meet the Captain in charge. He gives me amusing story about 17-year-old girl who will sail on the brides' ship with her mother. But it is her mother who is the GI bride. Aged 44 she married a US Private and now has a 15-month old baby boy in addition to 17-year-old Sarah. Owing to telephone delays in London, it takes me one and a half hours to put these few lines over the 'phone and so I have missed last good train back. I return to London with the two American press sergeants in the back of an open jeep. When they drop me at Marble Arch after the 80-mile spin in two hours from Wiltshire I am so stone-frozen with cold that I cannot even murmur thank you. I am bare-legged (still) and it is snowing tonight.

It was still snowing a week later when I went back to the camp. The brides were queuing in the snow, some with babies in their arms and tottering on stiletto heels. There was the usual sad little group of cameramen from all the papers; they're always very sad because they know that no one will be kind to them and no one will let them take the pictures they want to take. Besides we all had to stay and sleep at the camp overnight, in Nissen huts. I told them we would get fried eggs (2) on toast. 'All you think about is grub,' they said accurately to me. We had a fairly chilly night swapping stories with each other of the army camps we'd slept in. By the morning, more brides were arriving. About 400 had got their complaints ready for us.[...]

They stood in queues, clutching babies, or sat round the fire in the messrooms clutching them; hair-do and enthusiasm all a little reduced.

First snag was that the babies had to join the U.S. army for the duration of the journey from that day to New York. An army issue of baby food was available and mothers were forbidden to administer their own formula. The brides decided on immediate 'strike action'. They went secretly at first into the toilets where among rows of washbasins with hot and cold laid on, they mixed baby food of their own choice with lots of tears and oaths but not much hygiene. A thin snow was falling outside. Inside the problem was to stop the older infants from climbing out of the neat green steel filing-cabinet drawers which the G.Is had placed on the floors to be used as cots. Military-police patrolled the dormitories looking worried. What was to be done about twelve-months-old deserters who would not stay in their filing-cabinet-cots? No one knew. Moreover in the daytime there was nowhere to put the babies down, so we all had to hold them while brides powdered noses or drank American coffee. Childless brides weren't keen on holding the babies .... not with the new coat on ready for the arrival in New York and first meetings with in-laws. I held as many babies as I could during the long identification parades while brides had their fingerprints taken. In the end the G.Is themselves joined the 'strike' and rushed to the toilets to wash and scour the milk-bottles, mix the brides' own illicit formulas, apply the teats firmly and race back to the long queue where Mom, sagging slightly on her frail, high heels, clasped a squealing American citizen to her breast. By late afternoon, the Army Orders were rescinded, the mutiny was over and the brides had won.

So of course it looked like a jolly good story to me and on the third day I phoned it over to the paper. Later the Editor sent for me. The American C.O. in Britain was not too pleased about that story. I got a dressing-down from the Editor; but he got a lunch from the Colonel. Americans are like that. They bear no grudges.. and for that I'll always be on their side.

Love, Oggi

May 1946
21, rue du Sommerard
Paris 5E

Dear B,

I never thought I would find Nobby's family ever again.*

But someone gave me the address of the Red Cross office in Paris where they keep enormous lists of all French citizens missing in the war. They told me to come back in a few days and I went away without very much hope. Then came a message.

They had moved from the Bastille quartier before the war but now they have a lovely flat almost next door to his old factory in Vielle du Temple where they are moving soon. Let me tell you what Anna has given me to take home ... if I can get it past them at Dover. Two kilos of salami, half-lb of cheese, half-lb of butter, one bottle of Armagnac and a half-bottle of brandy, five tins of French sardines in real olive oil, huge box of Lipton tea; box of Carolina rice; lentils, raisins, almonds, large tin of Cristo fat for frying; several kilos of magnificent oranges and large bunch of bananas as well as two packets of Lux toilet soap, two pairs of first quality DuPont nylons and a long beige suedine raincoats, small quantity of sweets, chocolates and nougat I bought myself. There!

We talked and ate, and then started all over again. We must have got through five small roasting chickens and I drank the best part of a large bottle of Martel brandy! Oh dear, I know it must be unbearable to read about it ... but I will bring...!

Each meal was served in this way; hors d'oeuvres is standard and consists of plate of salami ungarnished, plate of herring ungarnished, plate of sliced tomatoes dotted with onion fragments in olive oil; sardines in olive oil, endive or beetroot or lettuce, chopped liver; next course is white fish (usually plain and steamed for Rudolf who is not well) served with thick home-made mayonnaise; next course is dish brought on with sliced beef or grilled steak (lamb chops for Rudolf) and roast chicken already hacked into large portions. (Note this method of serving chicken which saves the trouble of carving at table where the chicken gets cold); this is served with tiny fried potatoes for my nephew Marcel, with mashed potatoes for Rudolf, and dish of Kasha or petits pois. Sometimes there was leek soup or noodle soup as well; other occasions there was jambon (or ham) with salami; later comes oranges and bananas and pears served with Benedictine, and finally Swiss Gruyere or cream cheese or other cheeses and Russian tea. Thus do the middleclass French eat in Paris, exactly one year after the war. When I told them how we eat in London, on powdered egg, spam or bits of whale .... well they didn't believe me, as the old song goes... So I told them our rations and having one egg each per month, and they didn't believe that either.

I noticed that all this food seemed to require little time for cooking and preparation, and left a minimum of washing-up; much use being made of steamer pans or pans which cooked while standing one upon the other; there were also of course innumerable eggs and a huge apple pie but petit fours Anna bought. As though all this were not enough, they have a French maid named Ginette who gets about £2 a week for doing everything; she is the kind of treasure nowhere to be found in Britain. She comes at 7.45 each morning and stays till 5. She can prepare everything from a schmaltz herring to a stuffed chicken's neck. She washes snow-white every scrap of linen, tablecloth and towel in the place.....

It was a shock to meet Marcel again who is now over 13 and six feet tall and though somewhat darker, looks exactly like Norbert. In disposition he is an angel, though his parents do not think so and have a slight bias in favour of his sister Ruth, although they do not altogether approve of the American boy she married. They were not happy in America and Marcel prefers everything French to everything American which shows he is intelligent beyond his years. He has been moved about too much from innumerable schools. On their return soon after the Liberation, he was sent to the American school in Paris but hated it and got himself transferred to the Lycee Voltaire. I will write you more tomorrow.

Love, Og

* *During the war, Olga had, not surprisingly, lost touch with her late husband's family*

who had lived in Paris. Many French Jews were deported to their deaths during the Nazi Occupation. The Frenkel family remained in France for a few more years but eventually the whole family moved to America.

May 1946
21, rue du Sommerard
Paris 5E

Dear B,

Anna & Rudolf do not want to return to America but if they stay more than two years they will lose their passport. Their standard of life and business must fall heavily if they return to the USA because Rudolf found it nearly impossible to do business in America where the going is hard and every fifth person a crook or a bounder. Whereas in France he has good status after getting back his factory and having a good name in the leather business after 25 years. People live quite openly on the black market in France if they can afford it; it is apparently semi-legal here, so you can live very well, with the addition of food parcels from Ruth.

Rudolf told me how he actually fell into German hands in May 1941, a year after the Fall of France, when he tried to cross the border from Vichy France to get to his business in Paris. The Gestapo gaoled him for a month, starved him and he went to a Shadow; then by some strange, unaccountable miracle, let him go. After a month's recuperation in the country, he got to Marseilles where he hung round the docks trying to get a ship to take the four of them to U.S. The story of his attempts at business in America would fill a book. Yet in some odd way the years have not touched them. Anna is gentle and pretty as ever. His dark thick hair has not a single strand of grey and they are both very slim with no middle age spread. But what happened to Norbert has given Rudolf an overwhelming, unreasoning horror and hate for England and everything English, so he will not be coming over to see you and Frank I'm afraid. I will give fuller account of my Paris journey when I come over to see you all ... and bring some of this glorious food with me. I arrived in Paris on May Day and at first I didn't notice how shabby everything was ... though of course nothing like London because they have no bomb damage there .... because the streets were lined with flower-sellers holding baskets of lilies-of-the-valley. Oh oh, the streets

232

were snow white with it; you'd have gone mad with joy to see. Hope all children well and that the flu stays away from your doors.

Best love, Og

7th May 1946
c/o Daily Sketch
Room 311, Kemsley House
Gray's Inn Road WC1

Dear B,

The wind was not cooler yesterday than the reception given to the Minister of Town and Country Planning, Mr. Lewis Silkin, when he drove through Stevenage, the doomed 'Domesday Town.'

With a coloured map of its territory on his knee, he drove through streets and lanes and passed old-world farmsteads, where children peered behind scarlet notices bearing the slogan of their passive resistance, 'Hands off our Homes.'

Only in one road did people come forward to meet him. Then it was to stop the Minister to plead with him. With shaking hands, an old-fashioned pair came out of an old-fashioned country house called The Red Cot and drew him towards their gate, saying, 'Come into our garden.'

Mr. Silkin stood in their cabbage patch in the back garden, between the pear trees and the raspberry canes, between the ripening gooseberries and the rhubarb.

Mr. and Mrs. Arthur Preston, retired, who have lived at The Red Cot in Fairview-road for 20 years, said to the Minister: 'Save this road.'

'We must consider,' Mr. Silkin began, 'that you will get another house, just as good if not better.'

'We don't want another house,' said Mrs. Preston, and wept. 'We want this one.'

Mr. Preston interjected: 'But you can't put up houses for the people who have been bombed out.'

Putting a hand on the Minister's shoulder and pointing to an apple tree laden with blossom, he asked: 'Can you put in a tree like that? It is 20 years old. You can't give me back my fruit trees.'

'No, that is true,' replied the Minister, his hands nervously tying and untying the chain on the old couple's gateway.

Asked whether he would consider any alternative plan which would save the beautiful countryside of Stevenage, Mr. Silkin replied: 'An alternative has been put forward and will be considered. If it fails...' the Minister's voice failed.

'Believe me,' he said, 'the plan will be carried out with a desire on my part to avoid trouble.'

The whole day was like that. Heartbreaking. Many people in Fairview-road had just finished buying their houses. 'We wanted these freehold houses for our children,' they told the Minister.

I was at the Caves last night. Rita was there, also Freda and Jane. I have fibrositis ... from having to march with the Whitehall charwomen in the rain. Ha! ha! Stafford Cripps and his farthing rise...

Was it true what you said about Richard coming top in his exams, or did I dream it? Perhaps you'd better put it in writing again.

Best love to all, Og

PS. Rita Cave and her brother's new wife don't speak.

PPS. I went for an interview with the editor of the Daily Herald, but they say they have no vacancies. Expenses on the Daily Graphic nowadays are not a living at all.

August 1946
151, The White House
Albany St, NW1

Dear B,

Thanks to Rosalie who found me this tiny flat ... I am very cosy for the first time in London. What a mean swine I am .... always saying spiteful things about Rosalie, yet she is always so nice to me nowadays, it makes me blush to think. I suppose marriage has changed her. I suppose when you get what you want, you can still turn into a different person no matter what your age?...

No sooner am I so cosy ... trouble begins again. This time it is our Expenses! Business is very bad in spite of the paper always having a double-page spread of photographs of delicious kittens, dogs and things – I was told to interview every single cat at the first Cat Fancy show since the war even those with no proper pedigree at all – so Lord Kemsley has made some sweeping cuts to try and keep Costs down. He has ordered no more Entertaining, hospitality, tips or gratuities; all these will be disallowed to everyone in future from the Editor downwards. If this should stand, it would mean like a cut in wages for everyone of from 50/- to £5 a week. It is absurd, everyone says so; we cannot work under these conditions; it would mean for us reporters being constantly out of pocket or getting no story at all. Meanwhile we are lobbying together and this is one time the Editor and all his minions of assistants are praying the Union will do something. We aim to tell the Chairman it would be equivalent to the Daily Graphic (everyone thinks changing the name from the Daily Sketch is a stupid mistake) going out of business. The old boy must be dotty or else the dollar crisis has him worried about some of his millions.

We have a perfectly ghastly new News Editor named Dixon from Glasgow. He is known as Fix-it Dixon. He is, I'm afraid, quite mad but Lord Kemsley it is said likes only Scotsmen or Welshmen. To give you an idea:

First he tells me to get ready to go to Germany on the BAOR wives story on August 30.*

I get my passport from the Soviet Consul, go along to the Control Commission and deposit it in order to get permit for Germany. Next day, however, he has brilliant brainwave; wants me to fly straight off to Sweden before lunch on story of Russians experimenting with German V-rockets and sending them over Sweden. (Perhaps you saw Chapman Pincher's story on this in the Express last Friday?) Dixon sends me flying round to get visa for Sweden and Denmark. Back I go to Control Commission, again get passport, get visas, etc. But no seat on plane; so he gets on to the Foreign Office; insists on Priority Air Transport for me to fly to Sweden. At present I am still waiting for it. I am told to be ready to fly any day. When I ask him what kind of story he wants, he says use your imagination, I want the low-down on Flying Saucers; so you get to Stockholm; you sit outside a cafe; you hear bang-bang and there you are.

No wonder the staff are worried how long this paper can survive. Our sales are expected to drop like a stone when restrictions are lifted on circulation. Meanwhile they've put my wages up by 2gns to 16gns. Sweden is off and I go to Germany instead. Meanwhile the Viscount Kemsley is in Rio and rumour has it that squatters will take over his estate in Dropmore.

Love, Ogg

*On 30th August 1946, the first British wives and children of serving men in Germany were allowed to sail with the British Army to live with their husbands in Germany.

August 1946
c/o Daily Graphic
Room 311, Kemsley House
Gray's Inn Road WC1

Dear B,

The anxiety about the paper is having an effect. Some of my colleagues have got anxiety symptoms.

We assemble at the Bar in Theobalds Road of an evening and discuss the uncertain future. Dixon likes to hold court with a little group of his cronies around him. Sometimes chaps join us from the Sunday Times or the Sunday Empire News. Jack Fishman is the Empire editor and full of gossip. Robert Robinson* drinks alone at the Bar. There are usually three of us girls, my beautiful colleague Ingrid Etter, who is married to the Polish editor of the Dzennik Polski, and a racing motorist woman named Kay Petre, very elegant and nice, showing no signs that her face was smashed in a car smash-up. The boys are all very depressed; there is talk of a strike, so help us! Later on a little man from Extel (Exchange Telegraph agency) comes to join us. He is Alan Whicker and very shy but he likes to hang around us and pick up a few tips. Sometimes some of the van-drivers come in with some bananas or eggs for old Fix-it.

I had to go in to see our new Foreign Editor, a man called Ian Fleming.** Handsome, but the coldest blue eyes I ever saw. Something so chilling. But Victor Lewis likes him; remember our cricket man Victor who thought it was the 'end of his world' ....They appointed a man, the one who usually covers diplomatic stuff and UNO, to go to Washington. So this chap lets his flat to my colleague Ingrid and her husband Tadeusz Horko who also gets his job (Ingrid gets it I mean) going round the Foreign Office and all that. So this man takes his wife, packs his bags and leaves for the station last Friday morning en route for the Washington boat. At eleventh hour they recall him to K.H. Back he comes to Gray's Inn Road, large fat, fiftyish man, in tears, no job, no flat and no place to go. I tell you they're mad. I'll feel a lot safer when I get to Berlin...

Was at Rosalie's on Friday. She and Paul just returned from Sweden. Rosalie has bought four bags and six pairs of shoes. The shoes, about 6 gns a time, she displays to Rita, Jane and Sally. Then the blouses, trinkets, etc. Imagine! She goes on displaying for an hour. And has not bought one hankie even for Rita or Sally. Rita wept when she saw the shoes. Imagine, showing your sister six pairs of shoes and you haven't even bought her a pair of pumps. Ros never turned a hair though. Greta Garbo was staying in their hotel and guess who else? Mrs. Oscar Deutsch and Uncle and the two boys, Ronnie and David Deutsch.

It looks like we shall be an all-girl reporting team to sail to Germany. The papers want lots of 'heart' in it or something. I bumped into Monica, the Reynolds News girl who is coming with us. She says she'll give them 'heart' when she meets all the starving German children. 'We're doing it again,' says Monica, 'just like 1918. Starving the Germans; we've got no hearts.'

Love, Oggi

Robert Robinson (1927–2011) became a popular TV and radio presenter.
**Ian Fleming later wrote some books about a chap called James Bond. Alan Whicker seems to have lost his shyness in front of the camera.*

15th September 1946
c/o the Am Zoo Press Camp
Kurfurstendamm, Berlin

Dear B,

We were an all-women army when we set sail for Cuxhaven. What you might call a Strong contingent. This included three demure ladies in hats, me for one, also Florence Keyworth, nice, refined, rather attractive for the Daily Worker; and a Quiet Lady named Miss Phyllis Deakin for The Times. Monica, of course, clutching everybody's sweet ration which she insisted on collecting from each of us, in little bags, including bars of chocolate and anything else we'd brought along either as rations for the journey – or as give-away presents for we none of us know what to expect in Germany. We also have two males, one in British Army uniform is Willi Frischauer, looking very plump and Viennese and Ronnie Camp for the News Chronicle. A lovely dark-haired girl named Mea Allan represents the Daily Herald and so on....

Trouble is the British Army officers shrink away in terror at sight of us. They keep giving us Orders of the Day but only by putting up little printed notices all over the ship. It seems they do not want us to go to Berlin but only to Hanover, Hamburg, and their reason is that Berlin is flattened to the ground and there's no place for us to stay or to sleep.

After that we issue our own instructions saying we refuse to go anywhere else except Berlin.

This brought the C.O. and his Officers out of their hidey-holes below decks. By afternoon of the first day, they called a Press Conference. The C.O. spoke. He said that he and his Brother Officers were very 'glad we are not married to any of you Ladies.'

Silly-billies. After that..... having got it settled that we were free to go to Berlin, quite a few of the girls decided not to.

The train journey to Hanover first was quite slow, on account of much of the railway line having been destroyed; Monica stood at the open window and hurled our sweet ration on to the railway-line so that the German children could run on to the line and collect. Eventually a Stationmaster appeared and shouted 'Achtung'. He wanted us to stop hurling sweets because it was too dangerous for the children.

It was raining when we got to Berlin and very muggy warm. The smell of dead bodies under the ruins was awful. In the Kurfurstendamm close to the Zoo (or where the Zoo used to be), the hotel housing the international press corps was the only building standing. Inside a lot of famous names were sitting about in armchairs just staring dourly into space. I was told they were waiting for the London newspapers to arrive by air. Some nice, friendly ones among the Famous invited us to have a brandy which we did. They included Sefton Delmer for the Express, William Forrest for the News Chronicle and Ian Coulter for the Daily Telegraph.

In the afternoon I hire a big car and call on the newly-appointed Control Commissioner (Army) Colonel Guy Hughes with whose beautiful blonde wife and four gorgeous children I'd travelled on the train. I take the four children on a sightseeing tour in the Grunwald which is the only part of the city with houses more or less intact. Then we go to the Wilhelmstrasse and go up to Hitler's balcony to have a look. Awful mess, with documents still lying about or anyway scraps of books and papers. We play games on the balcony, giving Hitler salutes and playing the fool until the two Soviet Russian sentries on the ground floor call us down because a little crowd has gathered and seems rather annoyed.

So we get back in the car and drive around until we see some nice clean German children walking on stilts through the rubble and they let us do it too.

Love Ogg

April 1947
151, The White House
Albany St, NW1

Dear B,

Don't have a new-look coat or suit or at least not too new looking. I think when women realise how awful they looked, they will be dropped. You'd think they'd have a glimpse of themselves in windows passing-by, but most girls wearing the long sweeping skirt stare grimly ahead and try not to see the tortured faces of onlookers trying not to laugh. Hats are even worse; I have seen several women (two at the office) even more middle-aged than I am and wearing a bonnet like Dolly Varden tied under the chin. It's one way of supporting the chin.

At the Linguists Club near Hyde Park Corner, there were still more middle-aged ladies determinedly speaking French. I had tea at their snack-bar on Friday and the ladies all used the word 'oui oui' with such fire and verve that our cakes trembled on their plates. Friday was also Russian day but I saw no fellow-travellers about except for a few sinister slav faces, from which a great deal of Polish came forth, though when the ladies cried 'merci merci,' it was scarcely distinguishable except as one of the Slav languages.

I was so sorry I had to rush away from the canteen on Wednesday when Frank came to see me. I got sent to Bishops Stortford to look for the home of Mrs. Valerie Lea, the woman who fell off a train at Liphook last week. It would have been simpler if I had been given the dead lady's address; as it was I rode around the county in a taxi for several hours. It was 11pm before I found the village of Ugley, pronounced ugly.

One night a photographer and I got sent to do a picture story on The Poetry Society near Marble Arch; because someone had seen a similar idea done in Picture Post. The photo-man and me were very nervous; the poetry-reading was timed for 8pm and just before it started, we were ushered into the 'committee' room where the poets, three of them and one 'reader' in a low-cut floral gown, sipped a little sherry and talked about Byron. The Society's secretary in a green new-look suit assured me that she was not at all anti-traditionalist and I said, 'I'm so glad.' She introduced me to 'our rising young poet' who had a very white face behind thick tortoiseshell glasses and a strong Yorkshire accent. 'He is so virile,' she assured me. Tony, that's our photo-man who usually fights with me over everything, kept very close to me as we were ushered into a big room, with some 30 people sitting in rows on hard chairs. There was a dim light from candle-shaped globes and a big notice – 'no smoking.' One woman wore a long black velvet cloak, and then all the chosen, that is the four members of the committee, took front seats because they knew the reader would have the good sense to pick THEIR poems to be read. I sensed that the other 30 faintly hoped some of their contributions would be included, but I guess their luck was right out. Everybody shrank modestly from Tony's camera. The floral gown began to read, though it must have been an eyestrain in that dim light. Favourite poems were about the blackthorn and love and one was called 'on being dead'. When the front row had their poems read, the authors blushed and everyone clapped. After one hour the Chairman made a speech and said he had never heard poems read 'so lovingly'. Then all the 30 poets filed out silently.

There was the most tremendous crowd at the Women's Press Club in Carey St, to see Danny Kaye and I was glad I had no new-look clothes to spoil in the crush. Danny looks kind and intelligent and gentle and almost too modest to be true. Even three serious representatives from the Soviet News Agency turned up to see him. And people could be heard saying, 'If they were ALL like that, there'd be no Palestine problem' and similar nonsense. Still I felt awful having to go to see Lady Barker* at her Cobham home after receiving the Stern gang's bomb. She wasn't in, thank goodness, but the rest of the army was.

Love, Og

* Lady Barker was the wife of Sir Evelyn Barker who was the British Commanding Officer in Palestine. The Stern Gang had sent letter bombs to many prominent British figures, including Cabinet Ministers. Sir Evelyn survived the bomb that blew up the King David Hotel in Jerusalem and caused uproar by forbidding his troops to have any contact with Jews. Many years later it was revealed that he had had an Arab mistress and was deeply anti-Semitic.

25th July 1947
151, The White House
Albany St, NW1

Dear B,

Thanks for ringing me last night; but you shouldn't; it costs 3/6d which you should not waste on me. I am not phoning back because I can't afford 3/6d at the moment, and also the Operators here listen in on the phone which I always hate. I don't say they do it all the time, but they do very often. Though one can't say much in three minutes.

I did not go away for my holiday week but put the money in the bank instead. Partly I expect the general economy wave everywhere has affected me too. And for me travelling is so much like work, it was a pleasure to stay here with nothing to do but cook myself three meals a day, which was easy in this flat.

After the newsprint cuts, things went from bad to worse at the office. Last week 30 people were sacked altogether. Perhaps Lord K was trying to get back at the Government. I don't know. Anyhow, the Union took fright & decided it was time to do something.

Yesterday at a chapel meeting of the Union together with representatives of the Federated House Chapel (which means everybody, the machine-men, comp operators, printers, drivers, news-vendors, everybody 'who touches or distributes a newspaper') decided to send an ultimatum to Lord K, giving him 48 hours to rescind the dismissals. Up to time of writing, which is Friday night, there is no news of his weakening. If he doesn't act, there will probably be a strike meeting next week; a vote will be taken and then a 21-day strike notice given. I haven't the faintest idea whether it will come to that; but anyhow the place is in uproar. It was a pity (perhaps) that the representative from the Union who spoke to the chapel meeting was my old pal (from Reuter days) Harry Cousins of Tass Agency, but of course he came in his capacity as Chairman of the Central London Branch of the N.U.J., and not as a Communist. Nevertheless if Lord K should get to hear, he might see himself in the role of defender of the freedom of Kemsley House from the red danger. My colleagues at the office are worried in case a strike breaks before they collect their holiday money next weekend. These be stirring times ... A lot of people will regret the necessity of striking, which nobody likes, but we do have to think of our 30 colleagues with literally nowhere to go in these hard days, and so we have to stand together or fall.

I wish the heat would break; it is killing me, near. I hope you have settled down comfortably at home again and can cope with the garden, the house and the children. I suppose Richard has broken up from school now for the holidays.

Cora & her new husband Max called to see me and had tea. They took me to see the Winslow Boy. They seemed very happy and Cora never stops giggling. However, Max behaved very well. I thought Cora looked marvellous with her hair down to her waist almost at the back, and hanging loose like Ophelia's because Max likes it that way.

Our van-driver brought me 20 dozen fresh eggs, and then young Tom turned up out of the blue with another half-dozen! Everyone at the office complains about my clothes; nothing 'summery'. I am spending nothing, neither money nor coupons. Talk about mean.......

I had to go and see David Niven and the children. I liked the children.

We are all nervous in case the other papers print anything about us and our problems. That would upset Lawd K who is very vain. Strike pay from the Union is about 50 bob a week which certainly won't even pay my rent here which is one thing I would hate to say over the phone here, with the operators all agog.

Best love to all, Og

14th December 1947
151, The White House
Albany St, NW1

Dearest B,

Very many thanks for parcel which much appreciated. Also Much needed .... but thereby hangs a tale. Orange Juice especially joyfully received.

Please tell your Nanny Brenda that the jumper fits perfectly. The knitting is so much admired at the office that to repeat comments would only make her conceited.

Even Rosalie and Sally admired it! I saw them yesterday. Also heard the news that Harold is to wed next Saturday at Marylebone registry office, followed by discreet lunch at the Dorchester for twelve. The girl is a Miss Marsh, a blonde (rather taller than him) who accompanied him to a recent Ladies' Night.

So... how come you never noticed her? Also he has a flat, and says Rosalie, They Understand One Another. Everyone is more or less Thrilled.

Now there is talk of disposing into wedlock, Rita and myself with more or less despatch. But I said No, I would insist on Sally being also despatched, also Jane, before I fain would consent. However, there is evil talk of another newspaper cut in January, so it looks as though I shall have to Marry or go down a mine. Do you think I could wield a Pick when my cough is better?

My cough is not better.

I hope you will do the necessary and either phone your congratulations to Mr. Cave or send a telegram to the Dorchester on Saturday. They have a cold converted flat in the Hagley road, says Rosalie, so you will be Neighbours.

Cora made me leave off my boots and Frank's bed-socks, and hat because my lack of glamour offended her. So with Brenda's death-taking jumper I am almost New or shall be when my cough is better. My cough is not better. How is Bettina? And what is her social news? Has she finished her Midwifery? . . . .

I told Paul that we adored the cake. He made a lot of things for the Royal wedding last month. I was not at the royal wedding; Mr. Dixon was not pleased. I was in bed from the after-effects of a 'miscarriage' as it is sometimes politely called.* I know you will be very angry. I was angry too, and so ashamed. I do not even speak to the man responsible because I do not want him to know anything about it. I drew every last penny out of the bank, almost £90 but it was not enough. Cora loaned me the other £70 and I have promised to pay it back in six months. I was very frightened ... not being able to tell anyone about it ... and having to keep on at the office; it was in the middle of another Gas strike so I had to dodge between the doctor and the Union meetings on freezing street corners at Barking. It serves me right and I hope it will teach me a lesson. Mr. Dixon was not pleased because it meant there was no one to stand at the door of the church** asking guests for their full names with proper spelling. It is just as well; supposing Prince Philip had spotted me and recognised me, looking like hell and damnation which is what I deserve. I hope the children are well and being Good. When I have saved up to pay back Cora, I will save up to come to Brum and you.

Love, Ogg

*Abortion was illegal in 1947 (Olga's note).
**St Margaret's for Princess Elizabeth's wedding, November 1947.

March 1948
c/o Daily Graphic
Room 311, Kemsley House
Gray's Inn Road WC1

Dear B,

I've got to go and live in the Onslow Court Hotel in South Kensington, damn it, because the police are expected to be making an arrest there any day now. You may have read about the acid-bath murderer (he melts elderly rich ladies in a bath of acid) and I have got to live in the hotel and lurk in the lobby, witness the arrest and then chat with the guests to find out what Mr. John George Haigh* ate for breakfast, lunch and dinner. I told Duncan Webb, new news editor, I couldn't see why one of the Crime boys couldn't go and live there instead of me, but he said they want a Colour story, all about the hotel and especially the Food. I have to go in disguise, i.e. pretend to be ordinary Housewife holidaying in London for the shopping. The hotel porter looked pretty fed up when I arrived with my little overnight bag (one lock missing as usual) considering that the Press have been practically living in the place the past 3 days. Going up in the lift he said (very sarcastic this) he hoped I would enjoy my stay. I notice every little table has its own private pot of marmalade; I hope I don't get what's left of Mr. Haigh's.
    Love, Oggi

*John George Haigh was convicted of the Brides in the Bath murders and hanged in 1949.

November 1948
Flat 169, The White House
Albany Street, NW1

Dear Beryl,

Rosalie's girl friend returned from abroad and wanted her flat back. Luckily there was just one vacant, No. 169 further along the corridor, so I was delighted to move in here. It is just as tiny but I bought a little gilt Florentine-reproduction table and feel that at last my wanderings are over and I have my 'own place'. There is a swimming pool downstairs, restaurant and newsagent, hairdressing, which makes life easy.

I took a new boyfriend John whom I met at the Linguists Club round to Grove End Gardens but the evening at Rosalie's was not perhaps an unqualified success. Rosalie thought John too thin, which of course he is, as you barely see him sideways. John and I were disappointed in the hospitality which was even thinner. We got only one drink each, and then Rosalie put the bottle firmly in the cupboard. Nor did John shine socially so to speak, though he defended himself to me later, declaring he did 'not know much about baking anyway'. This means that Paul was in a showing-off mood on Friday, partly because of all his confectionery work he does for the Palace ...but chiefly because he was televised recently and is now determined to be in 'Life' with a middle-page spread of pictures or Die in the attempt. John promised to find out for him the name of the Editor.

The television scene showed the famous hands deep in the dough and Paul is quite intoxicated with success. John was made to read all Paul's cuttings from 'The Baker and Confectioner'. Paul showed him the pictures of all his cakes in the shape of Disney animals and toys and said his life-story for 'Life' will be called 'Fun in Cakes' and will tell how he started life in Vienna as a mere stockbroker.

'And did you fail then?' I asked,

'Fail?' said Paul and nearly exploded so that the dog Angus whimpered and ran into a corner.

There is no doubt I do not know how to handle Great Men. And Paul went on showing the pictures and John, rather tactlessly I thought, kept saying, 'terrific pictures, but where are the cakes?' His thin, pale face looked hungrily round the sideboard. But when it came it was just a plain sponge and we did feel a bit disgruntled.

Also, John did not seem impressed with the Family who were admittedly not at their best. Sally who looks her best with her hair up, wore it down which makes her look like dismal desmond. Rosalie, as always right up to the mark, was smart with the new curly-cut which suits her and looks 10 years younger than Rita who wore a huge black, heart-shaped halo on her blonde hair. Rita informed us that she is travelling first-class on the newly-swept Queen Mary to the USA in a couple of weeks. John stared at Rita all the time in a way I thought as tactless as his remark about the cakes. Rita looks very raddled and makes me more afraid than ever of getting old. John asked me why Rita looks so 'strained'.

Then we went home and I reproached John for not talking enough, which was unfair because he could not have got a word in edgeways anyway, although Jane was not there, having flown to Cannes to see some relative named Goodman I think, but I kept on so that John, who went to London University and has diplomas in Economics and Sociology, said he would not have minded Hearing about the Cakes if we had been given some to eat.[...]

However, John makes a nice platonic friend who keeps my interest only by his air of total mystery and by the fact there are no other men who want to take me out. We went to see Ruth Draper the other night, with free tickets of course which I got from the office, but John bought the supper, the gin, flowers and chocolates. I shall never be able to call him mean again after our visit to the Family last Friday.

Oh and I nearly forgot to mention that Paul has sent every member of the family (Jane, Sally, Rita etc) several tins of orange marmalade which he bought while in Dublin lecturing, some weeks ago.

But when I thanked him passionately for my two tins, he said, 'Oh, but you have to PAY for it. That will be 4/3d' And when I handed it over, allbeit [sic] rather sourly because I don't like marmalade anyway (so you can have the other tin, I'll bring it) Rosalie said rather crossly: 'I TOLD you Paulie, that everyone would think it was a Gift.'

By the way I have run out of sugar, suppose you can't REfund me half a pound or so?

My little flat is nice and warm, and I wish you would come up to town and see it some time.

I hope Lucy is better now and I DO hope that you will stop having troubles for a bit, as I think you get more than your share.

I have SUCH a cold, caught at the Cenotaph, atishoooooooot.

Best love to all, Og.

1949

29th January 1949
Flat 169, The White House
Albany Street, NW1

Dearest B,

I long to see the children; are you all well? What news of Bettina? Why no word from you?

I tried hard to get another job, but nothing doing yet. I had an interview with the Observer who said he would like to give me a job but couldn't as he has no extra paper for the Sundays. Don't ALL the papers look awful nowadays? Julius Silverman M.P. tried to get my Russian teacher Mrs. Grun into the Palestine debate on Wednesday, but it was hopeless; no room at all; but she spent FOUR hours quite happily standing in the cold outside hoping, along with a great queue of Palestine students. Today she has a big cold for our lesson.

Rosalie and Paul are in Paris this week; Rita has returned from New York; I was there last Friday when she arrived; but it turned out that poor Jane had done something wrong with Rita's egg ration and there was an enormous row, with Paul whistling shrilly throughout to try & remind the Girls they were Ladies Please!...... but no use, it was like a thrush song in the jungle.

I have not forgotten I promised to send you a cheque for the grey coat; I am positively sick of having it admired. Everyone says it is the smartest coat they've seen.

Tell Richard I had to go and interview a sick chimpanzee at the Bertram Mills circus last week. Was I scared when I had to go in that cage to shake hands with that chimp who is only Lucy's age but was fighting mad like Richard when you turn off the Dick Barton programme.

I am now reading Dostoevsky's novels in the original Russian and they are all so sad that I cry all the time like I used to do over the yellow pages of 'Beulah'.

Sally had a letter from Aunt Becky thanking her for the clothing she sent; apparently they haven't a rag to wear. Neither have I, that's why I could not go to the Anglo-Palestine ball, but I am trying hard to save. All my Paris food is gone now, and I am on lean times again.

Best love to Frank and Richard and Lucille and Tina and you. Og

July 1949
c/o Daily Graphic
Room 311, Kemsley House
Gray's Inn Road WC1

Dear B,

Thanks for yours. I thought I would have to 'do' Wimbledon all next week and the week after and was quite hysterical all week-end in anticipation (unlike Auntie Cora and Uncle Max I hate tennis, football, golf, and in fact all games and exercises of any kind; you could not persuade me even to a game of ludo) .... but it looks today like I've been saved by the gong or a kindly fate.

I was to have spent the coming week closeted in between matches with Miss Nancy Chaffee, the one they call the poor man's Gussie Moran, and when I pleaded with the Editor that it was 'bad for the paper' put tactfully, to send me to do Miss Chaffee because I knew nothing about tennis except that 'love' came somewhere into the score, the Editor replied blandly that it was not necessary for me to know anything about TENNIS.

Now it appears the Tennis Associations of G.B. and U.S.A have banned all the girls writing for the papers; (old Og was to write it, Reader, but Nancy was to get the cheque for 30 guineas and her name on it) so we may have to make do with Nancy's life-story in one issue, which someone else will write. The regulation is she must not mention one word about Tennis, Wimbledon or even England.

I met all les girls at the Queen's Club championships last week; both Nancy and Gussie are Beautiful and Terrible.

Gussie wears big brass ear-rings and a red-henna dye in her hair and looks wonderful and awful, if you know what I mean; something like a Bayswater landlady with a Bohemian gipsy touch before starting to take in lodgers just for the fun of it. But I didn't have to bother about Gussie because Rhona Churchill got her for the Daily Mail. I got Nancy who is equally beautiful, friendly, efficient, faintly masculine, even more faintly jewish (oh you Chaffas) and quite overwhelming. She told me how to have her cheque made out in the opening sentence. She has bronzed and beautifully toiletted legs from which all the hairs have been removed; rough, ugly boys' hair and wonderful green eyes, she is 21 and looks 36. Why do all American women look so old?

I had to watch her play Mrs. Todd; it lasted an hour, and I nearly fainted with exhaustion. Why do they do these things to me?!

As I have said, I was hysterical anyway. My Russian teacher says I have a 'thing' about Americans; she says it is worse than anti-semitism. She is quite right; but it was just the combination of Tennis and Nancy and all that batting, when I have other things on my mind.

After all I turn up to the office punctually and regularly every day; I don't think I should be expected to work as well, what?

You'll get no sympathy from me over Richard; I think Rick is o.k. Mrs. Grun says, after seeing his letter, she thinks so too. She says the grammar school will knock him into shape and all he needs is a lot of love.

I had to interview Anouk; she looked like Gussie Moran would look like after all those lodgers had finished with her. She made me feel quite Tidy.

Best love to Ricky; tell him if he had a basin-full of Denis Compton, Gussie and banned girl sprinters, he'd feel like pore old Arnty.

Love to all, Og

6th August 1949
Flat 169, The White House
Albany Street, NW1

My Dears All,

I am enchanted by your picture of the castle of Chateaubriand which you sent me.* Is it by a lake or on the seashore, or is it a sort of islet? I believe Combourg is a historic town and after seeing your postcard and hearing your raptures about the town and hotel I certainly shall hope to go there for my holiday and follow in your footsteps.

Am delighted you had the good sense to leave Le Touquet which I hear from many sides is an awful place, and still more happy that you joined up together, with Anna and Rudolph and Marcel.

Beryl, I wrote you once to Le Touquet but I don't know if you received the letter, saying I was unable to get the tablets you wanted because my chemist says they are most dangerous and advised me not to let you have them. So I owe you ten shillings.

Have been out of town three times this week and did a 150-mile journey each day, but got little out of it. One was a silly story about a German Prince, Prince Waldemar zu Hohenlohe Ohringen, who was invited by a poor butcher's assistant in a Gravesend slum to have a holiday here. We had to chase other press cars about 70 mph and my nerves were in a frazzle when we got back in the early hours of the morning in a terrific rainstorm. Yes, it has been cool and thank heaven, wet all this week over here.

An even sillier story was out at Leighton Buzzard where a young Methodist probationer parson had been sacked from his church for getting married three years before it was permitted.

About 30 pressmen and cameramen descended on the remote farmhouse set in muddy fields where the young couple were spending their honeymoon. The cameramen, who were determined to get a picture, parked their cars in the muddy lane leading to the farmhouse and declared they 'would not budge until the couple appeared'. And the Parson, who was an Oxford don and intelligent and knew what it was all about, was determined we should not put his picture in the papers. They sent the farmhands to put up barricades and they kept watch with pitchforks. Then it was decided to send a special delegation of the only two women in the Press party, that was me and Mabel Elliott of the News Chronicle. The rain was pouring down and the farmer was sorry for us and let us into the front parlour. But then the young man and his tearful bride appeared. They were very angry and cursed us and threw us out into the rain again. It was not nearly so funny as it sounds. So we all decided that we would ignore our Editors' instructions and return to London, which we did, but unfortunately my photographer and driver wanted to stop at every pub on the road back and it was early in the morning again before we got back, and me sulking all the way.

After that I got one story at Holloway prison and another interviewing a 14-year-old Miracle Boy called David the Miracle Healer from Indiana, Indianapolis who is to try and convert Londoners to Christ. He told us he had had a mystic vision when he was nine years old, went to Heaven, met Jesus who told him to go back and preach which he has been doing ever since. The little boy, whose voice was hoarse and breaking from preaching, wore a green and white check suit, called me Ma'am and gave me a bar of chocolate. I assume I am now Saved.

I am expecting to have Vivienne for a weekend soon. I am very cross because she has had her hair cut. Love to Anna and Rudolf and Marcel and you and Frank and the children, whom once again I implore to be Good. Write me again.

Olga

The Jaffa family had holidayed in Normandy with Olga's French relations, the Frenkels.

1950

By now Olga, now 38 years old, is established and settled (so far as one could ever be) in Fleet Street and working on her autobiography. The Labour Party had recently won the Election and the BBC ran the pilot for a radio series called The Archers. Princess Anne was born.

June 1950
Flat 169, The White House
Albany Street, NW1

Dear B,

Was at Rosalie's Friday night, Sally and Jane also there. FREDA is engaged to be married and is nearly off her head, but story too long to be told here. It will have to wait.

I am sitting here in my tiny flat, staring out at the stone wall opposite. Am watching the woman on the floor below in the flat opposite hanging her newly-washed net curtains.

Hers is not a rented flat like mine; she has her own bits and pieces.

The radio is playing 'Bewitched, Bothered and Bewildered' which fits my mood.

I met a man last Sunday whom I liked very much. Let's call him A. I sit here and wonder if he will telephone me today. The woman downstairs; she is a well known comedy actress but I forget her name, has finished hanging her curtains.

Love, Og

July 1950
Flat 169, The White House
Albany Street, NW1

Dear B,

I love being so near Regent's Park, the beautiful white Nash terraces, the shadowed, tree-lined avenues, the lake, the zoo and the shouting of the sea-lions and seals at night.

Oh Unfair, Unkind, Unkind, Unfair; to mention Caroline, the poor

251

girl who is always being frustrated just as she climbs into bed. I can assure you I never had the Faintest Intention of putting my so-called 'romances' on this level, as you suggest, in the autobiographical chapters of my book.* For one thing they never were Romances; I only wish they had been and I'd have fewer regrets. You ask, Why then does one 'do' these things? Well I shall tell you; one 'does' because one is lonely, bored, with nothing better to do and, as you say, often frustrated because there is an empty hollow at the very centre of life. I consider myself very lucky that I am on duty morning, noon and often night (it's a happy night that the News Editor or the Chief Sub doesn't ring up to say they don't understand my 'copy' or to query Some ghastly mistake I may have made ... like the woman M.P. and Holborn Counsellor who sued me and the paper in the King's Bench Division simply because I thought I was being nice, for once! I said she was devoted to the Local Authority Sewing-class because they made all her beautiful evening-dresses for nothing....! Even the subs didn't spot that one in time, alas, and she was awarded £3,000 for defamation)....

So THERE, you see! I think about what happened to me on some cold damp grass late one night, uncomfortable and perfunctory at least for me, which ended in a terrifying pregnancy and how I deserved every moment of agonising punishment. Sometimes nowadays, I think my trouble is that I cannot love anyone. And I want to so much.

I wrote the book for Betty; because she wanted to know what our family life was like before she was born, at home with our awful and yet marvellous parents. She says she can remember nothing before she was five. Having written one chapter, she was keen for me to continue, so I did.

As I say above, I am lucky to be able to sit in Queen Mary's rose garden and watch the ducks and mallards scuttling across the lake and oh the divinely sickly perfume of the voluptuous roses. I was pursued all week by a Spaniard I met there, a law student. He swears he is not pro-Franco.

I got a £5 prize from Lord Kemsley for the story on the Polish refugee shoemaker. His ludship also sent a letter saying, 'I see your name again in the list of prizewinners ... etc.' I would like to say thank you but what about a rise?

This week I had a cable from a journalist friend named Jimmy Hays who went to Korea for the fun of the battle because he disliked peacetime England and I warned him he wouldn't like it at all, at all. The cable says, 'How right you were about everything. Shalom, Jim.' He is a staunch

Tory and couldn't stand living here under Attlee, Bevan, Cripps and Co. I suppose his cable means that the Korean war is a mess and a shambles as I told him it would be.

I bumped into Aunt Sally who said she spent nearly the whole winter being very ill in bed and had neither heat nor food and no one (not even Jane) came near her. I felt very guilty because I knew nothing about it, having kept away from Les Girls for a bit in Grove End Gardens.

Then she said, looking hard at me, 'all old women should be married. You should do it .... do it now, before it is too late; otherwise you'll end up being as lonely as I am.'

Isn't it sad?

Best love to all, Og

Olga published her first book, Born Twice, *in 1951, which combined some family history with her own love story and its tragic end.*

1st September 1950
c/o Daily Graphic
Room 311, Kemsley House
Gray's Inn Road WC1

Dear B,

As you can imagine the approach of Freda's wedding-day (Oct.8) has caused a great stir among all us Girls, whether we are the Few (very few) who have 'made it'; those still hoping to make it or those who are almost past-hoping.

Even these latter combatants have a new lease of life, as it were, for there is no doubt that what Baltimore's Mrs. Simpson did for the over-forties, Hampstead's Freda has undoubtedly achieved for the nearer-fifties.

Not that Freda has put it quite like that. He is 42. Freda, who must now be nearly 47, has confessed to 45 and insisted that the wedding-day must not be delayed by one single hour more than need be, because she 'intends to have a baby before the year is out'.

Mind you ... we Girls are so impressed with her efficiency to date that we have no doubt she will be able to perform this extraordinary feat as well, since we are all agreed that Love will find a way.

Freda, who is fond of telling each of us in turn in four-hourly sessions, exactly how she Did It; I mean getting him to propose, claims it was all done by what she calls the Melting Method. No ... this is not an alternative method used by John George Haigh with his acid-bath system; it is simply a piece of advice given to Freda it seems by an itinerant Irish woman she met in the street. 'Be melting,' the Irish woman is alleged to have advised Freda. 'I was Cocky, and I lost mine. Give in – always.'

This was advice right up Freda's street and recommended itself highly to a woman of her sympathies whose main problem so far has been the difficulties of finding a sufficient number of men to give in to.

Rosalie, however, is a little annoyed with Freda who, finding Paul at home alone one evening before his wife returned from work, (her little hat shop in George Street) made to him the same lengthy revelations that she had already done to all of us in turn. Paul was later discovered in sadly wrecked state and, his wife suspects, missing some of his tender illusions about the reluctance of women to accept a proposal of marriage.

Paul, it appears, had learned unwillingly enough of the lengths to which Freda had gone during the six agonising weeks of doubt and struggle, to extract the proposal. She had described to him in palpitating detail how she had decorated her substantial mouth in the plummiest new colours, painted her eyelids with cosmetic in green and silver and dyed each silver hair blacker than the raven's wing. When Rosalie did get home, it was Paul who was doing the melting, into tears of deepest disillusion.

Luckily for all, however, Freda's Intended is not averse to these intimate confidences. Indeed, on the night of the Proposal, staring deep into Freda's green-and-silvered eyes, studded with lashes so heavily mascaraed they seemed like enormous guns pointing at his heart, more menacing and apparently more dangerous than any mere Cupid's arrow .... he made the Proposal on condition that after the nuptials she would continue to attire herself with the same careful attention as she had done that very evening; hinting darkly that he had seen 'some others who had let themselves go – afterwards.'

Freda, rising to the occasion, promised bigger and better eyelashes and brighter and more succulent eye-shadow for the Day and all the days to follow. Rosalie and Jane are in despair because Freda's mother, having agreed to pay for the wedding OR for a trousseau, Freda has plumped for a Wedding that will make Princess Margaret's (who we are told, is to engage the young Duke of Buccleuch shortly) look somewhat shoddy. Freda went the morning after the proposal to Upper Berkeley Street, which is as well known for Swank Jews, and registered. 'When I had to write Freda Levine Spinster,' she said, 'a cold shiver went up my spine; think of being THAT unutterable thing.'[…]

Even when her Intended (I forget his name which is slightly Spanish like Da Silva, or De Costa or something like that) met with an accident and bruised his spine; he is a Night-Driver for a car-hire firm, Freda, while passionately sympathising with his somewhat painful injuries, could not really think or talk of anything else but her Achievement and the Day.

The bruised spine is anyway probably a bit of luck for both of them, because any tender experiments while not exactly ruled out, are and have been somewhat limited since the accident; the young man, very tall and greying, indeed appeared to think that he ought to behave with the respect required of a real Chosen, but Freda, in spite of her transports at getting her man, was not quite willing to go as far as that. But, Freda informs us, she will not really Show him anything much until after the Day, or rather the Night, so as not to frighten him.

The Intended had, it seems, a mother until recently, and he saved his money and bought a nice little house for her and then the mother died and there he was, all alone. Freda, who has spent the past year touring London dance halls as far out as Wembley and Wimbledon, saw him standing alone at one of these, and said to herself, 'That's mine!'

But after picking him up she despaired of interesting him and rather than lose the Chance altogether, introduced him (Freda has an exceptionally kind heart) to her best girl friend, a blonde. Until the blonde opened Freda's eyes one night at another dance by saying, 'But he loves YOU, I can tell by his eyes.'

At this point, Freda assures her audience, that it was quite true; she too had noticed his eyes. They followed her, she says, like a hungry dog. Freda in war paint, as she herself is the first to claim, would make any eyes roll.

There followed six weeks of anxiety and sleepless nights. The strain was so great that the insomnia is now quite chronic; Freda can neither sit, lie nor sleep and a doctor is keeping her heavily dosed with barbituric opiates.

The wedding is to be Slap Up, with a suitable man invited for each of her girl-friends including our Cousin Jane (who is worn out too with all the excitement) Rita Cave of course, Rosalie's girl-friend Anne and myself; and the generous Freda declares airily that she doesn't want any presents; we should spend the money on tarting ourselves up (green and silver disguises are indicated) and we should concentrate on Melting.

Freda's mother (divorced) who is also in a state of near-collapse; (the house is either full of women listening spell bound to Freda's tale of her campaign or Freda is on the telephone reporting minute-by-minute accounts of how she did it) .... has now washed her hands of it and leaves all to Jane. Latest reports are that Freda will wear the traditional white bridal gown with the traditional white veil. I quite see her point; the veil will come in handy driving through Maida Vale in case the carriage passes any old friends or 'customers'.

The Chosen, says Freda, is a nice simple soul, not an intellectual it seems, but charming enough. Only snag is so far that his house furnishings offend her artistic soul, but she intends to turn one room into her own nest to express herself. Meanwhile Freda has been expressing herself freely to her young man with a wealth of detail and a confessional flow that has him quite fascinated and tends to prove that Honesty after all is the best policy. Melting or not, Scheherazade had the right idea; just keep talking.[...]

Paul says if anything were to go wrong now, Freda would have to be taken away to an 'Erdington House'.*

Now for some confidential gossip about another branch of the Family; strictly in confidence so don't let me down. Rita Rainbow has left Gerald and hopes to buy a house in Cornwall for herself and Rosemary. Aunt Sally showed me her letter, where she asks her to sell her ring, etc., because her brothers refuse to sell the house for her. Now .... not a word PLEASE.

I don't know whether I did wrong or not, but on the request of my Russian teacher I introduced her to Sally, who was here yesterday, so that Sally could introduce her to spiritualism. Time will tell. Mrs. Grun's husband died in a German concentration camp in the war and even worse if possible was the loss of her favourite sister, the husband and child killed in Jugoslavia but whether shot, gassed or beaten to death, no one knows.

Am a bit lonely this week without my various boy friends who always leave me (must try melting sometimes) ... both having flown to various fighting-fronts in far distant parts of the world.

Best love, Og.

PS. Freda has hand-picked a boy friend for Sally too, to dance with on the Day.

PPS. Mitzi was invited too on her return from a trip to America, to hear

All About It. But she didn't turn up and the gossip is that she is sulking. It appears she met some people at Cannes who invited her out to the USA for a visit, and everyone said oh goodie you'll get a husband there. And now she is back without one, everyone is saying, what no husband, why not? Which you must admit is damned annoying, particularly in view of Freda preening herself everywhere, sleepless yes but Satisfied.

* Erdington House was the mental hospital in Birmingham to which Olga was committed after her suicide attempt in 1937.

9th October 1950
c/o Daily Graphic
Room 311, Kemsley House
Gray's Inn Road WC1

Dears,

Freda broke down under the Chuppah [wedding canopy]. The crowded, beautiful and exclusive schule at Upper Berkeley Street (seven guineas extra) and the American rabbi Reverend Rinehard were frozen into silent immobility for more than five or six minutes.

What began with a touching sniff and a tear or two ended in a torrent of sobs that rang out across the heads of the massed congregation. But the more the hysterical bride tried to control herself, the more her strangled sobs caught her by the throat and in the end, Rev. Rinehard took her in his arms, white net off-the-shoulder gown spangled with tiny gold stars and white and silver crown and all, and comforted her. It happened while she was signing her name in the book after the ceremony while standing under the Canopy to do it, and a ray of sunshine shone down on the radiant white figure, turning her exotic ugliness into sudden beauty. But it was all much too much; and when the couple finally left minutes late to the strains of here-comes-the bride, Freda's elaborate make-up was gone forever.

Nevertheless if you expect me to describe the whole long elaborate wedding day yesterday with its fantastic Chassanic [sic] ritual and luxury, you are mistaken. For it was all so much more touching than I expected. The truth is that everyone there, and the schule was packed with Freda's friends & relatives, jew and gentile, young and old, male and female, ex-boy-friends and girl-friends she had made haphazardly everywhere, all love the bride so much that they were not only ready to forgive her for dressing up like a bride of the orient, but were even pleased about it because it was Her Day, Her Moment of Triumph of which she had spent nearly 46 long years dreaming.

To begin at the beginning therefore, I went to Freda's flat on the Saturday night. Only single people were invited and Harold Cave was there, so you may draw your own conclusions, but I am under oath to Jane to keep secret what little I know, except that you were right and all is over with the marriage and has been for a very long time; all that remains is to wait the 3-year period for a divorce by desertion now. For once ... I was tactfully silent and Harold seemed to make faint efforts to be not gay but placid. Jane even believed that he is quite specifically relieved.

The bridegroom turned up late for the eve-of-wedding party and Freda amused us all by wringing her hands and pretending she was CERTAIN he was not going to turn up for the wedding. He proved to be shy and simple, but seemed to me a good enough soul and possibly Freda can yet make something of him.

Freda wore herself out trying to make the single boys and girls get together, but without much success.

She even had a Stepney Green blonde for Harold posed on the couch. We left the bride and groom sitting up all night writing out the names of the guests for the tables at the reception the following day.

On the Day ... Freda's bridal outfit would have been, well, exceptional even on a young and beautiful bride which Freda, alas, is not even to her best friends. Yet because she is pure-in-heart and totally unselfish (although everyone well knew that the synagogue could have been filled from pew to pew by Freda's ex-chosen lovers) .... everyone admired her to such an extent and she herself was so radiant with happiness that we all suffered a strange trick of eyesight yesterday; and when we all yelled in chorus 100 times that she looked gorgeous, wonderful, beautiful, glamorous, heavenly, we all (men as well as women) really meant it. It was a triumph of mind over matter.[...]

I am almost convinced that ugliness instead of being a handicap is a positive benefit because not only had Freda developed strong personality and charm ever since childhood, I suppose in order to distract attention from her physical handicaps, but also people went out of their way to flatter her more and more tenderly than they would bother to do to a better-favoured girl.

I know you will not believe me but it is true that radiance and the admiration of all did transform her so that you believed and she believed, and it was certainly clear that her bridegroom also believed, she was a young and beautiful princess. You did not notice the dark purple skin or the hook nose, the lines round the eyes. I know, only in romantic novelettes can defects like these fade from sight but I tell you they did. If it crossed your mind at all, as she entered the schule on the arm of a friend who had been picked to give her away because he was tall, good looking, and had a dress suit (her own father is separated from her mother and her own uncle did not have a suit) that she looked a pathetic freak, it was only for an instant. You were caught up in her own belief that she was beautiful.

From the schule the whole large congregation of about 200 people walked up the road to Bryanston Square and the reception began in the Mayfairia. It went on until 7 and the bride was the very last to leave, dancing every dance. The catering, according to Jane, was a guinea a head, and the Mayfairia are building up a comfortable clientele, as the schule send them all their customers and they began resoundingly enough with the Earl of Harewood's wedding.

It was beautifully catered, there was buffet eats with gin and advokat, followed by full sit-down tea downstairs, a huge wedding cake and orchestra. It began with large salad and smoked salmon and savoury rolls and cakes and pear melba, and after sherry toasts and speeches we all trooped upstairs again, where there were chocolates and ice-creams and more drinks.

But .... upstairs Harold Cave and I both got it in the neck from the witch in the mink coat, our Rita, who wanted us to come right away to the follow-up buffet party at her Park Lane flat nearby afterwards. Harold, declaring that 'these affairs are simply torture for me', excused himself and walked out on the blonde specially provided for him by Freda. When I heard this, I found the courage to excuse myself rapidly too; (frankly after so many hours of gruelling entertainment, I was a bit tired). Oh dear, you should have heard the Witch scream and call me all the names under the sun including her brother. 'I'm on duty ... I think,' I murmured and hurried away. Actually I would like to meet her boy-friend Hans May, the Viennese light-operetta composer who is working on a new Show to be called 'Carissima' who is expected to attend her Park Lane party but really I just wanted a cup of tea and a nice sit-down.

I forgot to mention there was a red-coated Toast-master (5 guineas) among the many extras. The silver head-dress and veil looked like: this.....

Love, Og

9

Alone but no Longer Lost

*A different phase of Olga's life began as she met Alfred W. and started a relationship
that would continue until his death thirty years later.*

December 1950
Flat 169, The White House
Albany Street, NW1

Dear B,

I found out (via the electoral list at Mill Hill library) that A had been
misleading me and is in fact a Married Man. Surprise! Well, no, but he
did not lie to me as you appear to suspect; nor can he be blamed for
so innocent a deception. After all I never asked him whether he had a
wife or not! On the contrary, I was keen to impress him with the image
I have of myself … i.e. the hard bitten Fleet Street Girl. So .. when I
did at last ask (because it had begun to matter awfully) he replied
immediately Yes he was married and living at home with a wife … he
was naturally astonished at my floods of tears and stared uncomprehendingly
at the hard bitten one reduced to sodden jelly, prostrate upon the floor
of this highly-sophisticated block of flats inhabited by well known stars
of stage and musical hall, with a prostitute on each floor it was claimed,
at least during the war years.

His astonishment turned to annoyance when the tears of the melted
one stopped abruptly and turned to screams of laughter instead. I laughed
so much I could not stop when he said that V was actually his second
wife; having divorced the first one, reluctantly though, just before the
war when she refused to accompany him on his flight abroad.

'What's the joke?' he said. 'I don't see anything funny in it.'

He failed to see that because I had agonised at the thought of a Wife,

261

it was a perfect scream to find he had Two. I went on loudly laughing and chuckling until he stopped it. This is probably the clue to our relationship. I do as I'm told. I am more than a bit afraid of him and I like it.

Oh ... how often I've sat on duty in the Divorce Court listening to barristers or judges arraigning bad husbands; 'the husband was a dominating, domineering man who demanded from the wife total subjugation to his wishes at all times.'

For years and years I felt lost and adrift, with no restraining hand, no one to say 'put on the kettle and make my tea'; 'bring me a whiskey, cigarettes, soup'; 'make our bed'; ... for lost girls like me, The Dominating, Domineering Man is someone to treasure. It shows he is interested, involved, with all his feelings, however bizarre, continuously engaged.

It even makes me feel slightly, slightly less guilty towards the wife.

A is never likely to leave her or even to want to do so; she is therefore safe under his domination which five years ago she chose and I can well understand why she chose it.

In novels we are called Victims. I am a happy victim. I have waited so long for this. Life turns out to be exactly like the romantic novels we used to despise.

A took me to Paris for a weekend of reconciliation (What for? We hadn't quarrelled) for mutual confessional and understanding. We had a suite in the Hotel du Nord which had pink cabbage roses on the wallpaper, a tall grandfather clock in the corner and a large bed with white lace counterpane. On the last evening we saw Boheme at the Comedie Francaise, a special Easter series of operas for tourists like us. Watching Mimi loving and dying on the stage was glorious and moving; yet somehow flat and common place compared with our own drama, sitting there in the stalls holding my bunch of violets, drunk with the music, the voices, wondering what our own end would be and hoping that, unlike Mimi's, it would be far off, very far...

Back in the office, my Features Editor is pleased because my greyhound Frankly Yours is doing well at Haringay. I find my desk covered in beer mugs, silver-chrome decanters, cut-glass fruit dishes and every kind of chromium plated rubbish. I'd like to go home early but he says I've got to do new stunt for next week's column. This time I have to work as an all-night lorry drivers Mate and take a lorry load of steel ingots from Surrey Commercial Dock in East London to Liverpool.

Will write when I get back.

Love Ogg

January 1952
c/o Daily Sketch, New Carmelite House
London EC4

Dear B,

Marylebone High Street is quiet under smog. I've been in fog round here before but never like this one. You can taste it, rather evil, thick and murky. People walk along coughing or muttering 'sorry' as they bump into bodies, lampposts or cars.

We were sold overnight by Viscount Kemsley to Viscount Rothermere. I must say it's a big improvement. Kemsley House was nearly falling down and full of rats, especially down in the basement among the printing-machines and the canteen where the air was always like this smog only smelling of bacon and chips in some fearful oil.

Our new offices are quite splendid, huge and spacious and light with windows overlooking the Thames and the white masts of the Ship 'Discovery'. Trees too and gardens which belong to the lawyers who inhabit buildings of charm which lie between a green lawn and the river. We're in Carmelite House.

It is a great relief to have a job at all. Many of the older staff were just sacked and it wasn't at all nice to see them go, very despondent. It has left people feeling horribly insecure, but then they felt that way all the time. One colleague, a charming, gentle reporter who always dressed in black, legal clothes because he hoped to be taken off Crime and the Ministry of Food and put into the Commonwealth or Colonies or Diplomatic department, worried far too much about the job and his four children, then fell in front of a tube train and was killed.

For the first time in years I have a News Editor who is a Sweetie. He was more than 4 years in a German prisoner-of-war camp, for a short time with Douglas Bader; loves telling stories of Bader's grisly tricks with his artificial legs. He is lovely to all us girls. I never had a happy News Editor before but this one, named Ronnie Mogg, is actually happy. Mind you, he thinks women are tougher than men, so Ingrid, Kay Petre* and I … we get all the sticky jobs. Tonight he's sending me out in the office car 'to find out which part of the Home Counties has got the thickest smog'. 'Then what do I do, Ron dear?' I ask.

'You keep right on till it's black as black and you can't see a dam thing, then you sit there and write me a colour story.'

Love to all, Ogg

Ingrid Etter, former wife of the editor of Polish Daily; Kay Petre, woman racing motorist, famous in the 1930s.

Sunday July 1952
c/o Daily Sketch, New Carmelite House
London EC4

Dear B,

Well how do the children like being home again? Hope you had a good trip. I find I have been given a rise, but it is only 25 bob, nothing to shout about.

Mrs. Grun says ... she was disappointed not to meet you, especially as her favourite sport is going round the art treasures, museums, pictures, etc, and hopes to do it with you next time. I told her you left London two days early like a couple of refugees. Today is nice and cool; please come autumn or winter next time, otherwise it is not worth it, to sit & droop in a hotel.

Mrs. Grun says ... dieting is not a good idea for many reasons. One is you cannot eternally battle with nature because it is boring to concentrate too much on food or take it too seriously. Secondly, she says, to get the best out of a diet you must constantly change it... even to the extent of going on a diet of fats for a while and then back to the old salads. Thirdly, she says, and I agree with her, that being plump is quite different from obesity. Plump women were the only beauties 50 years ago when thin little meerskite* girls were despised; it is only fashion & Monsieur Dior, and who the hell cares for fashion? Not me. So please don't take it all too seriously and make yourselves miz. Fourthly, for your information, A likes fat women; swears that I diet at my peril; he likes big rounded stomachs, the lot ... he says women ought to look plump and healthy. After all this I'm changing my views a bit, and had some very solid meals the rest of this week.

Mrs. Grun says... she has found an excellent tailor who does some remarkably good work, and charges only £20 for the making AND the material. I passed on the name of Jane's doctor for her friend, and she finds he charges 250 guineas for the breast operation.

264

Had a grand time up north; business was excellent so A was a large radiant ray of sunshine all the way there and back.

Please give my love to everybody. Don't forget, arrange to come up to London again, when the north wind blows a bit; I know Cora will have the kids, or Bettina will. How are they all? Don't forget to tell Tina about the ballet. Yes, Mrs. Grun was very disappointed, she said. I told her you and Frank were both too weak for London. Probably because you don't get enough to eat.

Best love to all, Og

* *meerskite – Yiddish slang meaning plain or ugly.*

1953

4th Feb 1953
c/o Daily Sketch, New Carmelite House
London EC4

Dear B,

Was dragged from bed on Sunday at dawn to go to Canvey Island; it was just high tide when we arrived and frankly, I was terrified. Our cameraman had high rubber boots and I had not, but he got soaked to the waist just the same. I was lucky enough, however, to be allowed to come home that night, and other men were sent out from News Desk to replace me.

I just cannot understand how people were able to survive the cold; I was frozen in top coat, costume and woollen twin-set, and most of the survivors were half-naked, having been nearly drowned while they slept. It was the same old sordid war-time evacuation scenes and made one ache with pity.

It makes one feel guilty to come back to a warm bed and enjoy a hot bath, after seeing the misery of people left without anything. I have in mind a big healthy looking man like a farmer in a cap, barefoot with a blanket round him weeping like a child; and a woman who had lost her little girl and could not keep her borrowed stockings up because she had no corset.

Mrs. Grun's son George handed my manuscript to a girl named Katharine Whitehorn* who is Reader for the publishers Methuen and she liked it so much she is going to recommend it. She and George are old Cambridge colleagues; of course it does not mean there is any hope at all because Methuen's average age is about 100 and they are Serious publishers, but anyhow I thought it was very nice of her, don't you?

I sent you a bit more Brie; please let me know if it arrives in good condition from Selfridges where I now have an account;

I am delighted with Betty's news. I knew Louis would get a practice quite quickly, it sounds really exciting.** Cora seems to have had an awful time, with everyone being ill; I hope Max and the children are better and mind she doesn't have a breakdown herself now.

Going to drop into bed now, as I am on duty at 9am, but I am such a slow dresser, have to be up at 7 to get my hair up in time.

Best love, Og

Katherine Whitehorn became a very popular columnist, married to the novelist Gavin Lyall.
**Olga's brother-in-law-to-be, Dr. Louis Mintz, was a GP who had just established his practice in Tile Cross, a working class area of Birmingham, where he continued until his death in 1985.*

Friday night 1953
c/o Daily Sketch, New Carmelite House
London EC4

Dear B,

Felt rather poorly; bad tummy. Probably a cold, or bad food. I had the tummy-ache the morning of the railway smash.* It was bad luck for me to be the reporter living nearest to the scene as ....living near Baker Street station, I was the first one from our paper to get to the scene and it was a grim sight; they were still bringing out the bodies, with many more still trapped. I've been at disaster stories before, as you know, but never, no never anything like this. As the three trains collided head-on, two of them telescoped into each other, leaving one whole train or part of a train standing in the air vertically right where the overhead bridge had been a half-hour earlier. For the first time I decided I'd made a mistake ever to want to be a news reporter. I just wanted to turn and run ... and run without looking back. I had to stay for the first two hours or so, running to the telephone with the news, until Hayes sent out a team of men to replace me.

Yes I will try and come over a few days before Betty's wedding-day to see if I can be any help. Am not eating anything myself, I just nibble humbugs, but tell Tina I will show her how to make Green Peppers stuffed with rice when I come over. How is Richard the Songbird?** Did you like the Dybbuk? Mrs. G says: 'Of course your sister won't understand it'... Hope your cold is better and love to all. See you next weekend then.

Love, Og

Three railway trains were involved in an horrific train collision near Harrow.
**Reference to the fact that Richard had recently had his Bar Mitzvah.*

April 1953
c/o Daily Sketch, New Carmelite House
London EC4

Dear B,

My series on Diana Dors was a great success so now I've got to do one on Lady Docker.* Hooray, it means I can spend a few days with you in Brum at the office expense. Cousin Harold tells me that our Norah Docker was the prettiest, most popular girl in the Bristol Road .... only a few years before our time. All the boys wanted to take her out, he says, when she was all gold curls and very sporting. Do you think you could ask the headmistress at Edgbaston College about her? She probably won't know much because Norah was only there for a couple of terms before the family moved but there may be lots of neighbours in the Bristol Road who knew the family.

Love, Og

Sir Bernard and Lady Nora Docker were almost the Posh and Becks of their day, appearing almost daily in the gossip columns for their conspicuous consumption. Sir Bernard had been Chairman of BSA in Birmingham and Nora had been a barmaid in a Birmingham pub before she married him.

2nd May 1953
c/o Daily Sketch, New Carmelite House
London EC4

Dear B,

Did my duty and spent the usual Barren evening among the Barren ones, at Flat No.6 Grove End Gardens, St John's Wood, it being our usual Friday night get-together with Les Girls.

There is something, nowadays, faintly depressing to contemplate Nous Girls Tous Ensembles Sans Enfants, so to speak, and all of us also caught up in the sad process of ageing at one stage or another. Indeed, Freda (yes she was there) underlined the situation for Paul by stating that a woman friend had called on her for assistance; Paul being still mystified, Freda explained the friend needed a Tampax, and to this Freda replied: 'What a compliment; you flatter me.'

We were all together at last, a rare occasion in these days, Rosalie, Jane, Sally and the inimitable Freda who had managed to dispose of both mother and husband for a rare Friday evening out. There was also Me, no less barren, no less ageing and of course the solid figure of Paul Gottl, now spelt Gough, a little more aghast than usual. But do not ask me what he was aghast at.

There was first La Grande Dame Herself, a little pale owing to some unspecified heart trouble which the doctor cannot find, and with strawberry blond waves longer and free-er and more Swinging than formerly, rather the Rita Hayworth style and certainly in the famous Hayworth colourings. She's neatly encased in a smart tweed dress with, if I noted correctly, brown velvet lapels and cuffs. It was clear that the presence of the much blonder, much smoother figure of Cousin Jane, curled in utter exhaustion in Rosalie's favourite chair, was a source of intolerable annoyance to the hostess who bristled visibly every time she passed her. Rosalie, angular and sharp-cornered is capable of a bristle, whereas Jane's only bristle is on her chin, discreetly tinted to match her rather pretty ash-gold hair and therefore almost invisible under the kindly lighting arrangements of the living Room chez Gough.

Paul is in shirt sleeves and dressing-gown comfortably relaxing from his double toil of earning a living and looking after the domestic affairs of the home. As Rosalie wisely has never even pretended to be able to Cook, the kitchen side of things goes fairly smoothly and Mrs. Rosalie Gough is clearly happy to leave her digestion in hands which have pleased the royal family and especially the Queen Mother, as this gives all the evening meals a certain cache even on Paul's slightly off-days which don't occur often.

The grey figure of the oldest inhabitant, Aunt Sally, seems to breathe out an atmosphere of negative goodwill, like some sober pacifist dressed for a Sunday go-to-meeting who finds herself by mistake at a meeting of warriors in armour. Yet the absence of the cosmetic armoury on her own person renders her own ageing processes less noticeable, whereas the paint and powder on the faces of us girls, seems cruelly to accentuate each line and wrinkle.

Then there is me, the eternal-schoolgirl in dusty beret from which strands of hair are gleefully escaping; a button missing from the shiny black jacket disclosing the opening in a black jumper held together by two, it is hoped, invisible gold safety-pins which in turn protects a faded candy stripe blouse, breast-tight from its twelve years of existence.

Finally there is Freda, star guest and even more star-performer. Freda is groomed as never before. 'Joe makes me take a bath once a week, isn't it awful.' Slim as never before – the result of a gastric flu which attacked the happy couple recently – and a matt face radiant under the flattering lighting, with black hair innocent of grey and face innocent of hairs whether of black or grey, and with crimson lipstick not unpleasing.

The conversation turns mainly on the interesting necromania of the murderer Christie whose habits have been fully described to Freda by her doctor, with additional detailed explanation from Jane who has read the Sunday papers very carefully and has also gone to the trouble of consulting experts. Rosalie and Sally shriek in turn that they cannot bear any more but they are angry when somebody changes the subject.

As I was on duty in the Court when Mr. Christie* made a brief appearance on remand… I am asked for my first-hand description of the murderer. I begin to give this to the best of my ability, in a rather loud voice which is necessary in order to be heard above the din, but I am interrupted by Jane who has a much better version. But Freda who is in the happy position of knowing exactly what necromania involves and is determined to tell us, is outshouted by Rosalie who is over-excited because she is trying to listen to all three of us at once, while adding a few comments of her own as well.

Freda's excellent and musical voice declares that she asked her doctor for his opinion; It is Passivity the murderer craves and that on a dramatic repetition of this word passivity, rolled round the rims on lips, the case of Mr. Christie is at last dismissed.

We turn to lavatories. Freda has a story to tell us of What Happened to Joe in-the-toilet the day he got gastric flu. How Mr. Burridge, the most attentive neighbour from next door came to her aid, and how Joe was saved from a fate 'Worse than the Third Man who got lost in the Vienna sewers'.

Freda began her story as always by pointing the moral. Although pulling-the-chain may be a matter of taste, according to the individual household, 'Never, never,' Freda pleaded with us, 'you must never lock the lavatory door or bathroom door no matter what your reason for retirement behind it.'

Although the story of what happened to Joe in the lavatory has a reasonably happy ending, it might not have had because Joe with charming inexperience did in fact lock the lavatory door. Interruption here from Rosalie who declares that she never locks, from Jane who hardly ever locks and Paul says he never locks either. This appears to pacify Freda's anxiety, but unfortunately Sally and I were not asked whether we lock or not, though I think I did hear Sally say faintly that she leaves the door wide open but I was sitting next to her and I don't think anyone else heard. I mean we were sitting together on the couch. It might be better for the gentle reader not to read on.

To return, however, to Poor Joe in the lavatory. Joe's visit to the little room followed a fairly small tiff between the happy pair. He marched to the toilet, LOCKED the door and, it is presumed, took up the traditional position common to other races too, at least in the western world. There followed a short interval, length not specified and there was no sound from Joe, which I thought was very thoughtful of him, but which apparently caused some alarm in Freda's breast. This polite silence which followed – and which in other circles might well be taken as a mark of good breeding – began to get on her nerves. Finally Freda rattled on the door.

'Joe,' she said, 'what are you doing?' The silence was unbroken. Joe, obviously, was smoking. Another interval elapsed. Freda tried the door again and called out. No reply. She tried to peer through the keyhole, but was unable to catch a glimpse of Joe in any position whatever. The image of Joe sitting smoking happily, albeit a little sulkily, in the traditional position, began to fade from Freda's loving imagination. Something terrible must have happened to Joe. He did not normally shmull** as long as this.

Freda lay flat on her face and tried to look under the crack of the door, sniffing for smoke, flame or other disaster. Was Joe on fire or had he fainted? The last possibility filled her with an anguish of anxiety. My

Joe, in danger, in the locked lavatory. Joe was weak after the gastric flu and she ought not to have crossed him.

At the point of despair she remembered the faithful neighbour Mr. Burridge, who is likewise devoted to Joe. Mr. Burridge, solid, capable, comforting figure arrived pronto breathing goodwill and helpfulness, and Freda – taking advantage of the situation to some extent, fell on his bosom, imploring him to save her Joe. Mr. Bee then obtained a ladder and with calm despatch, he mounted to gaze at Joe, or at whatever remained of Joe, through the lavatory window. 'He thought of breaking the window with a brick,' said Freda, but the glass would have fallen on poor Joe. Mr. B took one peep through the window and was quite overcome. He dismounted from the ladder.

It appeared that Joe sat crouched in a dead faint in the exact position as recent victims whom Mr. B had rescued in a train smash, or rather he had not rescued them because they were already dead. This gave Mr. B quite a turn. Joe, Mr. Burridge said, had also been sick. Freda comforted her neighbour as best she could and as soon as he felt stronger, he went away to collect some tools. He soon returned with the contents of his workbox including a cutting-tool and having cut out the entire lavatory window, he fed Freda's newly-slim form through the window to the rescue. Freda unlocked the door but was helpless to lift the form of her loved one from the seat of the toilet. Again Mr. B came to the rescue, and gathering up the prostrate Joe into his arms, carried him back to the bed, while Freda telephoned for assistance. 'It was only then,' said Freda, 'that I noticed the poor boy had got his knickers down. So while he was still unconscious I pulled his knickers up and Joe was saved. Oh it was a terrible experience. Never, never lock your door.'

'How terrible for you,' said Rosalie, who had followed the story with deep interest. 'I never lock, nor Paul, do you Pauli?'

There was a short interval as Rosalie rose and said it was time for tea and cakes. But, passing Jane, she was this time unable to subdue her rancour that Cousin Jane had the right to sit and do nothing while she, poor slave, had only recently had all the trouble and work of clearing the dinner-things off the table from which three people had eaten. 'It is a great pity' said Rosalie icily, 'that YOU can't do something for a change. Sitting there, after doing nothing all day....'

'You're the hostess,' said Jane sharply, 'do it yourself. I'm not your servant.'

Rosalie rounded on Jane with all fangs showing, and some hissing ensued, with a great deal of shouting on both sides which continued until Paul ended it by shouting louder and telling Rosalie to be quiet. Jane seated herself more deeply and firmly in her armchair. (Normally she does make the tea on Fridays, I don't know why .... but as you know Jane enjoys allegedly poor health and does not work at anything as there is no necessity since I understand nowadays that a certain modest income has become available to her from Uncle Abe's fortune).

Freda sprang up to put the kettle on, followed by the reluctant Rosalie. I made a half-hearted move and lifted myself as far as the arm of the divan. Calm was restored as the macaroons and fruitcake laced with Paul's own homemade marzipan was handed round. Freda set out the cups and brought in the tea.

Sounds from the kitchen indicated that Jane's character was being discussed out of earshot. Rosalie was on her favourite theme of 'the laziest good-for-nothing-in-the-world.' Rosalie maintains the only possible candidate for this post is Jane herself, while Jane considers Rosalie much lazier than herself and entirely without her bachelor-girl's right to BE lazy.

We sipped our lukewarm tea, ate the excellent macaroons and turned to a discussion of Freda's father who died recently on a sick bed tended by his last mistress and who left a most un-satisfactory amount of money to Freda and her mother whilst leaving the bulk of his money to the mistress who also has a husband in a ménage now reduced from three to the more orthodox number of two. However small the sum inherited by Freda's mum who is the legal wife, this lady has recently given up cards to devote herself entirely to the Stock Exchange with results so disastrous that even the un-satisfactory little sum is now extinct.

After a description of Joe's stomach which is not strong, the evening draws to a close as Rosalie puts her coat on to take the poodle round the corner. I try to transfer the conversation to its former jollier basis that existed before Freda's marriage, and hinted at the life of adventure and enterprise she had exchanged for Joe's weak stomach. Freda declared she preferred Joe's stomach, and that her tastes in pleasure were so changed that even his rare lovemaking was 'too much' for her. I'm a reformed Tart, says Freda. Then we discussed Muriel (Mitzi Metz) who has captured a married man's fancy and is much transformed although unfortunately he is a Christian.

'If you call him a sheigetz,*** she'll kill you,' says Freda. Muriel's captive, surprisingly enough, insists on marriage and Muriel, rising 50 like all us Girls, carefully concealing her own surprise, has agreed to accept him.

'He must be mad,' says Freda to us. 'We only bumped into Muriel for a few minutes in Circus Road and she never stopped. On and on, about

Life, Love and the Pursuit of Muriel, as though we hadn't heard it all before. The man must be a Big Dope.'

Finally I was escorted to the tube after midnight by Freda and Jane. Freda's send-off caught the attention of all the male occupants of the tube train, which being the last of the night, remains stationary with doors open for several minutes. Clinging to the open door I prayed for them to close on the shrill gestures of Freda and Jane, apparently drunk with the night's emotional refreshment but certainly not with any alcohol which is almost never provided at Flat No.6. Both Girls, with the ravages of time and of art now painfully revealed by the unkinder lighting of the platform, stood at the open door, calling ribald and affectionate greetings to me to the huge delight of the audience.

'Don't forget,' screamed Freda, 'N.Y.F. N.Y.F. Ha ha ha ha.'

The men sitting in the train could not by any stretch of imagination have known that these initials bore the quite innocent interpretation of Nice Yiddisher Fellow – which Freda insists is the only certain basis for happiness and she wishes all of us an NYF, with all the good kindness of her kindly heart.

Soon it was clear from the sniggers all round me that Londoners gave a wholly other meaning to Freda's repeated calls of NYF. And when the doors finally and all too slowly closed before my perspiring face and shut out the dreadful sounds, I did not have the courage to sit down and face the fellow passengers on either side, and stood crouched in the doorway right to Regent's Park station. And so to bed.[...]

* *John Christie was found guilty of six murders at 10 Rillington Place and executed. Earlier Timothy Evans had been hanged for the same crimes. It was a major influence on the decision to end the death penalty.*
** *sulk*
*** *sheigetz – a disparaging Yiddish word for a gentile man.*

May 1953
c/o Daily Sketch, New Carmelite House
London EC4

Dear B,

We have a new Editor named Herbert Gunn ... used to be a top Beaverbrook man, ed of the Evening Standard. Romantic sort of chap, tall, greying. His wife fell in love with his news editor who subsequently fell in love with someone else, so the wife killed herself. He himself launched a beautiful girl reporter, married to a vicar, named Olive Melville Brown and so it goes; very involved story; glad I don't have to write it.

He's brought some of his own protegees to the paper. One is to be our new Drama Critic. Kenneth Tynan, tall and fair and rather odd and attractive in a slightly alarming way. What I find odd is that he's a Brummie too; went to my old school King Edward's though after my time. Tynan is absolutely nothing like any other Old Edwardian.

I'm off to Paris for a few weeks. Everyone says, 'Oh lucky you,' but it's a horror really. I've got to snoop around Princess Alexandra, visit her Finishing school, sit in on her music lessons, find out what she buys, spends, etc., etc. She rides around on the Paris metro and why not? The democratic royal whom everyone loves, schoolgirl with the common touch, that's my brief, oh oh.

My Features Editor Walter Hayes is madly keen on everything royal. He says only Kings and Queens are really worth writing about and when we asked him why, Hayes said because their experience is unique. He said there's only one of them usually and masses of us so we can never be unique, only ordinary. I go on Sat.

Will write, love to all, Og

July 1953
Daily Sketch
c/o Paris Office

Dear B,

You'd like the Finishing school in Paris; it has those yellow wood desks where you lift the lid and hide your head inside like we had at Edgbaston College. The desks are a bit dusty though and slightly shabby in an elegant sort of way. The 'Maitre' in charge pretended she didn't know what Princess I'd come to see. 'We have FIVE royal Princesses here,' she said.

Princess Alex is staying with the Count of Paris, Pretender to the French throne, his handsome wife and 11 beautiful children at their country house at Louveciennes, so I took the train, thinking the Princess could hardly give me the slip out there in the country … and if she does I can always grab hold of Princess Helene or Princess Isabelle or the youngest boy Thibaud. But when I get there, Alexandra has got the mumps, so has Helene, Isabelle, Thibaud and all the other little pretenders to the throne. All I've got for my fortnight's researches are the lessons in the music school and I've got to get a full 4 features out of it. Help!

Love, Og

PS the little maid swore Alex not pretending about the mumps.

2nd September 1953

Dear Beryl and dear Bettina,

(I've put a carbon in so I can write to Tina same time.)

How are you ... I mean You the Bride? And how is the Doc? Und wieviel patients? I hope tausends and tausends*....

As you may have noticed from my many moans in the post, I am much overworked. Perhaps it will be better when people start coming back from their holidays. I have a terrible new boss who is a Driver. He never eats, never even rises from his desk to go behind a door Looked or Unlocked. Don't know how he manages this, but I did ask him once, and he confessed that yes he was nearly Bursting. I should think so too. I was the same way at the Coronation. There was just no way ... once you'd pushed through the crowds, and the driving cold and rain of a nothing-like-June day about 6am, because the police informed us either we took our allotted seats opposite the Abbey at that early hour or they couldn't allow us through not with all the Special Passes with our photos on them or whatever. But even missing breakfast and anything else either, didn't help.

By about 10 am I was in torment as well as freezing to death and when I complained to the police, they told me it was part of their training to hold their water for hours and hours and I'd just have to put up with it. Our cameramen suffer too, but then they die young anyway just from the sheer weight of all that camera equipment which cripples one shoulder as well as the bladder.

Anyway my new boss, News Editor Mr. Jack Starr, is the conscientious kind... won't even get up from his desk unless the Editor calls him. Worse still, he said of me, while paying tribute to my working-speed, that I was much given to using cliches.. Me ... Me ... my bowels nearly burst with fury ... I told him icily I would rather he had called me

Unchaste. The beast. I have lain awake at nights, plotting, nurturing my hatred, oh I'll think of something awful. He has no wife, so he never goes home but just sits and sits, and works and works ... watching and watching to see how we work too. Monster. And I used to be so keen.

I take back all I said about Nature Diets. I have just seen Rosalie after a month's Nature Cure, living on nothing but orange juice, yoghourt, St Ivel cheese and steamed vegetables and eggs. She is starting a new Girlhood, radiant and revitalised, and never falls asleep while you are talking to her any more like she used to do.

Love to Beryl, Frank, Rick, Luce, Cork, Max, Viv, Anne, Louis, Tina and You, Ogg.

She is hoping her brother-in-law Louis has acquired thousands of patients at his new practice.

1954

March 1954
c/o Daily Sketch, New Carmelite House
London EC4

Dear B,

Sunday I crawled into work hoping for a quiet day in the warm, wrapped in woollies from head to foot, ankle socks, head scarf, two cardigans and top coat. Sunday morning duty is always a bit grisly on account of no cleaners to remove the debris. My desk littered with the Saturday leavings of the Sunday paper staff, cigarette ends in coffee mugs and scraps of veal and ham pie and the news editor's desk awash with some unknown liquid containing fragments of egg and chips.

Mind you, I preferred that to my day's assignment. By 9.30am comes the news that a British ship with homegoing servicemen, wives and children is on fire some miles off Algiers. I'm to fly to Algiers for the day ... a 9-hour flight by a French Breguet plane (that's one with an upstairs/downstairs). 'Don't argue,' says Robinson when I point out that by that time someone may well have been able to put out the fire.

When we get to Algiers it's evening with sun blazing down. Big press party makes for the docks but no transport available. Algiers very glamorous but distinctly uncomfortable when you're in ankle socks, extra cardies and winter overcoat, not to mention head warmer and outsize woollen scarf. I begin to shed the socks, scarf, cardigans, etc, but when we get to the ship in harbour, there's nowhere to put any of it down AND hold on to notebook and pencil. So I weave in and out of British housewives and small children who are hanging their soaked clothing, sheets, etc, plus nappies and trousers out to dry, and I just drop bits of my winter outfit wherever it falls. It gets hotter and hotter.

Walking back to the hotel I shed the last bits down to my blouse and skirt, so no wonder the Sheikhs stare at me in the lift as we slowly rise to the 3rd floor of this blazing white, super-deluxe hotel. Down in the bar the boys are busy phoning their stories to London. Dizzy with heat I fail to notice until too late that one of the boys has got firm hold of the telephone line to London and though he's finished phoning his copy, he won't let go because he's just realised it's the only free line and if he can hang on a bit longer, my story will be too late for the first edition. There's a bit of a tussle .... he's a big, stout Irishman and a No.1 Enemy of mine because we often compete like this. Finally I get through to London but I have to cut my story short after being cut off from London several times while I'm dictating. I realise I've probably been beaten on this assignment. Robbie will hate me for it; he may even think I was late with copy on purpose. My rival is swilling whiskey in the bar, grinning with satisfaction. The ship's fire's been out for hours; no one hurt and there's a 9-hour flight back to London. There's only one consolation for this trip. I jump into a taxi and ask to be taken to the British cemetery just outside the town so I can see Ivan's grave among the RAF servicemen killed here by the Luftwaffe in 1943. Please tell Cora I'll write her a full description soonest.

Love to all, Ogg

May 1954
c/o Daily Sketch, New Carmelite House
London EC4

Dear B,

We're saddled with a new News Editor ... comes straight to us from the Daily Mirror, with red hair and riproaring reputation. He is quite insane, and terrifies me.

A few weeks ago I was ordered to fly to Cyprus again and keep an eye on the battles there from Nicosia with the rest of the press party sozzling themselves silly. Casualties have been high and A was not at all pleased for me to get this assignment. Anyway it was cancelled at the last minute; don't know why as nobody told me.

But now! Oh to be in Cyprus instead of what I've got. The redhaired one, with his wild eyes, called me to him; handed me a tip-off address of some allegedly intimate friends of Princess Margaret. The red-hair believes that Group-Captain Townsend (don't tell me you haven't heard) .... is in hiding there ... and I'm to call round and find out, if you please. 'And what,' I asked, 'am I to say?' 'You say,' says Red-hair, 'that you want to come in and discuss the 'Townsend love-affair. Say you're an intimate friend.'

I stare back at Red-hair uncomprehendingly. As though I didn't suffer enough with Fix-it Dixon and his Flying Saucers...

'Tell them,' Red-hair continues, 'that you cannot go back to your paper without getting the story because you'll get the sack if you do....'

When I get back to my desk, everyone can see there's something badly wrong. Neville Randall who sits next to me stops going through the baskets of morning post to pick off the stamps which have escaped being stamped on. He's rather mean and it makes his day if he finds a couple of unused postage stamps, but he's terribly nice. 'Don't worry,' he says, 'I'm sure you won't get the sack. The man is being quite unreasonable.'

Instead of going to look for Princess Margaret's 'intimate friends', I go home. What else is there to do? I keep rehearsing speeches to make to someone to get me out of this mess. No sleep but I go back to work next morning, determined somehow without actually confronting anyone to get myself out of this mess. Red-hair is not in the office so I go around among my pals... 'What would you do, chum?' Suddenly the Features Editor comes into the general office, holding a piece of Press Association tape and he just looks at all of us and says, 'My God.' He shows it to two good friends of mine, Sidney Butt and Bert Pack, who are both deputy news editors. Bert goes a bit pale then he comes over to me with the bit of tape. It is a two line report from a South London news agency saying that my red-headed boss has just been found dead on the line at some South London underground station, after he jumped from the platform in the path of the incoming train. There's a one-line follow-up about his being one of the more brilliant discoveries of the post-war Daily Mirror group. As I told you in an earlier letter, I think, things are getting rough in the Street. This is the third man in our group to go mad in the past 5 years. Two are dead and one in his early thirties is in a Nursing-home having treatment.

Love, Ogg

June 1954
c/o Daily Sketch, New Carmelite House
London EC4

Dear B,

Glad to have your news. The answer to your question is 'no'. I'm a one-man woman now. Yes, I'm a changed character. A lays down the law and I obey. I like it.

What I don't like is another dam trip to Paris within weeks of the last one. Now the family have packed up and gone to live in America,* there's no one for me to talk to of an evening. I sit in expensive caffs and write out my expenses. This job is much worse than the last one. Hayes says now that the Duke and Duchess of Windsor have moved into their mill-house at Gif-sur-Yvette, I've got to crash in somehow, snatch an interview and do quick inventory of the carpets, fittings, etc, without treading on any of the Duchess' little dogs ... including Trooper, Disraeli, Ruffles, Thomas, Whiskey, all poodles like Rosalie and Paul's own Angus, sometimes called Peppi...

Hayes said to stop moaning and if I had any trouble to go round and see the Sketch correspondent in Paris (newly-appointed) living with wife and a couple of children. He turned out to be very nice, American, name of Rothenburg and he'd got his mother staying too, who was most encouraging. She knitted away, chatting all the time but it did me good. 'I don't know what you're so worried about,' said Mrs. R., 'I bet the Duchess'll be thrilled to see us all. What d'you bet we get invited to lunch and some real home cookies.'

Bernie Rothenburg couldn't see any problem either, so I didn't mention that in fact the Windsors were refusing all press requests for interview, no matter what. As the Duke's own secretary in Paris told me on the phone for a start, 'His Royal Highness is under contract to the Ladies' Home Journal,' and if I talked to him, it could jeopardise his contract.

Bernie thought it would make a nice trip into the Paris countryside for the whole family. Mom sits in the back of his car knitting away and we take a French cameraman named Abie who sits pale with fright,

279

holding on tenderly to his camera bag and flashlight. Off we go into the Seine-et-Oise department, with its nucleaire station, a 13th century church, a nice village with bistro en route for the Duke's pad called Moulin de la Tuilerie.

Even old Mrs. Rothenburg stops being encouraging after that. Every mile or so we encounter huge signposts rimmed in cat's eyes, 'Moulin de la Tuilerie' with the warning, 'You are forbidden to pass this point under penalty of a fine.'

Abie's not worried about the fine; only about the gendarmerie posted hereabouts with orders, so Abie says, to shoot on sight especially at press parties like ours.

We drove on, bravely, keeping our heads down except for Mrs. R who went on knitting and chatting. I kept an ear cocked for barking dogs. When the mill-house was in sight, we stopped and decided to put Bernie's mom in a derelict barn standing in the empty fields. Not a soul about. Not a sound.

I crept out to reconnoitre. I knew we were at the right house because of the smashing black lantern hanging at the tall yellow barn-door gate which looked straight out of Windsor Castle as well as a black and white cow and stately white duck guarding the gate. I lifted the latch softly and with Abie on my heels, we crept inside. We looked about in awe. Gleaming white house, low-lying in a sort of hollow and spread in an L-shape around a courtyard. Spotless lawns, golden pansies and American beauty roses climbing up the walls. The cuttings in the Paris archives had told me the Duke was a topping gardener and mowed the velvet lawns himself.

Another large notice on the lawn this time. To be careful about not running over the little dog; probably a mechant** one but it didn't say so. The silence was nerve-racking. Not a living soul to be seen or heard.

Then I spotted a gardener in black beret bending over the pansy bed not far off but he paid no attention to us. I didn't realise that no one would suspect any unauthorised stranger would get inside the gate because no one would dare ... no matter how keen they might be to see their favourite lover 'Edouard'. We called out 'Hi' then 'Monsieur' but he didn't even look up.

Housekeeper Madame Lucienne Molin spotted us from her front window and greeted us with big smile and a lot of French. Hooray ... at least we were inside, and not a single shot fired. I explained our business. To see Son altesse royale or failing that Sa altesse royale.*** A quick glance at the elaborate burglar alarm switchboard put me on my guard. I noticed that it lit up and sounded a buzzer when any door or window was opened; now it was buzzing like mad. It also had a chart below showing the private telephone numbers for the two royal suites, Son and Sa. Said Madame Molin, operating the switchboard, 'I shall send for Sydney, he will know what to do.' She confided that Sydney who was only Assistant Maitre d'hotel was the Duke's favourite, almost a confidante.

Sydney arrived, black as night, from Jamaica, in gleaming white coat. Very friendly, very nice. This always makes me nervous; it means things will not go well.[...]

I was right too. The reason the delightful Sydney can't go fetch HRH 'righterway' as Sydney puts it is because, oh Lord help me, the worst. In other words, the Competition are right in there, this very minute, my enemy, the columnist who wrote rude things in the Evening Standard about me for asking 'trivial' questions of Comrade Malenkov at his big London press conference the other day. Randolph Churchill is in there, having a lovely hot dinner specially chosen by la Duchesse. Randolph didn't bother about Ladies Home Journals; he was in and I was 'out' and would have to make do with Sydney, at least for the time being.

All right, you've heard enough. But it needled me. And after giving Sydney a note to give to the Duke and a long chat with Madame so I could have a squint at the carpets, accessories, etc. Yes, Very nice. I went back and made threatening call on HRH's secretary. She said to calm down, there was a loophole in the contract. Provided I encountered the Duke on a railway station, airport terminal or ship's landing-dock, the LHJ did not draw the line at any interview recorded with HRH under these circumstances.

Trouble was when I got the interview in the end, by bribing the Golden Arrow guard to give me the first class Sleeper right next door to HRH for his overnight trip to London that weekend to see his mother, Queen Mary .... it didn't really make a Good Read.

I barely recognised the Duke as he came on to the platform at Gare du Nord walking briskly with a little posse of bodyguards in a sort of close circle around him. He looked smaller than I remembered, awfully thin, somehow withered, his green velour trilby hat was pulled down deeply over one pale blue eye. Both eyes stared, almost unseeing and slightly bloodshot, at the wet platform.

As we moved into our sleeping-cars, I snatched the 'interview'. He wanted to know.... was I the lady who called to see him the other day? He was so sorry, etc. Previous engagement and then there was this trip to London already arranged. He looked at me kindly; a great aroma of Whiskey was in the air. We talked about the mill-house. Greatly daring, I asked .... staring into those despairing, bloodshot eyes, was he happy? He told me that he was. 'Very happy.'

In gratitude for all this, I ordered a treble whiskey for him, 'Not on me,' I simpered, 'On your good friend Viscount Rothemere.' He accepted it gratefully. Afterwards I dined with his valet in the dining-car. The Duke stayed in his sleeper. 'He's had enough whiskey for one day,' said the valet.

It was a sad journey. But with the dawn as we puffed slowly into Victoria station, a little crowd of English, well wishers for the Duke who, the valet told me, always got up at dawn on these occasions to 'welcome HRH home again', cheered thinly and waved warmly.

Back at the office, I learned that someone 'high up' had put the bar up. My 'story' would not be printed. Nichevo. I'm home. I collect my expenses thankfully and go home to do my washing.

Keep well and love to Lucy and Rick & you. Og

Olga had no one to talk to as her French family had had enough of anti-Semitism in France and decamped en masse to the USA.
** nasty.*
*** A French equivalent of HRH.*

July 1954
c/o Daily Sketch & Graphic, New Carmelite House
London EC4

Dear B,

I've become such a Weeper. Always was, remember? The Editor has asked me for a series of 6 articles on Prince Charles and Princess Anne. When Bert Pack, our Copy Taster this week, caught me snivelling, it all came out. Lots of sympathy but not much help. Herbert Gunn shook hands with me after my briefing and it felt like having to go 'over the top'. He's specially keen on what the kids have for breakfast, etc. It could help with advertising. I rang the Palace as per usual and the Colville chap said, 'Yes, call round Tuesday about 11 but we can't tell you anything.'

Of course, I know I've been spoilt lately, having lovely easy ones like Dors, Docker and James Mason's family in Huddersfield. (I thought the schoolmaster Mason brother much better looking than the film star). But the royal children really are a stinker one to do. You can't get near Nanny in the park; rows of cameramen fill up the whole battleground. Besides there's nothing new in it.

The Editor just strolled by, tall and elegant, his folded towel over his shoulder on his way to his own private lavatory. Such a gracious, trusting smile for me. All right for some, eh?

Then I remembered Rosalie and Paul! Every time I appear at Grove End Gdns., he's on about his 'intimate' friendship with the royal housekeeper. Said she gave a Christmas party for him at Clarence House. Hooray: The children have been staying there with Gran and Princess Margaret for weeks while the Queen's abroad.

I ring Paul at his office ... near Hammersmith I think ... it's a sort of Bakery where he makes this special marzipan. He's going to help. The relief! Paul, being Austrian, doesn't tremble at the thought of Publicity. In fact, he likes it.

In the end I make an appointment to take Mrs. Alma McKee out to dinner, for no better reason than I'm a cousin-by-marriage with 'good friend Paul Gough.'

First I have to do a Think. What do I tell her? My usual spiel 'I'm from the Daily Sketch' might send her screaming out of that good restaurant in Jermyn Street ... or shall I take her to the Savoy Grill or the Hungaria? Royal servants have to sign something saying they won't talk to the hated Press.

I decided to tell whopping lie. I go as 'wife to a Canadian journalist,' etc. No mention of the Sketch. Rotten. Of course it's rotten, but what would you do Chum? At least if she were to get in trouble, she could say I was a low-down filthy liar and she'd be right but this is war. The whole of Fleet Street is beavering away day after day on the royal nursery. And I'm the only one with a ghost of an 'in' with Cousin Paul so it would be mad to throw it away.

The royal housekeeper turns out to be an immense Swede, so tall I have to learn over backwards to see her pale strong face and white hair. Terribly nice though. I felt even more of a black betrayer. She adores the Queen and the Queen Mum and much preferred her life at Buck House in spite of the terrible, old fashioned and not very hygienic kitchen. Now she works for the QM and Princess Margaret at Clarence which is more comfortable with a nice little flat of her own (where she 'receives' people like Paul for a sherry, some gossip and talk about recipes, etc.) but the pay is poor and she doesn't like having to get out of bed in the middle of the night because Margaret has brought a crowd of 'palties' home from the theatre and wants a giant Smorgasbord made on the instant. This is the bit though that fascinates me because it's all about how to make one of these great salad dishes with a minimum of ingredients. Her budget tends to be frugal but the genius part is she can make it look good with a bruised bit of carrot, some squashy tomatoes and the odd bits of stale veg, fruit etc. It's an Art ... and the Scandinavians have it. We don't.

Thank God she cooks all this month for the royal children and her titbit about what Charles likes for brekkers gives me my first headline. He likes Uglis, sprinkled with brown sugar and warmed up under the grill. Oh and he calls her 'the Lady-in-white' because she appears in the nursery in her white chef's coat. Lots of this stuff. I begin to feel lightheaded with sheer relief. After dinner, I take her home to the side door of Clarence House in a taxi and she thanks ME for a nice evening. Me ... she thanks!

Of course she wanted to talk about Paul whom she much admires and his wife Rosalie but I manage to keep the talk focussed. Not quite enough about Princess Anne who appears to do as she's told by Charles and has no mind of her own. So she eats the Uglis too. So much more chic, mind you, than plain bloody grapefruit which the hoy polloy eat.

What with a week of crawling about spying on Nannies, interviewing the royal children's dancing class and with the help of my colleague Alan Gardner (who is quite merciless and would interview Anne in her pram if he could catch her for one unguarded minute) I get enough stuff, with pictures, to make up 5 articles. Mr. Gunn is in raptures. I get a Special Mention in the daily bulletin on the notice board and all that's left is to pray the Queen won't have any more children.

I went round and told Paul the truth ...about my disguise and all with his bosom friend Alma, the Swede. He approves of the whole thing. 'Alma is a sport,' he says, 'as well as a genius. She'll understand.'

Love, Ogg

From Royals to Russians

May 1955
c/o Hotel Beau Rivage, Geneva

Dear B,

Hardly had time to wash my undies, hair, etc. Very pleasant here among the blue lakes. Somehow, though, it's all different. I think of those innocent days with Cecil Asbridge cycling around Lake Como. Still the same utterly clean prosperous, efficient Switzerland as it was back in 1937, yet the charm's gone. Where has it all gone to?

Mind you, it was rather 'pretty' in the old Lancashire sense of that word, when Messrs. Bulganin and Krushchev arrived and drove through the streets looking like two white-haired benevolent Great-Uncles, side by side in a huge beige open touring car, in beautiful Panama hats and what looked like shantung jackets, all of it straight out of a Turgenev love-story deep in the Black Forest of the 1870s. The sheer amiable charm of it. How cunning, how clever; they drove around through the cheering, waving crowds, hugely enjoying themselves.

Then towards evening, General Eisenhower does the same. But this time, it's not an open car but a closed one and there are two bodyguards or outriders, clinging perilously to either side of the car and their guns are plainly visible.

So ... the first round of the Geneva 'peace' conference goes to the Russians. Krushchev is clearly the boss; every time Marshal Bulganin opens his mouth, Krush actually steps in front of him, shuts him up and starts to orate.

Night after night, all this week our big international press party has gathered outside the various villas, Anthony Eden's or the French, Americans, Russians ... hoping against hope for a Statement, a Handout, ANYthing to give to our News Editors to keep them quiet.

By Thursday I was so exhausted after hanging about all night or drinking with the boys or dashing by cab from one Villa to another, I thought, hang it, we're not going to get anything until the end of the Conference. Like an idiot, I went to bed. The phone goes about 3am. It's that terribly nice, dark, handsome American press chappie named

Daniels whom I'd been chatting up ... not knowing he was courting Margaret Truman. He tells me that the Russians, Molotov and all suddenly came out into the grounds, threw wide the gates; by the time I dressed and got there, it was practically over. But Daniels, the sweetie filled me in, read me his own notes of K's speech and what Molotov said and the vodka toasts and all. I can't think of any British or French journalist who would show such kindness to a silly, lazy girl reporter for going to bed when she ought to have stayed on the job till the bitter end. Only an American, I think, is capable of such generosity, magnanimity. Mostly, they're all like that.

They give, asking or expecting nothing in return. They don't hate each other's guts like we do. Of course, I know and everyone knows there was absolutely nothing in the press conference inside the villa that mattered. The papers would use the Agency material because it would probably get to London first. So, you'll ask, why am I worried, why am I ashamed? Because something MIGHT have happened; Molotov might have had a stroke or Bulganin got a salmon fish-bone stuck in his throat. It could have been a scoop, and I'd have missed it. End of me.

Next day I had a bit of luck I didn't deserve. Up very early ... and out to Eden's villa. Lady Eden (Clarissa you know, cool tall blonde) had been out for a very early swim in the lake and I don't blame her; only sensible thing to do at this boring Conference. But when she gets back: to the villa, in her wet things still, the body guards won't let her in. Where, they want to know, are her credentials. No one recognises her. They were Swiss police and no reason on earth they should know what Clarissa Eden looks like; lots of English people don't either. So she stands there while someone goes racing like mad on a motorcycle to get clearance.

Meanwhile she manages to push past the guards eventually, but boy, is she mad?! I cable 300 words straight off to the Sketch, and they're thrilled to bits. It not only makes the Front Page Lead for the following morning, it's exclusive and makes a big black headline. Lady Eden Locked Out. I keep it to myself. I'm no sweet, kind generous Daniels; can't afford to be.

Damn it all, there isn't a moment's peace! Phone call waiting for me back at Beau Rivage. I make a dash for the phone box in the foyer watched by that stone-featured, chalk-white visage of Randolph Churchill on his way to the Bar ... it's the News Ed. Want you back in the office right away, to get a visa to fly to Moscow with the Wolverhampton Wanderers who are to play Spartak in July. Football in the sweating hot

July heat of Moscow. Poor Billy Wright, poor Wolves, poor me.

Love, Ogg

To Moscow with Billy Wright and Wolves; Olga puts her foot in it and realises that Russia actually is a police state. Her month in Moscow paints a vivid picture of life in post-Stalin Russia. She is the only Fleet Street journalist fluent in Russian and this long letter tells more than a hundred newspaper stories.

July 1955
c/o Savoy Hotel, Jdanov Street, Moscow

Dear B,

I know you expect me to use this trip to go looking for Grandma's old farmhouse at Utyan but at the moment I'm busy with looking after Billy Wright and his famous Wolves, not to mention the Team Managers etc, who all go about looking a bit anxious and who can blame them?

For one thing the heat in Moscow is intense. The sun beats down from about 6am, which is when I start telephoning Room Service in this shabby-ornate hotel where the ceilings are quite beautiful with naked nymphs whose breasts hang down over the dining-tables and attract the attention of passers-by in Jdanov Street who are clearly fascinated not only by this erotic marble splendour but also by me and a disgruntled team of football reporters from the Mail, Express, Reuter, Telegraph, etc., waiting at the spotless white tablecloths for the dinner that never comes.

So ... you see, Gran will have to wait. Also the Prayer House in Minsk which nurtured Grandpa until he was fit for marriage; that must wait too. Waiting is a way of life in Moscow. Reporters, especially football ones, are not the patient kind so every now and then there are raised voices and someone (usually me) starts a 'Skandal!' It is the only way.

Actually Waiting for Dinner is a lot more comfortable than waiting for morning tea from a department laughingly known as the 'obslujivanye' or Service. The morning ritual goes like this.

I wake before six. The blazing sun has heated the parquet floor of my room so that it is already too hot to patter on it barefoot from my curtained bed in an alcove which is even hotter. You would love the curtained, canopied bed straight out of Dostoyevsky's Brothers Karamazov. If it were not so horribly hot and me so dry and thirsty I could almost fancy the stale, warm water in the bedside jug. I'd see myself as the voluptuous prostitute Grushenka rising from her bed certainly of about the same era, same style and furnishing. Nothing has changed in Moscow since our Grandma departed this land about 1870 and sailed for Grimsby instead.

The maids are charming to look at, in frilly black and white aprons and caps with black ribbon streamers down their backs. Alas, they appear to be only for looking pretty for I have still to catch them serving a meal, making a bed or carrying a tray with what I long for with all my being ... a glass of tea. Tea, heavenly tea. They grow it here in the Soviet Union. Red Square has a tall electric sign, the only advert visible here, which says, 'Drink soviet tea.' Oh I would ...I do .... if only I COULD!

Every dawn it is the same thing. I take the long walk across the hot parquet floor of my suite from the narrow bed enclosed in rich, heavy crimson velvet curtains to the desk with its telephone. I am hoarse from sheer thirst but thank God, I have my tea coupon ready out in my hand. (Bread is still on the ration here; food is scarce but who wants food?!)

'Please Comrade, put me through to the buffet.' I am husky with it, hardly able to speak.

'It is six o'clock, citizeness,' says the ice-cold voice of the hotel clerk six floors below, 'and the buffet does not open until eight.'

The cold tap in the bathroom runs warm; the hot tap runs cooler. So I drink from the water carafe on the desk; it is not good.

The uncertainty is the killing part. I am only a week or less in Moscow but I already know that if the buffet is advertised as opening at eight, it means nine at the earliest.

Still I try at eight. It is getting hard even to whisper but at last I am connected with the 'buffet'.

'Please bring me tea.' I know it sounds like the moan of someone in pain. I am. The sun is much hotter now. 'Immediately please, please:'

'Tea?' says an astonished voice. 'What tea?' She says this every morning.

'Tea, just tea,' I say painfully.[...]

The first morning I thought perhaps they don't understand my Russian. But I can't help noticing that my accent is better than hers. Having learned to speak it from a White Russian rather gives me away. Did you know there was pre-revolution speech and grammar and post-revolution which is rather basic; you would call it 'common'.

No, she understands the word 'chai' (tea) all right. But there is a ritual in Russia which all must obey. They will, I have already found, never give you today what they can put off giving until tomorrow.

I am still moaning painfully into the receiver. 'Tea, just tea ... as soon as possible please.'

'Do you mean a glass of tea or a pot of tea, citizeness?'

'A pot, of course, a pot, a big, big pot but quickly.' (This will take 3 of my coupons I notice.)

'A pot? But what kind of pot. For how many people? I do not understand.'

This has gone on like this, every morning for almost a week. I can hardly bear it.

'A pot, a pot!'

'Do you mean a pot for six or a pot for five or a pot for four?' Ha, I am getting cunning at last.

'A pot for four, of course.' I am screaming now, hoarse but screaming.

'Will you pay for a pot for four with money or coupons, citizeness?' says the calm voice in a tone which shows its awareness that a pot for four paid for in money is big business, whereas coupons are ... just a lot of coupons.

I hesitate. For money she may come quickly, that means within say 45 or 50 minutes. For coupons .... she may not even come at all. On the other hand I am going to need every rouble and kopek for bread, taxis, tips. It is an expensive town.

'Coupons,' I say humbly.

'So ... on coupons,' the waitress says, 'So, you will have a pot for four people ... but do you only want a pot of tea for four; do you not also want lemon or milk or cream with it?'

There is no way to cut it short. Russian rituals are sacred.

'So ... you want a pot of tea for four with lemon and I suppose sugar; do you not also want something to eat with it?'

'Yes, I will have some bread.'

'Ah bread, so ... you will have a pot of tea for four with lemon and sugar and bread. How much bread, bread for four or for one?'

'Bread for one.' I am gasping now.

'Ah, so you will have a pot of tea for four with lemon and sugar and bread for one, but will you have black bread or White bread?'

Every morning at this point, I know that I must try to get the conversation under some kind of control. It is not worth the effort though. The thing must run its course. If you interrupt, you may get

289

no tea at all. There will in any case be an hour or an hour and a half to wait anyway, so you might as well spend it in this way.

'I will have black bread,' I say firmly. 'Choirny hleb, and quickly please.'

'So ... at last I understand, you will have a pot of tea for four with lemon and sugar and black bread for one, but will you not also have butter with it?'

· Next morning, on reaching this point, I gasp in quickly ... 'and cheese for one.' I am getting quick off the mark now. You are unlikely to get another meal this day.

'Pardon, citizeness, I did not hear, you will have WHAT?'

She sounds very cross. I have upset her ritual. That was the day I got nothing.[...]

I got my chance to ask about Grandma & Co. Fat, blond, podgy Mr. Popov says, 'no;' he says no one can go to that part of the northern Baltic country; something about it being 'strategic' or out-of-bounds ... perhaps later, etc. I got distinct impression it was a bad mistake to mention Grandma's Father's farm or the little Lithuanian horses no bigger than ponies. When I got to the National Hotel for drinks with the boys, Roy Peskett* of the Mail said, 'You're a bloody lunatic ... get us all put in jail ...why don't you just sit here and help us get some dinner.'

Yes, it was a mistake. A bad one. I'll tell you later just why. The heat is still killing and I dread the nightly walk to the Central Post Office to get my cables past the censor.

We seem to be about 5 hours behind Moscow time. The maid woke me at 3am with a cable from the news ed. which read: 'Get an invitation for the Queen to visit Moscow.' It added, 'Do 500 words on polygamy in Russia'!!

I think the 'prislujenka' still in her pretty frilled cap (at that time of night!!) thought I must be having a nervous breakdown because I took a sort of flying leap into the crimson velvet alcove and started biting the nice white pillow (Moscow seems to have super laundry, even the women sweeping the streets wear startling white pinnies). When I calmed down a bit, I said 'Nu?' hoping she had no more bloody stupid cables like that one. 'Nichevo,' she said. 'I was always told that English people are calm, polite and do not scream. You are not calm, not polite and you scream.'

'Of course,' she added, 'you are journalists. I heard all about YOU. Terrible people. Ujass!' (Horror).

She was right of course, so I went back to bed. Not to sleep but write, in imagination, a really rude reply to Walter Hayes … who should know better. I mean, why drag the Queen into it?

It's bad enough here for the Wolverhampton Wanderers … no whit impressed by Red Square or St Basil's. They go around saying they prefer Wolverhampton.

Next morning therefore off I went to Comrade Popov and did my sweetly feminine-helpless act which seemed to work. They're cunning, these KGB men in the Ministry of Foreign Affairs in Smolensk Place. They pretend they're ever so glad to see you and as for the Queen, it's a lovely idea and he felt Comrade Nikita Krushchev would be charmed, etc. Being a much better interviewer than I ever could be, he led me on and in no time at all, I was pouring it all out. My plans, in between the football matches with Spartak and Wolves, to visit various old friends and relations no one had seen since Czar Nicholas II abdicated, to put it nicely so no one would be offended. I rattled on about the old family friends I was planning to call on, the Ephraims and the Fagins, etc., etc. Oh, how nice. He was SO interested.

The bastard. It just goes to show that Olga the pride of the Dynamos is a stupid, ignorant little idiot not worth a penny of that Union-minimum. How could I have been so crass, so dim-witted! No, don't tell me luv. I suppose deep down I hoped against hope that all the propaganda we've all grown up with about the soviet police state, etc., was, well, exaggerated. I'd seen myself as cosy little peacemaker who was going to come home and write beautiful articles about how it's no different really from Home and that Herbert Morrison should go wash his mouth out before he starts spreading nasty tales about Stalin not being as dead as he looks down there in the freezing vault in the Kremlin. (I must say I thought he looked rather well; not a grey hair to be seen and not many wrinkles neither.)

The truth is Roy Peskett was right and even the Wolverhampton Wanderers know more about Communist realities than I do. Oh oh. I've fallen flat on my face again … just like I did in 1943 with Mussolini's eldest son and the boxing match in Budapest … remember?

To save money I walk back to the Savoy from Smolensk Place, knowing in advance that I'll get stopped every few minutes by citizens wanting some more conversation. Every few yards, pushing through the crowds and a bit unsteady on my high-heeled Italian sandals with yellow and blue raffia flowers on them which are not good for crossing these wide streets with their steep cobblestones … someone confronts me head-on.

'Citizeness, where did you get those remarkable shoes? Are they expensive?'

'Citizeness, may I look at those beads you are wearing. They must be very valuable!'

'Citizeness,' says one old woman, regarding me severely, 'I'm not at all sure that your hairstyle suits your face. Have you tried?...'

'Leave her alone, Evdokia Agafyevna, you'll make her cry with your criticisms...'

Does everyone know everyone else in this godforsaken town? Yes, I reckon.[...]

The trouble is that everyone else stops too, right in the middle of Gorki Street and wants to join in the conversation. There's a crowd round me now, inspecting my white blouse and black cardigan (twelve shillings in a sale in Oxford Street).

'Those shoes are quite outlandish,' says someone. A young man is almost down on his knees inspecting them.

I apologise for shoes, beads, hair, etc., and explain I'm an Angliohanka and therefore know no better.

The crowd grows. Evdokiya Agafyevna is fingering my cardigan. Thank goodness, up comes a policeman, rather a pretty boy in white uniform. This is the 'milizia' not the KGB and usually very flirtatious. But not this one.

'What is going on here?' he bellows. 'Get along there ... all of you. Go about your business.'

After that I stop at the little kiosk which sells 'Information' for sums varying between 2 roubles and 5. I hand over several names of friends which Mrs. Grun gave me before leaving London. She wanted me particularly to visit a doctor's daughter who used to live in Moscow in 1919. And I am still playing the part of the Innocent Abroad. 'You see,' (this is how I put it to Comrade Popov, thinking in my abysmal foolishness that he would be impressed by such honesty, such frankness, such truly ENGLISH common-sensibleness) 'you see I've not seen or heard of Miss Ephraim for about 40 years or so, but it would be so nice to renew the acquaintanceship and pass on greetings from family and friends.

Oh oh. I can see you tearing your hair, old girl. Roy Peskett did that when I told him. Only he has less hair to tear.

The blond in the kiosk (they're called Spravochnoye Buro and they're a sort of substitute for telephone books which are only to be found in public libraries or hotels and are in any case some 35 years out of date) looks entirely un-interested. She cares nothing for my hair-style, my Italian yellow sandals (she can't see them behind her kiosk grill and tiny window)

.... cardigan, beads, etc. She looks bored. I am just another customer and behind me is a queue of about 8 or 9 more people waiting.

'Pay 2 roubles and come back here in 20 minutes,' she says.

Ah, that did make me stop and think. Is that all it takes to find a missing person? In this great, overcrowded city? How very odd.

I go and sit in the gardens outside the Bolshoi theatre. The thing is to keep moving. To stand still is to attract a crowd, then a policeman who is always on the look out for 'Prostitutki'.

11pm. The crowds were still thick when I passed by the underground tube station, The Sverdlova, to the left of Red Square. A tiny boy with golden curls, long tight trousers and bare feet, was running, twisting in and out among the people, holding high above his head a small bunch of blue cornflowers.

I hesitate. With those blue eyes and curls, he could be Oliver Twist in an early edition my father gave us, with beautiful coloured illustrations.

Three roubles! One-and-sixpence to a Russian but nearly six shillings to me, with the tourist rate of eleven roubles to the pound.

To hesitate for two seconds in a Moscow street is stupid. A group of men walking by, have spotted me, the boy, the cornflowers. They start to shout at me.

'Go on, citizeness, buy the flowers. You can't disappoint a child, can you? Only three roubles; he's only a little child, innocent small boy. You can't treat a child like that.'

Now the boy has seen me too and fixes his great blue eyes on me. I get out my purse and buy nervously. It takes so little to start a conversation, then a commotion. The boy snatches the note and is gone in a flash. I follow to the corner of the street where a young woman, fair hair covered with the kosinka or headscarf is crouched over a basket of mixed wild flowers and I say sharply; 'Grajdanka (Citizeness) your little son should be in bed at this hour.' (Blimey, dear B, they've got me doing it now, interfering!) A sunburned face turns to me. 'He is my brother, Citizeness, we've only just started the night's business.' She tells me she is 12 and her brother almost 8. It is the height of their private-enterprise season and their basket is already full of roubles and kopecks.[...]

'Meat is off,' says Zvetlana. She looks exhausted, clean and tidy with great black circles under her eyes. The waitresses appear to do a 16-hour shift and then have a day off.

'Fresh salmon then,' I say.

'Salmon's off,' she says.

That leaves the Flowering Cabbage (cauliflower to us). It's rather nice but no cheese, only fried breadcrumbs.

'Flowering cabbage is off too,' says Z, shifting from one foot to the other.

Her expression is somehow implacable. She reminds me of a girl I used to know in the ABC in the Strand. Same golden edifice of curls, the same set lipstick, the same indifference.

After a long wait, she brings me Fried Savruga fish and a few greasy chips. And some red and black caviar. I devour the caviar; the fish is dry and tasteless. Am still hungry.

Zvetlana reappears bearing a plate. On it are two slices of white bread, two slices of black. No butter.

'No butter?' I say.

'You never asked for butter,' Zvetlana cries aloud. She sways a little so that her frilled, white Victorian cap slips to one side over her tall curls.

'I am tired, all worn out,' she says. 'My feet hurt.'

Saturday afternoon.

This morning I was thrown out of the synagogue in Spassoglinichevsky Street.

My fault, for getting mixed up in a Conversation again. You will say, dear Sister, why do I do it? I think there must be some way, if only I could discover it, of actually STOPPING a conversation.

It happened this way. I promised the news-ed I would visit as many churches, chapels, cathedrals, synagogues, mosques and houses-of-prayer as possible to find out how many citizens still practise a religion in this godless country. I've already done the Russian Orthodox Cathedral which was marvellous, packed the roof with people and ikons and a massive queue at the door, all struggling to get inside. But it's standing-only anyway and I was soon tottering on those silly sandals. Then coming down here, the usual crowd of women start following to spy on those wretched raffia sandals again. I stand on one foot to let them feel the other which I take off and it is passed from hand to hand. After that, they follow to the doors of the 'schule'. It is just as crowded as the Russian Orthodox and the same crowd of would-be worshippers or rubberneckers standing on the steps and filling up the porch, entrance and hall. (None of the churches can close their main doors because of the crowds pressing between them).

I manage to push inside; it looks exactly like Singer's Hill, Edgbaston, Birmingham only shabbier. The men wear caps; hardly any women here, even the gallery upstairs has only men in it.

Soon a man in a battered trilby hat of the kind worn just after the first World War notices me. A deputation of three bearded ones move towards me. I feel more conversation coming; oh oh!

But no, it is much worse. One of the women who followed me in the street has sent a message to the Verger or someone, saying I'm a black-marketeer, that I have been trying to 'flog' my yellow sandals in the street, etc.

'You should be ashamed,' says the bearded leader of the three-man deputation to me sternly, 'to come here to this house of prayer on shabbos to do your low, degraded business.'

I start to protest my innocence but am not allowed to speak.

The deputation sort of shoulder me backwards to the door, through it and on to the steps. My disgrace is clear for all to see and a small cheer goes up from some of the crowd. I make to get away as fast as possible, uncomfortably unsteady on those blasted high-heeled sandals, but it is not easy to push through the crowds. Embarrassed and full of outraged innocence, I lurk behind one of the doors, intending to go back and explain that I am a pure-hearted English reporter, not a black-marketeer.

Suddenly I notice an extremely handsome young man standing half on the step and half on the pavement outside. He is golden-blond like so many here, pale, blue-eyed, looking if you can imagine it? a sort of golden Valentino in an Apache-type of floppy cap. He keeps going up and down the steps and glancing up and down the street anxiously. This time it is me who feels like some conversation; I may need his protection. Surely he is too good looking to be a Secret Policeman?[...]

Ah, a protector? 'Are you also waiting to get into the Service?' I smiled in my most ingratiating manner, I hope.

'No,' he said gloomily, 'I'm waiting for the Shadchan (Matchmaker). I waited for him last week too and the week before. I've nearly given up hope!'

I was stunned, as you can well imagine The Shadchan... in Moscow!!....in 1955! Was it possible?

He was young, perhaps 27 or less. Was he pulling my leg?

'I should have thought,' I said, 'someone like you could have found yourself a wife .... without waiting for the Shadchan?'

'What?' he said. 'How? The Jewish girls don't go out; they stay close to their mothers; you can't get near them. I was counting on an introduction by the Shadchan. Today he promised.... ' He was still going up and down the steps and staring hard up to the top of the street which was empty, quite narrow, except for the cluster of people round the open doors of the synagogue through which came the sound of a Cantor singing...

It seemed unbelievable. Yes, I know if it hadn't been for the Shadchan from Minsk in 1860, Grandma (who was no beauty) might never have found a beau and I'd not be here today, being thrown out of Schule in Spassoglinichevsky Street, and Stalin barely cold these past two years in the Kremlin vault.

I said well if he didn't want to wait for a wife, why not a Russian girl?

Oh no, he said, thank you very much, if I can't find a Jewess, I'll do without. But I'm fed up, he added, living at home with Mama and her new Russian husband. I want my own flat, he said, and you can't get on to the housing list unless you've got a family.

This was true; I knew that much. Most of the apartment blocks in Moscow have got tiny one-room or two-room flats with sometimes as many as three or four families living in them. Opposite my hotel room in Jdanova Street there's one window filled with green plants. Behind the plants is a sort of sheet hung across the room to divide one family off from another.

He wanted a young wife, children, a good cook to look after him, etc. Russian girls couldn't cook and besides.... It was clear he thought they were also no better than they should be...

'Well,' I said coyly, thinking it was time to reveal myself, 'you'd better come to London. Lots of us girls would be keen to marry a good looking chap with prospects.' ... (I thought of our lonely-hearts in Grove End Gardens who would eat him alive...)

For the first time he stopped searching the horizon for the shadchan and stared straight at me. Was I married? he asked and when I said no, a widow, he looked doubtfully, searchingly like a man who was not going to be sold a pup.

'How old are you?' he said. He looked sort of hopeful suddenly...

'About thirty,' I replied.

His face fell; he was gloomy again.

'That cursed Shadchan,' he repeated. 'He's let me down again!'

Sunday evening

I took a taxi out to the address given me for 2 roubles at the street kiosk. On my way to see the Doctor's daughter, friend of Mrs. Grun in

London. It was a suburb of Moscow, quite a long drive outside the city. It looked more like Grandma's 'stetl'** than a city suburb. I noticed there were no shops or stores; soon there was not much pavement either. Wooden houses and huge, dark blocks of flats with broken fences and loose bricks lying about. The scene was almost rural in its vast emptiness as though we'd left the city far behind. No, we were still in Moscow, the driver said. When he stopped, he turned to me and said, 'I'd better come upstairs with you; it's a bit rough around here.' Also it was getting dark.

I said I could manage but he insisted. It seemed to me an interesting sort of slum. Inside I could understand what he meant by 'rough'. There was no lighting and he took my arm; part of the bannisters seemed to be missing. We climbed four or five flights of stairs; then I knocked on the door. Dead silence. He knocked for me, more loudly. Someone pulled back a bolt; I heard a key being turned in the lock and then another; then more bolts were removed; a latch was lifted. It all took a long time; then the door was opened just a crack only. In that thin crack I could see four or five anxious faces one above the other, staring out at me. 'I've come from London,' I said loudly, 'to visit Miss Ephraim.'[...]

The faces disappeared immediately but the door did not open wider. After a pause, Miss Ephraim appeared, opened the door. She was neither middle-aged nor elderly but somehow both at the same time. Her face was severe and like most women here, terribly tired. I suppose the daily struggle to get enough bread and cabbage, milk or lemons to sustain life through each week – with the occasional sliver of garlic salami or sardines – must tire the women out, especially as it means trudging across the city each day looking for a street market. The shops in Gorki Street marked 'Milk' or 'Bread' are besieged by queues but have very little to sell. The chickens or carp or bunches of grapes in the shop windows are painted dummies.

But, clearly, Miss Ephraim is not only tired, she is distraught. As she with some reluctance opens the door to admit me, she puts out an arm and pulls with great force at the arm of my 'chauffeur' who has left his taxi in the bare, broken street outside. 'You must come too,' she says, 'otherwise I cannot speak with this lady.'

'No, no:' says the man, 'it is nothing to do with me. This is a private conversation.'

'You must come, you must. You must listen to all of it.' She is speaking with a kind of terrified urgency which terrifies me. My God, what have I done?

'I tell you no,' says the man. To me he says; 'She is upset; there is nothing to worry about. It is all right. I shall wait for you downstairs in the car.'

He manages to release himself. She is on the verge of tears. And so am I. We are left standing in a quite roomy square hall. Through the open kitchen door I can see a clean, shining gas oven and some kitchen equipment but no sign of any food. All round the hall are doors which stand open only about an inch through which people are peeping at me again. The flat is comfortably large enough for a family but here there must be at least one family and probably more in every room.

Miss E is struggling to compose herself. At last, she says, 'You may come and talk in my room but you cannot stay. A few minutes only.'

I protest that I will go immediately rather than cause her distress. 'No, no,' she says, 'now that you are here...'

She takes me into a room so tiny that there is room only for the two of us. It appears at first glance to be entirely empty. Then I see a camp-bed against the wall and a small table facing one wall, covered with papers. Also one chair. She sits at the table and talks rapidly about her life. 'There is not much to tell. I earn my living doing technical translations into English. Sometimes I get work from abroad; this pays me better but it sometimes makes my situation difficult. I believe I am entirely trusted by the authorities but now that you come .... no, don't say anything. I understand. It is not your fault. I am glad that you brought me messages from friends and family but I want you to go now. Ask them not to write to me; it could cause trouble. You were not to know what would happen. I have been expecting you. Ever since I was summoned a few days ago to appear before an investigation at the Ministry of Foreign Affairs in Smolensk Place.'

Ah, that bloody Popov: I feel such shame; wish for the earth to open and swallow me. She is still talking. 'My personal life too has been unsuccessful. I am an unhappy woman. For some years I loved a man who had been married but his children came between us. In the end he preferred his children and now I am alone, quite alone. As you see.'

In spite of my shame and embarrassment – which I shall always feel – I think I could see why he preferred his children. She was out of a Chekhov short story; not a Duchechka though because for her, life could never hold any compensations. She asked me to forgive her. Me .... to forgive HER?! I went forlornly downstairs. The flat was still and silent with all doors closed .... and locked. In the taxi, the driver (I had imagined he was employed by Intourist but now decided he worked for

298

the KGB) was in a bad mood. 'Silly woman,' he said, 'there was no need for her to make all that fuss. She behaved as though Stalin were still alive. She thought I would report her for talking to a foreigner. Nonsense. I report nothing; I say nothing. It was a private conversation.'

Well, I shall know it in future. There is no such thing as a private conversation in Moscow. Back at the Savoy, I found the restaurant closed and only the huge, stuffed bear still on duty at the entrance. The aged uniformed commissionaire took me up in the rattling old lift whilst he read his book of Chekhov short stories. Anton Pavlovich lives in this godforsaken country; about the only thing that DOES live here.

Love Ogg.

*Roy Peskett was one of the leading sports reporters in Fleet Street in the post-war years. He was one of the founders of the Player of the Year Award, an editor of Rothman's Football Yearbook *and wrote several books about cricket and football.* ** stetl, a small Jewish town or village formerly found in Eastern Europe.

31st July 1955
c/o Queens Hotel, Huddersfield

Dear B,

Sorry I was not at home when you called. I got back from Moscow two days ago rather gladly. After nearly a month there, we were all relieved to get back to the corrupt and capitalist West.

Found the News Editor buzzing with ideas and decided the only safe thing to do was to get out of town and – rather daring this – leave no address behind.

As I think I told you, A makes regular trips here on business. As a Consultant to some printing works at Halifax. It means we can have sometimes two or three days and nights together which makes a kind of honeymoon.

Jolly Jack Lewis, genial crime reporter who caught me creeping out of the office with my overnight bag, suspected I was off to Venice, Florence or somewhere 'glamorous'. No, Huddersfield, I said, but don't tell the news desk. I did tell my dear old pal Tom Halfpenny though; he comes from Redcar and is one of those dear, generous, loyal people always on the lookout to protect friends from the News Editor. Tom and Jack were sympathetic! 'In this glorious weather, Huddersfield! oh you poor kid!'

I waited for the train on Kings Cross platform and thought about how A has changed my whole life. To me, Huddersfield is a special kind of heaven nowadays. Then I thought about being in Venice, Florence, Paris or wherever; no, I preferred Huddersfield. For one thing it is so private. Not even the blasted News Editor would think of looking for me there, in the grey streets with the grey stone buildings and the 'gardens' (they call it a park) where I sit on a bench and wait for dinnertime when A will come back from work.

The gardens are dark and secret and no-one goes there, except for the Park-keeper or the gardener. I'm the only regular customer. Like a desert island. Quiet. Hazelnut and Sycamore, laurel bush and cypress; holly with bottle-green, greasy leaves. Even in high summer, it feels damp, dank, a little dour and I love every bit. Why not Huddersfield for honeymoons then? I sit on the bench and giggle to myself. You always said I was a queer cuss, always wanting to be different from other people. Not really, only here I feel safe.

Nice people too. I always did like the North. The country hotel newly furnished and decorated in wine and grey. She is a homely white-haired Lancashire woman; with taste and charm and she smiles at us as we say 'goodnight' and go upstairs to bed, though I feel I want to hide from her and from everyone because I fear they may all die of envy.

And all this luxury and joy comes out of what seemed one evening like disaster.

One of the chambermaids caught me going into his room and A was furious with me for my carelessness. After all this is a Small Town and Mr. Womersley of Halifax is a well known business-gentleman probably known to the local gossips. But that was almost a year ago. Next time we arrived here for our rendezvous, we found the Manageress had made things easy for us by providing a double-suite with an adjoining door. So now, if we get here from London early enough, we can make love before dinner as well.

When I say over the soup or the melon, that it's surprising what a lot you can get done in a day with a little effort, A laughs a lot. He is the kind of man who likes to laugh as often as possible.

Why am I telling you all this? After many, many years silence, discreet, sensible? To try and give some sort of necessary explanation for what you must see as my 'wickedness'. I know it makes you laugh, and that's fine. But in your more reasoning moments, I think you feel quietly horrified. Or sad?

Imagine the relief of being here after Moscow. Here there is privacy, content; no one interferes or says anything much except, 'Good morning, another fine day!'

In Russia, the streets are awash with conversation, with exhausting and exhaustive interference from its citizens. I think they wear each other out; however, there's not much else for them to do. Except of course to go to the cinema; but there were long queues for tickets which had to be booked in advance. Even the 'Chroniki', the News Film Theatre had long queues and had to be booked in advance.

What with the Moscow heat, the total lack of food (I lived on beautiful black bread and tea) I've lost over a stone in weight. A said I looked thin and haggard. That put me in a panic. Was he tiring of me then? I sit in the Gardens and think about him, and wait for dinner;

Wicked? Yes, but it is a good life. By the way, I have started to have gout in the big toe of my right foot. So ... the punishment begins.

If the News Editor rings you up to enquire where I am, please say that I was ill with flu and then left; you don't know where.

Love, Ogg

1956

August 1956
c/o Queen's Hotel, Huddersfield

Dear B,

Career crisis again. Walter Hayes was promoted, I think I told you, to be an Assistant Editor on the Daily Mail some months ago. Barely thirty years of age, he zoomed to the top on the Sketch after his demob in 1948. All the Girls like working for Hayes because he likes to discriminate in favour of the women. It's clever, cunning, canny. It also means that he can count on such a passion of loyalty no other editor can hope for. He can also take Decisions, get things done....For this he needs his women.

He likes only Kings, Queens, princes and women reporters. It means of course we girls get the most ghastly jobs to do because he knows that if he sends us to get some impossible interview, we'll stick on it until the massacre and shooting starts and get some kind of interview, no matter what. Whereas the men ...Even the tough experienced ones draw the line at some things and tend to wilt on the job much earlier

301

... unless reinforced with lots of cash, beer and cartloads of praise and... 'You did a super job, Bill'. Hayes doesn't waste time and breath smooth-talking us girls. Just the quiet hand on the shoulder, 'I knew you'd get it, luv.' The whole of Fleet Street is amazed by him, and puzzled too. They want to know how it's done. Without threats or sex. He has just married a rather attractive, quiet, slightly superior girl from Hull. He's a little mysterious, enigmatic; that's what gets them in Fleet Street.

One reason why he is greatly feared is that when he moves...to a new department, new paper or whatever, he likes to take his women with him. Naturally! That's how empires are built, nicht? The reason I can't just go and work for him on the Daily Mail, alas, because now that the Daily Sketch belongs to the same Rothermere Group, Associated Newspapers, it makes it impossible to move to a better job on a sister paper. Herbert Gunn would never allow it. Neither would the management...what to do?

Hayes hit upon a solution. A letter just came from him and I showed it to A and he is rather panicky about it. Hayes' suggestion is that I should apply for a reporting job on the Daily Herald who are looking for a Bright Girl. Upon getting the job, I would then send my letter of resignation to H.Gunn and accept the Herald job. Whereupon Hayes would go to see the top Editor of the Daily Mail, Arthur Wareham and, wringing his hands in despair, would report this tragic event, together with HIS proposal how I could be saved from the jaws of the Herald by Mr. Wareham making me a Better Offer to come and work for the Mail instead.

A shook his head over this letter. Apparently they don't do things in this underhand way in the Printing Business! He sees the dangers too well for me to fall flat on my face. He also remembers those weeks when the fate of the Daily Sketch hung in the balance in 1951 and he had to pay my rent and keep me. He is something of a Hayes himself when it comes to moving his staff about on a dicey chessboard but he is more cautious than our Walter.

For once I hold my own and I get on the blower and fix up an interview to ask the Daily Herald Editor for an interview. I'll keep you posted with the results.

I know you'll agree that I need a change from the Sketch. I must try at least to get away from the eternal Kings and Queens and Princes, etc. and on the Mail there should be more interesting stuff to handle. In the past year or so I've done Prince Peter of Yugoslavia, King Farouk of Egypt, King Zog of Albania and a host of minor princes, margraves etc.

Poor old King Zog. He went and died of a heart attack right after I went down to spend a weekend with him near Cannes. His wife Queen Geraldine is very nice and pretty but our several interviews with Zog were rather strained. For one thing he was so tall. I never really got to seeing the top of his head even when sitting down. Zog and our cameraman David Johnson got on very well at first until David starts talking about the time he was posted with the RAF to Tirana, 'My poor capital,' King Zog called it. 'And how did you like my poor capital?' asks the King. 'I didn't,' David replies, 'it rained every day of the fortnight I was there.'

After that we did Peter of Yugoslavia and his bride, also in the Cannes area, and flew back to London, David moaning all the way that I'd left him no time to go souvenir hunting. David has been to everywhere you can think of, and likes to collect souvenirs.

31st August 1956

Hooray! When I got back to London, I was offered the job by the Herald, resigned from the Sketch whereupon Hayes made me an offer, an interview with Arthur Wareham followed; I then rejected the Herald and I start with the Mail in about a fortnight. Mr. Gunn is rather 'pained'.

Love, Ogg

1957

January 1957
c/o Daily Mail, Northcliffe House, Tudor St
London EC4

Dear B,

From now on I'm to have my own Column. Fame at last! William Hardcastle has given it the title 'Frankly Yours' and every week he and Hayes and our new Features Editor, Marius Pope, think up a new 'stunt' for me to do. Marius is from South Africa, tall and dark and looks like Oscar Wilde though he is never quite sure whether he's pleased about that or not.

He says girls all want to be air hostesses nowadays so I've got to go and be one for a few days. Try BOAC, he says but when I ring them, their Press Relation man nearly has a fit at the mere thought 'of letting, one of you Fleet Street lunatics loose on our precious passengers'.

So Marius says, well ring Pan-Am and their chap said; 'What a marvellous idea. When d'you want to start?'

I have to go through all the various stages, being interviewed, etc., and measured for one of their rather glamorous pale blue uniforms. Horrors I'm a 39½ hip suddenly and their very largest is 38. So they find me a second hand uniform in the 38-hip that's been stretched a lot. I'm to fly out to New York starting about 6pm from London airport on one of their super-planes, so as to get the maximum publicity. It's a turbo-prop double-decker and takes about 16 hours to get to New York.

There are three other girls and a steward and the work is hellish hot, taking the hot dinners out of the oven and racing up the air-ship and back with all the Orders on this President Luxury Special. The girls all change into slippers because walking to New York on deck, as well as up and downstairs to the Bar, is, they've reckoned it out, more than 5 miles each trip. 'You'll find your feet swell at 30,000 feet,' Judy tells me. She's one of the glamorous, beautiful stewardesses. I wish she'd warned me though that I would swell all over because soon I'm not just hot, even in white blouse, without the jacket, I'm bursting all over and that bloody zip on my skirt comes spurting right off 'ping'. One large party looks at me as though wondering if they've caught the Economy Tourist instead of the President Special, but they keep me running all evening for drinks and smokes and hot milk for the baby and a fizzy drink for Nanny. It turns out to be a family from the U.S. Embassy going home on leave.

After the 7-course dinner is served .... and me hoping for a sit-down and feet-up so I can sew up my skirt instead of safety-pins, there's more drinks to be served and then the sleeping-bunks to be lowered, the children have to be put to bed, late-night hot drinks and biscuits and by that time, the trays have got to be got ready about 3am for 6am breakfast, just before we fly into New York. Never worked so hard in my life and when I ask the girls why they do it, they say the money's terrific, they share a luxury flat in New York and only work about one week a month!

At New York, coming in to land, I can see a group of photographers on the airfield itself, waiting to take pix of the celebrities. It turns out to be me, the Imposter-air-hostess ... and me trying to keep that dam skirt from slipping right down to my slippers.

The return trip that week was made as a Passenger. Not nearly as much fun. A was pleased with my picture and story in the paper. The thing is for A to be pleased, which is all I care about.

After that I've got to go on a diet, under the Queen's own diet doctor. I'm also booked to be a Clippie for a few days' work on a No.14 bus from Holloway to Kensington. The uniform is terrific, a well-cut blue serge with paler blue stitching collar interest; this time it fits like a dream.

The paper is to buy me a dog, a greyhound to race at Harringay. I think that's because Marius is keen on betting on the dogs. She's an all-black hound, with good pedigree, age two and her name, of course, is Frankly Yours. I'm not so keen on being famous as I was; the phone never stops with people ringing to ask is Frankly Yours running at Harringay tonight and how much should they bet on her and of course I haven't a clue as you know I'm not strong on arithmetic anyway but Marius says I've got to learn.

Love to all, Og

8th May 1957
c/o Daily Mail, Northcliffe House, Tudor St
London EC4

Dear B,

The most difficult people to interview, apart from Wimbledon tennis stars, are Writers. They are sensitive. Ethel Mannin was on edge in Wimbledon; so was Beverley Nichols* though he got braver on seeing that I was even more timid, faded and ageing than himself, but my favourite hero, Charles Morgan** claimed to be terrified .... which seems to me a bit extreme coming from a man who'd survived the first World War and written it up so beautifully in The Fountain.

Mr. Morgan even warned me on the phone beforehand that I must 'not mock him'; as though I would. Some of the reviews of his new novel 'Challenge to Venus' probably wrecked his nerve a bit. I've always thought of him as your truly Romantic Novelist in the nicest possible way because his heroines are always translucently beauteous and his heroes... sort of Godfrey Tearle types if you know what I mean.

So it was rather encouraging, on arriving at his house in Campden Hill-Square (a super tea with scones and jam) to find that he and his wife, although quite old and yellowing at the edges like the rest of us, were still good looking, even beautiful in that elegant, aristocratic way which we shall never have even if we lose weight and wear loose cardigans and pearls. His new book has sold awfully well; the first impression of 25,000 copies went in a few days but there seems just no way of convincing this nice, modest type of English author that we all love him. He was just as much on the defensive as Ethel or Beverley. 'People say that I live in an ivory tower, that I am a snob, a romantic. They say that I have always lived aloof. But I must write what is in me. It must have a glow.' He said that he thought, 'present so-called crude writing is not true art; that he didn't believe at all in giving explicit lovemaking scenes.'

His tall, pretty wife Hilda, also a novelist, comes in again with more scones and jam. I can't help feeling – though it may sound a bit grudging – that it is easy for him to stay romantic with Hilda who seems terribly shy and even though she must be nearer six foot and her lovely soft hair just gently tipped with pale grey, she has that eternal schoolgirl look of abashed tenderness. I think some people would call her a startled faun. I liked her, and him immensely, especially when he told me he couldn't give his heroine a happy ending in the new book. All his women are doomed by fate to reject the happiness they really want. We both agreed, on talking it over, that Life was often like that and much more long lasting than satisfied domesticity. A doomed unhappy love can last a lifetime. Perhaps that's what's worked so well for Charles Morgan and Hilda, by keeping them both so beautifully preserved and elegant. I dismiss this thought as too cynical, possibly even jealous!

The Features Editor wanted a contrast story so I had to go next day to Albany to interview Edgar Lustgarten*** who didn't seem sensitive at all, had my tea removed when I'd hardly started let alone finished, and sat cuddling his 12-year old cat Tush ... so he can't expect more than a couple of prosaic pars from me and that's what he got.

I hope you're not too bored with the above about Mr. Morgan; I realise you're not one of his fans, but I am. I just love reading about love.

Love, Ogg

* *Ethel Mannin (1900–1978) was a prolific novelist and at one time in relationships with W.B. Yeats and Bertrand Russell. Beverley Nichols (1898–1983) was a popular author and journalist.*
** *Charles Morgan (1894–1958) was a novelist and also, for many years, literary critic of* The Times.
*** *Edgar Lustgarten (1907–1978) was a crime writer and broadcaster.*

September 1957
c/o Daily Mail, Northcliffe House, Tudor St
London EC4

Dear B,

I used to think women reporters were as good as men any day, if not better. Last week I burst into floods of tears right bang in the middle of the News Room.

Now I think I may have been wrong all those years ago when I used to prowl around the Night News Desk at Reuters complaining that male Editors in Fleet Street were unfair to women because women were equal as Workers and ought to get Equal Treatment.

William Hardcastle who is Assistant Editor to Editor Arthur Wareham and therefore senior to my boss Walter Hayes, was heard to say; 'Why is that girl crying?'

I was snivelling at being sent flying to Copenhagen at a moment's notice to board the Soviet vessel carrying the now purged and forgiven Soviet Russian athlete Nina Ponomareva home to Leningrad. You'll have noticed she was arrested well over 3 months ago for pinching 5 woolly hats from C & A Modes at Marble Arch and promptly went into hiding where Fleet Street could not get at her. We, like the other papers, have had a team of crime men plus photographers camping out in Kensington Palace Gardens, more or less eating and sleeping under the hedges and any big stone they could find in the road with occasional forays to the front door of the Soviet Embassy residences until the police came to move them on to someone else's tradesman's entrance. It was a bad time for us all including poor Nina who might well have been hiding somewhere else. At last the weary pursuit was over; Nina gave herself up, was bound over at Gt. Marlborough St, police court where she upset everyone by guffawing foolishly when the Magistrate enquired what was her religion, and was then rushed by Soviet bus down to Surrey Commercial dock followed by the usual rabble of high-speed photographers hanging out of car-windows, and me.

Alas, it was not as I had hoped, the End. Someone spotted the Daily Express girl Shelley Rohde with overnight bag also going on board. 'But the boat has sailed,' I moaned to the News Editor, 'I saw it go, an hour ago.'

I should have known. Any reluctance on the reporter's part makes the News Editor all the keener. He can sense there's blood and pain in it

307

somewhere, and that's what he's after. Women are often, though not always, good weepers and it is tears with the occasional shriek which is thought to sell newspapers. A somewhat humbling thought ... that we women who prided ourselves on being accepted as equal workers are simply wanted to be wet.

I had even let my passport lapse for the past week or so, simply in order to avoid being sent abroad this past week ... when I had an appointment to meet A in the North Country for almost a week's tour between Huddersfield and Glasgow. There was no way of letting him know that I could not be there because I would be in Denmark awaiting the Soviet boat to take me on to Leningrad with Nina Ponamareva, known now as Nina-of-the–5-hats.

You may well say, serves you right old girl, for leading an irregular life, for having as the Tabloids put it, 'a secret love' which I cannot, dare not, Tell. Oh I agree. I do! But the whole thing has taught me a lesson I'll not soon forget. Women are not equal to men, not as Workers nor as People. A male reporter would have said to the News Editor that night, bugger you old chap, I've got a prior date in Huddersfield, send somebody else or dam well do it yourself! You don't believe me? I tell you, this is true. A chap told to go to New York when he doesn't feel like it, goes off to Amsterdam instead with or without an excuse, though he might pretend he's got a better story already laid on in Holland and really cannot spare the time. Me ... I do as I'm told. I'm timid, and that's the truth. Most of my women colleagues are too, I assure you.

Nina spent the voyage sulking in her cabin, except in the first two hours after dawn when she skipped around the deck, running and exercising and kicking her legs in the air, with me skulking after her, now and then catching up, with the help of the Russian Purser who was my friend. At least he was my friend after a few vodkas.

A sad story. I managed to keep Nina and her dawn exercises to myself by lying to the Express girl sleeping peacefully below. I also cheated by getting off the boat at Stockholm to telephone my story, thereby making the competition's story one day late at Leningrad next day. After that I filled up with vodka too and flew home again, guiltily. Women, you see, are not as good as men. Men don't waste their time and strength feeling guilty.

What d'you make of all this? I hope it reconciles you somewhat to the life of a Real Woman.

Love, Ogg

6th February 1958
c/o Daily Mail
London EC4

Dear B,

I was just congratulating myself ... in that hardboiled way that leg-reporters like myself often do ... at not being sent off to cover the Munich air crash and the ghastly deaths of so many of the Manchester United boys, and Matt Busby himself was hurt. Then, listening on the radio in my little flat to all the names of the dead, I somehow knew in advance it would include my old pal Henry Rose. The nicest men die the most often and the soonest. Last time I saw Henry, he said that now he was over 60 he didn't really mind what happened because he'd had a good life.....

Love to all, Og

15th August 1958
New York

Dear B,

The nice thing about New York is that you feel you know the place.

I've seen it all at the pictures, and they speak the same language and everything. I mean, you know what to expect; those taxi-drivers for instance, who never stop talking.

New York is like an oven at 7 a.m. I prattle on about the weather. But my cabman never opens his mouth.

On and on we go. I think: Is this a kidnap?

Now and then I hit the cab roof. New York's streets are pitted with craters only they never get into the pictures. That photo of the driver with his number below it. Gosh, it looks fierce. Alf Bernstein, it says, licensed by New York City Police.

I tap the cabman's shoulder. 'We lost?' I say.

'Lady,' says the driver, 'if you'd stop talking, just for one single minute I could figure out where your hotel is.'

It gets hotter so I go to Sterns on 42nd-street to buy a dress. You can get any size outfit here, no trouble at all, I've heard this too. Only this is for sure!

There are a lot of other women buying too. But I fight on until I find Miss Shaw to attend me.

'I'm a forty hip,' I say. 'Sure, sweetie,' she says. 'This is your size,' and she runs off.

Despite the air-conditioning it is that hot. Half-way in the dress I get stuck. The zip is at the back. Help. I'm going to strangle. The darned thing is over my head and stays that way. Someone comes up to inspect me.

'Gee, honey, you look cute,' she roars.

'Fetch Miss Shaw,' I'm shouting.

'Miss Shaw!' screams what sounds like the whole third floor Women's Dress Department.

'She can't come, sweetie,' someone yells back. 'You'll sure have to go and find her.'

All right, if they want to play blindman's bluff they can have it. I stumble out.

'Hee-hee!' everyone cackles. 'For heaven's sake ... look at her.'

Up comes Miss Shaw. 'You said size 14 sweetie,' she says. 'How dyou get in there?'

'Gee, these foreigners,' she says, addressing the crowd. 'You can't understand them.'

She gives me a little tug and the dress bursts wide open right down both seams, which are only lightly tacked. The crowd cackles again.

'You from London, England?' says Miss Shaw. 'Now you tell me in English what you want and I'll go get it.'

Mind you, there are some English innocents abroad who don't even know what Americans eat. Me ... I've seen it on the pictures, so I am pretty keen. Until I see the prices.[...]

It's a relief to find a chain of restaurants where you can order a nice steak for, say, a guinea without tip. Well, how am I to know they'll bring me a whole sirloin of beef – bone and all – enough for a week-end joint for a family of four, with French fries and trimmings?

Of course I know New York is full of millionaires. But I'm flattered to get an invitation from multi-millionaire publisher Victor Weybright*, who sells 50,000,000 books a year.

He is a mountainous man, very sophisticated.

'Hello,' he says. And out from the mountain comes a voice as English as Mr. Macmillan's. Well, it seems he picked up an English accent from Brendan Bracken and people like that during his war years.

He takes me to the Brussels Restaurant on East 54th-street, where the top people go.

Mr. Weybright talks about his parties in the Carlisle Hotel where, with Mrs. Weybright's help, he seats 30 celebrities to dinner every Saturday in the season.

People keep coming up to talk to us. 'How is Mr. Weybright?' 'What news, Mr. Weybright?'

Other chat is discouraged because he explains he's got to look after me. Manhattans Martinis, etc., prove that he's doing it. I do hope when they bring on the chickens they will be teeny-weeny ones.

Frankly it's all going to my head a bit. This sure is the life.

Suddenly Mr. Weybright brings out snaps of his four grandchildren to show me. 'I know what you're after,' he says. 'I'll send for a cab take you back to your hotel for a nice quiet cup of tea.'

Well, New York or anywhere, there's nothing like a nice cup of tea.[...]

Victor Weybright was called 'America's literary gatekeeper'. Having worked for Penguin in the USA, he went on to establish the New American Library.

24th August 1958
c/o Daily Mail, Northcliffe House, Tudor St
London EC4

Dear B,

Oh my feet hurt. It's hot, been chasing after Groucho Marx, staying at the Dorchester; won't see anybody, won't give interviews. Alas, Groucho don't know my Features Ed who won't take No for an answer. For one thing Marius Pope is a Fan. Marx fans never give up.

So I plod up and down Park Lane, resting my poorly feet in the park now and then. Then the Editor gets wind that Groucho has gone down to Stratford-upon-Avon to do the Hamlet matinee. I'm whizzed down there; can't see him anywheres. The whole audience is American, all in check caps.

Back to Park Lane again; feel a bit nervous of The Girls around here; sure to think I'm trying to collar their Beat. Suddenly I spot Groucho, right there in Park Lane in front of me. Check cap. Walking like he does in pictures, knees bent. His pretty little daughter is with him in white Dutch bonnet. I keep them under observation until Marble Arch, then I sidle up.

'Mr. Marx?' He stares straight ahead. One fierce black eye rolls sideways, takes me in. 'See me at my place,' he says. Without the cap he looks sad, rather bored. 'I've nothing to say,' he says. 'I'm Greta Garbo.'

'Make it quick,' he says. 'I don't like interviews. You're the only one.' He was going home tomorrow. He'd offered the BBC a film of his TV show for FREE and they didn't want it. He'd also offered himself at about one-eighth of what he gets back home. They said they were sorry, all full up. He looked sadder and sadder. He'd been offered 100,000 dollars to do a nightclub show at Las Vegas but he'd turned that down.

Not while people were EATING. Yes, he knew Noel Coward did it and so did Jack Benny. Not for him though. 'I'm a serious man, I'm old and tired. I just wanna be left alone. Play my guitar.' He hated himself anyway. Until 4pm each day.

'Don't you hate yourself?' he asks me. He thought everybody hated themselves.

He liked his little daughter best. By his second wife. They understood each other. England seemed a spiteful, cruel place. Why, said Groucho, he'd even heard spiteful talk about My Fair Lady.

His sad, sad eyes swivelled to follow a pretty girl. He didn't want to spend his holiday giving interviews, doing his stuff for nothing, for the BBC or for me. He wanted to enjoy himself. He'd been to the theatre, seen lots of shows, couldn't understand a 'woid'. So it wasn't much fun really. He wanted to go home.

Still Features Ed was dead pleased. An exclusive. Everyone else, even the photographers, had just Given Up.

It was nice to Get my Feet Up at last. I really know how Groucho feels. It's not much fun really bumming about....

Love, Ogg

September 1958
c/o Daily Mail, Northcliffe House, Tudor St
London EC4

Dear B,

Marilyn Monroe, who arrived here this week with husband Arthur Miller, is extraordinary. A woman with two faces. Perhaps we're all like that? Only her two faces seem to contradict each other somehow.

Her first appearance was with someone's overcoat over her head ....you know the way they smuggle criminals into the Old Bailey, to avoid the cameras.

Inside the door when they pulled the coat off, she was safe because no one could recognise that this was the star. Easy to see why she is renownedly unpunctual because the make-up and hair-do must take a long time. She looked like one of those girls who used to work in the old A.B.C. cafes before the war, with white, exhausted face, with sweaty, messy hair dyed too often. Then our cameraman sent me climbing on the stair bannisters high up to hold his flashlight and I got a shock, looking down, seeing the famous blonde head was clearly bald on top, with the pink scalp showing through the sparse hairs.

A few days later we were all in respectful attendance again, but this time at the studio, in orderly manner but fenced off ... so that the two 'royals' Miss Monroe and Mr. Miller strolled in front of us as we were held in check behind a barrier.

She was talking in a pleasing, high but unmistakably English accent about the sort of thing she liked to prepare for Mr. Miller's dinner when she was 'playing' the housewife at home. This was in answer to a question shouted out from our massed ranks of reporters, photographers, publicity pushers, etc. She was calm and poised, quite unlike the first time, and her reply was that he particularly liked having fish like whitebait; the word pronounced in an impeccable English accent which amazed me.

Her looks were even more astonishing. The crumpled ABC waitress with no looks to speak of was gone, not a trace remaining. The hair was freshly washed and set exquisitely with two soft loops forward over her cheeks, leaving still enough hair for a chignon behind. The face too was transformed and was not just beautiful but with a luminous prettiness and charm. She looked tall, slender and fragile in an attractive cloak which hid any hint of voluptuousness. A great groan of delight went up from the cameramen who'd waited a long time for this, as I had. I too was charmed by her and the soft un-American manner about the whitebait.

She was a work of art, a living tribute to the cosmeticians, couturiers and yet, under the subdued lighting, there was never a wrong note nor a hair out of place. Except for Mr. Miller who seemed to have no place there and was ill at ease even at the prospect of more of his favourite whitebait.

I suppose it is all this collective effort which marks the difference between European performers and American ones. The latter are almost the result of a team effort whereas our own or Continental ones are self-made, individual products. I think this must be why the European product is superior because each one is different and cannot be repeated so that even their flaws and weaknesses add to the general impression without damage.

Poor Marilyn, in ten years' time she'll be almost bald and have to wear a wig. The price of fame? There is a big price, I realise now I'm getting too famous myself to walk into a caff in the Tottenham Court Road without being recognised. My rough, coarse hair I think won't let me down but I have other troubles. The Features Editor says I'm far too podgy and must be dieted down ruthlessly; that my disposition is a bit spoiled too and 'I'm getting nasty' ..... even with my hair pinned up right on top, as shown in the paper's weekly cartoons on the column, I have a shifty, hangdoglook nowadays. Even A has noticed. Smarten yourself up a bit, he says. Please write me lots of good advice.

Luv, Ogg

1959

August 1959
Flat 169, The White House
Albany Street, NW1

Dear B,

I was glad to get your letter. Felt I was not very good hostess; it was cold and you ate almost nothing. I do understand only too well how Frank feels about Alfred. Frank was all his life the Good Husband. I was glad that you found A 'devastating'. Of course, he knows that women like him too much so I shall not tell him what you said about him.

I am sorry though that your ambitions for me will be disappointed. Now that you know I can never marry. A says that a 'sacrifice' is worthless unless it is a willing sacrifice. I am willing. He sometimes says funny things like that; says he got it this time from a Mary Renault book, 'The King must die.' We both admire her books, oh so much.

In our thrice-weekly Russian lessons Mrs. Grun and I discuss Love in Russian. It does wonders for my Russian grammar. Also we go to West End matinees on saturday afternoons if we can get seats and Mrs. Grun who is mad about Theatre, makes very stern criticisms in loud Russian. Naturally it makes people stare at us, especially in the intervals ... or they follow us into the street and to the coffee-house where we often

314

find ourselves mixed up in debates with bent ladies and gentlemen of enormously great age who join our table, insisting they don't care what it is about as long as they are allowed to listen! Once we found ourselves sitting behind Somerset Maugham and his companion Alan Searle whom I know quite well since he wrote me a fan letter. Mrs. G wanted to know (in Russian) why Mr. Maugham looked so sad as though he might burst into tears. Alan whispered (why whispered?) that Maughan had left his hearing-aid in their hotel and refused to have it sent for. So there they sat in the front row, throughout the whole performance of a Henry James adaptation and was not able to hear a single word. No, not masochism; I think it was intended as good manners as he did not discover about the hearing-aid until the curtain went up.

A says that girls like me are called 'betthupfele' ... which I suppose means bed-jumpers; isn't that awful? When I point out that I am a reformed bett-thing thanks to him and that I am now saved forever and ever, he says I had better be or else. It is all said good humouredly (usually!) but he is very strict with me. A letter came from that nice so attractive British Amy Sergeant I met in Newcastle named Tom Handford and I was foolish enough to mention it to A who simply went mad, and shouted. I was frightened and promised to meet Tom downstairs in the foyer by the swimming pool and not to allow him near the flat.

All this would not be worth mentioning. Except that it is humbling to think that those boring moralisers like Aunt Ray and Aunt Sally for instance (not to mention Mrs. G, bless her!) who said 'One day you'll be sorry you made yourself cheap' and all that stuff .... to think they were right all the time! But how was I to know that one day I would meet someone who minded about my having been a bed hopper from time to time and that I would oh so terribly MIND his minding. Can you make sense of all this?

Love, Og

September 1959
Flat 169, The White House
Albany Street, NW1

Dear B,

I do hope Betty and Louis will get a house soon. Looking after three small boys in that rickety pre-fab in Tile Cross is no joke.* Her nursing training makes her far too pernickety as a mother just as it did to our own mother but neither Bettina nor Louis will ever push for anything, as you well know ... though it seems a poor do that any citizen let alone a doctor and his family should be coping in a draughty pre-fab and the war over these almost 15 years! The trouble seems to be that the City Council are spending all their money rebuilding the city centre ... and having caught a glimpse of THAT on my way back to New Street station upset me very much. Brum never was a beauty spot (though it was always a lot nicer than most Londoners think) ... but now they are making it truly ugly. No joke any more; it hurts to look.

Nice to have a bit of 'family life' for a change. The weekly stunts get a bit wearing. In case you didn't see the paper at all, I 'worked' as a teacher in an East End school, a waitress at the Connaught Rooms, a trainee-seamstress at the best couturier house in Bond Street, trainee-policewoman, private detective, film star, pop-record-maker, etc., etc., to name just a few you may have missed.

I simply had no time to send you copies of the paper but I will try in future. The sweatiest job was last month when I was a deck-chair seller on Margate beach. They've never employed a woman before; for one thing the customers consider that sixpence per chair per day is too expensive and they get very aggressive and refuse to pay. One is supposed to insist. In that heat too; just lugging the ticket-machine and bag of money around was too much for me.

I went in to see Marius Pope and screamed not long ago. I screamed I'd had enough, doing lousy rotten stunts and not knowing what he'd think up next. 'You'll tell me go dig a hole in the road next,' I screamed. The whole editorial could hear me through the glass partition. Marius says my screaming gives him headaches and he has to take codeine for it every morning before Conference. But this time he just grins and says the hole-in-the-road is a super idea. 'Look,' he says, 'you've given me a marvellous idea. Go and join a navvy team building the M1. You'll need an Excavator and all the works. Take Jimmy Jarche with you.' (That's our top camera-man; he's in his Sixties and won't thank me either for putting him in a hole in the road. Last time I was out with Jimmy was at Blenheim doing the Duke of Marlborough. Terrible temper the Duke has; first he tries to throw us out, then he pretends we're not there at all. Most uncomfortable interview but Jimmy did get a picture of the Duchess who was nice and rather sorry for us, as well she might be...)

Marius just came over to my desk to say, 'When I've finished the hole in the road job, (at Stony Stratford about halfway up the M1 motorway)

316

I've got to get ready to fly to New York.' This time though it's a good story. Nikita Krushchev, as you may have read, is off to the U.S.A. Big stuff; first time a Soviet leader has ventured so far, right to Camp David to meet Eisenhower. Isn't that terrific?

I never thought I'd be sent because they've got Don Iddon in New York, as well as a man in Washington and all over the place. But the news is, according to Marius, that Comrade Krush is to take his Missis and all the family, his daughter Rada who's married to Alexei Adjubey, editor of Izvestia, his older daughter Julia by his first wife who died of t.b. early in the Revolution and his son Sergey who's married, I think, to a Jewish girl. Anyway it's going to be Family stuff, so all the papers will be sending a Woman probably. Will write again soon with all details.

Love, Oggi

By 1959 Betty had had three sons, first Henry (now a doctor like his father), and then twins Simon (a barrister) and Bernard (a chef). The lack of housing meant that for several years the five of them coped with a prefab, which was one of many built in this working-class area of Birmingham after the Second World War. Betty, who had been a midwife, then became an expert on family planning.

24th September 1959
New York

Dear B,

The main point about New York is you gotta keep moving...

Someone said, 'You oughta meet James T. Farrell. He's America's famous author of Studs Lonigan, a monumental work about a Chicago boy in the '30s – he's really something.'

Before I could stop it someone phoned James T. Farrell to say I'm on my way. I hadn't the energy to protest in a temperature of 84 degrees, so I sat dumbly in a taxi, thinking: 'Ah well, just another Yank intellectual. They're all alike.'

Arrive at West 85th Street, full of coloured Puerto Ricans and grim lines and ugly shops, but it makes a change from Fifth-avenue glamour and luxury. Crawl exhausted to the eighth floor, ring the bell.

A pale, thin woman in a dressing-gown over a frilled nightgown opens the door ... 'Sorry to be undressed at teatime, but it's hot. Come in and meet Mr. Farrell: he'll be delighted to meet a lady reporter from England.'

A big, hot room, airless and stifling. There's James T. Farrell, the great man, lying prone on a sofa.

The pale woman, with a 19th-century topknot on top of her head, prods him awake. 'Meet the lady from England.'

'What does she want?' says the great man. I stammer that I'm looking for personalities.

The great man wipes his sweaty face and shouts kitchenwards: 'Dorothy, come back here. Hear what the intelligent English lady said. She said I'm a personality – hear that, Dorothy, I'm a personality.'

The great man seems overcome, lies down again, and fans himself with a hankie. This commotion brings two more persons into the stifling room. One a dark, handsome lady in brief knickers and sun-top, the other a handsome young man who says he's an Israeli and speaks with a strong Glasgow accent.

Suddenly the great man sinks back in depression on the couch saying: 'No one reads me any more – they don't buy my books; they don't want stories, and I'm broke.'

We all sit down and wipe sweat from our faces while Dorothy goes back to the kitchen to prepare iced coffee.

'D'you know what's wrong with the world?' says the great man. 'I'll tell you what's wrong with the world.'

I get out my pencil and notebook and write down, 'What's wrong with the world.' But the great man has lost interest in the world.

A long pause follows. He says he wants to give Dorothy a kiss, because he loves Dorothy. He shouts for her to come to him. Dorothy drifts in holding her trailing nightgown and he kisses her.

'More coffee,' he roars. Dorothy disappears.

'Take Lebanon,' says the great man suddenly. 'I could tell you what's wrong with Lebanon, but I won't – why should I?'

'Take Sweden, too – people all have lots of free sex in Sweden, but they don't enjoy it. No, sir, they're miserable – they don't enjoy it one bit.'

'Are you writing a new book?' I ask timidly.

The great man, who has written scores of good books, says: 'Of course I'm writing a new book. I'm always writing a new book, only nobody wants 'em.'

The great man lies down again. Dorothy returns, says I must understand her husband works hard and when he's not working he likes to enjoy himself, so this is his day of enjoying himself, talking to me.[...]

The great man pops up again. He did have a job once, he says, for a few months, but never again. He gotta work for himself even if no one printed him ever again.

Mr. Farrell also explains the handsome woman in long bare legs and knickers. She's his secretary.

'I'm Mrs. Luna Wolf,' she herself says. I gather she's divorced. She works for the great man. No, not typing; just looking after his general affairs, plus correspondence.

Dorothy brings in a second round of iced coffee laced with lemonade or something like that. We are all wiping our faces and sweating.

I say I think it's time to go now and the great man gives me an armful of his books.

Dorothy says they have a son named Kevin; but he's not her son. 'You see, we've been married twice,' she adds.

I ask the great man politely about his other wife. Dorothy, who's of Irish origin like her husband, says: 'No, you see, we married twice.'

She explains that after their first marriage about 1931 James left her to marry another woman. Then recently he returned to her and they got married again.

'How marvellous,' I say. 'That means you forgave him.'

'Well,' says Dorothy, 'I couldn't see why he left me in the first place. I know this other wife he was married to between our marriages quite well. We have a nice entente. I'm not saying there aren't other women I like better than her; but we get along well enough – sometimes she comes shopping with me – we're quite friendly. Maybe the Arabs are right about men needing a lot of wives. Then there's plenty of women to do the work.'

I go down to 85th-street and crawl into a taxi. Temperature now near 90 degrees. When I get back to my hotel there's a party waiting to take me to a new party that has just broken out on East Seven-street in Greenwich Village.

'You wanna go to your room and rest! Are you crazy?'

So we all pile into a huge car that looks like a gigantic bulldozer and we go on to the next party.

You gotta keep moving.

A LETTER FROM OGGI

October 1959
Hollywood, Los Angeles, California

Dear B,

People told me I'd be able to relax when I got to Hollywood. That was the place FOR it. I only wanted sleep, but Americans never do. So I just hoped I'd got the right information therefore about the film city.

It was a place to dream, they said – where dreams came true. Shimmering pools and palm trees, and I might even catch a big producer's eye.

The big negro taxi-driver who took me to the airport for the 9-hour flight from New York to Los Angeles said: 'What for you says ah gotta sleep? Ah's a busy allaways.' Work from 4pm to 4am, then he ran a Boy Scout club and a choir. Two hours a night did him, he said. He added: 'Doan getta no conversation outa youse; guess youse tired right out.'

Well, I thought I'd try to sleep in the plane. The airport chemist said: 'These pills will do it. Take no more than three.' The other passengers were wide awake and jolly, wanted to talk. It was a packed tourist flight, three aside. 'Let's see your pills then, something new?'

So they wanted to try them. I gave all my neighbours three each and they washed them down with Bourbon and slept. I took five. But I couldn't even doze. I was too tired.

At 6am next day we landed at L.A. 'Didn't you sleep? Shame. Those pills sure did for me.' We shared a cab and drove through shanty-town streets empty, lots of tin cans and cartons, huge fried fish and hamburger signs. We were doing 90 mph, which woke me up a bit. It was steamy hot.

At the Ambassadors Hotel I stumbled into the lobby, feeling awful. The room clerk had never heard of my reservation. He said: 'There's people in all of the beds, so you can stop shouting and get out of here quick; this is a good-class hotel.'

I trudged up the road between the palm trees and red and white hibiscus and into the Chapman Park Hotel, where they had a room. I just took one look at my glorious white bed. Then the phone went and it was a Mrs. Jane Stinchfield Lambertson, and she said she was public relations for the Ambassadors Hotel, which belonged to Mr. Schine, formerly the late Senator McCarthy's aide.

It was all a mistake, she said, and there <u>was</u> a room booked for me, so why didn't I come right back over? She wanted to show me the gorgeous suite where Mr. Kruschchev had slept. It was a poem … in blue, grey and black trimmed with gold, and all the toilets had different coloured telephones to match.

I was just going to say I was all undressed now when Mrs. Jane Stinchfield Lambertson's voice stopped and another voice in strong Californian said: 'I'm Mrs. George Yardley. How do you do?'

So I said how did she do and she said she was a friend of Jane Stinchfield Lambertson and her husband, Mr. Yardley, was a retired building contractor. But she just loved helping Jane with her public relations work because it was so interesting.

She said: 'I'm handing you back to Jane now.' And then the Stinchfield Lambertson voice started again, saying she was from Peterborough, England really but, oh, such a long time ago she came on a 90-day trip to Los Angeles and she met Dr. Stinchfield, but now she was a widow and organised society parties and helped Mr. Schine and 'Hallo, hallo, are you there?'

I'd only dozed for a second standing upright by that gorgeous bed, but I could still hear her voice in a kind of daze. We agreed to meet in half an hour. I lay down on the bed.

The phone woke me and it was another public relations officer for some agency whose name I couldn't catch, inviting me to a reception in Beverly Hills to launch Mae West's new book.

I said thanks awfully, goodbye, and lay down again but the phone went again and it was a publicity man who wanted to know whether I knew that the well known dancer Miss Julia Prowse was related to a Mr. Keith Prowse of England, and would I like to interview her?

So I unhitched the phone and lay down again. Banging on the door woke me and it was a messenger from Jane Stinchfield Lambertson's office to say the car was ready to take me on a tour of the studios.[...]

We arrived at Twentieth Century-Fox which looked like a factory. We were led into a cafeteria and given plates of food and cardboard knives and forks and sat on a bench. Once or twice I nearly slipped off and fell asleep on the floor, but one of the sentries was always ready to give support.

Then we were put in a studio on some more benches with Frank Sinatra, who looked like a thin sort of Teddy Boy in a tight suit, and he looked very angry about something. Maurice Chevalier came in looking rather uneasy but wearing a lot of make-up. A lot of other stars were sitting on the benches to watch the film being made.

Gregory Peck was sitting in front of me and Merle Oberon right behind. Merle kept saying: 'It's disgraceful.' I suppose she meant the benches we were sitting on which were awfully hard. I wondered why people said Hollywood was a luxurious place.

Then Henry Fonda came into the studio and said to me: 'Push up and make some room,' and I did, which was more uncomfortable than ever. Then the studio lights came on and people were shouting and we were all stumbling out into the yard and the hot sun. Mr. Gary Cooper, who had dyed pink hair, smiled at me, but I just muttered that I couldn't stop and I got into the first taxi I saw.

But when I got back to the hotel Mrs. Jane Stinchfield Lambertson was waiting. 'I've got good news for you' she said. 'By invitation from Mr. Schine I am going to take you in to dinner and then afterwards to the Grove Room's late-night special cabaret which begins at midnight; it's all laid on and we're going to have a wonderful time. After all, this is Hollywood, you know,' and she laughed.

I longed for bed. I didn't care if I never got spotted by a big producer now; what should I do?

Then I remembered a Hollywood thriller I saw at Camden Town Odeon. It was about a girl escaper who said: 'I'm just going to freshen up,' and then she vanished.

So I darted outside into the big lobby which was full of shining shops. I started to run. Footsteps behind me. Someone running. It was the gorgeous blonde secretary to Mrs. Jane Stinchfield Lambertson. She said she'd been sent to find me and take me to Mr. Schine.

Mr. Schine said: 'Glad to meet you. I do want you to enjoy your stay in Hollywood.'

So... as well as dinner and cabaret there was going to be something special for breakfast too, because after that was over we'd begin a rather full programme for the day...

And not a bed in sight.

We're going to San Francisco from here so I'll write you again from there.

Love, Og

October 1959
Flat 169, The White House
Albany Street, NW1

Dear B,

Good to be home so I can wash my undies... Heat was frightful; an Indian summer, everyone said. No one warned us not to take autumn tweeds, wools, etc. The smell of sweat inside the American army 'plane especially the trip from Fort des Moines to Pittsburgh, was only conquered only by the smell of whiskey-sour. Why does anyone think of these gigantic press tours as 'glamorous'? The Russians were flown more comfortably I think, in fast jets arriving always many hours before we did. I had to admire the fortyish blonde representing the New York Herald Tribune, six months pregnant and every inch showing in a form-fitting navy silk dress, who was the only cool party as we flew out of Ohio through a sudden thunder-and-lightning storm.

Wife to an American General, she didn't want to miss the fun, but then neither did anyone else. Our total press party must have been well over a thousand strong, sometimes many more than that and I could see by the names of newspapers, magazines and radio stations printed beneath the accredited persons' names and pinned on their breasts, that some were brand new, dating from the day the 'tour' started.

The French press party was the largest, the most active and the most annoying and intransigent. Especially a dark pretty French girl called 'Jane' representing the magazine Elle who'd been sent, so she told me, to cover the 'fashions'.

Mind you, she had her work cut out to find any, except at the luncheon given at the Waldorf Astoria in honour of Nina Sergeyevna Krushcheva, dressed rather provocatively I thought, like a London charlady in hair net covering an unsuitably long bob, home-made print dress, lisle stockings and heavy shoes. Funny thing was she looked rather young and innocent, despite her heavy bulk, sitting with Mrs. Richard Nixon who was got up like a Christmas tree reminding me of our own Rita Cave, in furs, feathers, flowers and a lot of scented silk streamers. The only 'fashion note' for poor Jane was Nikita himself (not at the lunch), dressed for each occasion in dressy, frilled shirt, handmade Italian suitings, elegant shoes, Pucci ties and trouser pleats so sharp they stood out from his little fat legs, with warm, loving smiles overall.

Elle magazine's Jane also stood out; she wore a long black hooded garment, split at the middle so you could see her white belly every time, which was often, she lifted up the top to scratch. Jane was agin everything she saw and ate, waving away the chicken maryland and blueberry pie untouched at every meal, crying out, 'Tek away .. pliss tek away! C'est 'orrible.' The men in the French party all nodded agreement. They despised everything they saw. American cooking was even worse, they declared, than they'd been told it was. They were very elegant Frenchmen, but I noticed they were more efficient than anyone else, always managing to get pictures and interviews better and quicker than other pressmen, including the native Americans.

Dissatisfaction came to a head on the long day's train journey from Hollywood to San Francisco. Until then the K family party was untouchable to the press, guarded by police, F.B.I., and Russian security police, ... not to mention the elegant Mr. Gromyko himself who kept waving us away, incredibly with smiles and almost friendly quips.

However, once seated in the train, packed together in the boiling hot buffet car where breakfast of what looked like hot, treacly muffins was being served ... the very loud American police voice sounded out over the tannoy, almost drowning our own unceasing moans and whines and complaints. 'Attention! Ladies and Gentleman of the Press, when breakfast is over Comrade Krushchev will be coming through the train to meet you. Do NOT panic! Stay in your seats.' ..... (By this time, cameramen and pressmen and women had already leapt from their seats to rush into the corridors; sounds of breaking glass as camera equipment was smashed in the melee, cries of pain as people were trodden underfoot....) 'Do not panic!' the voice came more urgently. Comrade Krushchev will speak with each one of you. STAY WHERE YOU ARE...do not...'

The train was in uproar; the corridor completely blocked. No one could go backward for that was where the Russian party and the police were accommodated; they could not go forward because the whole length of the rest of the train was a mass of arms, legs and smashed cameras....

However, I saw my chance immediately ...ducked between the writhing legs and eventually found myself wedged tightly between Comrade Nikita and his protector, Mr. Bruce Cabot Lodge. Krushchev was radiant in silver-grey suit, another exquisite embroidered white silk shirt. I got hold of his arm and hung on for dear life. I have never seen a man so happy; it was, clearly, his finest hour. But luckily for me, no one else in the vicinity could talk to him. That was how I got him to admit, when stuck in one section of corridor, surrounded by determined Frenchmen wanting to interview with pix, that he'd hated every minute of 'the Hollywood performance'. It was the news everyone was waiting for. The 'show' provided the previous day at 20th Century Fox studio had been a rather petty choice, prompted by economy obviously as they still had the costumes and dancers, etc., handy from the Moulin Rouge.[...]

At first all went spankingly well. Nikita K was thrilled to meet the stars; his wife Nina took it more calmly .... being a more intellectual type. She had been his 'teacher' (she told us at a more intimate tea-party, ladies only stuff, at Blair House just opposite The White House in Washington, that she liked reading Jane Austen in English; Krush as a young widower had attended her lectures on Politics. She's one of those rare, admirable women who look plain and dull until you look more closely)....

For example, Nikita caught sight of Gary Cooper walking across the yard and it wasn't easy to spot him with his pink-and-grey dyed hair and fallen cheeks – but Krushchev broke away from Gromyko and his police escort and sped, or rather tumbled tubbily, across the yard until breathless, he caught up with him, calling out in pidgin-English, 'Mr. Cooper! See you.... all your films, ALL!' Gary Cooper, looking old and frail and nothing like a hero of Westerns, looked pleased and they stood together exchanging banter. It must have done Cooper good to be recognised, especially as all the current 'stars' were clamouring to be presented, but I fancied he looked too tired to care.

But the actual 'show' was silly because from the little gallery high up in the studio, looking down on the open, upturned legs of Shirley Maclaine and the other girls, it must have seemed more like an insult to the whole Krushchev family party, even though to all of us sitting on hard benches on the ground floor, it all looked harmless enough.

In the train, however, as I clutched Mr. K's arm, he admitted to the crowd swirling around him that he himself and his wife had regarded the 'spektakl' as intended to insult their more reserved and puritanical prejudices. He called it 'beznrevstvenny' at which I gasped excitedly, seeing in my hungry mind's eye how the word 'immoral' would look in the cable I was aching to send to the Daily Mail in London, and all the more aching because we were then almost 9 hours behind London time and if we couldn't send our cables soon, it would be too late for any morning edition.

But the crowd of pressmen had caught my excitement and wanted a translation. They turned on me instead of him and though I struggled to break free... it was no good, we were all in the same boat. There were several representatives of the Cable and Wireless Company, Northern and other cable companies tucked somewhere in that gigantic Marx-Bros-type-melee. I had no way of keeping the story exclusive. One of the saddest moments of my life.

After that the crowd was better behaved. They'd got their scoop for mornings and they parted like the Red Sea and let me through, still hanging on to Mr. K .... until at last we came to the very last carriage of the train which was fitted out as a bar with stools and a few seats and of course it was almost empty, a haven of peace and quiet where Cabot Lodge, who'd then caught up with us, decided to give the proper 'press conference'.

The only press available was Jane of 'Elle' and she sat alone on a low seat looking rather divine, studying her open notebook on her knee. Mr. K intimated that he would like to be presented to THIS person and Cabot Lodge bent over her to say so. Jane looked up and then down again. 'Mais! Non, merci!' she said, loudly so that even the barmen behind the bar could hear every word, 'I do not want to meet 'orrible man; and 'is wife ... she 'ave 'orrible legs!'

A was waiting at the flat for me and seemed as glad to see me as I was to have him back....and even more pleased that he didn't want to hear a word about the American trip, about Hollywood or even my opinion of Frank Sinatra, or Maurice Chevalier, the latter wearing so much make-up and looking more like 30 than nearly 60.

See you soon I hope; much love to all, Ogg

November 1959
c/o Athenee Palace Hotel
    Bucharest, Rumania

Dear B,

I just had time, only just, to wash up after giving lunch to A, to get to the airport on Friday night, catch the flight to Brussels (where not at all easy to get a hotel room, everywhere full up) and then after a night in the suburbs, take the one-per-day flight to Bucharest via Germany.

Yes, it was the old, old story; me opening my big mouth too wide as usual. It was the hole-in-the-road thing all over again. Features Ed listened to me prattling on about Mrs. Grun's old uncle getting black hairs again and making love to his wife at 82, and said, 'Jolly good. I see a good 5-part series in it if we can get you into Rumania.'

I wasn't worried .. knowing THAT was pretty impossible. Ever since the Hungarian business a year ago, the whole of that part of South-East Europe has been a closed shop. Especially to the Daily Mail, after Noel Barber got shot in the head and was rescued by Tom (Sefton) Delmer and all that glorious space in both the Express and the Mail. Since then no visas are likely for anyone. Our Dip.Corr., was turned down recently. Stories coming out of Rumania are grim; interrogation with torture, etc., etc.

Then I'm told to telephone Dr. Anna Aslan direct at the Geriatric Institute from my flat in the White House and to my amazement, get put through immediately! She sounds very nice, says in German she'll be only too happy to 'receive the Daily Mail.' Can you beat it?!

So here I am. All Communist capitals are bleak but this is like a ghost town, under deep snow, pavements rocky with impacted ice. When I manage to get my shutters undone enough to peep out through the long lace curtains the silence is awesome. It is dark, street lights are dim; just stillness and snow. Not a soul about at about 8pm.

Next morning in the restaurant that overlooks the street, I am given a boiled egg, served cold in a glass. Everyone understands and speaks French and German here; the people look and sound like Italians.

My first day was curious. A long interrogation. They want to know my politics and if I know any spies. I am told I have been allowed to enter the country only because Dr. Aslan herself has promised I will cause no trouble. I am urged, nevertheless, to be cautious and to confine myself to my commission, namely to write about Dr. Aslan and her 'discovery of the youth-giving properties of H3'. I am also warned to pay no attention to shocking stories about Rumania because they are all lies, and so on.

By this time it is nearly afternoon and a car comes with my escort, Dr. Cornel David who fortunately speaks German. He is too young and goodlooking to be a patient. The car ploughs with difficulty through the snow. There are Turkish-style mosques or churches, wide boulevards with trams and those huge cinema-advertisement placards in French, then a tree-lined approach to a white house. It is the Clinic the Institutul. Still the same quiet, the same silence as the night before. Perhaps it is too cold for people to go out.

The first day is spent at a long Conference table, with doctors in white coats and Anna Aslan herself, about 60 but looking much younger at the top of the table. It is very tiring, all in German or in French. Unfortunately not in Russian which is my only fluent foreign language nowadays, but one of the doctors has some English, as well as Dr. David.

I am to spend more than a fortnight in the Clinic and to interview all the patients. Several aged patients are brought in to perform for me.

One who is over 80 has had a stroke but claims he is now cured by the drug H3. He does as Dr. Aslan tells him and stands on his head to show me how fit he is. Several elderly patients are sent for to do similar 'tricks' which I find worrying as some of them look as though they might expire any minute. Aslan says not to worry; they are used to it and they love doing it for me .. especially as I have come all the way from London. Tomorrow she is going to take me to visit a married couple in their nineties who have restarted making love after some 25 years or so. At about 8pm the Conference is still going on and I feel I could lie on the floor and expire too. Dr. Aslan says she will give me a series of H3 injections starting tomorrow and 'then you will never feel tired again'. She hints that they have restored youthfulness to Dr. Adenauer, Mr. Krushchev, the Chinese leader Mao Tse Tung and several highly born Egyptian doctors; also Hewlett Johnson, the English friend of the Communist world. She refuses to admit if she is having the injections herself. 'I will tell you later.'

My Features Editor said before I left London; 'Mind you have the Youth drug too; we are not letting it loose on our customers until you've had it.' He also said to try and bring some back for him.

love to all in Brum, and to you, Ogg

p.s. A cable just arrived from the office saying I must try and get myself a visa to stay a few days in Budapest .... afterwards. Am very tired but hoping to get my youth back soon......

November 1959
Flat 169, The White House
Albany Street, NW1

Dear B

Flew back from Budapest; did you get the card I sent from the hotel on St Margaret's island? In the dining-room, every little table even a single like mine, has a national flag. Mine was the only Union Jack, which brought a lot of attention and fond whispering from the Head-waiter. I was not grilled here as in Rumania, perhaps because I'm only here for the weekend. The city very shabby, looks like Manchester because of all the peeling masonry and holes in the walls from gun blast. Oh these deathly communist cities with the empty shop windows or as here with unwearable, dresses and faded lengths of material. I visited some friends of Mrs. Grun's whose address was given to me when I visited her old Uncle and his family in Bucharest. One never knows what to expect. Rumania was all secret and terrifying on the surface with spies in every doorway and whisper, whisper in the dining-room over the marvellous food, especially the spiced meats, the paprika dishes and herbs, fruits … though of course it may be only in the Athenee Palace, but somehow free and rather happy and carefree underneath.. as though the authorities are only making a jolly Good Show of imposing a totalitarian regime. Whereas in Budapest it really does seem a disaster-area, except for little coffee-shops where attractive people huddle together talking, talking and listening too with intensity as though scared to miss a word. The people I visited in a little flat gave me a meal and fancy jars of paprika, etc. to bring home and put me in a taxi saying not to talk to anyone until I was safely on the Borjom plane back to Brussels.

The Geriatric Institute was extremely jolly and the old people in such an overheated comfort that it made me think sadly of our own elderly who, according to Anna Aslan, are horribly neglected. On the other hand, it was clear that Aslan and her little corps of doctors had persuaded the present Rumanian regime that there is a lot of mileage, good publicity and even some unspecified political advantage to be got from her 'discovery' of the drug H3. Being a simple soul devoid of any scientific (or other) education, I had to believe her when she told me that her injections, pills, etc. cure everything, from cancer, heart disease, stroke and tuberculosis. It sounded unconvincing; if only she'd left something out but she seemed quite carried away by her own enthusiasm. A charming, eager and humorous woman who won me over by showing she could laugh at herself as well as at her rejuvenated patients in their dotage rediscovering sexual or allegedly sexual intercourse, though some could hardly walk across a room so I was glad that Aslan did not insist on their giving me a demonstration like some did, doing press-ups, hand-stands or singing gypsy love-songs for me.

I just wrote it all down in my notebook, my head in a whirl with all the attention and flattery I got from everyone thrilled with my 'Englishness,' etc.

Aslan used to be an ordinary G.P., later specialising in heart problems, until a friend 'in Government' heard about her interesting experiments, mainly injecting H3 into arthritic patients who appeared to be cured in no time and jumping about like Mrs. Grun's old Uncle.

I was out of my depth obviously but the odd thing was that Aslan chatted away as though I were some intelligent medico instead of an overworked reporter on Rothermere's Daily Mail. What I mean is...my impression was she was, so to speak, all woman first and doctor after. Sincere, not gushing or anything horrible but I still had the feeling that the Gentlemen of Harley Street would run away screaming out of her clinic declaring the Institul de Geriatrie was not 'ethical' or something like that. And yet.... how can I put it? ....the little doubts came creeping in from the moment I handed over the presents of Aristoc nylons (her favourites) I'd brought her. She was, well, very grateful. (Of course A has often told me that women of Rumania Jugoslavia, etc. have an absolute passion for receiving Presents. Well .. I like presents too, I said. All women do. He says that's different because Englishwomen do not EXPECT them; it was his idea for me to bring the nylons and he was right because they made almost too much impression).

I've been taken for rides in the snow-covered Carpathians where Aslan showed me an exquisite little church; she stayed to pray for the welfare of the Geriatric business, she took me for a super weekend to Sinaia and we slept in the house where King Carol and his mistress spent their weekends together; it is now a Rest Home for Writers.[...]

Olga wrote a book about her experiences in Romania and the H3 drug, published in 1964 by Arthur Barker.

11th December 1959
c/o Daily Mail, Northcliffe House, Tudor St
London EC4

Dear B,

I went to a party on the steamer Achilleus lying off Piraeus harbour yesterday; it belongs to Aristotle Onassis. He didn't turn up but all his family did ... countless sisters-in-law, brothers-in-law, etc., the women very lovely, brown haired, brown skinned in plain black dresses, hardly any jewels.

Nice Battle-of-Britain hero, Bill Simpson, who is now PRO for BSA, told our press party, 'We aim to make the Gulf of Corinth look like Clapham Junction with traffic.'

This party was to launch the third Comet aircraft...among other things.

One of the brothers-in-law named, Professor Gerasimos Patronikolas, who is vice-president of Olympic Airways, is buying some of the new Comets which, he says, will enable Britons to get package tours costing £85 for a fortnight. This seems odd because my airfare London/Athens cost that much, though of course it was paid by B.E.A., for 'publicity'. Meanwhile my instructions are not to hang about the hotel drinking free whiskeys but get 'on my bike' and go looking for General Grivas.

I didn't find him but I took his brother out for dinner instead. It's always Octopus out here.

Love Ogg

1960

February 1960
c/o Daily Mail, Northcliffe House, Tudor St
London EC4

Dear B,

At home having a sort of nervous breakdown or at least that's my story.

I'm persuading the Editor, Arthur Wareham, that I'm having one. The letters arrive by the sack-load, I now have a team of girls, and secretaries typing replies to those which are, to my mind anyway, too tragic or sad or terrible not to merit one.

Everyone pretends to be surprised. My feelings of guilt are terrible.

It never occurred to me that by publicising Aslan's claims to cure everything with her Wonder Drug H3 that anyone would actually believe it and insist on trying it. At first I tried answering the letters myself with long descriptions, explanations ... but the thing that people are demanding to know is just HOW can they get a visa to get into Rumania and have treatment at the Bucharest Clinic. I would start on the first sack of letters early in the morning and then new sacks would be carried in by the smirking Tape Boys until finally at the end of a fortnight, I just got the flu and collapsed.

Some of it is funny. Like the letters from Japan, India, Australia, Egypt, all from men wanting H3 to restore or promote their virility. At least I thought it was funny until a few days ago when some of the Japs, Indians etc started to turn up at the office, demanding to see me and get firsthand advice on how to continue their journey onto Rumania. They refused to leave the Daily Mail front hall without seeing me, so I had to be smuggled out of the back door at night; not even daring to go out to lunch.

Then, a few nights ago, the telephone calls started at my Flat 169, The White House. Silky-voiced males announced they were 'lawyers', 'doctors', 'accountants' representing the Duke of godknowswhat, or the Chairman of some Public Company wanting to take me out to dinner. Why, I replied, should the Duke of S want to dine me out, never having set eyes on me before, except for Emmwood's or Illingworth's or Jon's cartoons in the Mail, showing a distraught, overweight little woman with a bun on top shedding hairpins as she ran .... and ran ..... God knows where .... but away, away.

The silky ones were always mysterious, declaring it as far too confidential to express over the phone ... and how they all got my phone number? ... you tell me, since the Daily Mail staff are sworn to secrecy on such things.

One lady proved, however, inescapable. Barbara Cartland had taken up H3, which together with an approved supply of vitamin pills, is in her opinion a new Elixir of Youth, and she can prove it because she is feeding it to her husband, Hugh McCorquedale, poor man and she is even arranging a lunch or buffet party at her home in Hertfordshire, to be attended by high ranking Cabinet Ministers no less, where she will launch the project to rejuvenate us all, including the Government. Naturally, Barbara is more effective than the Dukes, Earls, etc. at actually obtaining supplies of the drug, for by devious means not quite clear to me, she has her own experts manufacturing an 'improved version to be called KH3' which is shortly to be marketed in West Germany where everyone hopes to stay beautiful and virile forever.

I am now very frightened of the whole thing. There are long discussions with doctors or with journalists who claim to be doctors and the Editor has put out feelers in all directions with the aim of getting Anna Aslan flown to London to address a Conference of Doctors about her discoveries, and thereby squash all sceptical criticism. Not that there is very much of this about; several doctors have written me stern letters of reproach for trying to corrupt everybody but others write or telephone every day with encouragement and have put their names down on a List of Practitioners wishing to attend the Daily Mail medical conference to meet Aslan (if she gets permission to leave her country) and examine her 'evidence'. So far there are 300 of these.

I am driven half mad by it all; I burst into tears as per usual; I even have hysterics. As yesterday for instance when one of the secretaries visited me at home with several letters claiming I was a saviour or humanity similar to Jesus and should be canonised. One sent a box of chocolates.

Yes, you and Frank can laugh. I hear that my medical branch of the family Dr. Louis Mintz and our Betty do not find it all quite so funny.

And Dr. Raymond Greene, the Harley Street endocrinologist brother of Graham Greene is not nearly so pleased with me. No chocolates from him. On the contrary, he claims to have done similar research to Aslan several years ago but discarded it as 'unproved.' He is preparing an indictment against us for the British Medical Journal, I think. I have nightmares... and are you surprised? The only thing that Dr. Greene agrees upon, with Aslan I mean, is that; it really does grow black hairs on white heads and smooth out wrinkled aged skin .... but that's all!

Oh, oh, if only it were ALL over, and I could retire to the obscurity from which I sprang until Mrs. Grun's old Uncle started making love to his wife again. SHE is quite pleased about it. 'Why do you complain so much, Olyeohya?' she says, 'you wanted to be famous....and now you are.'

Love, Ogg

December 1960
Flat 382, The White House
Albany Street, London NW1

Dear B,

How funny to be 48. Do you find as I do that Life gets nicer as it goes on. I even manage to look younger, feel healthier, fitter, etc. and the glooms have disappeared seemingly forever. How strange that is .. and do you agree with me about it? I remember Mother and all the Manchester Aunts looked on Being Forty as the end of Everything; the time to get to a nunnery, hide behind a veil, preferably thickly spotted; a time for swallowing disappointment, accepting that all the Miseries were about to begin. I do not find it so. It seems to me now that being Twenty was the hard part and all the best is yet to be. But I do wonder how other women feel about it.

Everyone says I look so young; and it must be due to H3!

For instance I have turned against Feminism; I no longer moan about those cruel, selfish men who do us down. Oh how we hated them all.

I remember Freda and Rosalie and Rita and Jane thought all men were rotten; dismissed like an overdue barrel of apples. Why have I changed? Is it simply due to Being in Love? I think it has something to do with finding that most men are fragile, delicate, sensitive and terribly worried.

All the men in our office for instance have problems like Sinusitis or Rheumatism, Headaches, Impotence, Skin allergies or lack of self-confidence. Whereas the women are so tough, so fit, so healthy, so bouncing with it.... and during pregnancy and lactation they seem fitter than ever and the males seem to wilt by comparison,

I have changed my views on sex-discrimination which, as you know used to infuriate me. Now I'm all for it. I want to see discrimination in favour of Males of all ages because I think life treats them most unfairly. Women are altogether coarser stuff!; they thrive on adversity. I think it may have something to do with women having babies. Pregnancy makes a woman stronger by pouring all those jolly hormones into her blood. Think how fragile you were until you had babies and each one made you tougher, except for the first one which died and that was a fearful, ferocious blow but you survived. Women are survivors and men aren't, I'm afraid.

Saturday. Something has just happened to shake my confidence in the foregoing. You know I go every Friday evening when in town to visit Rosalie and Paul at Grove End Gardens? They are so often alone now that Freda rarely visits, being preoccupied with Being a Married Woman And Doing it Properly; Sally rarely visits either because she doesn't feel strong enough to look after Rosalie since she is fairly helpless after her second stroke; and Jane doesn't come either for the same reason. I confess the visits are pretty cheerless nowadays... to see Rosalie sitting, always sitting, big-eyed and eager for any distraction like Angus barking because a visitor has arrived.. and then to see Paul, so devoted, so self-sacrificing, so tirelessly cooking, cleaning, caring for her.

Last night I found things changed much for the worse. She cannot even walk across the room without holding on to a frame, but she refuses to do even that unless Paul himself acts as the frame. So they stumble with agonising slowness across the sitting room to the dining-table; he moves backwards and all the time she cries out in fear, making strange little noises as she cannot any longer speak any comprehensible language. I find it a scene of horror, so sad after the ecstatic marriage and the fulfilment of all her hopes. Paul won't so far allow a television set because he believes that will be the last straw for both of them. And he is right. Last night Uncle Ernest was there on a visit from Haifa and he too was horrified with the tragic picture they made. Paul is seven years younger than Rosalie, he must be about 55. Now he is trapped, and so horrid. How cruel life is. Yet he says he doesn't find it so. He feels only sorry for her, never for himself because he thinks her marvellous.

I suppose there is a special breed of men with female qualities and instincts which help them to survive too.

Love, Ogg

1961

November 1961
Flat 382, The White House
Albany Street, NW1

Dear B,

We had a row. A shouted, I was terrified. He arrived here late one night, having driven through the deep snow from Huddersfield. I know what it's like; wheels get stuck in snowdrifts or skid about where it lies thinner below the moors in places like Barnby Moor. He fell asleep on our bed eventually; I knew I must try to wake him because this was just meant as a short stop on his way home to Caterham which is 20 miles south of here. I tried, not very effectually, to wake him; couldn't bring myself to do it more roughly because he looked so tired, a great fallen log, helpless after his long journey. In the early hours, I tried again and he woke, startled, then furious. Why had I failed him? Tricked him? Was it to destroy his marriage, to hurt someone else?

Petrified I couldn't speak; the tears rolled, still almost speechless I followed him to the door, trying to stop him leaving in anger, tried to plead. He struggled through the door and I heard his footsteps hurrying down the stairs. He was right of course; I had been careless, weak, sentimental in my own interests perhaps? Soon it would be morning; I just sat there, on the bed, unable to move. I felt that if I moved one inch from that squatting position, sometimes rocking a little back and forth as one does with a stomach ache, the pain would get worse.

I don't know what time it was, perhaps about an hour later, the door suddenly opened and he was standing there. He'd phoned home but she was asleep, slightly annoyed at being woken; she'd not been worried at all. He didn't say much, stroked my hair; told me to go to bed and not to worry. The relief was so great, I just fell asleep immediately.

You are quite right when you see my situation as one under constant threat. On the other hand, I have chosen it. It even has a plus side to it because everything seems to happen at fever pitch. As Frank would say, 'Never a dull moment.' Sometimes it makes the dull moments almost peaceful. A says we have found the grand-amour and must treasure it and see no damage is done to it. Still there are the dull times to relax in and as long as the phone doesn't ring and the news-editor want to ship me off to the ends of the earth somewhere I am all right. Except for being jumpy, nervous; even the phone ringing in the flat next door makes scurry into a corner like a mouse afrighted.

Love yours, Ogg

1963

May 1963
c/o Daily Mail, Northcliffe House, Tudor St
London EC4

Dear B,

Had nice letter (see enclosed) from Alan Searle, Maugham's companion from which you'll see that they enjoyed my 50-mile bicycle ride through Hertfordshire hills with Olympic British cycle team trainer Dr. Woodard cheering me on. I think what they liked was the Daily Mail photographer's back view of me and the good Doctor on the saddle. I apologise for this. I do see that my posterior has kind of spread. We kept one of the DM's yellow newspaper distributor vans following us all the way at a discreet distance ... hoping for us to collapse which would have made a much better picture. I did fall off on one hill right into a hedge full of nettles. 'Don't fuss,' said the Doc; 'you're not dead yet.'

Back in the office Bernie Levin says he'd rather die than do some of the daft things our Features Editor makes me do. 'It's your own fault, Grand Duchess,' he says to me (he always calls me that because Peter Black is sure I'm a royal refugee from the Kremlin).... 'If your poor Buba could see you now,' says Bernard when shown the pix of my posterior on the bicycle. 'Why don't you tell them go to hell when you're told to climb up Hemel Hempstead in your knickers.' Anyway the bicycle company who sponsored the 'ride' have given me a present of a Viking bicycle as well as one of their low-slung models.

The editorial office gets a new woman every week; the place is stacked with 'em so you can't get near the mirror in the ladies. Top rank of course is Ann Scott James who is very pretty and nice and Eve Perrick, and after that comes Fashion blond Iris Ashley and her entourage. A new girl works on the diary, Judy Innes, tall dark slender and divine with personality to match; a kind of Rosamund Lehmann heroine. Or so I thought until I heard the men giggling together about her new boy friend, Joe Kagan, a small round Lithuanian who keeps coming to the office with flowers and won't get off the phone. Everyone enjoys the daily gossip about it. Kagan is bosom chum of new PM Harold Wilson.

Harold Wilson Himself telephoned me at the office just now in an awful state. I am taking my new Soviet Russian colleague, the Izvestia man Melor Sturus, for a 'personal' interview with Mary Wilson at their flat upstairs at No.10. I've talked now and then to the Prime Minister's Dad Herbert who is a close friend of our Girl photographer Ann Ward, but I don't get that many calls really from Prime Ministers. Dukes, yes, Earls, yes. (They all want H3 rejuvenation injections and I can tell them, thank goodness, that 'all is safely in the good hands of Barbara Cartland'...and anyway it is all on sale in chemist shops in West Germany.)

Harold Wilson's call was disappointing though. In that earnest placatory voice of his: 'Miss Franklin, I'm ringing to ask you please to be kind to Mary. She's not used to press interviews with foreign correspondents; she has little experience of this so I rely....' etc etc.

Comrade Sturus is not the usual dour soviet man. Tall, dark, Georgian; claims his Father was President of the Republic of Georgia and a close friend of Stalin. He never stops talking; invited me to dinner at his huge, luxe flat in St John's Wood. He has a beautiful blond wife formerly married to a Russian lorry-driver until she was seduced by Melor Sturus. Now they have a small boy called George who is 10. A sort of Billy Bunter.... from sitting in front of the telly to learn his English, eating sweets, sweets and cream cakes. He can speak English with terrific Anglo accent learned from ITV ads. Every now and then he interrupts the general conversation with the remark that something is 'whiter than white' and do I know 'stork from butter?'... or 'hands as soft as your face' and so on and so on. The Sturus parents are madly proud of him and his 'perfect English'.

Melor turned up at No.10, Downing Street in an enormous great grey flat cap hiding his black crinkly curls. The policeman let us in but ..... several great detectives who seemed to be hiding behind the door, just fell on him. I suppose it was the cap; it scared me too. They shuffled us through the downstairs portraits and up the stairs to the P-M's flat where Mary is said to cook breakfast for her Harold every morning. I am holding a typed list of eleven permitted questions but when Mary, looking remarkably pretty and lovable, gets over her shyness and starts to talk, that list gets forgotten immediately. Melor puts on all his terrific Georgian charm which is pretty sexy stuff I can tell you.

July 1963
Flat 382, The White House
Albany Street, NW1

Dear B,

The White House housemaid went off with all my shoes. Except the pair I stood up in. I had several pairs of navy, high-heeled, open-toe shoes I was keeping for best. You know me...almost new, un-worn garments hung in the wardrobe. You don't understand; any time I dress up in my best, someone upturns a glass of whiskey on me. I told the head-housekeeper about my shoes and she gave me a funny look. The maid always comes once a week just to change the bedclothes, dust around; I always left a hefty tip; she's disappeared now and I'm left barefoot.

Had such an odd postcard from Rebecca West whom I've always adored ever since reading years ago her 'Thinking Reed' and 'Harsh Voice'. She writes to tick me off for something nasty I wrote about Christine Keeler. RW says she's on Christine and Mandy Rice-Davies' side!

Here in this tight little office shared with some of the busiest brains, I pretend I have no one in my life. This arouses a sort of angry pity. Peter Black who is nice, wise and kind, insists that if only I could use some black mascara on my tiny eyelashes, I'd soon get a man.

Years of coping with our Lonely Heart cousins and all Les Girls at Grove End Gardens, has made me no less chatty about Other Peoples Affairs but silent-as-the-grave about my own. Besides if my boss Mackenzie ever got wind of my occasional (frankly quite frequent) disappearance at midday or weekends, he'd soon put a stop....by sending me to the back of beyond.

Have you noticed that erotic love is fanatical? Like Religion. I think it explains why it is so sustaining. The fanaticism grows just as in old-time religion. So the proverbial bed-of-nails has no fears; quite the contrary.

We've all been stuck in such a tiny, hot little room just across the corridor from the Ladies. Hardly any room to swing an envelope, let alone a letter, so I'm typing this to you from home. We are a delicious mixture; Barry Norman, tense and dedicated to the showbiz page; Peter Black, telly-weary yet savouring his power to make even the Beatles cringe. (The named Paul McCartney rang up to protest, ha ha!) ....Julian Holland (I find it odd that Julian went to the same school as me, just like Godfrey Winn and Kenneth Tynan, Brigadier Slim, Selwyn Lloyd, etc., etc.) ...Roy Nash, trade union correspondent who came recently from the dead News Chronicle, but not least, Bernard Levin who is very nice; everyone loves him so because he's funny.....it makes an odd contrast with the outside world where he is, it seems, not loved at all. We are all Egos, big ones...so the room seems even smaller. A sort of Huis Clos(?)*...and very sweaty with it.

We get a lot of visitors but there's nowhere for them to sit. So everything happens in the corridor, outside the Ladies. That reminds me; we have lots of new Ladies. More about them anon.

Love, Ogg

*Huis Clos – literally 'an enclosed space', also the title of a play by Jean Paul Sartre

August 1963
c/o Daily Mail, Northcliffe House, Tudor St
London EC4

Dear B,

The hue and cry for Dr. Aslan's Youth Drug continues. So many doctors have asked to meet her that the Editor is arranging for her to fly from Bucharest at our expense and address a medical conference.

I feel it has got out of hand but can do nothing to stop it. The sacks of letters, 'phone calls, etc. are, if anything, worse than when it began.

Barbara Cartland has invited me to her Herts home for a reception to meet, if you please, Cabinet Ministers and other men of influence. If Barbara is a sample of Aslan rejuvenation – instead of the injections she has managed to get some tablets from West Germany and these are an 'improved' form of the drug, containing extra vitamins etc. – well she was an active lady before but now she's a time bomb; has already written a book about it all – in which I get honourable mention as the first Discoverer and all that – and has even formed a Company with publicity personnel and sales executives to market the improved product. I thought at first that this would solve all my problems because I could just turnover all my frustrated customers wanting to get into Rumania over to Barbara…but no, there are still several million who want Bucharest or bust. The articles are being serialised in the USA, Australia, from Sumatra to Singapore, from the Philippines to Hong Kong….the Youth Drug has aged me 20 years or more.

The newest customers for it are Vivien Leigh and her mother, the very charming Gertrude Hartley, who has a beauty salon in Knightsbridge. And now Paul Getty, who invited me to take tea with him at the Ritz where he lives.

Curious person Mr. Getty. So ugly with unbelievably red hair which had either been dyed, tinted or helped in some way because no one, surely, was ever born with it. A dead white lugubrious face. I was invited into his suite upstairs where he's been living quite a while now. The most interesting thing about him was the woman with him, a lawyer, young and very pretty, Miss Robina Lund in glamorous hat. I thought she was lovely and couldn't quite make out the relationship although he deferred to her and asked her advice before answering my questions and so on. His face and voice were curiously without expression, the features almost unmoving. We discussed what he had for dinner. 'I'm a big disappointment to the Ritz chef,' he told me, 'I only eat one meal a day and that never varies; I dine every evening on one potato baked in its jacket. Nothing else.'

He said it kept him remarkably fit. After about half-an-hour he begins to warm to his subject. Normally, he said, he never gives interviews, talked to journalists or answered begging letters. He didn't believe in giving money away; money had to be earned the hard way as he'd earned it himself and now his life was spent protecting it and his 'art galleries' at home, 'with the help of Miss Robin Lund,' he added graciously. This made Miss Lund smile because his 'art galleries' were really more like a small town. He was like Maggie's father in Henry James' novel The Golden Bowl. He was fascinated by beautiful things and felt it his duty to preserve them for the nation.

The waiter came to take our tea order but I said I couldn't eat in front of a poor creature restricted to one baked potato a day so I had a drink instead. 'The trouble is,' Mr. Getty remarked, 'the Ritz simply have no idea how to bake a potato. I tell them I want it simply on its own cooked to a certain degree but it's no use, the Chef doesn't seem able to manage it.'

It seemed a poor do, at Ritz prices and I felt quite sorry for him. I could tell by the way the waiter entered the suite and looked at Mr. Getty that he'd not much hope of a real order...let alone a tip. Then of course we got down to business. What interested Mr. Getty was...you've guessed it, the Rumanian Youth Drug.....not O. Franklin nor the Daily Mail. I said I'd try and get him some; gave Anna Aslan's address and phone number.

Love Ogg

August 1963
c/o Daily Mail, Northcliffe House, Tudor St
London EC4

Dear B,

A truly awful week. I was nearly sacked. Worst time I remember since I made that bloomer at Reuters about Mussolini's eldest son.

The cruel part is that this time...I am innocent! Truly! I did no wrong; made no mistakes; only did as I was told as always (Mind you, according to Quentin Crewe that's half the trouble. He says he thinks I must have a 'slave' mentality. 'As soon as the Editor calls you, you run,' says Quentin. 'Why do you run? Keep him waiting or tell his secretary to go to hell.')

He's right of course. Even now, at my age, I can't get rid of the slavish habits of the workers I learned at Austin Motors and Joseph Lucas and BSA Tools and Birmetals or worse still, the fear of the sack from refugee German businessmen who sought salvation in keeping nose to the grindstone and grinding up girls along with it. I expect you're fed up with this philosophy stuff? Right, then here's my tragic story. Don't laugh; it felt tragic to me. Everyone believed I was going to be fired and I'm being congratulated as though I missed the firing squad by inches...and all for what?

I upset Mr. Harold Pinter. A highly-sensitive man it seems, he even telephoned Lord Rothermere 'in the middle of the night' about something I wrote in the paper about his wife Vivian Merchant...which was to the effect of How talented she is, and how talented he is... and how marvellous they both are.....and aren't they just the Greatest! It was most sycophantic, slimy stuff as you can see from the enclosed copy.

341

Instead of being thrilled to bits to get the whole of the Daily Mail Leader page – the equivalent of about £10,000-worth of free publicity for the Pinter talents – he phones the Lordship to say he or she's been misquoted over something. But what could it be? I racked my brains. The only possible 'inaccuracy' might be that I had suggested Miss Merchant was both sexy and Scottish (she came from Glasgow, she said, though born in Manchester). My Scots boss, who was Features Editor on duty on the Friday actually rewrote this somewhat uninteresting 'quote' because he wanted it slightly hotted up. He's Scots himself, you see. The whole interview was based on Pinter's successful television play the previous night, 'The Lovers' (did you see it? Very good I thought, also very sexy). This was the angle that Mack wanted. And what Mack wants, I have to give. That's what I'm paid for. When I read the paper next morning and noticed that this little sentence had been slightly rewritten, I didn't mind a bit. It was so harmless, so totally uninteresting, so massively boring. But it was enough to upset Mr. Pinter who appeared to think that I had tried to show his wife's Scottish sexiness or sexy Scottishness (take your choice please!) was more important than his talent.

Rothermere naturally didn't understand a word of the crisis, and was rightly annoyed to have his sleep disturbed. He rang our new Editor Mike Randall. Now Mike is not only Rothermere's first THIN Editor, he is also rather edgy, nerves exposed, nostrils tend to flare at the very scent of danger.

I was sent for, told to sit down and shut up and listen. I started to protest that I wanted to know what my 'mistake' had been. What had I done wrong? Silence, shut up, don't speak. I was told that to upset ANYone was bad journalism. That 'sort of thing' was dead and gone. The era of gossip and hurtful comments. Fini. If I didn't learn that toute suite, I was out. He felt I should be sacked but 'others' had pleaded for me. 'No, don't say anything. I don't want to hear. Never do it again. Now go.' I opened my mouth but no sound came. He was busy shuffling papers. I was dismissed from his presence. I went.

I shall never forgive Harold Pinter for this. Dam him, dam, dam. The absolute swine.

Love Ogg

August 1963
c/o Daily Mail, Northcliffe House, Tudor St
London EC4

Dear B,

I took your advice. I tried asking the chaps on the Leader page subs-desk what the Pinter row had been all about. No one knew. 'Was something wrong then?' one man asked. Whereupon the others looked shocked. Sshush....better not talk about it, someone said. I began to feel worse, if that were possible.

I tried asking the Features Ed himself. What had upset the ghastly Pinter? His face looked solemn, lips pursed, schoolmasterish. 'Better forget it,' he said, 'it's over now. I was one of those who saved you from being fired. I thought you didn't deserve it.'

But what had I done? I was shrieking now, with everyone staring. What was the mistake? Was there a mistake? Would there be a correction? It was unjust, I said, to punish me for something and me not to know what it was!

I was informed that I was not being punished; I was being saved! When I try to raise the subject, everyone gets their heads down; not a word. I give up.

And to think that it was me who first put Pinter in the paper anyway. Way back, years ago, when Hayes sent me to interview the young man who'd had a successful play done on Radio 3 called The Birthday Party. It was a good play. It sounded to me more like the truth than drama.

I arranged to meet the entirely unknown Pinter in a pub in Charing Cross Road. He wasn't easy to talk to. He was grudging, taciturn, sulky and irritable. I admired him for that. Usually they all talk too much. I asked him at last about the dialogue between mother and son in the play. He agreed his own mother talked rather like that, repeating things; it stuck in his mind, like a gramophone record. I thought, here's a talent that's truthful and trustable; he'll go far. I wrote a piece about him, the first publicity he'd had.

I think now he probably went too far, too fast. If you tell a man he's genius, he's likely to believe you.

Real villain of this episode is Barry Norman who is our showbiz writer, not me. Barry knew only too well that Pinter can sometimes be too hot to handle. 'Send Olga,' he said. The moral is that Quentin Crewe is right. It's doing as you're told that gets you into trouble. 'Remember that,' says Quentin. And I said I'd try.

Love, Ogg

16th November 1963
c/o Daily Mail, Northcliffe House, Tudor St
London EC4

Dear B,

Am in trouble again, this time with the Beatles. Or rather with their fans.

After some interviews I wrote about these tragic boys and what a rotten time they have on tour, pursued by the fans to such an alarming extent that they are prisoners in hotel rooms, unable to relax at a cinema ... not even daring to put their heads out of window. The Beatles are back from a tour with the Vernon Girls, with whom they shared the same bill. The girls liked the Beatles and felt it was so unfair, especially as their health was suffering. I quoted Maureen Kennedy as saying: 'It's hard for them to relax or get any sleep. At some of the hotels where we've stayed, the fans surround the hotel screaming until 2am.' Some hotels have refused to take the Beatles in and two hotels at Cheltenham had turned them away.

I wrote; 'Life for the Beatles today is a cage-like existence, shunted from their Princess car (they can't even pop their heads out of the window) up the back stairs to their hotel rooms. They cannot have meals in the dining room; they cannot sit at a bar and chat. Hotels have to hide them to avoid too much damage. They couldn't see Sweden; whatever town they went to, they couldn't stop and look around.'

Maureen said the worst thing was that though the boys loved music, they couldn't hear a note of it above the noise of the screaming. They look forward to the show each night, but each night they go to bed disappointed. She said the Beatles get very frightened of the girls in their frenzy. 'Worst was in Dublin, most frightening of all because even the police turned round and asked for autographs instead of holding back the fans.'

A pathetic story. Until the fans' letters started to arrive. They hated me. Hate nothing! Their frenzy of loathing for me because of what I'd written was so frightening that I knew what Maureen Kennedy meant. These were schoolgirls of 13, 14, 15 and over. And they wanted me killed if possible but only after prolonged torture. English schoolgirls these? I can't believe it. A few of the letters were printed and Monica Furlong* wrote a piece in the paper about the horrors and dangers of pop music. This time it was the Beatles themselves who took umbrage. Paul McCartney rang Monica to give her 'a piece of his mind'.

What's happening? Everyone says, 'What d'you expect? It's a new era; it's 1963.' Monica said she don't like it much. Me neither.

I took Mrs. Grun to a new play which got fairly rave notices but she wanted to walk out after the second act. For one thing it had a real live lavatory on stage so the action was sort of punctuated by the sound of the lavatory chain being pulled and the pan being flushed all too often. However, the climax of the play came when the male lead puts the female lead on to the bed (which is next to the loo, you see) and has a premature ejaculation. Apparently this was the theme of the play...how, I mean, to avoid being premature. I thought Mrs. G would want to walk out again when she twigged this but luckily I think she missed the point of its being premature and the heroine upset about it. She just thought the girl had got fed up; so we went and had coffee and Mrs. G, who'd once studied the Drama in old Kiev, said Theatre is dead and sex has killed it. It wasn't a very good play in spite of what Bernard Levin said.

Love, Ogg.

Monica Furlong (1930–2003), journalist, author, moderator of the Movement for the Ordination of Women, was on the Daily Mail 1960–68.

November 1963
Flat 382, The White House
Albany Street, NW1

Dear B,

I am to have a home of my own. I meant to tell you 2 years ago at least when A started a joint bank account for us to save up to buy me a flat. Only I didn't, then, feel secure enough that it could ever happen.

Since then we've driven around to look at various places, but they were a bit poky and cramped.

Once day he phoned to say he'd seen just the right thing for us. A billboard on a hill at Caterham close to his own home said that a block of 12 apartments is going up; it sounded just right but was it wise? There? A said not to ask so many questions but to ring the Estate Agent immediately and make an appointment to view. At the moment, there are only a few bricks showing as work has only just begun.

I fell in love with the place. I think it's Peter Pan place right up in the tree-tops and no other buildings to be seen in the lovely little copse on the hillside...though the Agent said, 'There might be other houses later.'

I didn't even want to think about any snags. Only it all seemed too good to be true. I never thought I would have a home in the country....It's not really of course. It's right next door to the railway station and overlooks the charming village but from any aspect, there's nothing to be seen but trees and the green valley opposite where the Surrey Hills begin.

So we went ahead. It will cost £4,000 to buy with garage. A insisted that I must keep the money we'd saved for furniture, etc., and plunge in and ask the Daily Mail for a loan. This has now been approved, so you can imagine how rich I feel. I have to pay back the loan within 5 years, to be deducted from my salary but interest is at 5% declining. Isn't that marvellous? Several other staff have been given similar loans at 5% for a house or 3% for a car.

I went down to see the building on Saturday. So quick...it's nearly finished, except for the roof! Mine is a top flat with a balcony. I just stood there in the wind on that green hill and stared, only half-believing it will be mine one day. After living almost 16 years in the White House where the view from my window was always another concrete wall.... They're pulling Euston Road down now all around us... and the dust and fumes from those old buildings has turned the White House curtains an iron grey. It's the end of an era.

Was having my dinner in the Cafe Boulevard in Wigmore Street when one of the girl cashiers was listening to a transistor radio behind the counter. Suddenly there was a deathly silence and someone shouted; 'They've killed him. Someone has shot and killed President Kennedy.' People got up from their tables and starting milling about, slightly dazed I thought and the girl cashier started to cry.

For some reason it reminded me of the first evening of the war, Sunday 3rd September 1939. I was eating in a little caff further up the road; called the Dutch Oven in Baker Street. I'd gone in for a Welsh rarebit after a walk in Regent's Park on a lovely sunlit evening but when I came out it was dark. A new kind of dark with people shuffling about in it, shops all closed and too late to try and buy a torch.

Love, Ogg

Olga moved into the flat in Caterham and lived there for the rest of her life until her final illness. She adored it and the countryside around it.

February 1964
5, Bishams Court Church Hill
Caterham, Surrey

Dear B,

Like a fool I sat on the railway-platform at London Bridge wondering why my train for Tattenham Corner/Caterham never arrived. Sat for an hour and a half before realising that daytime trains and night-time ones leave from different platforms. And me....with my bits of belongings, a suitcase, an electric fire, a typewriter, some books and a swimming costume in a hold-all. First lesson on Moving House; learn the times and stopping places of Suburban trains. Mind you, I am still so excited; it's so unreal that I'm still in a sort of daze; hardly noticed the trains going by! I'm going home to my own home which seems so unlikely....after 23 years. And that one in Lordswood Road, Harborne in 1937 wasn't mine but only rented. Don't even know how to look after a home...you'll have to remind me. What do you use to clean windows, paintwork, the bath? Please tell.

Before I moved in on Saturday, A came with his own key and looked around. He seemed amazed and pleased. At my choice of elec. light fittings and lamps. Never trusted my taste before. Most of all he admired the view from every single window, said, 'Whichever way one looked, only beauty.' Yes, yes. Oh come please very soon, bring Frank. I know you'll be happy for me.

Love Og

PS. The weather is freezing still down here. Snow, ice. So beautiful too. The first morning I looked out from my bedroom, which has crimson velvet curtains and pink carpet, beneath my window clusters of snowdrops, those tiny green spots on their bells were showing through the snow flakes.
PPS. My nephew Marcel Frenkel is coming to see me in early March. He's now a high-powered doctor...isn't that splendid? Come, let's have a party. My place.

April 1965
5, Bishams Court Church Hill
Caterham, Surrey

Dear B,

You ask for newest news of the Family .... so here goes. Rosalie died at last. After almost 12 years of sitting, staring, unable to speak or understand very much, though her face always lit up when I called in on Friday nights which made it worse for me because I felt even more guilty at avoiding the necessity of a visit as often as I could .... especially when I had the excuse of living now 20 miles or more distant. She sat waiting for the devoted Paul to come home and cook her dinner, wash her, launder her knickers, sit with her and the little black dog Angus ... until the final scene I always found so terrible when Paul walked backwards to the bedroom holding her hands and drawing her after him stumbling, fearful, making strange little cries.

His devotion should have been beautiful to see but I only found it tragic, even distasteful and this too proves my meanness of character. He did nothing to win admiration. On the contrary, he Paul Gottl now Paul Gough, a Viennese Catholic from a background rendered horrific by the Hitler war and the Hitler influence, simply did what he thought was his loving duty, never complaining, never even expecting help from anyone else. The flat was almost resonant with past crowds of noisy friends, spongers and hangers-on like myself. Now Sally never comes; nor Jane, nor Freda (who can be forgiven for having disappeared the way contented wives tend to do into that long-sought marriage). Mitzi and Anne, even Phyllis sometimes call, as I do, formally, embarrassed, accepting Paul's eager hospitality and looking ready to depart at the very first opportunity.

I shall never have such loving care for my end. Paul never leaves for work each day until the moment that the equally devoted and patient charwoman arrives to tend her needs throughout the day.

I feel guilty when I visit and more guilty still when I don't. For one thing I never really liked her though, clearly, others adore her so I know I must always have been unfair ... especially after her marriage when she sweetened towards me and to the whole world. Do you see what I am getting at?

I blame Father... needing to shift the blame on to someone. He hated his mother, disliked all his sisters, abhorred his brothers and made fun of all of them, especially of Rosalie, eldest child of his hated sister Phoebe, for no better reason than her failed efforts in her eager twenties and thirties, to find a beau. I think Father read too much Dickens and saw everyone, especially his relations, as an eccentric Heep or Jingle, a Rosa Dartle or Micawber, a Mr. Dick or Dombey ... almost never as themselves!

Rita is another matter. Now she is in the London Clinic too. Some nasty operation. In much pain but spending her days on the telephone, attending to her thriving business. And she doesn't even need the money now. Her husband Hans May* left her enough so that she need never give up the sumptuous apartment in Park Lane. Funny? Yes, but heroic too.

Sally, since Jane her nearest neighbour and closest niece also fell ill, first with bunions and then with cancer, has given up answering the telephone for fear of too many demands she can no longer satisfy. She rarely leaves her icy little flat nowadays. A tiny one-bar electric fire in her room never penetrates the chill. I went there one night to talk about the Family and get more details as to why Grandmother, having escaped from Russian Lithuania, returned there with four of her children .. which seems such a mad thing to do. Sally, as always, is straightforward; says she never liked me, doesn't trust me and why in God's name don't I leave the family history in peace, safely buried along with the rest of the ancestors whom the Czars and the cholera harassed out of their lives. Sally claims that I am 'sexy' like my father and says truthfully and disarmingly that she tries nevertheless not to disdain me, provided I don't visit her too often or demand much of her time which she spends less with her circle of psychic seance friends (some disillusion has set in) but simply in dreams of her past unhappy girlhood (trying to make peace between the brothers) and her past, brief, romanticised marriage to 'poor John Willy' ...as our parents always called him.

Paul came out here to see me in Surrey, tried to show me how to liquidise carrots (he lives on them since his own operation on his one remaining kidney) and admired my new flat.

I now have a tv set ... which the Office pays for, as I am stand-in tv critic once a week when Peter Black is 'off'. Suddenly one night I switched on and saw the face of my one-time Reuter boss who gave me a 'career' in exchange for some rather rigorous lovemaking. Cole, big-eater, big drinker, big lover and enormously hard worker, is dead at 50.

So many dead. We are entering the last stage, you and I.
I feel enormous happiness.... and guilt, guilt, never-ending.
Love, O.

Hans May, Viennese composer (1891–1959), composed music for over eighty films, including Brighton Rock.

1968

July 1968
c/o Landsdown Court Hotel, Bath

Dear B,

A has been showing me the beauties of Bath and I am stunned. To me it is more beautiful than Paris or Rome. It is sheer delight. Today we toured the Roman baths. I confess it seems twice as delicious seeing it with A. He knows far more English history than I do. All foreigners are like this, I think.

Did you hear me on 'Any Questions' on Friday night? A came along to Wales too just for the ride; that is, he took me in his car. Funny to meet Mikardo after a long time; he is uglier than ever but somehow less nice; all that Socialist aggressiveness and knowingness bore a little; young David Benedictus was also on the team but A disapproved, seeing in him I suppose the new 'permitted' generation to whom all Things are permitted; the 4th man was tall, handsome David Price, a real human being, simpatica. David Jacobs handles everyone beautifully; he makes Smoothness almost a Way of Life, but I can see how it helps, especially with the BBC who are eternally and universally Anxious. A treated everyone to champagne and enjoyed being the hovering host. It feels so wonderful to have a Protector after so many years fending for myself. I revel in it...yet feel uneasy too.

Nowadays life is almost too comfortable, too smooth. No need to worry one's little head on how to introduce the Boy Friend. Fiance? Agent? Friend? Husband? It matters not a jot. It leaves space around each person, inside which you do your own thing and no one will even notice, let alone wonder what the hell you are up to. This is marvellous and, paradoxically, chilling. In the old days, one resented so much landladies, hotel managers, even railway porters, friends, relatives who were far too interested. There are no more speculative glances; no more social gaffes, no more yawning silences, embarrassment fear. Only indifference, which is such a relief yet it leaves a hole; a hole in the ground into which one might fall, hardly noticing. As I said, I am too timid by half.

We all are ... all of us sisters. Thanks to those Victorian Manchester Aunts who believed it mattered terribly what people thought ... or thought they saw. I remember Aunt Ray telling me once that in that huge family photograph at our Mother's wedding in Higher Broughton Salford.....some wretch moved and tipped Ray's huge picture hat slightly askew (you've got the picture somewhere in Manor Road North) and she never forgot it, never got over it. It was a clearer, sharper memory for her than running away with young Flying-Officer Joe Kennedy and scandalising all the Family!

Love to all, Ogg

Olga and many others were made redundant by the Daily Mail *in the 1970s. She made a new career for herself as a broadcaster and freelance journalist, and wrote a successful series of books about making money at home. She adored her Surrey home. She even passed her driving test in her fifties at the fifth attempt. She explored the Surrey hills, entertained her nephews and nieces and continued working. She came back to Birmingham for the last few weeks of her life so that her family could be near her in the hospice. Even in her final illness she never lost her joie de vivre. She gave her last interview on* Woman's Hour *from her bed in the hospice just a week or so before she died.*

Her relationship with Alfred continued until his death in 1982. They exchanged love letters throughout their time together. Olga preserved every one of them. Olga died in 1985 and her oldest sister Beryl in 1988. Cora lived on into her nineties and died in 2009 and finally, the baby of the family, Betty, died in 2012. Beryl, Cora and Betty's children stay in touch and often reminisce about the fun they had with Oggi.

Index